Story of the
AMERICAN
WEST

Legends of Arizona

*Told Through the Lives of Apaches,
Mountain Men, Hispanics, Soldiers,
Mormons, Cowboys, Blacks, Outlaws
And Others, Who Struggled in
Arizona's White Mountains, One of the
Last Untamed Regions of the West*

Story of the
AMERICAN WEST

Legends of Arizona

Told Through the Lives of Apaches, Mountain Men, Hispanics, Soldiers, Mormons, Cowboys, Blacks, Outlaws And Others, Who Struggled in Arizona's White Mountains, One of the Last Untamed Regions of the West

By Carol Sletten
& Eric Kramer

Illustrated by Carol Sletten

www.WolfWaterPress.com

PO Box 588, Pinetop, AZ 85935

Copyright 2010 by Carol Sletten and Eric Kramer

Library of Congress Control Number: 2010940443

Publisher's Cataloging-in-Publication

Sletten, Carol.
Story of the American West : told through the lives
of Apaches, mountain men, Hispanics, soldiers, Mormons,
cowboys, Blacks, outlaws and others, who struggled in
Arizona's White Mountains, one of the last untamed
regions of theWest / by Carol Sletten & Eric Kramer ;
illustrated by Carol Sletten. — Arizona centennial ed.,
1st ed.
p. cm.
Includes bibliographical references and index.
LCCN 2010940443
ISBN-13: 978-0-615-41476-8
ISBN-10: 0-615-41476-1

1. Frontier and pioneer life—West (U.S.) 2. West
(U.S.)—History. 3. White Mountains (Ariz.)—History.
I. Kramer, Eric. II. Title.

F596.S54 2010   978
                          QBI10-600228

First Edition, Second Printing

Manufactured in the United States of America

Dedication

This book is dedicated to the memory of Carol's parents, Pearl and Owen Sletten, who told her bedtime stories about the olden days, and to Eric's ancestor Aaron Mershon, who died in the American Revolution.

Contents

CONTENTS

Illustrations

Introduction

The legends of the American West — from Indian wars and massacres, to outlaw gangs and the struggles of settlers — come alive in the history of east-central Arizona. The forests, grasslands, mountain peaks and deep canyons have been witness to lost civilizations, conquistadors, Mountain Men and explorers. Cavalrymen battled the warriors of Geronimo and other famous Indian chiefs. Texas cowboys murdered Hispanic sheepherders. Mormons clashed with other settlers over land and the practice of polygamy.

Zane Grey, who did more than anyone to create the image of the Old West, visited regularly to collect material for his novels. But the rich details of the region's history are more powerful than fiction.

For thousands of years, bands of native people struggled to live in the wildly beautiful but harsh environment with its unforgiving climate. The Desert Culture became the Anasazi and Mogollon civilizations, which in turn produced the Hopi and Zuni tribes. The Kachina religion of the Pueblos started in the area.

After wandering through North America for 10,000 years, some Apache bands began to spend most of their time in the White Mountains, gathering plants and hunting game.

Coronado, searching for the legendary seven cities of gold, found hardship and death in the desolate White Mountains and moved on. His countrymen fought the Apaches unsuccessfully for centuries. The region was still inaccessible to Europeans when Mexico ceded title to the Americans in 1848. Fur trappers and explorers came to the area, but moved on quickly.

Apaches, long accustomed to raiding into Mexico, had divided loyalties in the latter part of the 19th century. Some under leaders like Cochise and Geronimo fought to remain free, while others enlisted as scouts to help the U.S. Army track down the renegades. Civilians massacred even peaceful Apaches at Camp Grant and Bloody Tanks before Fort Apache was established in the White Mountains. The Fort and the extensive reservation surrounding it gave the Apaches some protection. Still, breakouts by Apache bands were frequent as Generals Crook and Miles tried to subdue America's last hostile Indians. In the end, both the renegades and some faithful U.S. Army scouts were taken to prisoner of war camps to die in Florida and Oklahoma.

Chief Alchesay, who had been awarded the Medal of Honor for his work as a scout, had a wild side. He killed a rival chief in a drunken fight before leading his people to a more settled life. The Apache Kid gained fame as one of the last renegades, while a small band of Wild Apaches continued to haunt the mountains of Northern Mexico even into the 20th century.

Native religious movements sprang up. One led to a battle between Apache believers and troops. Another ended after the prophet asked his followers to cut off his head to prove he would be resurrected in three days. White authorities made sure a 20th century charismatic religious leader had to serve a long prison term.

Sheepherders and cattlemen fought for the opportunity to overgraze the semi-arid slopes. The Hashknife outfit, funded by eastern banks, dumped cattle over hundreds of square miles and fought with everyone.

The region continued to be wild and sparsely developed because of the difficult climate and the reputation of the ubiquitous Apaches. This gap in the fabric of civilization remained even after 1890, when the frontier was officially declared to be extinct.

Mormons, sent by their leaders to settle the area, found water scarce and the growing season short. Their early communal settlements soon collapsed, but since the region was secluded, it became a haven for their practice of polygamy. The Latter-day Saints braved Indian attacks, repeated dam washouts and outlaws as they struggled to build communities and make a living on small farms.

The family of William Flake was first ostracized because he bolted from a Mormon commune. Later he fought outlaws and became a patriarch. Flake purchased land for many Latter-day Saint communities before being sent to prison for polygamy. His son Charles was shot to death trying to arrest a bank robber, and a grandson was the first to die in the American Expedition to Revolutionary Russia. A granddaughter, warming herself by the fire in one of the Flake's Victorian homes, burned to death. Yet, his 15 sons and five daughters produced thousands of descendants.

In another heartbreaking incident, a seven-year-old Mormon girl was lost on the Reservation. Apaches helped in the desperate search, which consumed local communities for a month.

Scarlet fever, whooping cough, diphtheria and other epidemics swept through the area. In the tiny community of St. Johns, more than 150 children died in one outbreak. The plagues on the reservation were even worse.

Larger-than-life characters included Corydon Cooley, a gold seeker who saved peaceful Apaches from a massacre, married two Apache sisters and served as a scout to hunt down hostiles. He survived to become a famous host and storyteller. Another legendary figure was the trader Sol Barth. He founded a town, became a political leader, and went to prison for graft before receiving a pardon from the governor. Voters also forgave him, returning him to the Arizona Legislature.

The Udall clan became an important presence, providing two chief justices of the Arizona Supreme Court, four congressmen, a U.S. Cabinet member and three U.S. senators.

Timber was a resource for early settlers, but they were drawn into conflict with the government's first attempts to protect the forest. Still, sawmills flourished for a time.

Famed naturalist Aldo Leopold developed his theories of conservation in the area. Later, 20th-century conservation practices, based on his work, protected the re-introduced elk, after the original population had been hunted to extinction.

The White Mountains were part of what was known as the Outlaw Trail, a broken swath of real estate stretching from Canada to Mexico. The remote towns along the trail were generally far from railroads, which could bring in lawmen for surprise visits. Outlaws were able to hide out in the vast wilderness along the route and even hang around the towns with almost complete impunity.

The Pleasant Valley War spilled over into the White Mountains and ended in a gun battle in Holbrook. Desperados from the shootout at the O. K. Corral came to the remote wilderness to meet their fate, and the lynchings that inspired *The Ox-Bow Incident* occurred near Heber.

By the turn of the 20th century, residents wanted their Wild West reputation to be a thing of the past. So, when word reached St. Johns that five outlaws were operating in the area, townspeople were primed to go after them. Sheriff Ed Beeler, a blowhard and poor organizer if not an outright incompetent, deputized citizens to take up the chase. Within a day, the posse dwindled to only a couple of boys. When the inexperienced youths were killed in a rain of rifle fire after being ambushed by the gang of hardened criminals, law-abiding people were outraged. Those shocked citizens forced the Territorial government to create the Arizona Rangers and declare an all-out war on the remnants of lawlessness.

Butch Cassidy, one of the West's most famous outlaws, was sitting in the St. Johns Jail on suspicion of horse theft when the boys were killed. Although Cassidy's arrest had ironically given him an airtight alibi for the murders, he knew he had to leave. Cassidy caught a boat to South America shortly after talking his way out of the jail. He rightly sensed things were getting too hot for his trade in Arizona.

Modern contraptions started to arrive in the remote region, including telephones and electricity. One enterprising man bought pipe left over from the St. Louis World's Fair and provided running water. Many of the men who went off to fight World War I did not return. Tourists began to come, enticed by the spectacular wilderness. In addition to Zane Grey, other famous writers came to the White Mountains to gather stories and practice their craft. One was Edgar Rice Burroughs, the creator of Tarzan. The Depression hit slowly but hard, both on and off the reservation, before men began to leave to serve their country in World War II.

Arizona on the Equator

It took millions of years for nature to create the captivating beauty and austere climate that has brought people to the White Mountains and sent them away for thousands of years.

Two-hundred-eighty million years ago, east-central Arizona was near the west coast of a giant land mass that included all seven of the world's continents. The future American Southwest was just above the Equator and near sea level. Limestone was created when the land was under water and sandstone was formed from the beach at the water's edge.

Coelophysis, one of the earliest dinosaurs, lived in what is now the Petrified Forest. The carnivore was the size of a large dog.

Carol Sletten © 2010

According to the *Geologic Highway Map of Arizona*, these 280 million-year-old rock formations are exposed north and west of Heber. The sandstone has few fossils to document the changes that were going on at the end of the Permian period, but life was already more than three billion years old, and bigger things were coming. Early reptiles were appearing along with primitive mammals.

Following these Permian formations, there is a gap of about 40 million years in the geology of the area. Either there was no stone created or it was washed away. About 240 million years ago, Arizona sat on a low-relief coastal plain. Predecessors of the dinosaur dominated the food chain on land during the first half of the Triassic Period. The red sandstone, mudstone and gypsum beds of the Moenkopi Formation, with their fossil record, are exposed in the hills from Taylor to Holbrook.

Next, a giant river system flowing from the Appalachians rolled west across Arizona, laying down the Chinle Formation. This layer of mudstone, sandstone and gravel, which is exposed to the surface at the Petrified Forest National Park, gives us a window into life on earth 220 million to 200 million years ago. East-central Arizona was moving from the tropics to the temperate zone as the super continent drifted north.

The trees were giant conifers. When they fell into the mud, the wood was gradually replaced with minerals, leaving east-central Arizona with the world famous stone logs. There are at least 14 varieties of trees in the fossil record of the park. The pollen indicates the trees changed significantly during the 20 million year fossil record. Since scientists don't have information about the needles, it is hard for them to draw further conclusions about the trees. There was no grass, but an abundance of ferns and giant horse-tails fed the grazing animals at the bottom of the food chain.

The huge colorful rock logs are the park's most noticeable features, but now animal fossils are also being studied extensively, adding to the scientific understanding of evolution.

Scientists were very excited in 1984 when they discovered "Gertie," an eight-foot-long ancestor to the huge tyrannosaurus. At the time, the 225 million-year-old bones were considered the oldest discovery in that family line.

In addition to early dinosaurs, the Petrified Forest preserves other reptiles and amphibians. There are many specimens of crocodile-like animals, and as unlikely as it may seem, the bones prove they are more closely related to birds than to lizards. The early dinosaurs of the park made small evolutionary changes during the 20 million years of the Triassic period exposed in the Chinle Formation, according to William Parker, paleontologist at the park. A change currently being studied in the park involves the attachment of the head to the spine. The older skulls have openings for much larger muscles, but the later specimens have smaller spaces for the connecting tissues. The researchers hope to learn why.

Another important late Triassic site in the White Mountains is near St. Johns. Scientists, beginning with researchers from the University of California at Berkeley in 1930, have found skel-etons of 40 large reptile-like mammals called Placerias. Often compared to a hippopotamus, they were the grazing animals of the area 210 million years ago, becoming extinct shortly after the local specimens met their fate. Other residents of the riverbank or swamp included giant crocodile-like reptiles.

In the Jurassic Period, the western portion of the super con-tinent began to split away from the east as the Atlantic Ocean started to open between South America and Africa. This was the height of the age of dinosaurs. There is no fossil record of the Jurassic in the White Mountains. Again, either no stone was cre-ated, or it was washed away.

Around 140 million years ago, dinosaurs were turning into birds in the Cretaceous Period. Around the Mogollon Rim, a layer of exposed sedimentary rock represents the period. North

6

America was breaking off from Europe, the sea level rose, and much of Arizona was covered by a huge inland sea. Essentially, the Gulf of Mexico extended all the way to the Arctic Ocean, leaving the western portions of Mexico, the U.S. and Canada as an island. The Rocky Mountains then began to form to the east, raising Arizona on their western shoulder. The geologic record is again hidden for nearly 80 million years.

In the Springerville area and in the Salt River Canyon, another formation of sedimentary rock is exposed from perhaps 60 million years ago. This is near the time when large dinosaurs and other large land animals became extinct. A meteor usually gets the blame.

Arizona was deprived of its seashore about this time when volcanic islands off the coast of the continent were swept up forming California.

About 65 million years ago, Arizona began to split along a line from the northwest to the southeast. The Colorado Plateau maintained its elevation north of this line, but to the south the land was stretched. Deep valleys opened and sediments from the higher ground washed down into the valleys. This basin and range landscape covers the southern portion of the state, according to the *Geology of Arizona* by Dale Nations and Edmund Stump.

Debate continues about the reason for the stretching of Southern Arizona, but scientists believe it was related to the drift of the North American continent.

Scientists have determined that the original dividing line between the Colorado Plateau and the deserts was about 50 miles south of the current site of the Mogollon Rim, a cliff sometimes 1000 feet high stretching 200 miles across Arizona. The land in this 50-mile-wide transition zone gradually collapsed and eroded, moving the Rim northeast to its current site.

As the Rim retreated at about a tenth of an inch a year, separate forces began to create the mountains that give the area its name. The oldest volcanic rock found in eastern Arizona is nearly 30 million years old, but most of the mountains are the result of volcanic activity that began 15 million years ago. These eruptions lasted four million years and formed much of the White Mountain range. Large-scale volcanic activity ceased about 8 million years ago. There is, however, some evidence of volcanic flows as recently as 10,000 years ago.

Lava flows from this period are found high in the White Mountains and in basaltic rocks and cinder cones to the north. More recently, superficial sedimentary deposits were laid down, exposed from Clay Springs to Overgaard, and in other areas.

Glaciers, beginning about 125,000 years ago, sculpted a small area near Mount Baldy, but this is a mere footnote to the geology of the area. The glaciation was never very widespread and was largely ended 100,000 years ago, although there is evidence of a tiny glacier in the Baldy area as recently as 10,000 years ago.

The White Mountains give their name to a larger region, stretching nearly 100 miles from the peaks. It includes long stretches of the Colorado Plateau as far north as Snowflake, St. Johns and beyond. The area ranges south through the 550 square miles of the Fort Apache Indian Reservation and includes vast stretches of forest east of the reservation through Alpine to the New Mexico state line. The "White Mountains" extend to the west through Heber and Overgaard and into the canyon country of Chevelon and Clear Creeks.

Wind and rain shape the landscape and determine what vegetation can survive. The area needs the cooperation of both the Atlantic and the Pacific to get its annual precipitation, which ranges from 12 inches in the lower elevations to triple that on the peaks. The rain and snow support thousands of varieties of native plants, but the meager precipitation has often disappointed the agricultural hopes of humans.

Winter storms come off the Pacific, down from the Gulf of Alaska. They are brought into the area only when a high-pressure system in the Atlantic brings the Jet Stream far enough to the south. Changes in either ocean can send the storms north of the White Mountains.

In the summer the Atlantic provides the moisture. The high-pressure system moves north to a location near Bermuda and creates a giant swirl with winds stretching out nearly 3,000 miles. Moisture is captured as the air flows over the Gulf of Mexico and the Gulf of California, then drops when the clouds collide with the cold air over the Mogollon Rim or the White Mountains. In a good year, the summer rains come in late June. If the high doesn't arrive over Bermuda on schedule, the mountains can be bone dry until mid-July, when the brief growing season is already half over.

Good years have built up the hopes of farmers for centu-

8

ries, but the air masses over the Atlantic and Pacific have been uncooperative often enough to ultimately frustrate even the most determined agricultural efforts.

Native plants are adapted to the infrequent rains and short growing season. Mount Baldy rises 11,403 feet into a small area of Alpine tundra. Spruce, fir and aspens compete in the high forest below the tree line.

A little lower, the world's largest continuous stand of Ponderosa Pine trees stretches across the high country. Oaks mingle with the conifers. Some of the woodlands are textured in varying shades of green by moss and ferns.

Meadows are scattered through the upper elevations and sometimes flow around the base of the peaks, but grass doesn't become the dominant vegetation until the taller trees give way to pinion and juniper scrub in the lower elevations. Cottonwoods and willows flourish around streams and washes.

Cactus fight for a place in the sun from high peaks to the lowest elevations. The area is home to hundreds of species of wild flowers. They attract swarms of butterflies, bees and other insects.

Former Secretary of the Interior Stewart Udall, who grew up in St. Johns, once wrote, "As a matter of fact, except for scenery (and it is my belief that the Colorado Plateau contains the most stunning array of scenic wonders anywhere on earth) all resources are marginal in this region. Geographers accurately describe it as a 'scrubland'; the native trees are scrub cedar and juniper, shade trees must be watered if they are to survive, and late spring sleet storms make the planting of orchards a triumph of hope over scientific horticulture."

Still, the area remains a haven for wildlife. Bighorn sheep survive in steep-cliffed, less-populated regions of the White Mountains. Bear, elk, and deer frequent the forest. Antelope and javelina enjoy the lower stretches of plateau. Beaver, raccoons, skunks, muskrats, porcupines, cottontails, jackrabbits, prairie dogs, squirrels and lizards make the area their home. They are alert to the danger from mountain lions, coyotes, foxes, bobcats, and rattlesnakes. White Mountain streams abound in fish. The wetlands also host geese, ducks, cranes, shorebirds and bald eagles. On the dry land there are many species of birds, ranging from wild turkeys to hummingbirds.

Humans Arrive From Africa

People look at the wide Atlantic and Pacific oceans of today and wonder how the Indians got to North and South America. It has been a mystery even to generations of trained scientists. However, when the question is asked in the context of the world at the time of early human development and migration, the answer is obvious. Modern humans, who spent their first 5 million years in Africa, were still bottled up on the Dark Continent until something like 50,000 years ago. A few crossed over into the Middle East and the rest, as they say, is pre-history. When they stepped over or around the Red Sea, they were in the corner of a single landmass that included the continents of Europe, Asia, North America, South America and Australia, according to *Before the Dawn*, by Nicholas Wade. Sea levels were 200 feet lower than today. The "bridge" connecting Asia and Alaska was more than 1,000 miles wide.

These ancient people were hunter-gatherers, and there was much to hunt and gather.

A person walking 10 miles a day can make it halfway around the world in four years. Early modern humans did not make the trip that quickly, but they followed the opportunities that presented themselves and were in the Americas 25,000 to 35,000 years ago. In the grand scheme of things that is not long after they had migrated into Europe.

No one knows the exact itinerary of the Hopi, Zuni and Apache as they traveled the Old and New Worlds for tens of thousands of years before arriving in the White Mountains. But genetics indicates they came from Asia at different times and lived separately in the New World.

Most human genes are quickly mixed in the inheritance from mother and father, but two types of DNA remain largely unchanged from generation to generation. A billion years ago, an ancestor of plant and animal cells captured a living bacteria which it kept as something of a milk cow to supply chemical energy. The relationship was so successful that nearly all living cells have these mitochondria today. The DNA of mitochondria is inherited only from the mother and changes little from generation to generation.

Also, the Y chromosome, present only in men, is largely inherited from the father and changes little over long periods of time.

When a change does occur in mitochondria or Y-chromosome

DNA, it becomes a marker that identifies people as descendants of a common ancestor. American Indians are generally identified by five unique characteristics of mitochondrial DNA, known as A, B, C, D and X.

The D and C characteristics are both traced to the first group that came from Africa. These people apparently lived in north-central Asia before moving on to the Americas. Hopis have ties to this early group.

The A characteristic belongs to a second wave of people coming from Africa and is carried by Asian peoples, including Koreans and Japanese. It is found among Zunis.

The B characteristic, also from this second wave, is found among the Chinese, Tibetans, Mongolians, Central Asians and South Siberians. It is thought that the B characteristic came to the Americas somewhat later than A, C, and D.

Finally, the X characteristic is more of a mystery. It is common in Europe, leading some people to think mammoth hunters followed their prey across the ice of the North Atlantic to arrive in eastern Canada. A more likely explanation is that the X characteristic originated in India and spread east and west, arriving both in Europe and Siberia. It was probably carried into the Americas from Siberia.

The Athabascans, including both the Apache and Navajo, carry the A and X characteristics and are thought to have arrived from Siberia in the last migration, perhaps 10,000 years ago.

The Zuni and Hopi have been in the Americas much longer, perhaps as long as 30,000 years. Since archaeology picks up their trail only about 2,000 years ago, the vast stretch of time for their early wanderings in the Americas remains a mystery. Interestingly, a study by Frederika Kaestle and David Smith found that the Zunis had the A characteristic but lacked the D. The northern Uto-Aztecan, which includes the Hopis, were found to have the D but lack the A. Both the Hopi and Zuni have B and C, but no X, according to the study. It would be a mistake – frequently made when studying pre-historic Indians – to overanalyze the data. But if the study holds up, it would be safe to say the Zuni and Hopi lived separately for tens of thousands of years before becoming neighbors and sharing a similar culture on the Colorado Plateau.

The male Y chromosome DNA also tells an interesting story.

11

In an article published by the American Society of Human Genetics, author Fabricio R. Santos of Oxford traced early modern humans across the Red Sea to an area near the Caucasus Mountains. From there, one group of these "Caucasians" split off to Europe while another continued to north-central Asia and on to the Americas. Interestingly, this study about how male DNA came into the Americas lacks the East Asian (Chinese, Japanese, Korean) connections present in the female DNA. This could indicate that the "Caucasian" males, involved in thousands of years of expansion and warfare, took East Asian women into their tribes as they migrated to America. It will be intriguing to see whether this analysis holds up, as the scientists dig deeper and refine their theories.

We can leave genetics and pick up the story of the first residents of the White Mountains through archaeology. Scientists have combed the White Mountains since the 1800s, naming pottery types after local communities and developing theories about the pre-Columbian natives of Arizona. An old newspaper account says that Dr. Henry Yarrow, a Smithsonian archaeologist, was robbed of his watch in a holdup 12 miles north of St. Johns in 1885.

Archaeology says the first people to venture into America lived in small bands and hunted big game. They left behind only an occasional stone tool.

Evidence from other areas of Arizona and North America indicates they hunted mammoths, giant sloths, camels and tiny pre-historic American horses. This hunting may have contributed to the extinction of the animals by 9000 B.C. when grassland was disappearing and the climate was growing warmer and drier. Mammoth bones are occasionally found in the White Mountain area. A good specimen was uncovered in St. Johns in 1984.

No one knows when wandering humans first saw the beautiful White Mountains in the distance and tried to make the area their home. A grinding stone found near Vernon indicates people were in the area at least 9000 years ago. Other than that "mano" and a few stone points possibly linked to these Stone Age men called "paleo-Indians," little from this very early period has been found in the White Mountains.

The pre-historic Indians expanded their food supply to include small animals and edible plants, which changed their migration patterns. They began to move with the seasons, following the availability of wild plant foods, rather than the herds of large animals.

Archaeologists call this new pattern in the Southwest "the Desert Culture," after the ancient group's primary habitat, even though they also lived in the High Country of Northern Arizona.

Emergence of the Pueblo Cultures

About 2,000 years ago, the desert culture began making permanent inroads into the White Mountains. Those pre-pueblo people lived throughout the area and surrounding parts of Arizona and New Mexico. Their oldest villages were made up of small dwellings called pit houses. After digging a hole up to seven feet deep, they placed support posts around the excavation and covered the dwelling with brush. Their villages had from one to 50 houses with 15 being average.

Archaeologists divided them into two groups. The more southern branch is called "Mogollon." The northern is called "Anasazi." Although archaeologists have spent their careers arguing the differences and similarities between the two branches, people living in the area 1,500 or 1,000 years ago would not have recognized these distinctions. They probably would have realized they had many similarities to nearby villagers, while they were somewhat different from those living farther away.

The dividing line between the northern and southern groups runs right through the White Mountains. So classifying settlements in the area as Mogollon or Anasazi is almost a purely academic exercise.

Even the name Anasazi is controversial. It was derived from "Enemy Ancestors" in the Navajo language. When experts classify a village as Anasazi, as opposed to Mogollon, they look for things like the quality of their stone axes and the presence of two-handed stones for grinding corn.

Some say the Anasazi used irrigation more extensively than

Fourmile Polychrome, a type of pottery found widely thoughout the Southwest, was named for a ruin near Taylor.

By Carol Sletten,
© 2010

the Mogollon, and developed a more effective agricultural food supply, which allowed them to occupy their villages year-round.

Even these distinctions disappeared as the groups became more involved in trade, which brought changes to their religion and culture. Scientists say the two groups had largely merged by 1000 A.D. and it is difficult to distinguish between them after 1300.

Villages in the White Mountains were some of the earliest in Arizona to grow corn, which was first domesticated from wild grasses in Mexico. They also planted beans, squash and a variety of primitive cotton adapted to higher elevations. Although they continued to hunt available game and gather wild plants, the combination of corn and beans provided enough protein to allow them to do without meat when necessary.

Success in agriculture made advancements in food storage necessary. These pre-Pueblo White Mountain people developed large storage pits in the floors of their homes.

As intensive farming increased the food supply, the size of their villages grew. Pit houses changed from round to rectangular. After 900 A.D. villages were made up of stone and adobe apartment houses built above ground in valleys.

Trade became an important part of urban life. They exchanged goods with Hohokams, another group of pre-pueblo people living in the southern Arizona deserts, and with people living in what is now Mexico. Seashells, parrots and other items came into the villages from the south.

Kent Lightfoot, in a paper for Arizona State University, described the conventional archaeological wisdom on native populations in east central Arizona from 1000 to 1400 AD in this way: "1) the increasing aggregation of families into large Pueblos along permanent drainages ... 2) a widening scope of social integration ... 3) the adoption of more productive corn strains ... 4) the development of irrigation and other water control strategies ... and 5) a greater diversity and quantity of exotic goods being associated with large Pueblos."

He attributed the changes to an increase in springtime droughts, which caused the villagers to give up dry farming. He said, "There was a widespread movement toward large permanent streams such as Silver Creek and the Little Colorado River, which offered well-watered, arable land. The settlement shift toward large permanent rivers produced a pattern of population aggregation in a few settlements and increased the number of clan-like units incorporated within a village." Lightfoot went on to suggest that sociopolitical organization and trade should be analyzed as causes of change in addition to the question of rainfall.

The villagers had rooms called kivas for religious purposes. These rooms kept many of the characteristics of a pit house even when incorporated into large apartment houses. Great kivas reached a diameter of nearly 60 feet.

Archaeologists call early members of this group basketmakers because of the artistry of their weaving. They hunted small animals with a boomerang-like weapon and large animals with a spear propelled by a launching stick.

These native people were among the first in Arizona to make pottery, beginning around 400 A.D. They acquired great skill and creativity, both in shaping their pots and decorating them. Dozens of pottery types, named for local ruins, were traded throughout the Southwest and are often used to date archaeological sites hundreds of miles from the White Mountains. Woodruff Red and Forestdale Red pots were made from 600 to 700 A.D. They were created from gray clay and coated with yellow ocher, which turns red when fired. Black iron ore pigment was applied to the vessels to make geometric designs.

St. Johns Polychrome became popular from 1175 to 1300. It is sometimes called the most widely distributed pottery in the Southwest, with examples found from New Mexico to Prescott and from Colorado to Chihuahua, Mexico. It has the red color of Forestdale pottery, with the black designs, but also has white paint in its decoration.

Pinedale Black-on-Red was made from 1275 to 1325. Pinedale Polychrome is also dated from 1275 but extends to 1350. These local pottery types are some of the first in the region to have glazing, meaning that the fired pottery was coated with a clear mineral or vegetable substance and re-fired to give it a shiny finish so that the vessel could hold water.

Fourmile Polychrome, named for a site near Taylor, is dated to the 75 years before 1400. Some of the distinctive designs are believed to have significance to Kachina religious practices.

Pre-Pueblo people also covered the area with petroglyphs showing geometric patterns, animals and human figures. They created images by scratching and pecking away the dark surface of rocks to reveal a lighter layer beneath. While some have attempted to interpret these symbols, most scientists consider the effort highly subjective. Other early Indians applied paint to rocks, creating what are called pictographs. Although they are less permanent than the carved petroglyphs, particularly when exposed to weather, some pictographs still survive in caves and under overhanging cliffs.

As the bow and arrow helped early natives become more efficient hunters and agriculture tied them more closely to specific locations, they evolved into what archaeologists categorize as Pueblo Indians. Living in settled villages enabled them to devote time to long-term activities. They began weaving their cotton with looms around 700 A.D.

Towns grew in size throughout the White Mountains as many northern and eastern communities such as Kayenta and Chaco Canyon collapsed. Migration into the area "likely included individuals and small family groups as well as small communities, and such groups were accepted by local populations," according to an article in *Zuni Origins* by David A. Gregory and David R. Wilcox. The newcomers sometimes were used as guards, a necessity because of intermittent warfare. "Many existing hamlets were burned out."

One of the most interesting sites in the White Mountains is Casa Malpais near Springerville. Not only did it possess a large kiva for religious ceremonies, but also contains underground burial chambers or catacombs.

Some dispute the use of the term catacomb because they say it implies excavated masonry burial vaults like those under Rome. But others say the masonry work and related improvements under Casa Malpais are indeed extensive. The catacombs underlie an area of two or three acres, with some rooms 20 feet high and 80 feet long. The stonework includes vaulted ceilings and entryways to the fissures. They contain hundreds of skeletons.

The site, along with Kinishba Pueblo near Whiteriver, is on the National Register of Historic Places.

To avoid any facilitation of pothunters who are actively looting much of the archaeological heritage of the White Mountains, the authors have decided against listing the many important ruins in the area not currently under active supervision. Suffice it to say that the area was well populated. Nearly every running stream had pueblos at some point in time.

The Collapse: Where Did They Go?

Around 1400, the White Mountain pueblos collapsed. This disappearance has been a great puzzle to archaeologists, and the general public, who have been intrigued with the ruins for more than a century.

The dry climate and remoteness of the White Mountain region preserved hundreds of ancient structures, making the area one of the most fertile fields for archaeology in the world. Archaeologists coming into the Southwest at the dawn of their science in the 1800s were fascinated by the huge standing ruins and wondered where the residents had gone.

Modern scientists realize their predecessors were asking the wrong questions. Most dwellings built before 1000 A.D. are no longer inhabited, in America or elsewhere. The difference in the Southwest was that the arid climate and sparse population allowed so many ancient habitations to survive into the modern age.

Also, the early theorists were hampered by their own European concept of real estate value. But the White Mountains were not like populous Europe. With only a million residents in pre-Columbian America north of Mexico, land was plentiful. There was little reason to stay somewhere if a more promising area

17

This beautiful butterfly pot was found at Casa Malpais and is on display at the ruins' museum in Springerville.

Carol Sletten © 2010

beckoned.

Even when the Mogollon towns were largest, they continued to rely on hunting and gathering in addition to farming. Many locations were only occupied part of the year. If opportunities improved elsewhere, people did not return to towns where living was difficult.

With more than 90 percent of the pre-Columbian Indians of North America living in what is now Mexico and Central America, the area that is now the Southwestern United States served as a sparsely populated frontier to the dominant civilization of the continent. Settlements in this borderland would probably expand or contract according to forces operating on the dominant population centers in Mexico.

Some scientists speculate that some of the Pueblo people of the White Mountains retreated to northern Mexico, surviving today as members of the Tarahumara tribe.

Others speculate that the early residents of the White Mountains were unable to create the social structure to govern their expanding cities, leading to chaos that caused them to disperse. Still others consider the Zunis to be descendants of the Mogollons.

The Grasshopper site on the White Mountain Apache Reservation near Cibecue is a well-studied case in the disappearance of the Anasazi. The community reached its peak population around 1375 and was almost totally vacant by 1400. Archaeologists say the Anasazi were de-stabilized by a 23-year drought that hit the area in A.D. 1276. Lightfoot, the anthropologist, wrote a paper for Arizona State University, arguing that drought may be overstated in the population shifts among the pre-historic Indian villages. He said social, political and economic factors were also involved. In particular, he pointed to the amount of labor required to maintain extensive irrigation systems in the area. The rapid snowmelt in the spring turned tiny streams into raging rivers that ripped out primitive dams. After the flood, Pueblo residents were left with thousands of hours of backbreaking work to rebuild the dam, and no water for the current year's crop. Perhaps they didn't have the political structures to continually organize this work, or perhaps they just found it easier to live elsewhere.

In today's modern U.S. economy, people who make their living growing vast amounts of corn don't choose to farm the rocky arid soils of the Southwest. We tend to think of the villages of the Colorado Plateau as being isolated, but archaeologists have found artifacts that indicate trade routes extended into Mexico. Another major route started in California and passed through the White Mountains en route to the Great Plains. With the whole continent available to them and hundreds of years to adapt, perhaps individuals, or small groups, found better opportunities on their trading trips and didn't always return.

Today, scientists largely discount a once widespread theory that villages in the area were attacked by Apaches and Navajos moving into the Southwest. It is now thought that the pueblos were gone before the Athabascans arrived. Even so, there is some indication that the pre-historic Indians of the area were occasionally disrupted by hostile forces, probably other pre-historic groups from the south or east. Cannibalism has been documented at a few sites in the Southwest.

The dispersion of modern Indian languages offers some clues to the disappearance. It is clear from oral history and the White Mountain archaeological record that the Hopi are at least in part descended from these ancient Pueblo people. The Hopi language is a branch of the Uto-Aztecan group, which also includes tribes from the Aztecs of southern Mexico to the Shoshone of the northern Rockies. The language group takes in the Yaqui, Tarahumara, Pima, Comanche and Utes of northern Mexico, Arizona and Utah.

Perhaps some day we will know if any of the ancient ones from the White Mountains also joined the Yaqui, Tarahumara, Comanche, Shoshone or other people of the Uto-Aztecan group.

Linguists have not yet put together a timeline for the development of this language, but its roots appear to be somewhere in an area between Guadalajara and the U.S.-Mexican border. The Aztecs have a tradition of leaving the Southwestern United States or northern Mexico in A.D. 1168 before conquering central Mexico on the eve of the European invasion. Scholars do not know how closely the Aztecs are related to Arizona tribes and their ancestors, but Aztecs do have some cultural, as well as linguistic, similarities to the Hopi.

Hopis Pack Up and Move North

Hopis say many of their clans came from the White Mountain area. This ancient oral history helped scientists complete the world's first tree ring chronology.

In 1929, archaeologists were developing a method to date sites by determining the age of wood in ancient ruins. Trees grow a new ring each year as the trunk expands. The width of the ring depends on the moisture conditions during the growing season. The patterns of thick and thin rings are relatively constant throughout an area. By comparing a sample of wood to known patterns in ring growth, the age of a beam can be determined.

Scientists had already determined the pattern of tree rings going back from 1929 to the year 1280. They had also put together a 580-year chart of rings by studying beams from ancient ruins. However, they could not date the second chart because they did not know how many years there were between the two sets of tree ring patterns.

To search for that missing link, Dr. A. E. Douglass led a group to the Hopi pueblo of Oraibi. He thought they might find it there because the village is the longest continuously occupied town in America. The expedition gained permission to bore into beams of the oldest dwellings by promising to fill the holes with turquoise, a stone sacred to the Hopi. Although that information from Oraibi pushed knowledge of tree ring patterns back to 1260, it still did not link up to the ancient samples. When the Hopis heard the archaeologists needed to find a village even older than Oraibi, they told Douglass to go south to a place in the White Mountains where their ancestors had lived before settling on the Hopi Mesas. They directed him to the Show Low ruin, which was located where downtown Show Low sits today. The ruin had once been a thriving village, described as a multi-story pueblo of several hundred rooms

The Vernon Image is a human effigy of stone that was found in a great kiva near Springerville. It was identified as a Hopi water god and is in the collection of the Field Museum in Chicago.

Carol Sletten
© 2010

built in an 'E' shape around north and south plazas.

"The general area in which the men were working is one where modern things intermingle with ancient ones," Douglass wrote in the 1929 *National Geographic*. "There are 20th century houses, cisterns and stone walls, barns, chicken yards, and fences covering the site of what remains of the prehistoric buildings, most of which were razed many years ago."

There, near the 20th century town, they found an ancient log in the ruins and named it HH39.

"...Whereas the Oraibi beam could tell us nothing back of 1260, Show Low's HH39 did not stop there," Douglass wrote. "Here was its account of 1258, a hard year, and of 1254, an even harder one. Presently it told of 1251 and 1247, years when all the trees were singing, 'How Dry I Am.'

"We were getting down close to the center now, but the rings were clean and easily understood. Finally came the one at the very core, and from its central ring we learned that this charred old stick began its life as a promising upright pine A.D. 1237, just ten years after the Sixth Crusade moved eastward to compel the Saracens to restore Jerusalem."

"Later that evening we gathered under the spluttering old gasoline torch in the village hotel, and beneath its flickering light, by the use of my skeleton plots of prehistoric tree rings, we began to determine whether our historical chronology now extended back from 1260 to 1237 by Beam HH39 might not overlap the old chronology."

It did. Scientists now had an unbroken record of tree rings

extending back to 700 A.D.

Thirty-one years later, Dr. Paul S. Martin of Chicago's Field Museum of Natural History made another startling discovery, which linked ancient residents of the White Mountains to the Hopi. He was leading a dig in 1960 at Winema Village on the Hooper Ranch north of Springerville when his workers uncovered a stone-lined crypt under the great kiva of the ruin. After taking the top off the 12-inch, rock-lined box sealed with adobe, they discovered a stone figure nine inches tall. It was lying face down in the box with one arm broken off. A decorated clay pot containing 11 beads was buried with it.

Martin, who worked in the White Mountains from 1952 to 1972, wrote for a popular audience so his discovery was widely followed. A national news syndicate broadcast the story of the sensational find, announcing to the world that archaeologists had uncovered an early stone Kachina. It was named the Vernon Image, not because it was found in Vernon, but because Martin's field headquarters was near that community.

And the figure was not a Kachina. Hopi Kachina dolls are made of wood and used to instruct children about religion. A stone carving is of much greater significance – a wu'ya or clan deity – with both great beneficial and destructive power. When Hopis inspected the figure, they instantly identified it as Panaiyoikyasi, the god of the Water Clan. When the ancient ones decided to abandon the village, they were faced with a dilemma. The Hopis explained that the wu'ya was buried face down with its arm broken in order to protect the world from its immense power.

Though the pigment had largely deteriorated, archeologists determined that the image was originally painted with a black hood and rainbow stripes. It was taken to the Chicago museum for display.

A Hopi legend says two branches of the Water Clan, the Short Well and Deep Well people, lived near Globe before they split in a dispute between two brothers who both wanted to be village chief. The younger brother was able to call down rain by praying to Panaiyoikyasi, but the anger of the older brother caused him to take his people to the village near Springerville.

There they established one of the four corners of the Hopi

world, the Red Cloud House. Traditional Hopis believe that the other three corners are watched over by the Fire or Ghost Clan at Navajo Mountain, the Eagle Clan at Mesa Verde and the Kachinas in the San Francisco Peaks.

Tradition says each of the four corners has a god buried in a stone crypt, but only the one near Springerville has been discovered.

Though the inhabitants of Winema migrated to the Hopi mesas to the north, their descendants still have reverence for the White Mountains and their Red Cloud House.

The Ancestral Home
Of the Zuni Mudheads

Zunis, who now live in a New Mexico pueblo, also have a tradition of once living at Winema.

The Zuni creation story traces the migration route of a large portion of the tribe from northwest Arizona down into the White Mountains, stopping at Winema near Springerville, which they call Shohk'onan im'a. They regard the site as the home of Mudheads, deities who are impersonated by humans in Zuni dance ceremonies. The mudhead impersonators wear round black helmets and represent Zuni ancestors from an underground world.

Though the Zunis and Hopis have a long history of interaction and both absorbed clans from the White Mountain area, they speak different languages. The Hopis' dialect of Uto-Aztecan is spoken by most descendants of the ancient inhabitants of the Southwest. The Zunis speak a language that is almost entirely unique.

Another important Zuni site in the White Mountains is Koluwala:wa. It is located at a mineral spring near the confluence of the Little Colorado and Zuni rivers. The site plays an important part in the Zuni creation story, being the location where various bands of the tribe split before wandering in different directions and rejoining at the present pueblo of Zuni.

Traditional Zunis believe that when they die, they will join their ancestors beneath the water in the spring. A pilgrimage is held every four years with the Zunis walking from their current home to Koluwala:wa. The sacred site is the newest reservation in Arizona and the only one that is not inhabited on a regular basis.

The original Zuni village of Hawiku, which was attacked by Coronado, is also at the edge of the White Mountains. The abandoned pueblo is just inside the Arizona state line northeast of St. Johns.

There are Zuni religious shrines on Mount Baldy and several other locations throughout the White Mountains. Zuni people continued to have contacts with the White Mountains into the historical period, claiming all the land north of the Mogollon Rim even after 1848 when the Americans took the area from Mexico.

A Zuni trade route, in pre-contact times, extended through the White Mountains, crossed over the Mogollon Rim near present-day Show Low and continued on to the Gulf of California, where they obtained shells. The *Zuni Atlas* describes another route east of Mount Baldy, which headed south.

Early pueblo residents of the White Mountains lived successfully in the harsh environment for hundreds of years by valuing the balance of nature. If their beliefs were similar to the traditions of the Hopi and Zuni, they regarded all natural resources as gifts, and considered the mountains, lakes, streams and cycles of the seasons to be sacred.

Kachina Religion Emerges
In Little Colorado Area

Scientists believe the Kachina religion, which unites many of the Pueblo people of the Southwest, originated in the White Mountains or nearby. The society is an essential part of Pueblo life, integrating the members of diverse hereditary clans into a common society and cosmology. The Kachina Society cares for many of the spiritual and physical needs of the village. In addition to conducting ceremonies, the society distributes food to all the people.

In his book, *The Origin and Development of the Pueblo Katsina Cult,*

This design, on a bowl found at the Hooper Ranch near Springerville, helped archaeologists theorize that the Kachina religion originated in the White Mountains.

Carol Sletten
© 2010

E. Charles Adams argues that the religion began on the upper Little Colorado. By this description, he means the section of the river north of St. Johns rather than the actual headwaters near Greer. Adams bases his theory on the depictions of Kachinas in the Fourmile pottery of about 1300 A.D. Such representations of deities are not present in the earlier Pinedale pottery. Though the names of these pottery types are based on their first discovery in excavations in the White Mountains (Four Mile is near Taylor), pottery of both types have been found in wide areas of Arizona and New Mexico.

"The Fourmile style apparently represents a rapid and widespread shift in the decoration on primarily bowl interior bottoms beginning about 1340 in the upper Little Colorado River area and spreading north, south and east over the next century," Adams wrote. "Thus, its depiction on local ceramic traditions, such as at Homol'ovi (near Winslow) and Point of Pines (south of the White Mountains just below the Salt River), may signal local adoption of the Katsina cult."

In the most developed Kachina religion, practiced by the Hopi, the word Kachina, or Katsina as Adams spells it, refers to three different things. The dolls carved from cottonwood root represent the Kachina spirits and help children differentiate between the various Kachinas. Men wear masks and become the Kachina spirits in ceremonies participated in by the whole village. Finally, the Kachina spirits themselves come to this, the fourth world, early in the year and return in July to the third world, which is believed to lie beneath the Grand Canyon.

The arrival of the Kachina religion in a village can be dated by archaeologists based on the creation of a large central plaza for the dances, and the construction of large rectangular kivas. Kinishba, near Whiteriver, and Grasshopper, west of Cibecue, are mentioned as pueblos in the White Mountain area with large central plazas essential to the Kachina religion. These two sites, along with Forestdale, near Show Low, are mentioned as having large rectangular kivas.

Adams felt some of the elements of Kachina religion came from the south. He mentions both the architectural elements and the construction of large parrot cages in northern Mexico as being early signs of changing religious practice.

While scientists will continue to work on these theories, the creation of a new religion and its eventual spread certainly would explain many of the similarities between the diverse people we now call the Pueblos. Eventually, we may even learn what role, if any, this rise in theocracy played in the abandonment of so many pueblos.

Apaches Thrive in High Country

Apaches, who still live in the White Mountains, and their closely related neighbors, the Navajos, broke off from other Athabascan groups in Alaska and northwest Canada. It is believed they traveled along the Rocky Mountains to the southern Great Plains, the Southwestern United States and northern Mexico.

The Navajos were a Western Apache band before cultural changes set them apart a few hundred years ago. Even though the Athabascans were among the last Native Americans to arrive in the New World, they are hardly newcomers. They have apparently been in America for about 10,000 years. Athabascans were wandering the New World well before Homer wrote his poem about Ulysses being lost in the seas of the Old World.

That gave the Apaches a long time to wander. Some authorities put them in the Southwest by 1100 A.D. Others argue for a later entrance. It is possible that the highly mobile bands wandered in and out of the area a number of times.

As hunter-gatherers, the early Apaches were experts at living in the Southwest mountain environment. They seasonally migrated through a series of campsites at differing elevations to take advantage of food available in each location. Their custom of living in small bands made it easy for them to be mobile and to use the natural resources without depleting the environment. They planted corn in mountain valleys, moved to other locations to harvest wild plants, hunted, returned to harvest the corn and moved again. They gathered leaves of the mescal plant, acorns, pine nuts, manzanita, juniper berries, yucca fruit, cactus fruit, wild potatoes, wild onions and mushrooms. They hunted deer, antelope, quail, some waterfowl, small birds, rabbits and wood rats.

Agriculture

Before coming to the Southwest, Apaches harvested only wild plants, but through contact with the Pueblo people they learned the value of agriculture. Apaches grew corn in irrigated fields. They chose the time to plant by watching the emergence of wild plants rather than astrological events. In high elevations, corn was planted as early as April so it could mature before the fall frosts, but in lower elevations planting continued as late as July. Water was channeled onto the tiny fields from streams or springs. Apaches never planted in flood plains of rivers, according to *The Western Apache* by Winfred Buskirk. They rotated their fields, not planting the same spot two years in a row. "In early times men did not always participate in agriculture," Buskirk wrote. "Raiding and hunting took them away from home much of the time, leaving all agricultural activities to the women. When not otherwise engaged, however, men often helped with all forms of farm work." They cleared brush with fire and used sticks for tilling and planting. "The majority of the Apache preferred blue corn, although red and the soft variety of white were also popular," Buskirk wrote. Apaches returned to the fields to begin harvesting anywhere from late August to November. Usually they picked only ripe ears, but sometimes they collected green ears and baked them in a pit. "Rich people stored in pitched baskets, [plain] baskets, or pottery vessels," Buskirk wrote. "Poor people wrapped their corn in bear grass. Corn placed in grass spoiled if it became damp." They also grew various types of beans and gourds.

Like Arizona's pre-historic Indians, Apaches used matates to grind corn. Women placed the grain on the flat, concave rock, and used a second stone to grind it into flour. Matates were also used to grind acorns and other seeds. "As preparation for adult life, Apache girls began grinding corn when they were five or six years old," says *Don't Let the Sun Step Over You* written by Eva Tulene Watt and edited by Keith Basso.

Western Apaches made two kinds of alcoholic beverages. Tulapai was brewed by allowing corn to sprout and ferment. Tiswin was made by cooking, grinding and fermenting the heart of the mescal plant. The mescal brew was more potent and took longer to make. Because tiswin spoiled quickly, it was consumed as soon as it was ready, often in great quantities. Both beverages could be spiked with peyote from cactus found in the southern deserts. That psychoactive brew was used for religious purposes as well as entertainment. The names of the two beverages have been used interchangeably by both Apaches and whites.

Clothing

Apaches used deerskin for clothing. The hide was soaked in water, scraped with a bone to remove hair, meat and fat, and then soaked again. The brains of the deer were applied to soften the leather before additional soaking. "The thick skin from the sides of a deer's jaws was used for the soles of moccasins, skin from the middle of deer legs for the uppers," Buskirk wrote. Both men and women wore "leggings to mid-thigh, a breechclot for men, a long skirt for women, and optionally worn upper garments." Apaches also used coyote, mountain lion, bobcat, badger, fox, skunk, raccoon, beaver and squirrel skins for clothing, blankets and other items.

Baskets, Cradleboards, Pottery and Other Items

Apaches used baskets ingeniously for many domestic purposes because their light weight was compatible with a mobile lifestyle. White Mountain baskets were usually woven from mulberry because the dense hardwood was durable enough when moist to be used in cooking. Later, when other fireproof materials were available, willow twigs, sumac and cottonwood shoots were used. Devil's claw and yucca root were woven in for decoration.

Shapes included a coiled tray and a woven bottle, or tus, which was made of sumac and covered with pinyon pitch so it could hold water. The Western Apache flat-bottomed burden basket had sloping sides reinforced with pieces of leather to protect the contents. They also made large baskets for storage "jars."

Though Apaches created simple pottery cooking vessels, they never developed ceramics into an art form like their more sedentary neighbors.

Cradleboards were used to restrain and carry infants. They were made from a wooden hoop covered with strips of yucca or other plants. The inside was padded with soft moss and a woven canopy protected the child's head from the sun.

Apaches made music with gourd rattles, wooden flutes and buckskin-covered drums, beaten with a hooped stick. Violins were made from hollow pieces of walnut or agave stalks. They were strung with a single piece of sinew and played with a horsehair bow.

Beliefs

Ussen, the Giver of Life, is believed to be the source of all supernatural Power, the one who creates a spirit or life force in all things, both animate and inanimate. He provides some unity to the Apache cosmology, but there are few stories about him.

Other deities are more frequently mentioned, including Changing Woman, the Twins — Born for Water and Killer of Enemies — Sun, Water Old Man, the trickster Coyote, Spider Woman and the Mountain Spirits or Gans. Changing Woman has multiple names, including White Painted Woman and White Shell Woman. She is the mother of the twins and is associated with nature and cyclical renewal. The twins went on heroic quests to kill monsters that were plaguing the world. Sun and Water, the fathers of the twins, give light to the world and make things grow. Coyote is involved in many stories, often tricking humans. Spider woman, less important to Apaches than to Navajos and Hopis, is a benevolent deity who aided the hero twins.

The Gans are involved in curing and are represented by the Crown Dancers in ceremonies. There are four Gans, representing the four directions. The men paint their bodies and wear black hoods under elaborate wooden crowns. They carry wands or swords, painted with zigzag symbols of lightning, and are accompanied by an irreverent clown swinging a noisemaker called a bullroarer. "The concerned Giver of Life sent the Gan as his emissaries to teach the Apache how to live a better way," says *The People Called Apache* by Thomas Mails. "Now they learned in plain terms how to live decently and honorably, how to cure the sick, how to govern fairly, how to hunt effectively and responsibly, how to plant and harvest, and how to discipline those who failed to live as Giver of Life wished them to." Gans are similar to Hopi Kachinas in that they are mountain spirits represented by humans at dances. Unlike Kachinas, the Gans remain with the Apaches throughout the year and help and heal them on a more personal basis. The dancers within Apache culture are a very special group who receive extensive religious training.

One sacred story involves the repentance of the Apache people who have turned away from the path laid out by the Gans. When a boy is taken into a cave by the Gans his people begin to dance in an effort to get him back. When the Gans appear, the boy's spotted dog recognizes him among the holy ones.

Anthropologist Grenville Goodwin, the author of *Myths and Tales of the White Mountain Apache,* stayed with them and learned their stories. Apaches attribute his death from brain cancer at the age of 33 to his having learned too much about their powerful religion.

Stories are told only in winter months when darkness prevents the deities from seeing the Apaches talking about them. The tales lose much when translated into English and placed on the printed page. "He Goes to His Father: Slaying of Monsters" is a very important story. Much like Homer's Iliad defines the Greek pantheon, the Apache deities are introduced in the odyssey of the Hero Twins who go to find the Sun. Some stories are holy, but others, even though they mention deities, serve a more secular purpose, entertaining and instructing the listeners. Different bands have their own versions of their origins, which satisfy the need to center themselves in the natural world.

"Most Athabascan systems of cosmology involve a belief that both living and inanimate objects are invested with a 'Power' that inherently is neither good nor bad, but capricious, unpredictable, and potentially dangerous because of its strength," says *Western Apache Heritage* by Richard John Perry. "Such Power may interact directly with humans, generally through dreams, and affect them in various ways." Individuals sometimes obtain supernatural powers from an animal or natural phenomena, such as Bear Power or Lightning Power. These Powers, obtained through dreams or visions, often involve healing, but can also aid in hunting, war and other aspects of traditional life. Mountains, springs and some caves are especially sacred.

Ghosts were a source of dread. "They whistled in the dark, or appeared to people in dreams, or in the form of owls, and they could cause sickness through fear," says *Western Apache Heritage*. Traditionally, people took measures to avoid ghosts. "They removed the bodies through holes made in the walls of their dwelling and buried their dead with all personal belongings. Relatives did not mention the name of the deceased, and they destroyed or abandoned the dwellings."

Apaches believe that witches use Power to harm others. They are often older persons, almost always men and identified with unusual sexual practices, such as incest. Apaches believe witches cause sickness and death by using poison, spells and injecting foreign objects into the bodies of their victims. "Unlike medicine men, they do not conduct ceremonials, do not employ chants, do not make sandpaintings, and they use their Power to cause sickness," wrote Keith Basso in *Western Apache Witchcraft*. Medicine men, however, can turn to the dark side when tempted to use Power to harm others. Witches are little discussed because a display of knowledge about the dark arts invites suspicion. Generally avoided, suspects are ostracized and have even been killed.

The most powerful shamans acquire their spiritual gifts through dreams or visions. Medicine men are paid for performing curing ceremonies, which often involve administering herbs, chanting prayers and creating sandpaintings. Cattail pollen, eagle feathers, tobacco and other holy objects are important to the rituals. Young Apaches can be trained to be medicine men. Women sometimes have healing and other Powers, but don't lead ceremonies.

The Sunrise Ceremony is the most important event in an

31

Apache girl's spiritual life. When she first menstruates, the girl is ceremonially conducted into adulthood by her band, who drum, sing and dance. An eagle feather and a white-shell bead are tied in her hair, and pollen is rubbed on her face. The Gan impersonators come to bless her and the people who have come to honor her. The Sunrise Ceremony is important to the entire community. It ties the people to their traditions and reminds them of their place in the cycles of nature. During the puberty ceremony, traditionally four days long, the girl is dressed as White Painted Woman and believed to possess the healing Power of the deity.

"It is important," according to *Changing Woman of the Apache* by Sydele Golston, "because the rituals represent the constant recreation of the world and the renewal of the community. Days of song cycles lead her through all the periods of her life from youth and young womanhood to adulthood and old age as the girl actually personifies the first woman … she acquires goodness and strength from Changing Woman, which she shares with others through the blessing Powers that she holds through the duration of the ceremonies."

The medicine disk ceremony was used often in the past. It was directly related to healing. Medicine men created sandpaintings, up to 16 feet across, elaborately designed with signs, symbols and representations of Gans. The sick person walked in circles on the design or was sprinkled with the sand. The sandpainting had to be created and destroyed within one day. Other dances were performed to bless warriors and hunters.

First-time warriors were subject to taboos, including prohibitions against scratching their heads with their hands or allowing water to touch their lips. The youths had to carry a scratching stick and a drinking tube for days before going into action. Apaches had hundreds of taboos. There were prohibitions against killing snakes and bears, or eating javalinas, fish or other water-dwelling creatures. Taboos had a purpose. Fish, for example, were thought to represent the spirits of evil women, while bears were believed to be re-incarnated humans. Snakes were messengers to the deities. Men were required to avoid women's blood. The consequences of violating any of the circumscriptions could be dire. Taboos, particularly the dietary ones, were modified over time, especially during times of extreme need. Sweat baths are still used to prepare for ceremonies.

Games

Apaches played many games and gambled enthusiastically on all of them. In one game, a long pole was thrown into a small hoop. Both the pole and hoop were divided with markings, similar to a dartboard. The score was based on where and how the pole touched the hoop. Women were not allowed to participate or even watch. Western Apaches also played "dice." They threw three sticks, each with one flat and one rounded side. If three round sides landed facing up, it was worth 10 points. If the player's sticks landed with three flat sides up, he scored five points. Other combinations produced lower scores. Apaches wrestled and held contests similar to tug-of-war. Some games had sacred meanings. The moccasin game was one of those. Four shoes were partially buried on each side of a fire. A team put a bone in one of the moccasins and the opposing side had to guess which one. If they missed, points were awarded based on how far removed the guess was from the correct moccasin. They played until the score was 104 to nothing. If they didn't finish by dawn, participants blackened their faces and continued, according to *The People Called Apache*. Songs performed during the contest describe the first moccasin game between animals and birds, which determined whether the world would have daylight or perpetual night, according to *Apache Odyssey* by Morris Opler.

Weapons

Early Apaches used bows and arrows, spears, throwing sticks, hooked sticks and clubs. White Mountain Apaches made bows about three-and-a-half feet long from wood wrapped in sinew to add strength. They used sinew or rawhide for the bowstring, according to Buskirk. "Apache arrows were made of reed, with a wooden foreshaft," he said. "The Western Apache also used one-piece wooden arrows made of willow or other woods." The arrows had three radial feathers on the butt and a head of obsidian or hard wood. They used headless arrows for practice and hunting birds and small game. Some bands applied potions to arrowheads in a belief they would be more fatal to deer. Others used "poison" when going to war. The ingredients of the secret concoction varied from herbs and putrid animal organs to insect and snake venom.

They used wooden spears up to fourteen feet long. The points were made from hardwood or stone before iron became available. Straight or curved throwing sticks were used to bring down small game while a club made of bone, stone and leather was used "for dispatching an animal after it had been run down," Buskirk said. They pulled rats and rabbits out of their holes with a hooked stick. Boys in Cibecue were said to use the sling as a toy, but not for hunting.

Apaches also caught game in snares and traps, and made deer calls. They sometimes wore deer or antelope heads and covered their shoulders with skins to disguise themselves in the hunt.

Dwellings

Because Apaches moved through a variety of climates and stayed for varying lengths of time, they made several different types of houses. The gowa, or wickiup, was a brush hut. Small tree trunks were tied together at the roof with the opposite ends spread out to form a circle. In domed gowas, the branches stretched all the way across from the ground to the top of the structure and back to the ground. Each wickiup had a smoke hole in the center of the roof with an entrance to the east or northeast. In summer camps, Apaches put a brush roof on poles to form a ramada. These could be connected to gowas or free-standing.

Early Athabascans created wind breaks for short stays by piling up branches or placing rocks in a ring. Sometimes the rocks were piled into higher walls. There is no indication that these structures were roofed. Some camps were protected by low log walls.

They placed blankets over piles of dried grass to make beds. Dogs served as pack animals to help the band move between campsites until the Apaches obtained horses from the Spanish.

Social Structure

Athabascans were born into their mother's clan and sub-clan. The members of the sub-clan formed a migrating troupe, led by a headman and a headwoman, who counseled the people in the ways of living and organized food gathering by the women.

Apaches had to marry outside their clan, with the husband

usually living with the wife's family. Maternal cousins were considered siblings. And if they were of the opposite sex, they couldn't talk to each other unless they had their backs turned or had a barrier between them so they couldn't see each other.

Married couples often lived near the girl's mother in a wickiup built by her female relatives. It was taboo for a man to talk to his mother-in-law even though he had to live in close proximity to her. A man sometimes married two or more sisters. Twins were considered an indication of immorality, and one of them was killed at birth.

Little girls were given the same training as boys. They practiced with bow and arrows, slings and spears. But as they grew up, they took on the burdens of Apache women, doing the heavy work in the camp as well as farming, tanning hides and food gathering. Men were free to spend their time hunting, raiding and fighting enemies. Women would occasionally join in these activities.

The Apaches had periods of peace when they traded with their more settled agricultural neighbors, but they did go on raids if the need or opportunity presented itself.

Coronado Finds
White Mountains Desolate

Apaches would soon be meeting another group of raiders, a restless people who came from an area nearly 6,000 miles east of the White Mountains. The invaders had practiced settled agriculture for thousands of years, but still raided when the opportunity presented itself. The Spaniards had united most of the Iberian Peninsula, through wars against Moslems, before they sent Cortez to conquer Mexico and Pizarro to loot Peru.

After viciously subduing those areas, the Spanish had control over nearly 18 million of the 20 million people in the New World. Though the conquerors had stolen nearly all of the precious metals and stones ever mined in the Americas, they wanted more. So they focused their greed on the unexplored north.

In 1536, four men came to Mexico City with a fantastic tale, which helped touch off one of the most fabled misadventures in history. The men, Alvar Nunez Cabeza de Vaca, Alonso del Castillo, Andres Dorantes and his slave, Estevanico, had escaped a hostile Indian attack in Florida in 1528. They were then shipwrecked on the Gulf of Mexico before traveling overland across what is now the southern United States and northern Mexico. It took them eight years to get to Mexico City. When they did, they passed along rumors about fantastic treasures in what is now Arizona and New Mexico. The three white men declined to go back, but Estevanico had no choice. The viceroy purchased him to guide the priest and adventurer Marcos de Niza to the gold.

Estevanico was a man of African descent who has been variously described as being black or brown. He had spent much of his life as a Spanish slave and, for eight years, as something of a curiosity or celebrity among the North American Indians. The Spanish probably did not realize how little Estevanico enjoyed being a slave.

He went ahead with a number of Indian followers and a harem of Indian women. De Niza followed at what he figured was a safe distance until word came back that "Little Steven" had been killed by Indian arrows. It is unknown how far north Estevanico went, if he was actually killed or whether he simply said "no" to Spanish slavery.

De Niza apparently got cold feet near the current international border. He retreated to Mexico, swearing he had personally seen gold-paved streets in the Seven Cities of Cibola. His words were enough to launch another expedition.

Francisco Vasquez de Coronado, a well-educated man who had come from Spain to rule an area of Mexico's northern frontier near Culiacan, was recruited to bring back the nonexistent gold. On February 22, 1540, Coronado left with 225 men on his famous wild-goose chase, which was to initiate a 300-year war between the Spanish and the Indians in and near the White Mountains.

Scholars differ on Coronado's exact route through the White Mountains, but a growing consensus puts the expedition generally on the following route: When the Spaniards reached the site where Fort Apache would be built, they found a green, forested and well-watered country with fresh rivers and grass. Some scholars say the explorers saw the Kinishba ruin in the area and referred to it as Chiciticale. Next, they ascended the west bank of the main fork of the White River, generally along the route that Arizona 73 follows to the north. They stopped at an arroyo, which they called La Barranca. Later, it would be called Post Office Canyon.

The next night they camped along one of the small streams in the vicinity of McNary. They probably took a route generally along the Forest Service road from McNary to Vernon, passing Summit Spring and camping the next night at Bannon Springs.

Juan Jaramillo, a captain of the expedition, wrote about what happened there: "In the neighborhood of this stream a Spaniard, who was called Espinosa, died, besides two other persons, on account of poisonous plants which they ate, owing to the great need in which they were." These "two other persons" were probably slaves. The plants are thought to have been wild parsnips or water hemlock.

From the "Camp of Death," they set off on a more or less direct line toward Zuni, passing Malpais Spring, down the Big Hollow three miles west of St. Johns and on to a camp on the bank of the Little Colorado. They caught fish that they said were similar to those in Spain.

Some accounts say they saw Indians communicating with Zuni with signal fires. Zunis say the Spaniards may have encountered leaders of a pilgrimage to the home of the Zuni gods only a few miles away, west of present-day St. Johns.

An unpublished U.S. Forest Service manuscript tells how the explorers were visited at their camp on the Little Colorado by four Indians: "The natives made signs of peace, and using interpreters, they said that they had been sent to welcome the Spaniards. The next day, they would supply the expedition with food. The starving soldiers were ecstatic. ... Two Cibolans were held until Coronado could arrive. ... Coronado presented the Cibolans with little cloaks."

The next day, Coronado rode off to the east and captured the Zuni city of Hawiku in a chain of fruitless conquests that would take him as far east as Kansas.

Partly because Coronado did not report seeing any Apaches

in the White Mountains, some historians have denied the Athabascans a role in the pre-history of the Southwest, saying they moved into the area from the Great Plans after the Spanish arrived.

It is likely that Coronado and his men did not find Athabascan bands in the White Mountains because they were looking for golden cities, not wandering hunters and gatherers. Apache tradition says their ancestors were in the area at the time. Some writers even say that Apaches fought alongside the Zunis when those Pueblo people made their stand against Coronado.

While the Athabascans' role in the conflict may be in doubt, their descendants own some of the best physical evidence of Spain's early ill-fated expeditions in the area. The Navajos have a display of Spanish armor at their tribal museum in Window Rock.

The Apache term for Spaniards and Mexicans means "together walking," which hints at some contact with early military expeditions.

The Three Hundred Years War

Though Coronado found no gold, the Spaniards were still determined to get wealth from the northern provinces. Since humans were the only exploitable resource the Europeans found, they set out to enslave the natives. Some Spaniards raided Pueblo Indian villages and took the survivors in chains to work the mines of northern Mexico. Others used the guise of religious zeal to cover their plans, forcing the Indians to labor as converts for the benefit of ecclesiastical or secular authorities. Some natives worked on Spanish farms. Others worked their own land and paid tribute in food and clothing until they were naked and hungry. The nomadic Apache were less easy to exploit than the settled Pueblos.

By the late 1500s, the Spanish had pushed northward close to the present Arizona-Mexico border. As they were working to convert the southern Pimas, Opatas, Conchos and other tribes on the frontier, they started to have more contacts with the next tier of tribes. The Spaniards initially called these people the

Jocomes, Mansos, Janos, Sumas, Cholomes, Jumanos and Sibolos. But it is now believed those people were nearly all Apaches.

In 1598, Juan de Onate left Mexico with about 129 adventurers to set themselves up as the masters of New Mexico. They enslaved the Pueblo people, but had only limited contact with the Apaches of New Mexico and very little interaction with White Mountain bands.

Many Pueblo people fled the increasingly impossible circumstances to join Apaches, who welcomed anyone who could contribute valuable knowledge, skills and numbers to their tribe. The newcomers shared their colorful and complex sacred ceremonies, which they had been able to develop during centuries of living in a more settled civilization. The Apaches, whose ancestors spent more of their time trying to eat and stay warm, were like a thirsty sponge, drinking in the customs of their guests.

In the beginning, the Apaches had usually been peaceful traders with the Spaniards of New Mexico. One of the first flash points between Athabascans and Spaniards came in 1606 when Juan Martinez de Montoya was granted the right to enslave the people of Jemez, a pueblo in north-central New Mexico. Since the village had close contacts with nearby Athabascan bands, many of the Jemez villagers fled to live with Apaches. The Indians began to steal horses for food and transportation. Hostilities spread until the Apaches attacked San Gabriel in 1608. Martinez and Cristobal de Onate, son of the founder of Spanish New Mexico, launched a retaliatory raid against the Apaches.

In 1632, the Zunis were fighting the Spanish in the White Mountains. They killed Friar Francisco Letrado as he tried to Christianize their village of Hawiku near the present New Mexico state line. They attacked and killed another friar who was retreating toward Mexico. The *Zuni Atlas* places the site of the attack near present-day Show Low on the Mogollon Rim. Killed were Friar Martin de Arbide and two soldiers who were escorting him.

While the situation continued to deteriorate in the north, Fray Martin del Espiritu Santo made a peaceful but unsuccessful trip to convert Apaches along the upper reaches of the Gila River in 1626.

Later in that decade, a group of Apaches visited Santa Fe and made inquiries about the Catholic faith. When they left the city, the governor sent a force to enslave them. The leader and many of his people were killed before the rest of the Apaches were brought back as slaves.

Trouble continued to build. The Spanish attempted to defend settlements near the current Arizona-Mexico border and along the Rio Grande in central New Mexico. By 1662, Athabascans along the road between the Zuni reservation and Hopiland made it the most dangerous trail in the territory.

In summer of 1680, the Apache warriors helped the Pueblos throw off Spanish rule. Indians drove the priests and soldiers back to northern Mexico.

In 1692, the Spanish counter-attacked. With superior weapons, they regained control of the settled Pueblos. But the Apaches continued to attack. As the Spanish force reached Zuni, the Apaches stole their cattle. And as the Europeans headed east from Zuni, the Spanish were attacked twice by Apaches. One Apache was captured. He was forced to join the Christian religion, baptized and shot.

The Spanish recaptured the New Mexican Pueblos, but never captured the Apaches. The collapse of the Pueblo Revolt brought important changes to the Athabascans who were joined by Pueblo people escaping from the Spanish. After that, the Navajo began to be considered as a separate tribe and lost their identification as an Apache band because they absorbed so much culture and religion.

The Spanish gave the name "Apache" to all Athabascan speakers in the Southwest. Some historians said the name came from a Zuni word, Apachu, or enemy, which the Zuni used for the Navajo. But that is no longer believed to be the most likely explanation. In what is now central Arizona, Apaches had joined with Mohave Indians to create a band called Mohave-Apaches or Yavapais. Their word for themselves was Apatieh. Spaniards pronounced the word as Apache and gradually began to use it for all Athabascan groups they met.

In the first 75 years after the conquest of Mexico City, Spanish civilization had advanced nearly 1,000 miles up the North American continent. But after encountering Apaches, the Spanish advanced no farther during the next 250 years. Apache warriors prevented the Hispanics from establishing a population density that could have enabled their culture to hold the territory in the face of Anglo expansion from the east.

In 1630, Friar Alonzo Benavides reported that the Apaches were fierce raiders who preyed upon Pueblo villages, but did not attack Spaniards. In his book, *The Basket Weavers of Arizona,* Bert Robinson says: "A few years later, however, this did occur and, in raiding the Pueblos, priests were killed and churches and other property destroyed. By 1670, the Apaches were openly attacking rancherias and missions and killing all they encountered. Between 1670 and 1680, numerous attacks were made on Spanish missions."

Robinson gives an account of an early attack on a Pima mission settlement on the lower San Pedro. "Most of the friendly Indians of the mission were away when the Apaches attacked, and after killing their chief and some of his warriors, the rest were driven into the mission building. The Apaches climbed to the roof and set it afire; then thinking their victory complete; they slaughtered the horses and cattle of the mission and started feasting on the meat. Captain Coro, a Pima chief, lived at another of Father Kino's missions about three miles down the river, and, hearing the fight, came to the aid of his friends. When he arrived, the Apache chief, Capotcari, heaped insults on the Pimas and proposed that 10 men from each tribe be chosen to oppose each other in a mass duel. Capotcari headed his own group, but the Pimas, with their bows and arrows, were too much for the Apaches and soon Capotcari was the only man of his group left in the fight." The Pimas killed the Apache chief and then fought the rest of the Apaches, chasing them into the hills.

By the early 1700s, Spaniards began to apply descriptive names to the various Apache bands. If they saw Apaches gathering mescal, they became known as the Mescalero Apaches. The people of the White Mountains were called Coyotero Apaches by the Spanish, probably because they used dogs as pack animals. Though the Spanish tried to apply names to the Apaches based on where they lived, the groups were highly mobile and individuals moved from one group to another with no formalities. The groups had no fixed political affiliations

Apache raiders were going deep into Sonora, capturing women and children on slave raids as far south as Hermosillo and beyond. Edgar Perry, former director of the Culture Center at Fort Apache, said the White Mountain Apaches did raid into Mexico, but it is likely that the Indians who raided farthest south were those whose territory was closest to the border. After failing to stop the raids by punishing nearby Indians, the Spanish from northern Mexico began to believe that the raiders were coming from well to the north.

The Spanish withdrew from settlements in what is now southern Arizona and established a series of forts just to the south. The Apaches found it easy to slip between the forts, which were sometimes a hundred miles apart. By 1751, San Juan Bautista, then the capital of Sonora, was abandoned. Spanish raids into Apache country succeeded in the random killing of several Indians, but did nothing to reduce the raids. The Pimas of southern Arizona, friendly to the Spanish, were also raided by the Apaches. But the guerrilla raiders, interested in horses, cattle and food, avoided pitched battles with soldiers.

Spanish occupation of the American Southwest was sparse in the 1700s. Santa Fe, the capital of Nueva Mexico, had only 2,324 residents when the Marques de Rubi made an inspection of the frontier for King Carlos III in 1765. Northern Arizona was considerably less developed by the Spanish. A map made during this expedition combines the Salt River and the Little Colorado into a single stream calling it the Rio de Navajo. If the map were correct, someone could put a boat into the Zuni River, float by the Hopi villages and then paddle southwest a relatively short distance to join the Gila near present-day Phoenix. On this strange map, a mission called Aquicu is suggested in the White Mountain area. It is possibly what is now called Hawiku, the ruined Zuni village near the New Mexico state line. The area is generally designated as Provincia de Gila with a people called Yutos Saguaguanos living a bit to the west.

In 1772, Carlos III, King of Spain, ordered a war of extermination against the Apaches. More forts were built and Spaniards raided deep into Apache country. The Spaniards appointed a red-haired Irishman, Don Hugo O'Connor, who had spent 12 years along the northern border, to wage war against hostile Indians from Texas to California. He moved many forts to try to be more effective in protecting Sonora from raiding Arizona

Apaches. The presidio was relocated from Tubac to Tucson. His campaigns were mostly against the Mescalero and Lipan Apache, leaving the White Mountain bands largely untouched.

A new commander, Don Teodoro De Croix, reported casualties from Apache raids during the years 1771-1776 for the northern provinces. The account is given in a book called *The Spanish Borderland Frontier 1513-1821*: "Persons murdered, 1674; persons captured, 154; haciendas and ranches abandoned, 116; livestock stolen, 68,256; not included in these statistics were [military] losses in men and animals."

"The constant raiding of the Gila Apache contributed to the misery in Sonora," says Alfred B. Thomas in an article called "Juan Bautista de Anza in Sonora." "The Pimas and Seris were inciting a general rebellion and seeking an Apache alliance."

De Anza, who became famous for founding San Francisco, was in charge of the Sonoran frontier from 1777 to 1778.

In a report to higher authorities, he said, "I have never seen the province more exposed to total extermination than during the last four years, but most particularly the present time. It would be no exaggeration to say that it is hanging by a very weak thread. Its misfortune proceeds from the war waged unceasingly for more than 40 years by the cruel Apache, contemporaneously with those interior nations who are extremely expert in war, namely the Seris, Pimas and Papagos. Although subjected in several uprisings by punishments which has made them return to their towns, not much success has resulted because a considerable number of the rebels remain in the mountains. The latter not finding sufficient reason to keep the peace by themselves have made alliance with the Apache while keeping up at the same time contact with those in the towns. From this activity has occurred several thousands of favorable opportunities for the cruel murders and robberies they commit, as it is easier to attract their relatives with such successes."

The authorities sought an alliance with the Comanche and more troops from Spain to subdue the Apache.

An event far away from Arizona and the White Mountains dashed that plan. People living on the East Coast of America had bad feelings about their king, George III, who lived on an island even farther to the east. This led to war. At first, the Americans were defeated whenever they fought pitched battles with the better-armed and trained British and German soldiers.

But, perhaps through native ingenuity, and certainly from experience in fighting Indians, the American soldiers decided to fight only when conditions were favorable to them and decline battle when they were not. Using these tactics, which the Apaches would later use against Americans, the colonists were able to continue the war against England for many years. Sensing an opportunity to increase British suffering with little risk, the kings of France and Spain joined the war on behalf of America. So with commitments to join the French against the English, the Spanish could not afford to join the Comanche against the Apache in the American West.

However, it was only a few years later that Spaniards in New Mexico and Arizona were able to again muster the forces to raid Apaches on the upper reaches of the Gila River. De Anza, who had been appointed governor of New Mexico in 1778, decided to continue the war from his new base in Santa Fe. He had no love for Apaches. His father had been killed by them in 1739 and his famous 1775 expedition from Tucson to California had been delayed when Apaches stole the 340 horses that he had planned to use for the journey. *Anza and the Northwest Frontier of New Spain* by J. N. Bowman and R. F. Heizer is one of several works that mentions De Anza breaking up an alliance between the Navajos and the Apaches of the Gila River area. "In the five years after 1780, seven of Anza's commanders made nine expeditions against the tribes in southwest New Mexico and southeast Arizona," Bowman and Heizer wrote. "Spanish arms and aid brought a fair peace among the tribes devastated by famine, disease and tribal wars. Isolated depredations of the Apaches and some other tribes continued intermittently along the Gila River."

But no town was safe. A party of 300 Apaches made an unsuccessful attack on Tucson on May Day in 1782.

As both sides continued to raid each other's settlements, the Spaniards decided to add a new policy. They offered the Apaches free food and unlimited supplies of liquor if they would live near the forts in northern Mexico. The plan worked fairly well for 26 years. The Indians reduced their raiding and small numbers of Spaniards resumed moving into Sonora and southern Arizona.

Again, distant events had an impact on the White Mountains. When powerful kings in Austria and France began to covet the throne of Spain, liberals and conservatives in Spain began to compete for influence. As each party successively gained power in Spain, their opponents in the New World tried to tear Mexico away from the mother country. By 1811, the governments in Spain and Mexico were in such turmoil that there was no money to buy liquor for the Apaches. The tempo of Apache raiding picked up.

Later, after the final breakaway of Mexico in 1821, the new government offered a bounty of $100 for each Apache scalp. The bounty hunters were paid whether the scalp came from a man, a woman or a child. Mangas Coloradas, a leader of the Mimbreno Apache who had been friendly to the Mexicans, became embittered. Tubac was abandoned in 1848. Tucson came under increasing attack.

Apaches also suffered casualties. "Many women and children were carried away at different times by Mexicans," Geronimo later recalled. "Not many of them ever returned, and those who did underwent many hardships in order to be again united with their people. Those who did not escape were slaves to the Mexicans, or perhaps even more degraded."

Americans Arrive in Arizona

Portions of the White Mountains had been claimed by various English colonies and American states for more than 200 years before the first American stepped into the area. When an English king gave land for a colony, he would write the legal description so that the land grant started on the Atlantic Coast and ran all the way through the continent. James I gave the northern portion of the White Mountains to Virginia in 1609, while Charles II gave the entire area to Carolina in 1665. Then George II gave a portion of the White Mountains to Georgia in 1732. Since these grantees could have no influence over land they had never seen, the grants were soon forgotten. Though English-speaking people had long-since abandoned any claim to the area, Americans gave short shrift to the claims of Spanish-speaking people

45

who had never successfully settled northern Arizona. Americans began to enter Arizona more than 20 years before their government gained control of the region.

Fur was one of the first materials early humans used to keep warm, but by the 1800s fur-bearing animals had been hunted to near extinction in Europe. And since kings claimed a monopoly on hunting, fur was extremely valuable. John Jacob Astor realized the Industrial Revolution was creating a wealthy business class that wanted to ape the fashions of royalty. He emigrated from Germany to New York and opened a fur shop. He bought beaver pelts trapped on Long Island, N.Y., until they became extinct on the island. The demand for beaver hats in England was so great that new and more remote streams had to be found. In only a few decades, trappers worked their way to the limits of what was then the American West and they were anxious to move into Spanish territory. Astor became the richest man in the United States, so rich, in fact, that his family bought its way into top positions in the English aristocracy.

The fashion needs of dandies in London created an entirely new breed of men in the American West. The Mountain Men were highly skilled at hunting, trapping and storytelling. With the latter skill, they trapped many historians.

They honed the art of telling tall tales during many long nights in the wilderness with good friends and no other entertainment. Part of their storytelling ability came from economic necessity. They were the first illegal aliens in the Southwest. The Spanish, and later the Mexican bureaucrats, punished Mountain Men severely if they were discovered in the territory working without proper papers.

James Ohio Pattie may have been the first American to reach the White Mountains. Raised in Kentucky, Pattie traveled with his father to New Mexico to seek a fortune in 1824. They received a permit to trap, and on November 22 set out for the headwaters of the Gila. When they reached the mouth of the San Francisco River just inside the Arizona line, they headed north. They probably worked both the upper reaches of the main stem of the San Francisco River in Catron County, New Mexico, as well as the Blue, which starts in the White Mountains.

"The banks of this river are for the most part incapable of

cultivation being in many places formed of high and rugged mountains," Pattie wrote after he returned to the Midwest. "Upon these we saw multitudes of mountain sheep. These animals are not found on level ground, being there slow of foot, but on these cliffs and rocks they are so nimble and expert in jumping from point to point, that no dog or wolf can overtake them.

"One of them that we killed had the largest horns that I ever saw on animals of any description. One of them would hold a gallon of water. Their meat tastes like mutton. Their hair is short like a deer's, though fine. ... We traced this river to its head[waters], but not without great difficulty as the cliffs in many places came so near the water's edge, that we were compelled to cross points of the mountain, which fatigued both ourselves and our horses exceedingly." The expedition went back downstream to the Gila and followed it to the San Pedro before turning back to New Mexico.

Pattie took off down the Gila in 1826 with a group of French trappers. They were attacked near the mouth of the Salt River by a band of Indians that killed all but three members of the party. Pattie called them Papawars, which some historians believe were Papagos, or Tohono O'odham as they are now called. Others have called them Pima-Maricopas, Apaches or Yavapais.

Pattie and two other survivors met up with a party led by Ewing Young, a fellow American. Young's more experienced group included famous trappers Tom "Peg-leg" Smith, George Yount and Milton Sublette. In Pattie's account, perhaps somewhat exaggerated, they attacked the Indians, killing up to 100 members of the tribe and regaining horses lost in the earlier raid. Apaches hung on their flanks as they continued to trap down the Salt. The Indians would raid the camp at night, stealing horses. The combined expedition went to the area where Phoenix now stands. One group trapped up the Verde to its source, while Pattie and the rest of the men worked up the Salt River to the White River and on into the White Mountains. "It [begins] in mountains covered with snow, near the head of the left hand fork of the San Francisco [the Blue River]," he said. Then both groups came back down those rivers before joining up and continuing down the Salt to the Gila and finally to the Colorado.

When they arrived in Santa Fe, the Mexican governor said

they had been trapping without a license and confiscated all their furs. On his next expedition into Arizona, Pattie had to walk out through the California desert to San Diego. He spent time there in a Mexican prison for immigration violations before being released and returning to the Midwest via Mexico City.

When Young returned to Arizona in 1829, he brought along a greenhorn who would ultimately become one of the most famous men of the West. That was the 19-year-old Kit Carson's first trip west. The party headed north from Santa Fe to make the Spanish authorities believe they were headed back to the United States. But Carson said their true purpose was to look for Apaches who had attacked a trapping party earlier. They turned west and passed into Arizona near Zuni, traveling down the Zuni River to its confluence with the Little Colorado. Then they followed the Little Colorado to the mouth of Concho Creek, northwest of St. Johns. They probably passed quite near the area where Snowflake and Taylor would later be founded. From there, Young's party went southwest and crossed the Mogollon Rim south of Pinedale. After they crossed into the Salt River basin, they were soon in contact with Apaches.

"Here we met the same Indians that had defeated the former party," Carson said in his autobiography. "Young directed the greater part of his men to hide themselves, which was done, the men concealing themselves under blankets, pack saddles, and as best they could. The hills were covered with Indians, and seeing so few of us they concluded to make an attack and drive us from our position. Our commander allowed them to enter the camp and then ordered us to fire on them, which was done, the Indians having fifteen or twenty warriors killed and a great number wounded. They were routed, and we continued our march, trapping down Salt River to the mouth of [the Verde River], and up to the head of the latter stream. We were nightly harassed by the Indians, who would frequently crawl into our camp, steal a trap or two, kill a mule or horse, and do whatever damage they could."

The Young expedition's battle with the Apache band "on the headwaters of the Salt River," was probably on the White River, which combines with the Black River to form the Salt.

William Sherley Williams was known as Old Bill Williams by the time he was only a little past 30, probably having aged from alternating bouts of serious drinking and fervent missionary activity among the Osages on the Great Plains.

By late summer of 1826, he had arrived at Santa Fe with famous fur trapper Ceran St. Vrain and 35 others. They got approval to enter Arizona for trading, but were forbidden to trap beaver. They were trapping north of the Salt when Williams was captured by Apaches.

Williams said they stripped him of everything, "clothes, arms, traps and mule." He said they turned him loose and he traveled naked through the White Mountains until he reached Zuni where he was "treated with great veneration and almost worship."

He was heading back to the White Mountains in 1834, approaching through Catron County, New Mexico, when he went north to discover the sacred Zuni Salt Lake east of St. Johns. He continued on across the Little Colorado where he met a Hopi hunting party. The Hopis directed him to the Petrified Forest and Grand Canyon. After visiting those fascinating places, he went on to the mountain and river in western Arizona that would carry his name.

By 1837, the beavers were trapped out of the Gila and its tributaries and Apache contact with Americans ended for a time.

U.S. Takes Possession
Of an Enigma

Eleven years later, decisions made in a town called Washington began to affect people in the White Mountains. American troops were sent into a disputed border area between Mexico and Texas. War was declared in 1848 based on a claim that Mexican troops had attacked the U.S. forces.

The giant industrial nation easily took Mexico's lightly populated northern areas. This action by the United States is often viewed as an abuse of the weak by the strong. But Indians of northern Arizona had a different point of view. Apaches, who had successfully fought the Hispanics for more than 300 years, welcomed the American attack on Mexico and were pleased to increase their raids on their ancient enemies. But after helping to win the war, the Apaches were shocked to learn the terms of a treaty their allies had made with the Mexicans. It gave Apache land to the Americans and obliged the U.S. to end Apache raids on Mexico. After the U.S. gained possession of the Southwest, boundary commissioners were sent out from Washington to explain all of this to the Indians and make peace. The Apaches did not understand.

And the Americans had little knowledge of what they had obtained. An 1853 book published in Boston called *The Indian Races of North and South America* included an article on the Hopis and Navajos: "Not far distant from the Mawkeys, and in the same range of country, is another band of the same description, called Nabbehoes, a description of either of these tribes, will answer for both. ... They say the men are of the common stature, with light flaxen hair, light-blue eyes, and that their skin is of the most delicate whiteness." Americans generally knew even less about Apaches.

Nonsense from the Southwest was to be a steady diet of some eastern publications for decades. As late as 1887, *Century Magazine* published an article by Frederick Schwatka, which claimed that Geronimo was a captured Mexican child. He also gave this fantastic account of an early Apache attack: "Way back in the '50s an emigrant family, winding its toilsome way through the burning desert of the Gila valley, on the road to California, found themselves, with an exhausted team, at the bottom of a steep hill, which they vainly essayed to ascend. A band of Tontos Apaches, bent on some fiendish foray, passing that way, came upon the scene and at once willingly offered their services to carry the effects to the top of the hill. Not only did they do this, but the empty wagon was spared to the exhausted horses and hauled up by hand. This wonderful act of kindness was terminated by the massacre of the owners on the crest of the mesa, while all unawares they were reloading their wagon, the only object of the pretended friendship being undoubtedly to throw the victims off their guard." Presumably, the magazine's fact checker was satisfied that the writer got the story from the murderous Apaches since the emigrants in this tale did not survive.

It was about this time that Francis X. Aubry, something of a latter-day mountain man, at least as far as storytelling is concerned, passed through the area. He told a tale about being attacked by club-wielding Yumas near Flagstaff, where he and his party of 18 fought off 450 Indians without losing a man.

Aubry's stories only got better as he got closer to the White Mountains. In his account about meeting a band of Apaches on August 27, 1853, he said, "We obtained from them over fifteen hundred dollars' worth of gold for a few old articles of clothing. ... The Indians use gold bullets for their guns. They are of different sizes and each Indian has a pouch of them. We saw an Indian load his gun with one large and three small gold bullets to shoot a rabbit."

Fantastic accounts like these were published in newspapers as far away as St. Louis.

Real Indians had to live in a real world that didn't understand or respect them. While some of the White Mountain Apaches wanted peace, other Western Apaches wanted war. Meanwhile, Hispanics and Anglos began to move into the area.

Conflict and Peace Talks

One of the first major conflicts between Apaches and Americans came after a man named James Johnson killed an Apache chief in southwestern New Mexico. Johnson, who had been hired by Mexicans, killed Chief Juan Jose and many of his followers after feigning friendship and luring them to his camp. Johnson's men fired a hidden cannon and then shot the survivors with rifles. Apaches sought revenge.

Mike Burns, an Apache boy captured by the cavalry and raised by Capt. James Burns, wrote a book called *The Indian Side of the Question*. He tells a story, which he heard from an old man named Ha-lo, or Rabbit, about the first meeting of the Apache and whites near present-day Prescott in 1847.

"One day four young warriors decided to go into one of the white men's camps to see if they could not trade some skins they had for something. ... The older people shook hands with the Indians, but the young men got on their horses and acted as if they were going to corral the young warriors. They rode close to them, holding their pistols and guns in readiness, and commenced shooting at the young Indians, only one of whom escaped.

"Ha-lo said that when he was a young healthy man he could run so fast that he could catch a young fawn, but that he never ran so fast as he did in trying to escape from these white men. A few days after this massacre, and after the white men had left the camp, some of the Indians went to the place and found two of the young Indians' bodies mutilated so badly that they could not tell who they were, and the bones of the third Indian were found nearby, having all the appearance of his having been boiled to death."

By 1850, the number of whites entering Apache territory was increasing in response to the discovery of gold at the Santa Rita del Cobre copper mines in New Mexico. When Mangas Coloradas tried to tell the prospectors there was more gold to be found elsewhere, they beat him up.

Franz Huning trapped into the White Mountains in 1851. He said even though members of his party robbed an Apache cache of corn and beans, they were not punished. The Apaches made it fair by stealing two mules as payment.

In 1852, the U.S. made its first treaty with Apaches. The peace commissioners met with a group of Apaches at Acoma Pueblo in New Mexico. Historians believe those Apaches were from the White Mountains. The Americans, expecting the Southwestern Indians to have the formalized structures of eastern tribes, probably thought they were dealing with a political authority greater than an individual band. They didn't understand that an Apache chief was usually the leader of only a relatively small group that lived with him.

John Rope, an Apache Scout who recounted his 1850s childhood in *Arizona Memories*, said there were 10 groups of White Mountain Apaches. "The western White Mountain people had six chiefs, and the eastern White Mountain people four."

He recalls how his band, under a chief named Hacke-Idasila, made peace with the soldiers at Goodwin Springs on the Gila River near San Carlos. "The head officer at Goodwin Springs told Hacke-Idasila that he wanted him as a friend. He said, 'We white people are far from home here, but you Indians know all this country, where the water is, and where the best lands are.

Your people should settle down and live around here in the good places. If you keep on living your old way, you will never eat this new food like we have, but if we are friends, we will all eat it. I see your people eating the guts, legs, hoofs, and heads of horses. If we are friends we shall have lots and eat only the good meat parts.'

" 'All right,' Hacke-Idasila said, and now he told where he lived, at a place where two streams come together. Then he and Guc-Hujn [The Apache name for the leader of the soldiers] embraced and were friends. From that day on they were like brothers and had no more trouble. It has been like that with all of us since that time, and it was Hacke-Idasila who made it this way with the white people for us."

Looking for Ways Across Arizona

Meanwhile, Washington was interested in establishing transportation routes through the area. In particular, the government wanted to know whether the Zuni and Colorado rivers were navigable in case the U.S. went to war with the Mormons in Utah. Captain Lorenzo Sitgreaves of the Army Corps of Topographical Engineers set out from Zuni in 1851 to find the answer. His expedition was made up of topographers, naturalists, artists and 50 infantrymen.

"They traveled along the Zuni River southwest to its mouth and then headed northwest along the Little Colorado, intending to follow it to the Colorado," according to a website "Southwest Explorations." "When they reached Grand Falls [northwest of present-day Winslow] their guide, Antoine Leroux, advised them that it was impossible to follow the river any farther because it flowed in a deep canyon for the rest of its course."

Leroux left his name on one of the seasonal streams in the area, and the group headed west. They passed north of the San Francisco Peaks and continued to California.

The next American expedition to arrive in the area was led by Lt. Amiel Weeks Whipple, a graduate of West Point. He had already surveyed parts of the border between Maine and Canada, as well as a section of the Mexican border. Finding a route across northern Arizona would seem fairly simple — just go west from Zuni and avoid the mountains near Flagstaff. But the actual terrain made the task difficult. Without construction equipment, a 10-foot drop off could be a problem. A stand of trees in the way could mean much manual labor. Finally, the surveyors needed to find a route that came near streams and springs frequently enough to provide water for men and animals.

The expedition started from Fort Smith, Arkansas, and headed west. By late November 1853, they were near Zuni, where diarist John P. Sherburne remarked on the tame eagles. "They are caught in the cliffs when young, and become quite domesticated. The people are not willing to part with them."

He wrote in a diary, which has been edited by Mary McDougall Gordon. "Camp flooded with Indians from Zuni, some with fresh marks of small-pox on faces and hands. The Gobernador, his war-chief and Lieutenant came today in their war dress and had their portraits taken. ..."

"There is a great peculiarity here in this climate," wrote Sherburne. The Ther[mometer] ranging from 9 degrees to 30 degrees at sunrise and from 50 degrees to 70 degrees in the middle of the day."

While the expedition camped on the Zuni River about nine miles west of the Pueblo, an advance party returned from the west and said the expedition would have to cut down trees for as much as 20 miles to make a wagon road. It rained all night and all day, so they remained in camp while teamsters began to fell the timber.

"A delegation of several Indians from Zuni came in Camp just before dark, with information of a good road," Sherburne continued. "It appears that after we left they had a meeting to discuss whether or not 'twould be for their benefit to tell us of a proper and best road. Coming to the conclusion that 'twas best, they sent a delegation to bring the information and offered two of their men as guides."

The new route took the group along the Zuni River to its confluence with the Little Colorado near the present-day hamlet of Hunt. From there, they followed the larger stream to the northwest. Later, Sherburne was to report, "Plenty of water but no wood in Camp. The ground in the vicinity is covered with pieces of wood, petrified into agate, flint and some a species of jasper."

There is a mention of the White Mountains themselves in the diary. "On the left of Camp, about 20 miles distant is a range of mountains, snow-capped."

As they journeyed west, the teamsters were falling ill with smallpox, despite inoculation. Approaching the area of present-day Flagstaff, the Zunis attempted to find Hopi guides, but the Hopi were too devastated by smallpox to lend any assistance. It took the group until March to reach Los Angeles.

The next explorer was Edward F. Beale who came in 1857 to build a wagon road across northern Arizona. He was a friend of President Buchanan and had survived some difficulty in his previous position as Indian superintendent for California. The wagon road was to start at Fort Defiance and end where the Mojave River joined the Colorado, which was impossible because the rivers did not actually meet.

According to *Edward F. Beale & the American West* by Gerald Thompson, Beale was told to "make all watering places and fords easily accessible to wagons." And he was to attempt to conciliate Indians through presents and acts of kindness. But it was pre-arranged that his cousin Gwin Heap would take over in the event of his death.

The group stopped in Texas to pick up camels, which would make the expedition famous. They eventually reached Fort Defiance, just west of what is now the Arizona state line. Beale set off for Zuni with approximately 70 men, including soldiers, Hispanic laborers and assistants. He frequently consulted Aubry's fantastic descriptions and notes from Whipple's 1853 expedition.

Beale entered the White Mountain area by passing through Zuni. He reported wood, water and grass at Indian Wells, and the same conditions when he camped 14.43 miles from Zuni. Twelve miles farther, he came across Jacob's Well before continuing on to Navajo Springs.

The party headed west toward the San Francisco Peaks, near present-day Flagstaff.

His report, published by the *Southern Vineyard* in Los Angeles in 1858, concluded that this route would "inevitably become the great emigrant route to California." His prediction was correct.

Beale's work was strongly criticized, mostly by those who had a strong economic interest in other routes. The camel experiment, though highly successful, provided no economic benefit to established interests and became only a historic curiosity. His route, slightly modified in later decades to run farther north of the White Mountains, was to become the nation's major east-west corridor. The Santa Fe Railroad, the fabled Route 66 and later Interstate 40 followed the path surveyed by Beale.

In 1866, the Santa Fe Stage Co. was sticking pretty close to Beale's route, running through what is now the St. Johns area up the Zuni River to the Little Colorado and across to Ash Fork.

Apaches Raid Mexico

In 1857, Apaches raided deep into Sonora, molested some Arizona settlers and killed the Indian Agent on the Navajo Reservation. Americans knew they needed to have the support of a strong Apache leader if they wanted violence to stop. They met with Cochise, chief of the Chiricahua Apaches, and made peace.

Cochise agreed to permit the Overland Mail to run through southern Arizona. American government officials also met with bands of Pinal and White Mountain Apaches who agreed to maintain peaceful relations and allow travelers to pass through their country. But the Apaches refused to stop raiding Mexico and did not want whites to settle in their territory.

In his 1859 annual report, Indian Agent Michael Steck said the White Mountain Apaches were the most reliable and most advanced in agriculture of all the Apache bands. He said a party of gold hunters went into east-central Arizona and wrote about receiving good treatment from the Apaches. White Mountain Apache leaders made frequent trips to forts in New Mexico to pledge their peaceful intentions.

The shaky peace of 1857 did not last with other bands. It ended four years later when a young officer betrayed Cochise. During a peace conference, Lt. George Bascom decided to try to recover a captive from the Apaches by taking the chief and other leaders as hostages.

"Cochise denied that his people had perpetrated this raid

and when he was told that he and his group would be held as hostages until the boy and the cattle were returned, he slashed the wall of the tent and escaped," according to Bert Robinson's book, *The Basket Weavers*. Bascom was killed by the other Apache leaders as Cochise escaped.

Cochise "and his band went on the warpath and when three of his relatives, who were held as hostages, were hanged in retaliation for murders perpetrated by his band, he set out on a frightful campaign to avenge their death," Robinson wrote. "It is said that he killed more than 25 white men with his own hands. Some he bound and dragged to death behind his pony; he cut chunks of flesh from the bodies of others until they died. Another fiendish act practiced by his band was capturing a wagon train and driving off the mules and oxen, then tying the men to the wagon wheels and setting the wagons and contents on fire. The women and children were held as captives to await a worse fate."

Geronimo, who rode with Cochise, had this to say: "After a few days' skirmishing we attacked a freight train that was coming in with supplies for the Fort. We killed some of the men and captured the others. These prisoners our chief offered to trade for the Indians whom the soldiers had captured at the massacre in the tent. This the officers refused, so we killed our prisoners, disbanded, and went into hiding in the mountains. Of those who took part in this affair I am the only one now living.

"In a few days troops were sent out to search for us, but as we were disbanded, it was of course, impossible for them to locate any hostile camp. During the time they were searching for us many of our warriors [who were thought by the soldiers to be peaceable Indians] talked to the officers and men, advising them where they might find the camp they sought, and while they searched we watched them from our hiding places and laughed at their failures.

"After this trouble all of the Indians agreed not to be friendly with the white men any more. There was no general engagement, but a long struggle followed. Sometimes we attacked the white man — sometimes they attacked us. First a few Indians would be killed and then a few soldiers. I think the killing was about equal on each side. The number killed in these troubles did not amount to much, but this treachery on the part of the soldiers had angered the Indians and revived memories of other wrongs, so that we never again trusted the United States troops."

Other Apache bands began raiding Anglo settlements throughout Arizona. The raids reached a peak just as the U.S. Cavalry was withdrawn to fight Civil War battles in the East.

Apaches Raid During Civil War

Though Arizona was far from the main action, the Civil War's currents rippled through the remote Southwest. Leaders in both Richmond and Washington needed gold to buy guns and pay soldiers. They looked to the rich mines of California. As Arizona was a strategic buffer between the Confederacy and the West Coast, Confederate Texans attacked from the east and the Union's California Column came from the west to drive them out. While northern and southern forces were fighting their way across Southern Arizona, the Apaches took a toll on both. Four Confederates were killed by Apaches as they fled east to escape Northern troops, who were preparing to recapture Tucson. The Union troops were constantly attacked by Apaches as they headed east to drive the Confederates from New Mexico. In addition to running the Rebels out of New Mexico, Union soldiers also killed Mimbreno Apache leader Mangas Coloradas. Geronimo relates how the chief and many of the Chiricahua were led into a trap in New Mexico by Gen. Joseph West who made promises of food and gifts.

Mangus Coloradas "and about half of our people went to New Mexico, happy that now they had found white men who would be kind to them, and with whom they could live in peace and plenty," Geronimo said. "No word ever came to us from them. From other sources, however, we heard that they had been treacherously captured and slain. In this dilemma we did not know just exactly what to do, but fearing that the troops who had captured them would attack us, we retreated into the mountains near Apache Pass. ...

"We discovered four men with a herd of cattle. Two of the men were in front in a buggy and two were behind on horseback. We killed all four, but did not scalp them; they were not warriors. We drove the cattle back into the mountains, made a camp, and began to kill the cattle and pack the meat.

"Before we had finished this work we were surprised and attacked by United States troops, who killed ... seven Indians — one warrior, three women and three children. ... At first I had a spear, a bow, and a few arrows; but in a short time my spear and all my arrows were gone. Once I was surrounded, but by dodging from side to side of my horse as he ran I escaped. It was necessary during this fight for many of the warriors to leave their horses and escape on foot. But my horse was trained to come at call, and as soon as I reached a safe place, if not too closely pursued, I would call him to me. During this fight we scattered in all directions and two days later reassembled at our appointed place of rendezvous, about fifty miles from the scene of this battle.

"About 10 days later the same United States troops attacked our new camp at sunrise. The fight lasted all day, but our arrows and spears were all gone before ten o'clock, and for the remainder of the day we had only rocks and clubs with which to fight. We could do little damage with these weapons, and at night we moved our camp about four miles back into the mountains where it would be hard for the cavalry to follow us. ...

"A few days after this we were again attacked by another company of United States troops. Just before this fight we had been joined by a band of Chokonen [as Geronimo called the Chiricahua] Indians under Cochise, who took command of both divisions. We were repulsed, and decided to disband. ...

"After we had disbanded our tribe, the Bedonkohe Apaches reassembled near their old camp vainly waiting for the return of Mangus Coloradas and our kinsmen." When he did not arrive, Geronimo was appointed chief of the Bedonkohe band.

Arizona Apaches took up the fight in earnest with Cochise becoming the most prominent leader. By 1863, most white settlements, except for Tucson, had been eliminated from southern Arizona by Apache raids.

Just as the Apaches did not seem to favor the North or the South, both sides made war on them. The Confederate governor of Arizona, Col. John R. Baylor, ordered his men to trick the Apaches into coming to peace conferences, then to kill all the adults and sell the children into slavery. Gen. James H. Carlton, the Union military governor of Arizona, ordered all Apaches killed anywhere they could be found.

As the war wore on in the East, gold fever began to spread in the Prescott area. The prospectors' intrusion into the area pushed the Tonto Apaches into war with the whites.

Arizona's First Capital

Arizona's white settlers, adventurers and out-of-work politicians talked the federal government into creating the territory of Arizona in February 1863. A party of appointed officers headed out from Washington and arrived in the territory just north of the White Mountains. But they were not sure they were in Arizona yet, so they traveled west for two more days before taking the oath of office at Navajo Springs, just east of the Petrified Forest. Finding little to govern on the northern fringes of the White Mountains, they hurried west to Prescott. That town was established not only as the territorial capital, but also as the seat of Yavapai County, which stretched from the Mohave County line to New Mexico and from Utah to the Gila River. So Yavapai County covered half the state and included the White Mountains.

Because there were no quick riches in the White Mountains, white contact with local Apaches was limited. White Mountain bands remained in relative peace as Apaches farther west, south and east were being all but eliminated.

Bloody Tanks, Wheatfields

In 1864, Carlton realized he would need the Mexicans to help him subdue the hostile Apaches. He asked the governor of Sonora, Don Ignacio Pesqueria, to "put a few hundred men into the field on the first day of next June, and keep them in hot pursuit of the Apaches of Sonora, say for sixty or ninety days, we will either exterminate the Indians or so diminish their numbers that they will cease their murdering and robbing propensities and live at peace." The Mexicans agreed. There was war against the Apaches on both sides of the border.

Several hundred Pima, Tohono O'odham and Maricopa Indians supplied with government equipment also launched an expedition against the Apaches. They killed 200 Apaches and recovered much stolen livestock, but made no progress in bringing peace to Arizona.

The Anglos gathered near Prescott and carried on the war. Their forces ranged as far east as the Superstition Mountains, where state militia leader King S. Woolsey killed 30 Apache leaders in the Bloody Tanks Massacre. Woolsey arranged a so-called peace conference, but ordered his men and their Maricopa allies to start shooting the Apache leaders when he touched his hat. The Maricopas brought back 24 Apache scalps. Other accounts of the massacre say Woolsey fed the Apaches poisoned food. It is not completely clear what bands the Apache leaders at Bloody Tanks represented. Woolsey clearly did not care. Some Yavapais were massacred along with the Apaches.

A few months later, it was the White Mountain Apaches who were attacked, at Wheatfields, near present-day Globe. Eskiminzin, an Aravaipa Apache leader, related the story to Gen. O. O. Howard in 1872. "A band of White Mountain Apaches, . . . two hundred women and children and old men, was camped in Pinal Creek Valley, in the shadow of the Sierra Anchas," Eskiminzin said. "It was just before the cold time, eight winters ago. Corn and wheat were ready to be harvested. Harvesting is women's work, and so the men had gone to the high country to hunt the deer, that there might be meat for roasting at the campfires, and skin for moccasins, and for warm sleeping when the cold nights come. For three years there had been no warfare with the Americans. And the peace was there, the peace for which all good Apaches wished. This is why the men were not afraid to leave their women and children and old men in the valley, with the corn and wheat to be harvested.

"Americans, more than a hundred, maybe, climbed down into Pinal Creek Valley, from the mesa to the north. They were all American and many wore hair on their faces. Each was riding a pony and carried a rifle with many shots in it. The dawn-sun was just rising from the darkness, but the Apache women and children and old men still slept on their beds of hay. Much wheat and corn had been harvested, and was stored in baskets and in gourds, inside the wikiups. But there was more, much more, growing in the fields." The attackers included Woolsey's militia and soldiers from Fort Goodwin.

"The Americans rode swiftly, and the faraway noise of ponies' feet reached the ears of half-sleeping Apache dogs," Eskiminzin said. "Much barking made the camp awake, and women and children rushed from their wikiups, as the Americans stopped their ponies at the edge of the village.

" 'Where are your men?' asked their leader.

" 'They are gone to the high country,' said the women, 'to hunt the deer.'

"Then the Americans got off their ponies and, with pistols in their hands, brushed aside the women and children and old men. They went into the wikiups, and with the handles of their pistols broke the tus, the gum-covered jars that held the cool water. They took the corn that had been harvested and fed it to their ponies. Some corn they put into the saddle-bags on their ponies' backs and took it away with them." Before leaving, the Americans destroyed the crops in the fields. "During the winter that followed, many White Mountain Apaches died because they had no wheat or corn to eat," the chief said.

Mike Burns, the Apache raised by a cavalry officer, told a story about soldiers massacring Mohave-Apache.

"Two long strips of white sheeting had been put down for the Indians to sit on. Some of the soldiers opened some packages of tobacco, and some calico, and had taken some of it out to give to the Indians. The Pimas and Maricopas were closing in, pretending to be watching as the presents were given out. ... The Pimas and Maricopas and the soldiers closed in upon the other Indians, who attempted to escape, but volleys of shot were poured into them so that hardly any of them escaped sound in body."

Burns related another incident that he said occurred in 1864: Three Indians found a camp of white men in the Bradshaw mountains. "Two of them decided to go to the camp and ask for presents and tobacco. The third and older man tried to persuade them not to go to the camp but without success. [The whites] shot one of the Indians down. The other ran for his life, receiving only a flesh wound through the leg, but he paid no attention to the wound and made his escape. The third Indian who had refused to go to the camp saw the whole affair from the top of the bluff, and went to his own camp for assistance for the wounded man. After the wounded man had recovered there was quarrelling as to who first proposed going to the white men's camp, and thus causing an Indian to be killed. A lot of the Indians wanted to kill the two who had returned, believing that they were the cause of the other's death, but they finally decided to allow them to live."

Burns also told of a time when his family was surprised by soldiers. His father ran off to higher ground to lead the troops away from the rest of the family. "He was shooting down on them with his bow and arrow and rolling rocks down on them and in this way he kept them from climbing the mountain. The soldiers had not seen us, for they took after my father instead of charging up the canyon. … After the soldiers had marched away, my father joined us, and said that the soldiers must have killed my mother because he saw her running along on the side of the hill, and the soldiers were shooting at her, and then he could not see her any more. We all came down from the mountain then and camped in a cave, and early the next morning my father and uncle went back to try and find the body of my mother. They found her dead in a cave, full of bullet holes."

Though the territorial militia, federal troops and Mexican soldiers were able to inflict great harm on isolated Apache camps, they were losing the war and needed a new policy.

Plans To Remove Apaches

The U.S. government began removing Apaches to a reservation in New Mexico as early as 1863. A group of 400 Mescaleros were the first Apaches brought to Bosque Redondo, to what the world would later call a concentration camp. The Apaches were confined to a small area with bands of Navajos. When smallpox broke out, the Mescaleros fled.

In April 1865, Inspector-General N. H. Davis arranged a peace conference at the copper mines in New Mexico with Victorio, Nana, Acosta and several sons of the slain Mangas Coloradas. The Apaches said that they desired peace, but they would not agree to allow the government to confine all their people at the hated Bosque Redondo reservation. As the Walapais joined the Apaches, the war continued with new energy in their wide-ranging opposition to white settlement in Arizona.

Mike Burns told of another massacre: "A small band of Indians went to the camp of some soldiers just below where the mining camp of Superior is. This party walked right into the soldiers' camp, not expecting that anything would happen to them, but the soldiers saw that there were but a few Indians, and they grabbed hold of the men and cut their heads off and burnt the corpses. Some other Indians happened to see the occurrence from a distance, and after the soldiers had left the camp they went there to see if they could find the bodies of their relatives, but could only find small pieces of bone in the ashes."

Burns said this attack provoked the Mohave Apaches to retaliate. "So they went to the Pinal Mountains to tell the news, went up the head of the Salt River near where the Roosevelt Dam now is, and also to the Tonto Basin, and called a council of war to be held near the Superstition Mountains."

Though the Indians had only three old muskets, bows and arrows and a few spears, they set out to retaliate. They found a dozen soldiers escorting wagons near Florence. "So the chief told them not to be scared, but to be men, to fight as men for vengeance for the wrongs done to them by the soldiers and others. ... They saw a wide sand[y] wash on the road, and much brush on each side of the road in which they could hide. ... The Indians having the guns fired, and the others armed with bows and arrows commenced shooting at the horses, and also at the soldiers. Four of the soldiers dropped off their horses, and the others tried to escape, but several of them were shot with arrows in the back." The Indians took the tobacco, but destroyed the remaining contents of the wagons and headed back to their camp in the Superstitions. "When they reached their camp there was great rejoicing there that the warriors had returned safely and had been victorious."

A larger group of soldiers followed the Indians to their camp. "The soldiers could not see the Indians, and while they were dismounting their horses and preparing to set fire to the camp, the Indian boys opened fire on them and the soldiers were scattered in all directions. Some fell dead, and some ran away, leaving their horses. The Indians kept firing on the soldiers, and the soldiers fired several volleys in the direction where the shots were coming from, but could not see any Indians to shoot. Farther up on the bluffs, however, on the tops of the hills, could be seen groups of Indians waving red blankets at the soldiers and daring them to come up, but the soldiers only made haste to go back the way they came."

Burns added, "From that time on it was shown that the soldiers were not very good fighters; they could kill Indians when they came within gun reach and had no weapons to protect themselves. If the Indians were armed to the teeth like the soldiers were with breech-loading guns, pistols and sabers, with plenty of ammunition and a pack train, the soldiers would not stand up to them. ... For several years afterwards, on the upper ranges of the country, beyond the Matazal Mountains, many Indians came together and agreed to keep up the war against the whites in the western country."

Burns told of his band attacking a party south of Prescott. "On this road they met six white men, mounted on horses. They attacked them and killed four of them, and the other two escaped toward Prescott." His group of Apache-Mohave then went home to the Bloody Basin country.

Cooley Saves
White Mountain Apaches

Miguel, a band leader whose people migrated between Carrizo, Show Low and other parts of the White Mountains, was arrested in October of 1864 at Zuni on one of his peace missions. He was finally released in the fall of 1865, but had to work patiently for the release of other members of his band who were still being held prisoner.

Miguel told the soldiers that he and his people raised corn peacefully. He asked for a reservation to protect his band from the whites. He proudly carried letters of reference from soldiers

Corydon Cooley saved the White Mountain Apaches and served as an army scout. Cooley married two of Chief Pedro's daughters, Molly and Cora (facing page). Apaches often practiced plural marriage, especially when the women were sisters.

Carol Sletten
© 2010

he had met, including Gen. Carlton, the Union general who had once ordered the extermination of all Apaches.

Diablo, another White Mountain band leader, was also asking for a reservation, having traveled to Fort Goodwin on the Gila. He offered land at the junction of the East and North Forks of the White River for a fort. Five years later, the army camp that was to become Fort Apache would be built on that site.

The White Mountain Apaches were saved from being massacred in 1869 by Corydon E. Cooley, who entered the area from New Mexico seeking gold. Instead of gold, he found two new wives when he married into the tribe.

Corydon Eliphalet Cooley was born near Staunton, Va., on April 2, 1836, according to his biography written by Col. H. B. Wharfield. When he was in his 20s he drifted to Santa Fe, then on to Colorado, where he worked in a store owned by Mountain Man and fur trapper Ceran St. Vrain. There he met famous characters, including Kit Carson and Jim Bridger. During the Civil War, Cooley became a first lieutenant and regimental quartermaster to the 2nd New Mexico Volunteer Infantry, which fought against an invasion of Texas Confederates. He was also in a battle near Canada Alamosa on September 26, 1861, and another against the Texans at San Marcial on February 16, 1862. Wharfield says a bullet seared the end of Cooley's nose, but this was probably one of the stub-nosed Irishman's charming stories which often had little relation to fact.

After several more battles, the Texans were routed and Cooley shifted to the 1st New Mexico Cavalry, serving under Kit Carson. Cooley briefly engaged in New Mexican politics before he headed

Carol Sletten
© 2010

toward Arizona.

At Zuni, Cooley and his two companions met Miguel, the White Mountain chief, and accompanied him to his camp along Carrizo Creek.

"We were met several miles from the village by all the band," Cooley wrote. "Women and children all gave us a hearty welcome and escorted us to town. The village is on a beautiful stream finely timbered — walnut, sycamore, pine — in fact a finer variety of timber than I have ever seen in any part of the West."

"With a group of some forty Indians under Miguel's leadership they started west for the gold locations," Col. Wharfield writes. "When some distance beyond Cibecue Creek, a large party of Pinal Apache halted them, insisting that the prospectors turn back because white men were not allowed in their country. A big pow-wow took place amidst much threatening of violence and noise. Miguel protected his guests, and at first refused the demands. Then another group of Apache arrived on the scene as neutral observers. The headman, Chiquito, of the Coyotero band, advised Miguel to withdraw to avoid a fight."

A runner came in from the camp of Pedro, an Apache chief who had some authority over other White Mountain bands. Pedro had been expected to join the camp and settle the dispute. But the messenger brought bad news. "Soldiers had attacked a group of Pedro's people, wounded one, taken several prisoners and destroyed corn," Wharfield said. "The whites' fears were quieted by Miguel with the word that Pedro had previously warned his Indians to keep away from the place and it was their own fault.

67

"On July 30 another messenger brought word that the troops were in the vicinity of the Black River ford, and perhaps going northward and then coming over into the Carrizo Creek region."

Cooley, knowing that the soldiers were likely to consider all Apaches to be hostile, took Miguel and another prospector to talk to the cavalry near where Fort Apache was later built.

According to Wharfield's account, "The commander, Major Green, was astonished to see white men with the Apache, and 'inquired what the devil brought us there in this country among the Indians, when he had four companies and expected to fight every minute.'" The major suspected that the white men were selling guns to the Indians, but one of Green's teamsters recognized Cooley and vouched for him.

"Miguel, through an interpreter, told the commander that his people were friends of the whites, and intended going to Santa Fe to see General Getty about permission to live in the region," Wharfield said. Miguel also showed letters about his good conduct from Carleton and other officers.

Col. Green then ordered Capt. John Barry to lead a large detachment to Miguel's camp, reportedly with orders to kill all the Indians. One version of the story says that the Apaches greeted the soldiers cordially and offered them food, thus persuading Barry not to kill them. Another version says Cooley talked Barry out of killing the members of Miguel's band. We don't know for sure that Cooley personally talked Barry out of the massacre, but none of the accounts dispute the fact that he went to meet with the soldiers to head off the disaster.

Fort Apache Established;
Camp Grant Massacre

On May 16, 1870, Maj. John Green of the 1st Cavalry established a post at the confluence of the east and north forks of the White River. He called it Camp Ord, but its name changed in August to Camp Mogollon and in September to Camp Thomas, before becoming Camp Apache five months later. Though it never had a stockade, the sine qua non of the romantic conception of an Indian fort, it was christened Fort Apache on April 5, 1879, when the government ordered all military installations to be called forts.

In 1871, a massacre occurred south of the White Mountains at a peaceful Apache camp under army protection along Aravaipa Creek. As many as 140 Apaches were killed in the dawn attack by a gang of Tucson Anglos and Papago Indians, or Tohono O'odham as they are now called. Twenty-eight Apache children were kidnapped. This incident was called the Camp Grant Massacre, after a nearby army post. "This massacre was somewhat more extensive than most of the others carried out by Anglos and was widely reported over the United States," according to the book *Cycles of Conquest* by Edward H. Spicer.

"The whole nation was incensed at the brutality of this raid, but it brought the whole Apache problem squarely before the American people," Robinson says in *The Basket Weavers of Arizona*. "It resulted in improvement in both the number and caliber of the military personnel sent to cope with the situation."

President Grant was outraged. He took three actions to try to solve the Apache problem. He sacked Gen. George Stoneman and appointed Gen. George Crook to lead the campaign against the Apaches. He appointed peace commissioners. And he created a reservation for the Apaches.

The federal government filed murder charges against 100 residents of Tucson and nearby communities, but the defendants were all acquitted.

Chief Escanela gave testimony recorded by army interpreters: "His people were living here peaceably, receiving rations three times a week, up to the time of the massacre. He believes neither the lieutenant nor any of the officers knew of the people coming to attack them. It was about 4 o'clock in the morning when they were attacked; 128 killed, 29 taken prisoners. He and all the captains lost some of their families. He lost two wives, four children, three men, (one an old man), and two of his nephews were taken away. He also lost fifty of his band. When the Tucson people attacked him, his best wife got separated from him and he could not find her. It was dark. If he could have found her he would have fought and died with her."

"The fact that it had been carried out against obviously peace-

Fort Apache had no stockade. The oldest building there is General Crook's Cabin, which he occupied during at least some of the time when he was at the Fort in the 1870s and 1880s.

ful women and children roused Anglos outside the West and gave impetus to a federal Indian policy which the new Board of Indian Commissioners had been working out," says *Cycles of Conquest.* The new plan was called Grant's Peace Policy. "It was designed to replace the fumbling and frustration of the War and Interior Departments' handling of Indian problems."

The Aravaipas hid in the mountains until September, when their leader, Eskiminzin, learned that Vincent Colyer, a Quaker minister and member of President Grant's special Indian Commission, was at Camp Grant.

Eskiminzin went in to talk to Colyer. The chief's comments speak eloquently of the plight of the Apaches. Through an interpreter, Eskiminzin told Colyer, "The Papagos would not have killed my people if the white men had not urged them to do it. ... The people from Tucson stole twenty-seven of our children and made slaves of them. That is very bad. The girl children they have made worse than slaves." Using a tactic of the Washington bureaucrats that was old even then, Colyer promised to get back to him on the matter of the children.

Colyer also met with Unojo, the leader of the Tonto Apaches, at Camp McDowell near Phoenix. "We are tired of living in caves and on the tops of cold mountains," Unojo said. "My women carry water two or three miles, from the little streams. They get water at night because we are afraid of soldiers. Even rabbits are safer than my Tontos. We hide our children behind big rocks when we go to hunt the deer. But deer are not so many now. You say Tontos must not steal cattle, but we must steal or starve. White Americans have stolen our cornfields and our wheatfields. What are we to do?" The chief, with tears in his eyes, went on to describe how his four children had been killed by American soldiers.

Col. N. A. M. Dudley, the commander at McDowell, after hearing the Tontos' plea for peace, wrote: "I have been present at a great many talks with Indians during the past seventeen years, but I never have seen more feeling or good sense exhibited by an Indian than this Apache showed. If I remain in Arizona, I ask that I be stationed at a post overlooking an Apache reservation, for I know that a race of beings possessing the intelligence of the Apaches can be taught to appreciate the advantages of living at peace with the white men."

While waiting to hear from Colyer, Eskiminzin's warriors encountered an American looking for gold and killed him. A few of his followers tried to use the incident to convince the chief to return to the warpath. Eskiminzin said he was tempted by Cochise's example to go to war with the whites. "But then Americans would kill more Indians, and Indians would kill more Americans, and the cycle of death would be unending," the chief said.

The debate is described in *Apache Agent,* the biography of John P. Clum. Santo, a sub-chief, said: "Eskiminzin, you took my three daughters for your wives, and my blood is in your children. For many years, I have followed you as chief. What you have done, I have said was the right thing to do. After the Papagos and Mexicans and Americans killed many of our people near Camp Grant, you said we should forgive. We did and went back to our burned village. Then American soldiers killed Munaclee and tried to kill you. Then we came to the mountains. Many moons ago, you went to Camp Grant to see big nantan Colyer from Washington. He said he would help us, but no help comes. ... Now you say it is wrong for Aravaipas to kill Americans. But I think it is the thing to do."

Eskiminzin said he asked the sub-chiefs to wait for him while he went to Camp Grant again. Colyer was not there, but the chief met Gen. O. O. Howard, a personal emissary of President Grant. Eskiminzin repeated the stories of the Camp Grant and Wheatfields massacres. Howard was much taken with the Indian and his sincerity and desire for peace. Howard established a temporary reservation at Camp Grant and asked the president to establish a permanent home for the Apaches.

Cooley wrote a letter to Gen. Howard on Pedro's behalf, emphasizing the success of the White Mountain Apaches at becoming farmers, which the government had ordered them to do. "They raised about 20,000 pounds of corn and hope that next year they will be able to show you they are in earnest in regard to living at peace and are desirous of helping themselves," Cooley wrote in his beautiful calligraphic script.

Later, Howard wrote to the President: "If more kind words and fewer bullets were used in the Apache campaign, success would be achieved much sooner. A kind word to Miguel made a real man of him; Palone was conquered by the kindly services of an army surgeon when he was sick. It is not blows alone that bring men to reason — even red men. Eskiminzin demanded the return of the twenty-seven Aravaipa children that had been stolen at the time of the Camp Grant massacre. Citizens [of Tucson] brought in six of these children — all we could find in Arizona. The rest of them are declared to be in Mexico. I assured Eskiminzin I would do all in my power to obtain the return of all of them."

Crook, who considered Eskiminzin to be a liar and thought less of Howard, explained the fate of the children differently: "These children had been taken into many of the families, and in the year that had elapsed became more or less identified with their new associates, and had correspondingly become weaned from their people, in fact, dreaded going back to the Indians almost as much as white children. Most of the people who had them had been much attached to them, and were very loath to give them up.

"General Howard had induced some of the people to bring the children with them to [an April 1872] council under the promise, so the people claimed, that if the children had no parents living, he would not turn them over to the Indians. When he asked Skimmy [his derogatory name for Eskiminzin] if these children's parents were still living, he said, 'Of course not, they were killed by the citizens,' but the Indians wanted the children all the same. General Howard tried to talk him out of it, but Skimmy remained firm. So Howard decided to turn over the children.

"One little girl in particular, nicely dressed, clean, tidy, and nice looking was brought in to be turned over to the Indians. She shrieked, fought, and showed as much horror at being taken by the Indians as any white child would. There were many there with wet eyes. One old, gray-haired man ran out of the council crying, declaring he could not stand that. Judge McCaffrey, the U.S. District Attorney at Tucson, got up in the presence of all and denounced Howard as being a liar and a brute."

Apache Reservation Established

On November 9, 1871, President Grant, sitting at a desk nearly 3,000 miles away, doubtlessly with the help of many bureaucrats who had never been west of the Mississippi, made an attempt at carving out the borders of the White Mountain Apache Reservation. He started where the Mogollon Rim crosses the New Mexico-Arizona line and followed the rim west to the current western boundary of the reservation at a point due north of a mountain he called "Sombrero or Plumoso Butte." From there, he went generally south and finally followed the Gila back to the New Mexico line, taking in Alpine and the rest of the area in Arizona now east of the reservation. But the first attempt was to be modified many times as the initial 10,000 square miles was reduced to about 5,000 square miles, an area approximately the size of Connecticut.

On December 14, 1872, Grant added a strip of land 15 miles wide south of the Gila River to the reservation. On August 5, 1873, the south-eastern corner of the Apache reservation was restored to farmers who claimed they had settled the area and started an irrigation project before the reservation was created.

"The pattern of pressure and capitulation was to become all too familiar; white settlers demanded the watered river lands and claimed that the recently pacified Indians were not farming the lands in question," said Thomas R. McGuire, writing in *Mixed-Bloods, Apaches, and Cattle Barons.*

On July 21, 1874, a strip of land on the eastern edge of the reservation was removed. The eastern limit of the White Mountain Apache territory, which had always been vague, was now precisely 219/720ths of the earth's circumference west of a line someone had drawn on a stone in London, England. It was a difficult concept for Apaches to understand. They had no thought of the earth as a globe, no arithmetic for large fractions and no words in their language for London or England. This generous slice of the reservation was carved off to accommodate mining in the Clifton-Morenci area.

"Copper had been discovered on these lands around 1872, and the flourishing mining camp at Clifton had been established," McGuire wrote. "According to the claimants, their original mines had been believed to lie outside the reservation; they had thus acted in good faith in developing the resources. Territorial officials came to the support of the miners, pressuring federal officials to allow the claims to stand. Upon hearing the familiar refrain from the San Carlos agent that the Indians were not utilizing the eastern edge of the reserve, the Indian Commissioner proceeded with the recommendation for reduction of the reservation."

On April 27, 1876, the president removed areas on the western edge, including the present site of the town of Globe from Indian lands in response to the discovery of gold and silver. Indian Agent John Clum sent Apache police to arrest the miners who were trespassing on the reservation. But he had to give up that policy because it was wrecking the government's relations with Anglo settlers and contractors.

On January 26, 1877, Grant set aside an area three miles square around Fort Apache to remove the soldiers from the jurisdiction of the reservation.

On March 31, 1877, it was a new president, Rutherford B. Hayes, who gave the Apache Reservation something close to its final shape. He took away an area south of the Gila River and the northeastern slope of Mount Baldy.

There were still more changes to the boundaries to come later. In 1893, the south bank of the Salt River was lopped off at the western edge of the reservation. In 1896, the reservation was split along the Salt River. The southern portion became the San Carlos Reservation while the north remained the Fort Apache

Reservation. The Deer Creek Coal Fields area, lost from the San Carlos Reservation in 1896, was restored in the 1960s.

If it seemed that the fate of the White Mountain Apaches rose and fell with inept cartography in Washington, the adjustments on the Apache reservations were modest compared to the ill-fated Salt River Reservation. Hayes created a reservation covering Tempe, Mesa and Phoenix and extending up both sides of the Salt River to the Fort Apache Reservation but gave up on the idea six months later under political pressure.

Another vanishing reservation was created for the Chiricahuas in southeast Arizona in 1871. Cochise lived there until his death in 1874, but later the government would try to move the Chiricahuas into the White Mountains, touching off most of the fighting of the later Apache wars.

By the time the Fort Apache Reservation was first created, the politics of the Indian wars was already changing. In the 1600s, all British colonists in America lived close enough to Indians to fear them or covet their land. By the Revolutionary War, Indians still posed a threat to the "Frontier," which was only a few hundred miles from the East Coast cities. As settlers from Europe gobbled up the farm land of the Midwest through the early 1800s, the "Indian problem" moved farther and farther from the population centers of the East. By the late 1800s, great-great grandchildren of the people who had fought the Mohawks in Upstate New York and grandchildren of the people who had settled the land once held by the Fox in Illinois, were no longer threatened by Indians. Humanitarian sentiments were on the rise throughout the civilized world and vocal segments of the American electorate were beginning to gain sympathy for the Indian side of the question. Though the settlers in the territories were a vocal minority, they had little real political power, with no voting representatives in Congress.

Arizona Indians also faced less pressure from settlers than Native Americans farther east. If the Apache territory had been farmland like central Iowa, farmers who could till the soil more intensely would have gained ownership of the land through industry, economics, politics or force. However, most whites in the eastern United States and Europe were not willing to invest their time and energy in settling the wilds of Arizona.

Faced with growing romanticism about Indian life and sympathy for the early inhabitants of the continent, as well as confronted with a stream of press reports about atrocities against Indians, the aging Union generals who ran the White House and the War Department sought to be evenhanded. They had large tracts of what they considered to be worthless federal land to throw at the problem the way later federal administrations would throw money.

Spanish-Speakers, Sheep and Supplies for the Fort

The establishment of Fort Apache was a major inducement to economic development in the area. Not only did the garrison require vast amounts of food, but, being cavalry, they also needed even larger quantities of fodder. And the soldiers gave the settlers a sense of some security. While the army could not protect every far-flung farm, ranch or sheep camp, the Indians knew that there could be consequences if they molested people under the protection of the American soldiers.

Sheepherders from New Mexico were the first to seize the opportunity. It was easy for them to expand a herd. Sheep only need to be a year old to reproduce and frequently have twins. When the New Mexico sheep men realized there was grass and water along the route to east-central Arizona, they pointed their animals west.

Those sheep men left few records. They had been citizens of Mexico only 20 years earlier and still spoke mostly Spanish. The Homestead Act, which required "cultivation" of a 160-acre parcel, was of little interest to herders, who brought their sheep into what seemed like a limitless sea of grass.

The expansion of the sheep herding culture had begun in central New Mexico more than a hundred years earlier, probably around the end of the 1700s. The book *Spanish-Americans of New Mexico* by Nancie L. Gonzalez reports that the population was gradually moving out into the plains east of Santa Fe and also to the west. "But it was not until after the annexation by the United States government

76

This adobe church in Concho shows the community's ties to the early Hispanic settlers. The building, which was once a dance hall and store, replaced the original San Rafael that was deteriorating nearby.

that stock raising became really big business in New Mexico," the book says. "The Indians were gradually conquered – a circumstance which not only opened up new areas for settlement but created a market for meat, since the government agreed to supply rations to many of the formerly nomadic groups. ... The United States Army itself had to be fed. Continued and increased population pressure sent the Spanish-American population out into the grasslands, and even many of those who remained in agricultural areas turned to herding on a larger scale."

In 1850, there were only about 375,000 sheep in New Mexico, but by 1880, the sheep population had increased to four million. Clearly, if there was grass on the Arizona side of the line, there were New Mexicans who would move their sheep in that direction.

As sheep herding can involve considerable long-distance seasonal migration even now, the first herders probably came into Arizona to take advantage of summer grass and retreated to New Mexico to be nearer markets and supplies as the weather grew cold. This makes the exact date of the first arrival very difficult to pin down. The available accounts place the date anywhere from the U.S. conquest/purchase of the territory in 1848 to just after the Civil War in 1866. When Charles Hoffman, an anthropologist from the University of Arizona, spoke about Hispanic history at a ceremony honoring early sheep man Juan Baca in Springerville in 1987, he said the New Mexico Hispanics entered the area on a temporary basis as early as 1855.

A video tape produced by the Little House Museum says Juan

Baca drove sheep into Round Valley in the early 1860s to take advantage of the lush grass. Baca, who lived to be 110, told the *Arizona Republic* in 1952 that he recalled fleeing to the hills when Apaches raided Round Valley.

There is sharp disagreement on when Hispanics made the transition from being sheepherders to settlers. Some say Baca and others had homes in the Round Valley area before the Anglos, but Jack A. Becker, who has researched Round Valley history extensively, says the Hispanics did not settle in the valley until they accompanied William Milligan in setting up his farming operation in 1870.

When the Hispanics did settle in the valley, they built "a rock fort for protection against Indians in a grove of trees at the lower end of the valley," according to *On the Road to Nowhere* by Karen Miller Applewhite. "The women and children stayed in the tiny fort during scares, while the men climbed the nearby ridge to watch and shoot from behind rock barricades they had built there. These Spanish families together with others that followed farmed beans, squash, corn, chili and potatoes; and as a later settler remembered, cut their hay with butcher knives and scythes." The Little House tape says this early Spanish settlement was on a ford of the Little Colorado in the Springerville area.

Concho was another area visited early by Hispanics, and again, accounts of the first settlement of the town vary widely.

"Juan Candelaria brought a flock of 700 head of sheep from Cubero, New Mexico, to the Concho area in 1866," according to *A History of the St. Johns Arizona Stake* by C. LeRoy and Mabel R. Wilhelm. The Mormon regional history continues, "Shortly after he arrived his brothers, Roselio, Ambrosio, and Averisto, joined him. Thus it was that Juan Candelaria not only became the founder of Concho, but the first Caucasian to establish himself permanently in the sheep business in the state of Arizona."

While the Mormons generously credit the first settlement of Concho to Candelaria, even some of his descendants question whether their family deserves that much recognition.

The stake history, however, not only provides the story of the Candelarias, but also traces the ancestry of their animals. "The Candelaria sheep were the descendants of seventy-one head brought by their maternal grandmother at the beginning of the

78

nineteenth century from Vera Cruz, Mexico, to Cubero, New Mexico. Two years, from 1799 to 1801, were required to make the drive, the sheep in the meantime increasing from 71 to 141 head. Four convicts were released from the Ulloa prison in the harbor of Vera Cruz for the purpose of driving the sheep to Cubero. Due to the purebred Merinos — three ewes and a black ram — the Candelaria sheep become in a few generations the best in western New Mexico. The line has never since been broken, the blood of the four Spanish Merinos still coursing in the veins of the Candelaria sheep."

In *Concho, The Enchanted Pearl*, E. M. DeGlane provided the Candelaria story with compelling details of legendary proportion. He attributes the account to an *Arizona Silver Belt* interview with old timers in the area, published in 1923.

"Don Manuel Antonio Candelaria was in the Concho area in the 1840's as a captive of the Apaches," DeGlane said. "He remained a captive for several years, while still a small child he was given to an old Indian woman who adopted him as her son. He learned the Apache language fluently, as well as their customs.

"When Don Manuel Antonio became a young man he joined the Apaches in several raids. He referred to them as brothers. Later he got tired of roaming around and decided to leave the Apaches; be bid his Indian mother farewell and headed back to Cubero, New Mexico.

"The people at Cubero refused at first to recognize him as one of their own, until he recalled his name, Manuel Antonio Candelaria ... . Undoubtedly some may have remembered this family. From thereafter he was called 'El Cautivo,' the captive.

"Don Manuel Antonio Candelaria married Regina Baca. Several children were born to them. His flocks of animals were increasing. He remembered the abundant grass and water running in the Concho Valley area. In 1861 he and his family, driving 700 head of sheep and goats, settled in Concho. Once again his faithful Indian mother would come to visit him."

The *Enchanted Pearl* mentions that there had been an even earlier settlement of Concho. "When Don Manuel Antonio Candelaria came to Concho the second time in 1861, there were but a handful of pioneers living along the Concho creek. ... These early Concho settlers didn't come in organized groups or teams, it was mostly by individual families. As the settlers sent word to their other relatives in New Mexico, of an abundance of water and grass, they came to help settle Concho."

An article in the *Arizona Republic*, based on a reunion in Concho in 1991, said the New Mexican families from the Cubero area began moving westward to the Concho area in 1848.

The Mormon account continues, "As the Candelaria brothers began to establish themselves their success attracted other Spanish and Mexican sheep men who joined them to share in the abundance of the Concho range land."

Four members of a family from New Mexico — Melquiades, Jesus Maria, Antonio and Tranquilino Luna — each published notices in the Prescott paper in 1873 claiming large tracts of land around Concho and Vernon. Their claims included Malpais Springs, Concho Springs, Lake Springs and Mineral Springs. The date of their claimed settlement is unclear because land titles were sometimes filed years after a family moved into an area.

In his manuscript, *Background History of the Lakeside-Pinetop Area,* Ben S. Hansen says, "Before the establishment of official government surveys, squatters often moved into an area and waited for the government survey before officially establishing their claim." He adds, "Use of the range was obtained by first occupancy and was recognized by the ranchers." Livestock men dominated areas by controlling key watering holes.

A September 5, 1888, local newspaper article reported on a land dispute in which Cornelio Atencio claimed to have homesteaded the Concho townsite area. The local residents said they had been there beginning several years before July 5, 1883. On Dec. 5, the newspaper reported that Atencio had given up 40 acres for the townsite, but the residents wanted 80 more.

Nathan Bibo, a German Jew who settled in New Mexico, played a prominent role in the early trade with Arizona. Bibo's family came West in the 1860s and became traders in small New Mexican towns as the U.S. forced the Indians onto reservations. Originally working for his brothers, he realized Arizona was the frontier and set out to make his own fortune. In an article published in the *Albuquerque Herald* in 1922, Bibo explains how he opened trade between New Mexico and Fort Apache:

"When in 1870, I was living in Cebellita, I was informed by

some of the Zuni Indians, ... who came to do their trading at Cebellita, that their people had helped a government team out of the snow in the White Mountains.

"Upon further inquiry, I found that Captain Smith of the 1st U.S. Cavalry, had crossed the summit of the White Mountains, following some Apache trails, guided by an Indian and finally had reached this side of the mountain range after working through 3 to 5 feet of snow for many miles. With the help of the Zunis he finally reached their village."

Bibo obtained a contract to deliver 100,000 pounds of corn by following the same route back across the White Mountains. In addition to the 1st Cavalry, several companies of the 21st Infantry were camped in the area where Fort Apache was to be built.

"The first thing I did was to send a number of men with my brother Simon to follow the Indian trails as far as possible and locate a way possible for the heavy teams. He returned after one month's time had been spent and he reported a fair road up to the White Mountain range. In the mountains near the summit, the level spaces in the pine forest were impassable even on horseback and the only way was to cut trees and brush and use all the old fallen timber to build the road in these bottomless flats."

Simon Bibo obtained a promise of help from the soldiers in cutting the road.

"There was great joy among the whole command when Simon promised to fetch from this side some of the necessaries, including medicines and in particular Jamaica ginger which all asked for. Simon brought a few hundred personal orders along, all of which he could transport in a light wagon and which he did deliver before all of the snow had melted on the summit. The snowfall in those years seems to have been a good deal heavier than in recent years."

Nathan Bibo bought all the corn that was available in New Mexico along the Rio Grande and prepared for the trip to Fort Apache.

Bibo had obtained the release of five Apaches taken prisoner by Navajos. They repaid him by helping him establish good relations with the Apaches in the White Mountains. After seeing the mountains of corn Bibo had purchased in New Mexico, his

81

Apache guides were prepared to tell their people that Bibo was a great captain who controlled all the corn in the United States.

Bibo started out into the area, still described on the maps of that era as "terra incognita," with 12 men equipped with plows, scrapers, pick axes, spades and shovels. They reached the base of the White Mountains, after a difficult crossing of the Little Colorado.

"The summit was reached after about eight days of hard work and here where the bottomless level place commenced the real trouble began," Bibo said in the newspaper article. "Part of the place had been rip-rapped with logs, branches of trees, thick and thin, but when the heavy teams started over the same, many of them mired down to the axles, had to be unloaded and their cargoes carried on the shoulders of the men composing the train crew and help had to be asked from the post which was then only about 50 miles distant."

With the help of 100 men from the fort, more trees were felled to build the road and the freight was carried by hand over the worst places.

"When the wagons arrived, there was great rejoicing in the camp, not only of the officers and men, but also the Apache Indians, who were certainly a half-starved and hungry looking crowd," Bibo wrote.

The Apaches held a great dance to thank Bibo for the return of the captives.

Bibo said that he had delivered goods to the fort for 6 1/8 cents a pound, a substantial reduction from the 18 cents a pound it cost to get supplies from California, over a route that was subject to attacks by the still-hostile Tonto Apaches.

Life at Fort Apache

"Renegade Apache were active in the area of the new army post from its beginning in 1870 to April 1872," Wharfield says in his biography of Cooley. "In February 1871 a gang of young braves ran off a herd of a beef contractor's stock on the grazing grounds. Then several months later a group of the wilder ones stampeded the government cattle, making away with most of the herd. And the government mail rider was murdered along the south road toward the Black River ford. Previously in March a renegade called Handsome Charley walked to the sutler's store, and stuck his lance through Mr. Richmond, killing the trader instantly. It was not until two years later that the savage was again discovered in the vicinity. The post commander asked Cooley, one-eyed Miguel and Petone to capture the outlaw. They found him at a camp, and surrounded the man. Upon approaching, the vicious Apache snapped a revolver at Cooley; but before he could again pull the trigger, Petone killed him with a shot through the heart."

Often, troubles started with a tulapai drunk. Trader Nathan Bibo happened across one in 1872 on his way to Fort Apache. He was invited to participate by a chief he called Pittoon.

"Early next morning the concert started. Imitating all the animals of the camp, the howling began, and also canting in their peculiar whining way. The fellows went to a place where three large copper kettles were suspended over fires, each one of these kettles probably held 20 gallons. The water in two of them was still boiling, while one had been cooling off.

"They advanced, singing until they surrounded the cool one and Mr. Chief held a tin cup, with which, after dipping into the liquid stuff of the kettle, commenced to drink and thereupon handed the cup to the man next to him, who, doing the same in turn, handed it to his next man. So it went on and about 30 Indians stood in a circle around the kettle and Cigaski pulled me into the circle to do the same. It was disgusting, but they would have considered me a coward if I would have stood back. Round and round the tin cup went, without intermission and before long the drunken beasts commenced to drop.

"Every time a fellow would fall, the squaws and children would paint him with charcoal and anything else and drag him away. Finally, Cigaski thought he had enough and I grabbed hold of his leather belt, as I could not see anything else but stars, and the stuff which tasted like stale beer, mixed with something unmentionable, had made me sick, but if I had not done as they did, I do not know what would have happened. It may interest the reader to know, how the stuff called [tulapai] is made by them.

As soon as the corn is ripe, they either trade it through some of their people who speak Spanish, with the Mexican people of Sonora or Chihuahua, (I am, of course speaking of the time previous to 1872) or they would steal it from the fields. The corn is gathered and taken to certain localities in the mountains and buried. Whenever they were ready to use it for the purpose of making their mash, a trench is dug into the ground, large enough to hold the amount of moistened corn which they want to brew. The corn I saw spread on leaves or rags, and again covered in similar manner, sometimes without any cover but moist earth.

"After having been left sufficient time to swell and sprout and ferment, they wash it well, and immediately prepare for the feast, and the big copper kettles, of ancient hand-made manufacture, are hung on the iron high tripod, under which the fires were lit, by the thirsty savages. The roving outlaws of all the Apache tribes would not miss the occasion of this event, but would always return to participate, to do their share of disposing of the brew, which was consumed as soon as it was cool enough after boiling it."

In 1871, Bibo had a contract to provide 100 tons of hay to Fort Apache, but had subcontracted the deal to two men. While he was in New Mexico, a message arrived from the commandant at the fort, telling Bibo that the two men were using his hay cutting machine and wagons, but not crediting him with the hay delivered. Bibo set out immediately for Fort Apache.

The two men ran away as Bibo approached the Fort. Bibo bought new wagons and oxen and began hauling hay from the summit of the White Mountains down to the fort, but heavy snow began to fall, making further hauling by wagons impossible. Bibo was reminded of Napoleon's retreat from Russia as his party trudged through the snow down toward Fort Apache. He was rescued by Apaches, who took them to a rancheria and shared their meager provisions, including a squirrel thrown whole into the hot ashes.

"Then he ripped it open, took out the insides with his Bowie knife, and without saying a word, threw it to me, just as he would have done to a dog (but that is their way.) Of all the many delicacies that I ever tasted during my lifetime, I will always remember this juicy delicately tasting squirrel, something of the spring chicken flavor ... of one of the most fashionable French restaurants."

Not only was Bibo behind on the hay contract, but he had lost the $2,500 he had invested in the wagons. "I felt down and out and forlorn," he said.

The camp trader, Thomas Ewing, took pity on him and gave him new clothes and shelter. The camp commander suggested that Bibo order a supply of large butcher knives and give them to the Apaches to cut hay. "The squaws came in a constant procession — carrying from 60 to 100 pounds of grass on their backs, bundled up with strings ... wrapped around their foreheads, and besides the heavy burden, carried their papooses on top of the hay."

While the women were working, the men were idling around smoking tobacco, which they bought from the women's earnings before purchasing anything to eat. "It was not long, I had delivered every pound of hay on my contract."

Ewing sold the post store, but the man who bought the contract was soon asked to leave. Bibo was allowed to buy the store's contract and inventory by making time payments.

He finished the account of his life at Fort Apache with two stories. Soldiers were allowed three drinks of liquor a day, and Bibo had to keep track of each soldier's allotted drink, morning, noon and night. One soldier wanted more than his ration and took a shot at Bibo's head. The shot missed and the thirsty cavalryman was soon on his way to Fort Leavenworth.

After one Indian murdered another, the commander began to punish all the Indians, trying to force them to give up the guilty party. Friendly Indians snuck into Bibo's store at midnight to smoke and talk about the problem. Bibo set out the next day to help mediate the dispute, meeting Geronimo along the way. Though the Apaches had an elaborate plan to draw the soldiers out of the fort, the matter was resolved without further bloodshed, though the guilty party never did give himself up.

John Rope, the Apache Scout, tells a story of his early days at the fort: "While we were all camped here at Fort Apache, some eastern White Mountain people and western White Mountain people went on the warpath. They went south to Graham Mountain and stayed there quite a while. Then they came back and tried to make friends again with the white people at Fort Apache. Most of the Cibecue people and Tca-tcidn (a clan) were camped at this fort also on the east side of the river near the soldiers. All the White Mountain people were camped on the other side of the river. My family was living near the soldiers then. ... I think the white man in charge of the fort told the Cibecue and Tca-tcidn people to kill those men who had been on the warpath. They started to do this. They would kill one man, and in a few days they would get another. This way it kept on. One day they killed a certain eastern White Mountain man, and all the White Mountain people got mad and shot back at them. They killed nine Cibecue and Tca-tcidn men that day, and three of their own men were killed."

Martha Summerhayes, a proper New England wife who joined her husband at Camp Apache in 1874, took time from her concerns about the transportation of her dishes to make some observations about the Apaches in her book, *Vanished Arizona.*

"The Indians who lived on this reservation were the White Mountain Apaches, a fierce and cruel tribe, whose depredations and atrocities had been carried on for years, in and around, and indeed, far away from their mountain homes. But this tribe was now under surveillance of the Government, and guarded by a strong garrison of cavalry and infantry at Camp Apache. They were divided into bands, under Chiefs Pedro, Diablo, Patone and Cibiano; they came into the post twice a week to be counted, and to receive their rations of beef, sugar, beans and other staples, which Uncle Sam's commissary officer issued to them."

"Large stakes were driven into the ground; at each stake, sat or stood the leader of a band; a sort of father to his people; then the rest of them stretched out in several long lines, young bucks and old ones, squaws and papooses, the families together, about seventeen hundred souls in all," she said.

"This tribe was quiet at that time, only a few renegades escaping into the hills on their wild adventures; but I never felt any confidence in them and was, on the whole, rather afraid of them," Mrs. Summerhayes said. "The squaws were shy, and seldom came near the officers' quarters. Some of the young girls were extremely pretty; they had delicate hands, and small feet encased in well-shaped moccasins. They wore short skirts made of stripped bark, which hung gracefully about their bare knees and supple limbs, and usually a sort of low-necked camisa, made neatly of coarse, unbleached muslin, with a band around the neck and arms, and in cold weather a pretty blanket was wrapped around their shoulders and fastened at the breast in front. In summer the blanket was replaced by a square of bright calico. Their coarse black hair hung in long braids in front over each shoulder, and nearly all of them wore an even bang or fringe over the forehead."

"Once or twice, I saw older squaws with horribly disfigured faces," she said. "I supposed it was the result of some ravaging disease, but I learned that it was the custom of this tribe, to cut off the noses of those women who were unfaithful to their lords."

"The mail was brought in twice a week by a soldier on horseback," Mrs. Summerhayes said. "When he failed to come in at the usual time, much anxiety was manifested, and I learned that only a short time before, one of the mail-carriers had been killed by Indians and the mail destroyed," she said. "Our letters were from two to three weeks old. The eastern mail came via Santa Fe to the terminus of the railroad, and then by stage; for in 1874, the railroads did not extend very far into the Southwest. At a certain point on the old New Mexico road, our man met the San Carlos carrier, and received the mail for [Fort] Apache."

She recalled going to an Apache dance across a ravine from the fort: "We all sat down on the great trunk of a fallen tree, and soon the dancers came into the arena.

"They were entirely naked, except for the loin-cloth; their bodies were painted, and from their elbows and knees stood out bunches of feathers, giving them the appearance of huge flying creatures; jingling things were attached to their necks and arms. Upon their heads were large frames, made to resemble the branching horns of an elk, and as they danced, and bowed their heads, the horns lent them the appearance of some unknown animal and added greatly to their height. Their feathers waved, their jingles shook, and their painted bodies twisted and turned in the light of the great fire, which roared and leaped on high. At one moment they were birds, at another, animals, at the next they were demons.

"The noise of the tomtoms and the harsh shouts of the Indians grew wilder and wilder. It was weird and terrifying. Then came a pause; the arena was cleared, and with much solemnity two wicked looking creatures came out and performed a sort of shadow dance, brandishing knives as they glided through the intricate figures."

"Scarce three months after that some of the same band of Indians fired into the garrison and fled to the mountains," she added.

She described an interruption at an officers' dinner party. Her account included some of the stories she had heard about hostile Apaches, some apparently especially crafted to scare the young wives of officers: "It was lovely; but in the midst of it, we perceived a sort of confusion of moccasined footsteps outside the dining-room. My nerves were, by this time, always on the alert. I glanced through the large door opening out into the hall, and saw a group of Indian scouts; they laid a coffee-sack down by the corner fireplace, near the front door. ...

"I had heard tales of atrocious cruelties committed by a band of Indians who had escaped from the reservation and were ravaging the country around. I had heard how they maimed poor sheep and cut off the legs of cattle at the first joint, leaving them to die; how they tortured women, and burned their husbands and children before their eyes; I had heard also that the Indian scouts were out after them, with orders to bring them in, dead of alive.

"The next day I learned that the ringleader's head was in the bag that I had seen, and that the others had surrendered and returned."

Walter Reed, Fort Apache's Famous Doctor

America's foremost military doctor was posted at Fort Apache during the Geronimo wars, though his fame came later in his career.

Walter Reed was a young teenager when the Civil War ravaged his native Virginia. He entered the University of Virginia in 1867 at age 16 and through unbelievably hard work and considerable aptitude, graduated with a medical degree in two years.

After a stint working for the Board of Health in Brooklyn, he joined the U.S. Army Medical Corps. He married and was transferred to Yuma, and then Tucson. Soon orders came dispatching the doctor and his wife to Camp Apache. They set out with their small dog in a horse-drawn "ambulance," accompanied by a few soldiers and a baggage wagon. "There were no way stations or even houses along the trail which ran through the San Carlos Reservation, which they had now entered, but there were Indians," according to L. N. Wood's book, *Walter Reed, Doctor in Uniform*. "It gave Mrs. Reed rather a turn when, at their first halt in the open, an Apache came into the camp. He laid down his rifle, sat beside the doctor, and explained with unsmiling friendliness that he was on his way to Camp Apache and would like something to eat. … The way then gradually ascended into the White Mountains, and the trail became almost impassable, even to stout hearts and army mules. How to get up and down hills where the track was only a steep jumble of barrel-sized rocks became the major problem. Leaving the baggage wagon stuck on a tremendous hill with the soldiers who were to unload it and bring it up empty the next morning, the Reeds one evening pushed ahead with the ambulance." At one point, Reed, trying to hold the wagon on a steep incline, was jerked so hard the soles were ripped off his shoes. The young couple arrived at the camp late in the year 1877. "They were to live at this post, one of the most inaccessible in all this wild and inaccessible region, for the next three years," Wood wrote.

One night there was a knock on Reed's door. "When he stepped out on the porch, he could distinguish by the starlight two enlisted men standing there, one of them with a bundle in his arms," Wood wrote. "Before anyone could speak, the bundle whimpered." Geronimo's band had left a tiny girl, badly burned, behind as they quickly abandoned a camp. The soldiers, riding only at night for fear of the hostiles, got the child to Reed who was able to nurse her back to health. The Reeds named her Susie and raised her in their home. This kindness endeared Reed to the Apaches, who would come to him for treatment if the efforts of their medicine men proved ineffective. Susie stayed with the Reeds for 12 years. Later she went to live with the Apaches at Fort Sill, Okla., where she taught English. Susie died in 1902.

"The post Indians were fond of games, and the men, in their

free time, could often be found squatting in the shade playing cards, each with his little scrap of red flannel, which all Apaches wore for good luck, stuck in hat or belt or button hole," Wood wrote. "The cards, homemade from horsehide, were marked with crude sketches of men and animals, and with dots and Apache signs; stakes were a bit of tobacco, small coins, a knife, or perhaps a pair of canvas pants."

As medicine was advancing in the wider world, reports of Lister's experiments and antiseptic surgery even reached an army doctor in Arizona, 700 miles from the nearest railroad.

Orders came and the Reeds, with their son and the Apache girl, traveled 27 days to the north to flag down a train near Cheyenne, Wyo., and head back to civilization. A stint near Johns Hopkins in Baltimore allowed Reed to bring himself up to date on the latest medical advances.

The former Fort Apache physician became world famous when he led a team in Cuba that solved the riddle of Yellow Fever. Though mosquitoes had been suspected as a source of infection, it was very hard to prove the insect was the carrier. The team finally learned through many experiments how complicated the disease cycle was. Humans can only transmit the virus to insects in the first couple of days after infection, and the mosquitoes had to carry the virus for at least 12 days before they could transmit it to a second person. To make the task more difficult, only humans suffer from Yellow Fever, so animals could not be used in laboratory experiments. The doctors had to experiment on themselves and other volunteers. Reed lost a close colleague in the experiments. The Army Medical Center in Washington is named in Reed's honor.

Sol Barth and the Settlement Of St. Johns

Sol Barth, another Jewish trader, became a larger than life legend of the White Mountains after immigrating from Germany at age 13.

"He came to the United States from East Prussia in the early months of 1856 with an uncle who had espoused the Mormon faith in Germany," says an article by N. H. Greenwood in the *Journal of Arizona History*. "They went first to Grand Rapids, Mich., where another uncle was established, but the two soon joined a Mormon handcart company – possibly at Council Bluffs but more probably at Iowa City, which was the railroad terminus in 1856."

The carts looked something like a miniature two-wheeled covered wagon, and contained flour, food, bedding, extra clothing, cooking utensils and a tent, according to *Treasures of Pioneer History* by Kate B. Carter. They were as wide as a standard wagon, so that the wheels fit easily into the wagon ruts. Two people usually pushed and babies and ill children were allowed to ride. "It was very common to see young girls between the ages of 16 and 20 with a harness on their shoulders" to pull the cart, according to *Handcarts to Zion* by LeRoy R. Hafen and Ann W. Hafen.

The experience apparently cured Barth of Mormonism. He moved quickly through Utah. By 1860 he left San Bernardino, California, to work along the Colorado River for a fellow immigrant Jew. The store owner, Michael Goldwater, was the grandfather of the 1964 presidential candidate Barry Goldwater. Barth worked at Fort Mohave and La Paz, which was across from Blythe, California. The gold strike brought him to the Prescott area, and then he served briefly with the Confederates in Tucson. After that he entered the freighting business, obtaining a government contract to haul mail from Albuquerque to Prescott and then hauling salt from the Zuni Salt Lake in New Mexico to Prescott.

The lake, 60 miles south of Zuni Pueblo, has provided salt to the area for many thousands of years and is revered for being the home of the Zuni salt deity. A 1956 *Arizona Highways* article says the lake, in a volcanic cinder cone, is saltier than the Great Salt Lake. "Zuni Indians hold annual salt ceremonies on the rim of the cone casting 'Apache Tears' (small obsidian stones) and willow sticks decorated with feathers into the lake," the magazine article said. "When Coronado passed this way en route to the Seven Cities of Cibola in 1540, he traded with the Zuni acquiring salt which they obtained from this place."

Like Coronado, Barth had Indian troubles. "Sol and a few of his associates in the salt enterprise were captured by Apaches under Cochise and Pedro," Greenwood wrote. "The Indians stripped the party of all belongings, including their clothing, and left them nearly a hundred miles from Zuni, the nearest settlement. They survived exposure, fatigue, hunger and thirst and made it to the Indian village. Their only food during the arduous journey was a small dog that followed them from the Indian encampment."

Barth first crossed the Little Colorado near present-day St. Johns in 1864, operating a pack train carrying salt from the Zuni Salt Lake to mines in the Prescott area, the St. Johns Stake history says. "In 1870, he secured a contract from the government to haul supplies for the army from the railhead at Dodge City, Kansas to Camp Apache. ... To help with this and other enterprises, Sol sent for his brothers, Nathan and Morris, who had remained in [Europe]. ... The wagon train that Sol and his brothers built up to handle this contract was an awesome thing and hauled much of the supplies used by the armies which suppressed the Apache uprisings. ... Although the route used by the Barth train ran through some of the most dangerous Indian and outlaw territory in the West, it was so formidable, by size alone, that it wasn't in great danger of attack by anyone. At its peak the train was composed of 38 big Murphy Wagons."

"Everything about them was jumbo size," the account continues. "When loaded, it required the united efforts of eight big oxen to move each wagon. The number of animals that were driven along, as spares to replace the sick, lame and weary, averaged 200. Adding these to the 300 head that were required to move the train at any given time, we have an indication of the size and scope of this operation. The services of nine blacksmiths were needed to keep the train rolling. Much of their work was accomplished while in transit, since three of these big wagons were outfitted as repair shops to handle not only ironwork, but the woodworking as well. When we consider the number of bull whackers required to tend and drive the oxen, the blacksmiths, out-riders, cooks, and helpers it took to make up the support crew, it becomes evident that this was a veritable army and, in case of trouble, a force to be reckoned with."

The Mormon account of Barth's early wagon route says the road led from Dodge City to Albuquerque, then through the Zuni country to "El Badito," a Little Colorado ford near present-day St. Johns. The crossing was called El Vadito, which means little ford in Spanish. The stake history and other English accounts refer to it as El Badito, possibly because of the difficulty of English speakers in discerning the unaccented initial Spanish consonant. It is also something of a bilingual joke, meaning little bad place.

The stake history says the train went on through Valle Bonito Pass in the mountains, to Camp Apache. The first trip took six months to go from Kansas to Camp Apache, and back to Kansas. But as the railhead was extended slowly westward, each succeeding trip became a little shorter. Each time the Barth brothers crossed the Little Colorado at El Vadito, they saw large tracts of fertile bottomland and the constant flow of water. They decided it would be more profitable to raise hay and grain at that location rather than haul it all the way from Dodge City. So in 1871, they started a little farming community with a few Hispanic families from Cubero, New Mexico.

Barth's nephew, Jacob Barth, in an oral history published in *This Land These Voices* by Abe Chanin, gave this account of the settlement of St. Johns. "He went through here and needed hay for his teams, and there was plenty of wild hay here and water from the Little Colorado. And then he could raise his grain, too. He put his drivers – the drivers of the ox trains – to farming in this area, but they didn't turn out to be very good farmers."

The following year, the settlement was moved six miles upstream to the site of present-day St. Johns.

Arizona Was the West, by James R. Jennings, gives this account: "The first settlers were Mexican, bringing many sheep to graze on the lush grass of the rolling hills. Some small farms were established, about 1873, using water from the Little Colorado for irrigation."

In another chapter, Jennings said, "St. Johns was first established in 1872 by Jose Seavedra, who arrived in a two-wheeled cart. He built the first bridge in the area to assist in moving sheep across the Little Colorado. It later became a toll bridge, a fee being charged to freighters hauling freight from New Mexico to Fort Apache."

Greenwood mentioned that John Walker, a mail carrier, built the first cabin at the location of St. Johns, which was at the intersection of developing routes from Albuquerque to Prescott and Fort Wingate (near Gallup, New Mexico) to Fort Apache.

"About 1874 Sol Barth, a trader, accompanied by his two

brothers, arrived," Jennings says. The book goes on to say that Barth won the land from the Hispanics in a card game, a story that is not widely credited.

Barth married Rufugio Landavazo of Cubero, who came with a dowry of 4,000 sheep. Having already tapped out his supply of brothers, Barth looked to the countrymen of his wife to work his farms and herd his sheep.

He built a dam and irrigation canals to farm the area around present-day St. Johns, and constructed a huge manor house, establishing himself as one of the most prominent residents of northeast Arizona.

According to the *Arizona Citizen* of Prescott, Barth "killed a man named Charles Davis in a fight on the Little Colorado beyond Camp Apache, probably because of some incident involving his freighting operations," Greenwood wrote. "He had made plenty of enemies, including one lawless group which made up its mind to hang him. According to one tale, these outlaws captured what they thought was their man and took him to the appointed tree only to discover that they had 'Old Man Cooley' instead of Sol. They let Cooley go."

Gunplay was not out of character for Barth. The biography of William Flake tells about a dispute the Mormon had with Barth over the quality of a mare in an exchange of sheep for horses. "Barth was a small man but he pulled his gun and said, 'Colts make all men equal.' " Flake's answer was, " 'Colts can't make a man out of you. I was not born in the woods to be scared of a coyote.' Sol put his gun back and his brother Morris told him to behave, Flake was living up to the contract. They had other deals, but Barth never tried another bluff."

In other troubles, Barth's brother Si was accused of trading whiskey and firearms at Zuni. And "Sol was sentenced to twenty-four hours in jail for the same type of illegal trade at Fort Apache, where he was the post trader," Greenwood wrote.

A book called *Down Through Arizona* reports that Barth "claimed the Grand Canyon – and everything else in Northern Arizona from the Little Colorado to the Big Sandy" in Mohave County. Unfortunately, since the book makes so many mistakes about Barth, it is difficult to know whether the grandiose claim was actually made during Sol Barth's lifetime or came posthumously as his legend grew.

Expansion
Of Hispanic Settlements

The *Enchanted Pearl* tells the story of a temporary Spanish settlement in the Snowflake area. "Several families arrived in Concho, stayed for a while, then decided to settle in nearby areas. Don Benito Baca, and his family moved to 'El Rillito de la Plata,' Little Silver Creek, some 18 miles west of Concho."

The New Mexicans moved beyond Concho to settle Vernon as well. "In early May 1875, Don Casimiro Padilla and his family left Los Lentes, New Mexico in a covered wagon pulled by oxen and brought their possessions here," *The Enchanted Pearl* says. "It was about August 2, 1875, that they arrived in Concho. Here they rested and visited relatives for about a week. On August 10, 1875, this family settled at El Mineral, thus becoming the first family to settle in what was later to become Vernon, Arizona."

"The first settlers in the Vernon area were the Mexicans who settled in the mouth of the Mineral Canyon," says the St. Johns Stake history. "This settlement was, mainly, Casimiro Padilla and his posterity, probably about 25 people in all."

In addition to Cubero, *Enchanted Pearl* says the early Spanish-speaking settlers of the White Mountains came from Blanco, Los Lentes, Seboyeta, San Mateo, San Miguel and Dona Anna County in New Mexico.

In the mid-1870s, Hispanics from New Mexico were predominant throughout the White Mountain area. According to the Great Register of Yavapai County, which tracked only adult men who paid their poll tax, there were 91 Hispanic men in St. Johns born in New Mexico with only 16 non-Hispanics born elsewhere in the U.S. The Barth brothers were the only foreign-born persons showing up on the register for St. Johns. Springerville was more mixed, with 24 Hispanics, 17 U.S.-born non-Hispanics and six immigrants. Camp Apache had 64 New Mexico-born Hispanics and 19 non-Hispanics born in the U.S. The Mormon community of Sunset on the Little Colorado had a different mix. There were no Hispanics. Of the 29 registered, 11 were foreign born and the remaining 18 came from the U.S. No other White Mountain communities show up on the register. Either the residents were recorded under the larger towns where they may have received mail, or they were so remote that they didn't become involved with county taxes.

Anglos were also getting into the sheep business in the White

Mountains. "It is known that Felix Scott ... had established a sheep ranch around Woodruff prior to 1877, because he sold to Mormons in 1877 when they came," says Ben Hansen, in his manuscript *Background History of the Lakeside-Pinetop Area*. "Another big sheep man was Will Amos in the Lakeside area, from the late 1880s to 1905."

Cattle Culture Arrives from Texas

Cattle herds came to the White Mountain area on the heels of the sheep. In old movies, the cattle and sheep people just plain didn't like each other because of their choice in grazing animal. It was never quite that simple. There were ethnic divisions, with the sheep people being mostly Hispanic and the cattle people being mostly Anglo. There was competition for resources with both groups anxious to turn the area's grass into meat they could sell. Then, there was an abundance of really bad people with guns. And there were thousands of valuable animals walking around loose with little supervision. Violence between groups of cattlemen was at least as prevalent as that between cattle growers and sheep men.

Two of the most famous cattle disputes occurred on the fringes of the White Mountains. The principals of the Pleasant Valley War, fictionalized by Zane Gray, traveled routinely through the area from the Tonto Basin on their way to Holbrook where a number of them met their fate. And the lynchings that were the basis of the book *The Ox-Bow Incident* by Walter Van Tilburg Clark happened near Heber.

But most cattle of the day probably lived uneventful lives, being born in the grasslands, fattened and driven to slaughter without being rustled or seeing a gun fired in anger. Cowboys too saw long stretches of hard lonely work without encountering anything worth mentioning in a movie script.

Like much of the early development in the White Mountains, the cattle business was first driven by the needs of Fort Apache. The soldiers ate beef and also distributed it to the Apaches.

Dan Ming ranged cattle in the area in 1866 or 1867, according to *From Indian Trails to Jet Trails*, Snowflake's Stake history, by Albert J. Levine.

A videotape produced by the Little House Museum credits the Slaughter family with driving the first herd of cattle into the area, bringing them over what became known as the Slaughter Trail from Texas. The Slaughter family was big in Texas. The patriarch of the group, George Webb Slaughter, had been a messenger for Sam Houston when he was a young man and, according to *The Slaughter Ranches and Their Makers* by Mary Whatley Clarke, was the one who brought Gen. Sam Houston news of the death of the defenders at the Alamo. His son Pete Slaughter served as a Texas Ranger and made several cattle drives north to Kansas, one to northern Montana and three to California. Pete and his younger brother, Mason, set out for Arizona in 1882, passing near Clovis and through Lincoln County, New Mexico. "The Rio Grande was crossed below Socorro, New Mexico, where the herd of 1000 animals swam the turbulent stream and the chuck wagon was floated over on a raft of dry cottonwood logs," the Slaughter book says. "Magdalena was passed and the cattle trailed over the San Augustine Plains to Datil, then Luna, New Mexico. The herd was turned loose on Black River, Apache County, Arizona," near the Apache Reservation. The Slaughters lived on a ranch near Alpine until the children were of school age. Then they built a home in Springerville.

Some places could be farmed with irrigation, but vast stretches of the area were really only suitable for grazing. Mormons began to trade Utah cattle for land. Though driving the beeves in from the north was tough, the Mormons had cheaper access to cattle than the other settlers. Still, there were also non-Mormons who brought small herds into the area in the 1870s.

Ben S. Hansen, in his manuscript *Background History of the Lakeside-Pinetop Area,* relates a story he heard his uncle Dick Hansen tell about trailing cattle down "the very dangerous and winding dusty trail" to Lee's Ferry to cross the Colorado River. "Any unusual disturbance would have brought a stampede and almost certain disaster for the herd. Then towards the end of the trail the cattle were tired, dusty, and thirsty. It was at this point in the story that Uncle Dick began to bawl and bellow as though he was one of those cows that suddenly had come alive at the smell of water and began a mad stampede toward the stream. There was no stopping the cattle then until they reached the river. Luckily they were far enough down the trail that no losses occurred."

Two external events were making the cattle business boom in northeastern Arizona. Texas had been synonymous with cattle for decades, but the invention of a practical way of making barbed wire in 1874 rapidly sliced up the open range of the Lone Star State. Cattlemen had to look west for new opportunities. And the railroads entered Arizona and New Mexico, allowing shipment of beef cattle to urban markets.

The Atlantic and Pacific Railroad (now the Santa Fe) was built across the northern fringes of the White Mountain area in the early 1880s. The railroad asked the local cattlemen's association where to build a stockyard along the railroad, and they recommended Holbrook "both for grass, water and convenience of location," according to the *St. Johns Herald*. The railroad reached Holbrook in 1882. Another railroad reached Magdalena, New Mexico, in 1884, providing an alternative market to ranchers in the southeast portion of the White Mountain area. But Holbrook became the main shipping point, with cattle drives coming up from as far away as the Tonto Basin and even Globe. *The Crooked Trail to Holbrook* by Leland J. Hanchett, Jr. documents the eight-day trek from the Q Ranch in Pleasant Valley to the railhead. The herds would spend their first night in Red Lake, then move on to Canyon Creek, cross the Mogollon Rim to overnight at Gentry Station in Black Canyon, then move on to Wilford, Heber, Halter Cross Ranch, Bushman Homestead (later Zeniff), Crosby Tank and finally to Holbrook.

Just before the arrival of the railroad, two Englishmen, Henry Smith and Ernest Tee, brought 1,800 head of cattle to a ranch between St. Johns and Springerville, according to *On the Road to Nowhere* by Applewhite. They had a horse camp in the mountains west of Greer, and were later joined at the "Twenty-four" ranch by Thomas Carson, a Scotsman.

The longhorn cattle from Texas were basically descendants of Spanish cattle, which had come to the New World as early as Columbus's second voyage. They were mixed with some English breeds that had been brought to Texas from the East Coast. Applewhite described those longhorns as being able to "run like deer, keep up with a horse, and were able to cover as much as twenty miles in a day."

Anglos Move
Into East-Central Arizona

Settlers followed the sheep men and cowboys into the area when they saw there was unclaimed land, and money to be made supplying Fort Apache.

William R. Milligan, who had been supplying forts in New Mexico, delivered corn to Fort Apache in 1870. On his way, he passed through the area where Springerville is today and liked what he saw. So, before going back to New Mexico, he built a cabin to claim land in what would later be known as Round Valley. Marion Clark, another pioneer, accompanied Milligan on his second trip. Oren W. McCullough and Anthony Long joined Milligan in the beautiful valley. They established farms to supply the fort with corn and barley. On an 1872 visit to Prescott, Milligan told newspaper editors that there were 20 to 30 people in the settlement.

The Snowflake Stake history says Milligan and his men were the first permanent white residents north of Apache country.

Henry Springer, a prosperous New Mexico merchant (from Albuquerque with no association to Springer, New Mexico), opened a store in Round Valley in 1876. James Colter reminisced about those days in *History of Arizona*. "I was hauling goods one time from Henry Springer's store in Albuquerque and I told Henry Springer he had better come to Round Valley, as it was called then, and put up a store; that the people were coming in and we would name the post office and little village after him, Springerville, and that was old Henry Springer." But Springer extended too much credit and was soon out of business.

"The first map of Arizona (Colton's, 1873) shows Round Valley as 'Milligan's Fort,' " according to *On the Road to Nowhere.*. "Milligan was an enterprising sort. He established the first saw and grist mills; had a large farm, the first year raising 800,000 pounds of barley which he sold to the army at Fort Apache for five-and-one-half cents per pound and made a good profit. He, together with Tony Long, had the contract to erect houses for White Mountain Apaches (each costing the government $1,600, in which the Indians housed their livestock while they preferred living in their wickiups); and was a major freighter in association with Solomon Barth of St. Johns. ... Milligan's sawmill was the first that converted timber into lumber from the virgin White Mountain stands. The mill was fed its first log in October, 1876." The Little House Museum says Milligan's gristmill was in Water Canyon south of what is now Eagar.

Marion Clark planted corn for Milligan in Round Valley, then moved west to farm in the area near present-day Show Low, according to Cooley's biography.

Gustav and Julius Becker were working for a New Mexico stagecoach line in 1874 when two travelers told them about Round Valley, which Spanish settlers called Valle Redondo. "They fired the imagination of the two Becker boys so that one of them, Julius Becker, soon after saddled his horse and rode west to what is now Springerville and Eagar," says the St. Johns Stake history. "His brother, Gustav, followed in 1876. At that time there were very few wagon trails west of the Rio Grande. The Becker brothers came out on horseback, but passed a few scattered wagon caravans coming westward, following no particular trail. They settled in … Round Valley and began farming and later on, merchandising." The Beckers learned that the men who had encouraged them to move to the area were cattle rustlers. A run-in with the Texas Rangers prohibited the two Round Valley boosters from making it back to the area.

"Naturally people needed a place to trade, so Julius Becker opened a store on the west side of the Little Colorado River," the stake history says.

A ledger entry indicates the first sale at the Becker store was in March 1876 to one of the Bacas, according to *On the Road to Nowhere.*

The Beckers brought their goods from Belen, New Mexico, where their brother lived. He helped organize the shipments. "Oxen were used instead of horses at the outset, and therefore the first wagon trails of any consequence were laid from Springerville east, via American Valley, now known as Quemado, and thence from there directly to Belen," the stake history says. "It took the ox trains sixty days to make the round trip, one month each way, and, incidentally, as there was no post office in Round Valley, this was the method of carrying the mail. … The oxen were used until approximately 1890, when horses and mules were substituted because they could make the trip so much faster."

To start a buying trip, the Beckers would "put the gold in the saddle bags and the greenbacks in their boots," the stake history says. "They would then ride one of the fastest and best horses available out of Round Valley to Belen and would always travel at night because the outlaws were laying for them. They generally published their departure date, but never lived up to it, in order to throw the outlaws off the trail, but they were always followed after they were missed from their store."

The current route of Highway 60 was blazed by the freight wagons after the railroad was built to Magdalena.

"During that time the farmers in Round Valley had very little cash with which to purchase their wants," the stake history says. "They received credit from Becker Brothers and the other merchants and could only pay back in their farm products, which in those days were barley, oats and hay mostly. ... The Becker brothers tendered their bid each year to the United States Army, stationed at Old Fort Apache, and were fortunate most every year in receiving the contracts to furnish oats, hay, and sometimes wood. The farmers would deliver their products to Fort Apache on the Becker Brothers contract and were then given credit until their accounts were paid and then received cash for any balance."

"Naturally there had to be a road for these wagon freighters, so little by little the road from Springerville across the mountains, through Cluff Cienega [now McNary] by Cooley's ranch [south of Hon Dah], to Fort Apache, was established," the stake history says. "As most of these contracts were filled late in the fall and often in the winter, the freighters had a hard time of it and many times they had to devise means of pulling through the deep snows in the White Mountains in order to reach their destination. ... Oftentimes they would drive their horses back and forward through the snow over the trail in order to pack it down and in that way they were able to pull their wagons over the solidly re-packed snow."

Other towns also had early Anglo settlers. "Woodruff was first settled by Luther Martin, a non-Mormon in 1870," said Jennings in *Arizona Was the West*.

Gen. Crook Takes Command

Arriving at this point in history was Gen. George Crook, who labored in life, as well as in his autobiography, to provide a politically correct mix of toughness and fairness in his Indian policy.

Although he must have been hard to like — his autobiography dismisses nearly all of his military colleagues as cowards or incompetents and usually both — he is revered by many White Mountain Apaches for his military leadership and fairness.

Though the coming of the whites brought misery, disease, starvation, lost land, death, dislocation and cultural changes to the White Mountain Apaches — for nearly every other native group in the Americas the experience was much worse. Crook, along with Cooley, helped the White Mountain Apache escape the fate of nearly every other tribe. Few tribal members were killed by the military and they were able to keep a substantial part of their ancestral land.

Crook arrived anxious to boost his reputation, which, as always, was not as illustrious as he hoped. During the Civil War, while many of his contemporaries were moving up toward the White House, he had made a few mistakes. He was assigned to attack Virginia from the west while Grant attacked from the north. Instead, he fled back across the mountains to West Virginia after capturing an erroneous Confederate telegram that said Grant had been repulsed. Shortly after gaining the rank of major general, he was taken by Confederate guerrillas from a hotel room in Cumberland, Md., where he had been resting. The embarrassed general was exchanged for Rebel prisoners. At Antietam he missed an opportunity to crush the Confederate army when he spent hours trying to find a way to cross a creek, which was later found to be only three feet deep.

Though a bit proud, Crook was no fool. Despite his setbacks, he learned much during the dreadful years of the Civil War. When he led his men in the pursuit of Lee from Richmond to Appomattox to end the war, he was a tough, aggressive, opportunistic fighter. After that victory against thousands of Virginia's celebrated veterans, he was confident he could subdue bands of ill-armed Apache warriors. Since he was not shy about sharing his accomplishments, he probably told the Apaches the futility of opposition.

Certainly, he let the eastern newspaper correspondents, who nearly always accompanied him, know his thoughts. Desire for publicity was probably one of the least eccentric things about Crook.

He wore an unusual outfit and rode a mule in his campaigns. His men wrote a mocking, but affectionate, ballad about their commander.

"I'd like to be a packer,
And pack with George F. Crook,
And dressed up in my canvas suit,
To be for him mistook.
I'd braid my beard in two forked tails,
And idle all the day
In whittling sticks and wondering
What the New York papers say.

"I think that the Apache is painted in darker colors than he deserves, and that his villainies arise more from a misconception of facts than from his being worse than other Indians," Crook said. "Living in a country the natural products of which will not support him, he has either to cultivate the soil or steal, and as our vacillating policy satisfies him we are afraid of him, he chooses the latter, also as requiring less labor and being more congenial to his natural instincts. I am satisfied that a sharp, active campaign against him would not only make him one of the best Indians in the country, but it would also save millions of dollars to the Treasury, and the lives of many innocent whites and Indians."

Crook was placed in command in Arizona on June 4, 1871, but had to call off his campaign twice, first while Colyer tried to make peace with the Apaches and then when Howard was given his turn at negotiating a settlement.

An attack on a stage near Wickenberg helped turn public support away from the peace commissioners and gave the military its chance to force peace. "On November 5, 1871, Yavapai located on the tiny Date Creek reservation raided the California stage near Wickenberg," McGuire wrote in *Mixed-Bloods*. "Six Anglos died in the attack, including a young East Coast writer. Stimulated by reports of the massacre carried in eastern newspapers, many prominent pacific-minded individuals now became convinced that Apache affairs had been described inaccurately by those who have allowed their philanthropy to outrun their judgment and sense of justice. Public opinion turned against Grant's peace policy, and General Crook prepared for new campaigns against the Apache and the

Yavapai, who were consistently confused with Apache."

The War Department issued General Order No. 10, summarized by McGuire as follows:

1. All roving bands were to go upon the reservations at once;

2. If found away, they were to be punished as hostiles;

3. An army officer was to act as agent on each reservation;

4. A descriptive list was to be made of each male old enough to go upon the warpath, with the number in his family recorded, and a duplicate form was to be on his person at all times;

5. The presence on the reservation of every male was to be verified at least once each day;

6. A tribe, unless guilty of giving aid, was not to be punished for the acts of individuals;

7. The families of absent warriors were to be held in custody until captures were effected;

8. The department commander was to fix a time-limit for the inauguration of the new regime;

9. No whites except officials were to be allowed on the reserves without permission, and official escorts were to be furnished in all cases;

10. Each Indian was to receive a specific amount of rations, and the issues were to be supervised by army officers;

11. Vigorous operations were to be continued against the hostiles until they submitted;

12. Incorrigibles were to be hunted down with the aid of friendly scouts; and

13. Full authority was conferred upon the department commander to adopt such measures as might be needed to give full effect to the policy of the government.

In *General Crook, His Autobiography*, he described his first approach to Fort Apache: "From this point we scouted the mountains on either side of Aravaipa Canyon, but finding nothing, we continued our scouting over the Gila and up the San Carlos River to near the source of the western branch of it, but were still unsuccessful. Now being near Fort Apache, I became uneasy for fear I might mistake some of the friendly Indians of the latter place, I having been informed that there were some there. It was difficult to realize that there could be any of the Apache tribe who were friendly to anybody."

While the lore of the West is filled with the army defending against hostile Indian attacks, the war against the Apaches was almost always conducted with the army on the offensive. With the Apaches free to roam over hundreds of thousands of miles of rough terrain and attack at will, the army could not defend every place in the territory against Indian attacks.

To win the war, the army needed to go on the offensive, find the Indians and either kill them or force them to live where they could be supervised.

Crook announced that all Apaches should be on their reservations by February 1872.

The general planned his campaign well. First, he realized he needed strong forts throughout the area. Second, he needed a large number of Apache Scouts, familiar with enemy tactics, routes of travel and hiding places.

And finally, he needed roads so his men and mules could move rapidly against the enemy.

The White Mountain Apaches, who had been more or less at peace with the whites for years, were natural volunteers for Crook's ranks. The general, upon arrival in Arizona, hired 40 of what he called Mexicans to act as scouts, but by the time he reached Fort Apache, he knew he needed Apaches to fight Apaches. He sent the Mexican-Americans home to the Yuma area and began looking for Indian scouts.

"I had many long talks with the Coyoteros, White Mountains, and finally got them to join in my plans for subduing the hostiles, which was for them to enlist as scouts and act in conjunction with our troops. Old one-eyed McGill (undoubtedly Miguel) and Pedro were the principal Indians, or chiefs."

"Crook told the Indians that a rapidly increasing white population would put an end to their existence as hunters," Time-Life says in its book, *The Scouts*. "They would be much more content as farmers on reservations where the army could protect them against predatory whites. For this plan to succeed, however, all Indians had to come onto the reservations. Crook explained that he hoped to avoid war, but that after granting a reasonable grace period, 'he intended to start out in person and see to it that the last man returned to the Reservations or died in the mountains.' "

Crook, of course, couldn't lead the Apaches directly because he couldn't speak their language. Also, a celebrated Union general doesn't personally lead privates, let alone Indian auxiliaries.

Corydon Cooley, who had married into the Apache tribe, was well suited for the role. Familiarity and family ties helped Cooley become an effective leader to the army's Indian scouts.

With his scouts ready, Crook needed to organize transportation to complete his plans. Here is his own account of blazing the famous Crook's Trail from Fort Apache to the Prescott area:

"We left for Verde about the end of August, without a guide, being assured that there was a plain trail all the way, which I soon found out to be pretty much a delusion. Our route lay along the summit of the Mogollon Mountains. The trail, at best dim, soon ran out, and the summit was in places cut up by ridges and cross canyons. Not being able at times to tell the main summit from some of the minor ones that ran off to the east, principally, we experienced much difficulty in finding our way."

After the road was improved, it became important in Crook's campaign against the Apaches. He was now ready to begin, but Howard had made a peace treaty with Cochise placing a new reservation along the Mexican border off limits to Crook. The general began operations against the Pinalenos and other hostile bands.

"Crook's winter campaign of 1872-1873 sent troops from all of the posts to sweep through the Salt River Country and Tonto Basin to conquer the outlaw Apache bands and drive them onto reservations," Wharfield wrote. "Each contingent had Indian scouts and a pack train for effective field service." They moved out from Camp Verde, Camp Date Creek, Fort Whipple, Camp Hualpai, Camp McDowell, Camp Grant and Camp Apache.

"At Camp Apache, army scout Cooley and some thirty Apache Scouts were with Captain George M. Randall, 23rd Infantry, and detachments," Wharfield wrote. "The group left in late November 1872, moving out along the Crook's Trail country for some miles and then southward into the mountainous regions toward the Tonto Creek junction with the Salt River, and on to Camp McDowell. There were only a few scattered Indians discovered in the region."

One of the most celebrated of Crook's early Apache battles was the fight at Skull or Skeleton Cave on Dec. 28, 1872.

Crook set out with about 220 men from the 5th Cavalry in late fall. With snow covering the ground in the high country, the hostile Apaches were believed to be in the desert below. Capt. James Burns and several troops of the 5th Cavalry were en route from Fort McDowell to the Salt River when they surprised a small Apache village and killed six Indians while the rest fled through the canyons.

Burns captured a seven-year-old boy he later christened Mike Burns and raised and educated the child as his son.

The soldiers believed more Apaches were hiding in the area and made plans for a search. One Indian, Natanje, variously described as a Pima guide and an Apache Scout, told the soldiers that he had once lived in a cave, high up on the wall of the Salt River Canyon.

The soldiers split into two groups, one approaching the cave from the bottom and the other moving up on top of the cliff.

The party approaching from below fired on a group of Indians who quickly retreated to the cave. The Apaches hid behind a wall of boulders at the mouth of the cave and fired at the sol-

General Crook's success in the Apache wars came largely through the efforts of his Apache Scouts. Alchesay, also known as A-1, won the Medal of Honor and became chief of his tribe.

107

diers. After exchanging fire all night to little effect, the dawn began to show the flat roof of the cave. The soldiers decided they could fire into the roof, allowing the ricocheting bullets to search out the human targets within the cave. When the fighting continued despite the heavy toll taken by the ricocheting bullets, soldiers above the cave on the cliff noticed they could drop boulders behind the wall at the mouth of the cave.

"The destruction was sickening," said Lt. John G. Bourke in his book *On the Border with Crook*. "The air was filled with bounding, plunging fragments of stone; no human voice could be heard in such a cyclone of wrath; the volume of dust was so dense that no eye could pierce it."

The soldiers counted 76 men, women and children dead. Accounts differ on the wounded. One story says there were 18 mortally wounded and another 35 captives killed by Pima and Maricopa scouts on the way back to Fort McDowell. Other accounts say half of the 35 wounded died of their injuries and make no reference to any subsequent massacre.

The events that led up to the famous battle of Turret Peak started with Cooley's scouts looking for hostiles suspected of a recent atrocity.

"The trail of this band had been picked up by the Apache Scouts in the Bloody Basin, north of McDowell and west of the Verde River," Wharfield wrote. "Only a few days prior near Wickenburg Tonto Apache had slaughtered three whites. One of the victims, a young Scot by the name of George Taylor, had been ruthlessly tortured. His clothing was stripped and the naked body shot full of arrows, the Indians taking care not to hit a vital place. In his agony the helpless man rolled on the ground breaking off the shafts. Then he was finally put out of his misery by further torture, cutting off portions of his body.

"The fresh signs of the Tonto were followed for a distance mostly at night."

Crook described the action: "Capt. Randall's command ran on some fresh sign of Indians there, and was very discreet in his movements, moving after night, and watching during the daytime. But some of his pack mules got away and fell into the hands of the hostiles. They at once commenced sending up signal smokes, but evidently failed to locate us, our people understanding their signals, and consequently lay very low. One of our scouts, while prowling around and watching, caught a squaw, brought her into camp, and by intimidation made her tell where her people were, and took her along as a guide."

The Time-Life book *The Scouts* takes up the story: "Snow fell heavily in the high country around Turret Peak, southeast of Prescott in Arizona Territory during the night of Dec. 2, 1873. Fourteen Apache Scouts and a Hispanic tracker under Chief of Scouts Al Sieber, plus a handful of U.S. Cavalry troopers, plodded through snow that already lay two feet deep."

The scouts and soldiers climbed one mountain, but found no hostiles. "The Apache Scouts went out again, this time spotting a campfire in the gloom one half mile ahead," the Time-Life Book says. "At this news, [the captain] halted his column for the night, but the men got no rest. To keep from freezing, they marched in circles — fires would have given them away to their quarry — and warmed their rifles inside their clothing so that fingers would not freeze to triggers when the action started."

Finally, the soldiers and scouts got ready to go.

"Our soldiers, before starting out, wrapped their feet and knees with gunny sacks, so as to make as little noise as possible," Crook said. "Soon after dark the command started for the camp of the hostiles under the guidance of the squaw. Their route lay down the banks of the river Verde for a ways, and then it took up an incline of broken lava that had become detached from a high palisade of the same material. ...

"Here they met with a circular mountain running up into a column, with but one mode of ingress. This was caused by a piece of this palisades fallen down, leaving a notch by which, with great difficulty, our people could get up. On top of this notch was lying a huge rock, so our people had to crawl on their stomachs. ...

"Just at the dawn of day our people fired a volley into their camp and charged with a yell. So secure did they feel in this almost impregnable position that they lost all presence of mind, even running past their holes in the rocks. Some of them jumped off the precipice and were mashed into a shapeless mass. All of the men were killed; most of the women and children were taken prisoners."

Wharfield puts the casualties at 50 killed and less than 15 taken prisoner.

The soldiers "emerged from the engagement unscathed, although one Apache Scout suffered the anguish of finding his mother among the slain Indians," the Time-Life book says.

Crook's victory nearly ended the 1873 campaign. "I had some of the prisoners sent out to communicate with the hostiles, holding out the 'olive branch,' offering them peace on certain conditions, which were that they should all move in on the different reservations and abstain from all depredations from that time forward," Crook said. "They promptly responded to my proposition, and all within reach came in at once."

Crook recommended the Medal of Honor for four of the White Mountain Apache Scouts and six Aravaipa Apaches for their service during the campaign. The White Mountain Apaches given the medal included Sergeant Alchesay, who later became chief of his tribe. Others were privates Machol, Blanquet and Chiquito. All the citations were identical: "Gallant conduct during campaigns and engagements with Apaches." They were issued in 1875 for their efforts during the campaign of the winter of 1872-73.

Pre-Mormon Settlers of Snowflake

The Snowflake Stake history says Albert Franklin Banta, a civilian guide, was sent from present-day Prescott to Fort Apache with dispatches. The army then requested him to establish a wagon road between the fort and Horsehead Crossing, which was about two miles east of present-day Holbrook. This may be the first record of an Anglo passing through the Silver Creek valley, where Snowflake and Taylor would eventually be settled.

Other people began to notice the valley. "William R. Milligan and Marion Clark made a trip in June 1872 from Round Valley to Camp Verde with corn for the military post there," says the Snowflake Stake history. "They went by Silver Creek ... and found the bed of the creek dry, with only a little water in holes in the upper part of the valley."

"In these early days James Stinson and others had contracted to deliver cattle to the army posts of Northern Arizona and New Mexico," the stake history says. Stinson, who lived in Colorado, was to meet the cattle herd, coming from New Mexico, at a point on the Little Colorado. He found the river near present-day Winslow and headed east.

"Somehow he missed the fork of the Little Colorado and followed Silver Creek instead to the site of present-day Snowflake, where he camped," the history says. He eventually realized his mistake and backtracked to meet his herd, but the "Snowflake valley so impressed Stinson that he persuaded his partners to go in with him and establish a ranch at this place."

The partners were Dan Ming and a man named Evans. The stake history says, "These men raised cattle, selling the livestock to the army at Camp Apache. Dan Ming and Evans soon pulled out leaving Stinson to operate the ranch along with the aid of Mexican helpers."

He had his ranch headquarters on the northwest corner of what are now Stinson and Freeman streets in the town of Snowflake. "Stinson had a line of adobe rooms which contained on the south end Stinson's living quarters. Next was the room for the Mexican ranch hands, then the granary. The fourth room was the saddle or tack room and the most northern was the machine shed." The stake history says Stinson was just finishing another building – the one now known as the Stinson House — when he sold out to the Mormons.

During the five years Stinson owned the ranch he constructed "a mile of ditch which took out the waters of Silver Creek, enough to irrigate about 300 acres of land."

Nutrioso also had a pre-Mormon settlement. *Road to Nowhere* says James G. H. Colter settled briefly in Round Valley in 1873, then acquired vast holdings around Nutrioso. The St. Johns Stake history says Colter came to the area from Wisconsin to raise barley for the fort. "He had heard that barley was selling for eight or nine dollars a hundred pounds. ... The first year, with the help of Mexican labor, he cleared land and dug ditches so he could irrigate the fields. He raised a good crop that year and was able to sell his barley to Camp Apache. The next year he sent to Atchison, Kansas to get a threshing machine. It cost him more to get the machine across the plains than he paid for it."

Colter was also influential in Round Valley. According to *On the Road to Nowhere,* he was one of the area's first cattlemen, was the district's first deputy U.S. Marshal and was elected to the 1879 Territorial Legislature.

Alpine, originally called Bush Valley, was settled in 1877 by Elias Gibbs and Anderson Bush. Gibbs was one of the men who had come to Springerville with Springer. Bush built a cabin east of what is now the Alpine cemetery.

The first settler in Greer was Ambijorn Englevalson. (His name has been spelled many ways.) *The Road to Nowhere* says that he brought horses to "a place on the flat, at the south end of the meadow where the east and west forks of the Little Colorado join." Amberion Point is named for him. "Some say he was a freighter and raised the first grain in the valley. ... Since a threshing machine wasn't known of then, he built a round corral, tamped the ground hard, then drove horses over the grain, cleaning it by winnowing in the wind. He built a little one-room cabin and was believed to have slept there with his horses to keep warm. Most accounts agree on his end: He was killed by a horse near Springerville." The Greer book says Tommy Lang homesteaded near the Greer turn-off. Lang was killed by a cowboy named Youngblood from the "Twenty-Four" ranch.

The area that became Lakeside was called 'Turkey' in Apache. Some of the first white settlers were sheep men, with Robert Scott and his two uncles, James Scott and William Morgan, arriving in the area about 1878, according to a 1987 article published in *A Tribute to the Lakeside Pioneers.* "Woodland, sometimes called Hog Town, is two miles from the present site of Lakeside. It is a fertile valley owned by homesteaders. The settlers previous to 1892 were A. Young Sr., A. Young Jr., Aleck McCleeve and Abner Crandell."

An article by Leora Schuck in the same book mentions other pioneers who "stayed for a few years and left. There was Jim Porter whose homestead lay north of Porter Creek. The creek, Porter Mountain, Porter Springs and Porter Knoll were named for him and other members of his family. He sold out. ... Half a mile up Billy Creek was a small cabin, already half in ruins, which was built and lived in by a man named Springer, probably a trapper." After giving his name to Springer Mountain, he disappeared. Billy Scorse lived on Billy Creek and gave the name to the stream, which had earlier been called Sawmill Creek. An article in *Forever*

Frontier, the Visitors' Guide to Southwest New Mexico, West Texas and Eastern Arizona, said Scorse was an Englishman and ran the only store in town, selling liquor to the soldiers at Fort Apache. "He had 40 acres on the creek and squatters' rights to more land in [downtown] Lakeside," according to the 2006 article. And, "there was a settlement called 'Milltown' north of where Blue Ridge High School is now located."

The government was a long ways from the White Mountains and wasn't keeping very close track of what went on in the remote region. So its records give only a fragmentary view of who arrived in the area and when they came. Names on poll tax records give some indication of the years prominent people began to show up, or at least when they began to pay their taxes. The law required every male inhabitant over 21 and under 60 to pay $3 yearly as a poll tax. The counties got $1.50 for their operations and $1.50 was passed on to the Territory. Records in Prescott, the territorial capital and county seat for northern Arizona in the early days, show W.S. Wilson, William Clark and Corydon Cooley paying in 1873. In 1874, D. M. Scott, Morris Barth, Solomon Barth, C. E. Cooley, M. Clark, Wesley Clanton and C. B. Wilson paid. In 1876, the taxpayers included William L. Plum, Pionico Bacca, C. E. Cooley, M. Clark and Wm. Clark.

Milligan filed the first homestead claim in the White Mountains, securing his allotment in the Springerville area on May 15, 1880. James D. Murray followed with his claim on November 20, 1880, and Gustav and Julius Becker each filed claims on November 20, 1882. St. George Creaghe filed his claim on April 20, 1883, also in the Round Valley area. Antonio Gonzales was the only one who filed an early claim on land outside Round Valley. He filed Dec. 30, 1884 for a homestead east of present-day St. Johns, near the New Mexico state line. These homesteaders may have been farming on their property long before they filed their claims, partly because the government offices were so far away.

113

Struggle With Apaches Continues

The White Mountain area was a dangerous place for early settlers. Though Gen. Crook had forced the Apaches onto reservations, it remained to him to put down frequent raids. " ... the Indians at the San Carlos agency broke out and went into the San Pedro Valley and brutally murdered some families living there," Crook wrote. "They also killed some other people. The troops started out after them at once, had a couple of fights with them, killing a good many of their number. Some of them returned to the reservation and surrendered.

"I arrived there at this time. I refused to accept their surrender, but told them I could not harm them, as they had thrown themselves on my mercy, but I would drive them all back into the mountains, where I could kill them all, that they had lied to me once, and I didn't know but what they were lying to me now. They begged to be allowed to remain, making all kinds of promises for the future. I finally compromised by letting them stay, provided they would bring in the heads of certain of the chiefs who were ringleaders, which they agreed to.

"A couple of mornings afterwards they brought in seven heads of the proscribed. The same edict was sent out to the Tontos, which was also responded to with alacrity. Deltchay (a hostile Tonto leader) had two heads. When I visited the Verde reservation, they would convince me that they had brought in his head; and when I went to San Carlos, they would convince me that they had brought in his head. Being satisfied that both parties were earnest in their beliefs, and the bringing in of an extra head was not amiss, I paid both parties."

Crook now had the White Mountain Apaches, which he called "Coyoteros," on the Fort Apache Reservation. The Apache-Mohave and the Tontos were on a reservation on the Verde River and the Pinalenos and other bands went to San Carlos. By 1874, about 3,000 Apaches were on reservations and another 1,000 hostiles remained in the mountains.

Crook was proud of the progress the Apaches, particularly the White Mountain Apaches, had made with agriculture on the reservations. "The Indians at Apache had, with a few grubbing hoes condemned by the Quartermaster Department and fixed by the post blacksmith, and with sticks hardened in the fire, raised in 1873 some 500,000 pounds of corn and 30,000 pounds of beans."

But people who sold the government supplies to feed the Indians were not interested in having them become self-sustaining farmers. And Crook thought that those unscrupulous contractors had convinced the Interior Department to concentrate the Apaches on the hostile wastes of the San Carlos Reservation. "In the spring of 1874, the Indians on the Verde Reservation were removed to the San Carlos in the interest of some persons at Tucson, who were on the inside of the 'Ring,'" Crook said.

"During August 1874 Cooley with some thirty Apache Scouts and accompanied by Sergeant Butler of Troop B, 5th Cavalry with a detail of four soldiers were sent into the Tonto Basin in pursuit of several marauding renegades," Wharfield wrote. "The *Arizona Citizen* of Tucson, August 27, 1874, and the *Yuma Arizona Sentinel,* August 29, 1874, reported incidents of this scouting trip. On the 13th they surprised Chappo's group and killed thirteen. The Tucson paper laconically recounted 'no prisoners.' One of the scouts decapitated the leader and took his head along for an exhibit. This group of outlaws had recently stolen beef cattle in the Verde area and traded the property to a Moqui [Hopi] band.

"Moving southward into the Sierra Ancha range [west of the White Mountain Apache Reservation] the party on Aug. 21 jumped a rancheria of 11 wickiups. Ten more renegades were killed and 23 new blankets, perhaps recently issued by a reservation agency to the Indians, taken along with four rifles, powder and lead."

When Cooley returned to San Carlos with the hostile's head, the Indian agent, John Clum, sent a complaint to the Indian Commission in Washington. He wrote, "This is the fifth head brought to the agency this summer."

Wharfield wrote about a group of Petone's band killing some miners who were prospecting north of Fort Apache. The incident gave Miners Camp its name. "Throughout 1874 small groups of savages left the reservations to murder and pillage the miners, settlers, and other whites in the country. Crook used vigorous methods to control the situation, demanding that the heads of wrongdoers be brought in or all would suffer."

Molly, one of Cooley's wives, told a story about finding a pair of human ears in his blanket. That was the last time she aired out her husband's bedroll.

The government began to move the Indians from the Fort Apache Reservation to San Carlos. "These Indians at Apache were a mountain Indian, and the heat and dust of San Carlos agency was quite equal at times to that of Yuma, besides being malarious," Crook wrote. "There was plenty of arable land in the mountains about Apache and on the reservation set aside for these Indians. Their removal was one of those cruel things that greed has so often inflicted on the Indian. When the Indian appeals to arms, his only redress, the whole country cries out against the Indian.

"They finally succeeded in removing all these Indians except Diablo's band, who said they would rather be killed than go down to the San Carlos to sure death. For fear of an outbreak and an exposure of their infamous schemes, they allowed this one band to remain, provided they would become self-sustaining."

With the fighting nearly at an end, Indian matters were transferred to civil authorities, the Office of Indian Affairs.

"As soon as the Indians became settled on the different reservations, gave up the warpath, and became harmless, the Indian agents, who had sought cover before, now came out as brave as sheep, and took charge of the agencies, and commenced their game of plundering," Crook said. "Then there was a Superintendent of Indian Affairs for Arizona by the name of Dr. Bendell, a little General from Albany or Troy, N.Y. He obtained permission to establish his residence at Whipple Barracks, and built the house now occupied by the telegraph offices. It was generally understood that during his short stay in Arizona he carried off some $50,000 for his share of the spoils."

Crook said that Capt. Byrne watched distributions to the Hualpais and determined that Indians who were to receive 95 pounds of beef only received 15. "Upon investigation it came out in evidence that the Indian agent had sent wagon loads of Indian food to the mines, and sold them," Crook said. "And amongst many other little dodges practiced by these Christian gentlemen was to change the pea on the scales, so that a beef that would weigh three hundred pounds was made to weigh 1,300."

Crook caused the "Ring" some discomfort until he was sent off to command the Department of the Platte in the spring of

1875.

About the same time Lt. Jack Summerhayes was transferred to Camp McDowell. With two wagons called "ambulances" and some soldiers, the lieutenant and his wife started north. There was no major Indian action at the time, but there were enough hostiles off the reservation to make the trip dangerous. After passing through Snowflake, the party camped at a place called Walker's Ranch and then headed toward the Little Colorado near present-day Winslow. "Quite early in the day, we met a man who said he had been fired upon by some Indians at Sanford's Pass," Martha Summerhayes said in her book. "We thought perhaps he had been scared by some stray shot, and we did not pay much attention to his story.

"Soon after, however, we passed a sort of old adobe ruin, out of which crept two bare-headed Mexicans, so badly frightened that their dark faces were pallid; their hair seemed standing on end, and they looked stark mad with fear. They talked wildly to the guide, and gesticulated, pointing in the direction of the Pass. They had been fired at, and their ponies taken by some roving Apaches. They had been in hiding for a day, and were hungry and miserable. We gave them food and drink. They implored us, by the Holy Virgin, not to go through the Pass.

"What was to be done? The officers took counsel; the men looked to their arms. It was decided to go through. Jack examined his revolver, and saw that my pistol was loaded. I was instructed minutely what to do, in case we were attacked. For miles we strained our eyes, looking in the direction whence these men had come.

"At last, in mid-afternoon, we approached the Pass, a narrow defile winding down between high hills from this table-land to the plain below. To say that we feared an ambush, would not perhaps convey a very clear idea of how I felt on entering the Pass.

"There was not a word spoken. I obeyed orders, and lay down in the bottom of the ambulance; I took my derringer out of the holster and cocked it. I looked at my little boy lying helpless there beside me, and at the delicate temples, lined with thin blue veins, and wondered if I could follow out the instructions I had received: for Jack had said, after the decision was made, to go through the Pass, 'Now, Mattie, I don't think for a minute that there are any Injuns in that Pass, and you must not be afraid. We have got to go through it anyway; but' — he hesitated, — 'we may be mistaken; there may be a few of them in there, and they'll have a mighty good chance to get in a shot or two. And now listen: if I'm hit, you'll know what to do. You have your derringer; and when you see that there is no help for it, if they get away with the whole outfit, why there's only one thing to be done. Don't let them get the baby, for they will carry you both off and — well, you know the squaws are much more cruel than the bucks. Don't let them get either of you alive. Now' — to the driver — 'go on.' "

Though the day seemed like a year to Mrs. Summerhayes, the party made it through the pass without incident and prepared to cross the Little Colorado and leave Apache country.

The policy of concentrating Indians at San Carlos was, meanwhile, failing. Clum resigned in 1877, complaining of military intervention and under-financing. "Contractors found it impossible to supply the massive quantities of beef, flour, coffee, and sugar needed to ration the dependent Indians," McGuire said. "To compound the problem of short supplies, the Indian Office insisted on enforcing its regulation that no cattle under the weight specified in the standard contracts could be accepted. Local agents attempted to act on their own to procure the quantities needed with inferior-grade cattle, only to be charged, with some justification, with graft and collusion with the Tucson ring of contractors."

White Mountain Apaches were given temporary passes to go back to their traditional areas to gather food, then allowed to return for good.

Their return brought them into conflict with Mormons who had settled Forestdale, a high meadow just south of the Mogollon Rim. "Oscar Cluff hunted in the valley in 1877, and in the following spring, he chose to move down from his lands around Show low," McGuire wrote. "He and others, intent upon farming the meadow, consulted with the Indian agent at San Carlos. Agent Hart allowed the colony to establish itself, assuring the Saints that Forestdale was not within the reservation boundaries. ...

"A detachment of soldiers was promptly dispatched to remove the Indians from Forestdale. By the end of the summer, a colony of a dozen Mormon families had brought 180 acres under cultivation."

"It was ... a favorite camping area for Petone's band, and Pedro's

Mickey Free, who was taken from his Hispanic mother by Apaches, grew up to be one of their bravest warriors. Later, he became a fearless army scout.

people frequented the place," wrote Col. Wharfield. "Cooley confronted the people about his complaints of competing for his markets. They were gravely concerned by the rough attitude, and conveyed their fears post-haste to the Church headquarters at Salt Lake City. Brigham Young, ever solicitous about the welfare of his colonizers in new regions, wrote Cooley a letter of admonishment. It stated: 'I understand you are an influential man, and our people are colonizing Arizona. If you treat them right you will be blessed, but if you do not you will go down, become a pauper in the land and your family will disown you and you will die a miserable death.' "

Wharfield said Cooley had lived on the frontier too long to be scared. The letter made him angry. "He went down to Camp Apache to talk about the Mormons' encroachment on the reservation with the commanding officer and the civilian Indian agent, Mr. Tiffany," the Cooley biography says. "Thereafter word was sent to the Forestdale settlers to move off the reservation."

The story of life on the Apache Reservation in the late 1870s is told best by Tom Horn. Though he was most famous for being hanged in Wyoming for his zealous attempt to wipe out rustlers, Horn spent most of his adult life as an interpreter and leader of Apache Scouts in or near the White Mountains. [A mock re-trial of Horn in 1993 found him innocent of the shooting that led to his execution.] Horn was born in 1860 near Memphis, Missouri, just a few miles south of the Iowa state line and only 30 miles west of the Mississippi. He was raised in an old-fashioned Campbellite family, but often neglected church, school and Sunday school to hunt. Horn was beaten by his dad so badly that the boy had to stay in bed for a week. Though only 14, Tom sold his gun for $11 and started walking west. At farmhouses along the way, the women were usually happy to give the boy food. He got a job on the railroad and then was hired to drive a team to Santa Fe. His jobs soon took him into Arizona where he learned Spanish working with Mexican-American woodchoppers north of Prescott.

Al Sieber, the chief of Scouts, came to Prescott in the mid-1870s and hired the young man to be a "Mexican interpreter" for $75 a month. They set out for the Apache reservation in eastern Arizona. The "reservation was 60 miles wide and 120 miles long, and Sieber and I, with a few Indian scouts and police, were on the go all the balance of the year around the reservation," Horn wrote in his biography, *Life of Tom Horn, Government Scout and Interpreter.*

"Sieber was keeping an eye on the peace and conduct of the Indians," Horn wrote. "Sieber spoke Apache and Mexican both, and as there were always Indians with us, I began to learn the language very rapidly."

The autobiography, though generally consistent with other historical accounts of the period, reads rather well for a Missouri boy who spent his school days preoccupied with coon hunting and headed west at 14. A school teacher helped him write it while he was waiting to be hanged.

Horn said the first time he ever saw Sieber angry was when they came upon an Indian making tiswin. "The Indian was an old offender, and Sieber began to talk to him in Mexican, which Sieber said the Indian understood perfectly. The Indian, whose name was Chu-Ga-De-Slon-A [which means 'centipede'], spoke to Sieber in Apache, and told him that he was always watching around like an old meddlesome woman. Sieber said: 'Yes, I am always watching such men as you, that make devil's drink.' Chu-Ga-De-Slon-A said: 'I have a notion to kill you, Jon-a-chay,' and that was what made Sieber mad. Jon-a-chay in Apache means 'meddler.'

"Well, the Indian had picked up his gun as he said this, and

Sieber sprang towards him, and I guess must have pulled his knife as he did so, for he caught the Indian by the hair and made one swipe at him with his knife and nearly cut his head off."

Soon Sieber and Horn were at the camp of Pedro, the most important leader of the White Mountain Apaches. "Pedro said he did not want his men either to make or to drink whiskey, and that he would help Sieber at all times," Horn's biography says. "He also told Sieber that all Indians were not bad, but that some of them were as good as any man the Great Spirit put on earth, but that he had six hundred warriors, and some of them were as bad as a bad Apache could be, and that he could not do anything with them. He said that the bad ones never got killed, and they never got good, nor old and disabled, but just remained and were always in any and all trouble that came up.

" 'You see, they are part Devil,' said Pedro, 'or they would get old or get killed some time.'

"Pedro then commenced to talk to me in Apache," Horn said. "I was very much embarrassed at first, for Pedro, the great Chief, Warrior, Friend of the Whites, Counselor and Orator, was to me a great personage; but when once I got to talking Apache to him he made me feel at home. Pedro asked me to stay and visit with him a few days and go hunting with his young men."

Soon, Lieutenant Wheeler arrived at the camp with the 5th Cavalry, responding to reports that Horn and Sieber were being held against their will. Wheeler was led by the famous Mickey Free, another great leader of Apache Scouts.

Free had been born to an unwed Mexican girl in the Sonoran village of Santa Cruz in 1847, according to *Mickey Free, Apache Captive, Interpreter, and Indian Scout* by Allan Radbourne with research by Joyce L. Jauch. His mother gave him the first name Felix and he was given his father's last name of Telles. His mother crossed the line into the U.S. and married John Ward, an Irish immigrant who had established a farm along Sonoita Creek in extreme southern Arizona. In 1861, an Apache raiding party attacked the house while Ward was away. "Nine Apaches rush[ed] the house, intent on capturing the women and children, while another party pursued the livestock on the other side of the creek," the book quotes a witness as saying. "Most likely this later group came upon young Felix, some three hundred yards from the house. Neighbors who heard the story from Felix in his later years related that 'there was a big orchard and while the sheep and goats were grazing on the hillside [he was] … sittin' on top of a peach tree, and they told him to come down and he did.' " Americans arriving at the ranch drove off the Apaches before they killed or captured anyone else, but the Indians escaped with the boy.

If Free had been a little older, he would have been killed, but as a child, he was valuable booty from the raid. He was traded to White Mountain Apaches, while his stepfather and the army attempted to get him back. The biography says his kidnapping was the subject of Lt. Bascom's famous confrontation with Cochise, which ignited war between the Americans and the Apaches.

The boy experienced another raid while he was being raised as an Apache. This time whites killed many Indians. Free, who spied the attackers while fetching water, was criticized for not raising the alarm. Later, when the Apaches went on a raid, Free killed a white woman and her baby. He explained, "They did that to our Apache tribe." Free lived among his adopted tribe in the Canyon Day area until he became an Apache Scout for General Crook in 1872. He once again switched sides, though he was actually going along with the rest of his White Mountain people in opposing the hostiles. The soldiers assigned him the name Mickey Free.

"He now spoke both Mexican and Apache like a professor, and was the wildest dare-devil in the world at this time," Horn related. "He had long, fiery red hair and one blue eye, the other having been hooked out by a wounded deer when he was twelve years old." Whether the deer story was Free's hyperbole or Horn's, the Free biography says he lost the eye to disease as a much younger child. Free "was thoroughly qualified for a typical scout and guide in every sense, except the fact that he never had any regard for his own life," Horn said.

Pedro got his wish. Horn, whom the chief called "Talking Boy" — because of his youth and his ability to speak Apache — stayed with Pedro's band. At first Pedro kept him in his own lodge, but then the chief suggested that one of his sons and Horn get their own place.

"A word of advice, I may add, was the same as a command from Pedro," Horn said. When Horn accompanied his new brother to Fort Apache, they found a widowed half-sister to keep house for them.

"This woman, who was called Sawn, said she would be our housekeeper if we would keep grub in camp. Keeping house in an Indian camp meant to do our washing, cooking, to tan our buckskins, make our moccasins, herd our horses, and, in fact, do everything there was to be done. In those days an Apache buck did nothing but hunt."

About the first of 1879, Major Chaffee was appointed to take over the reservation from civilian control. He called Horn and Pedro down for a talk. Pedro "advised Major Chaffee to take his soldiers and go and kill off all the bad, turbulent Indians, and he offered Major Chaffee 200 good warriors to help him do it."

Chaffee asked Pedro if he should send Horn to live among the Cibecue Apache to help pacify them and convince them to live on government-dispensed rations. "Soldier Captain, you know soldiers," Pedro said. "I am an Indian Chief, as was my father and my father's father, and I have more influence with the Indians than any man on earth, and I know the Apaches as you know your soldiers. But the day you send this boy to the Cibecue country alone, will be the day he dies, for to you, I, Chief Pedro, do say no white man can go among them and return. They will burn him at the stake and send an old Indian woman in and tell you to keep your flour and sugar and send on some more warriors for them to burn."

Horn didn't go.

"There were many different branches of the Apache tribe, named as follows: Tonto Apache, San Carlos Apaches, White Mountain Apaches, Cibecue, Agua Caliente [or warm spring], and last and worst of all, the Chiricahuas," Horn said. "These Indians all spoke the same language, but were divided according to their dispositions. Thus a bad Tonto would leave the Tontos and go to the Cibecue or to the Chiricahuas, and a timid Chiricahua would go to the Tontos, so at the time of which I am writing you could find a good Indian or a bad one by knowing to what tribe he belonged. They all wore their hair different, and to one accustomed to them, they could be told apart as far as you could see them."

At the end of May in 1879, Tom Horn was mustered out because there was no more money to pay him.

The Real Story
Of the Naming of Show Low

Cooley said the central town of the White Mountains was named when his partner, Marion Clark, uttered the words "show low" in a card game in which Cooley won the land. The town celebrates the story with a grouping of life-sized statues of the participants. And though the old scout's colorful account is known throughout Arizona and beyond, it is, in fact, only a tall tale.

Cooley left Fort Apache and settled in the valley where the town is now located after taking on family responsibilities. "During the next summer, 1871, Cooley married one of Pedro's daughters, and bestowed upon her the American name of Molly," Wharfield said in his biography of the scout. "As was a frequent practice among the Apache, a sister joined the household. Some time later he also married her since the custom of more than one wife was acceptable with the natives. ... This wife was given the name of Cora." The family soon moved to Show Low.

A book entitled *The Show Low Arizona Stake: A Compilation of Ward & Community Histories* gives this account of how Cooley and Clark discovered the site. "Coming upon a beautiful little valley covered with flowers and lush grass, with a babbling brook flowing through it, they selected it as a promising place to settle. Log cabins were soon erected in the vicinity of the present town of Show Low."

The Cooley biography says Clark settled in the area first, a little before Cooley did, perhaps in the summer of 1873. "Arrangements were made with Clark for a partnership ranch deal, and to settle his growing family on a good location (present-day Show Low). This area was also one of the favorite seasonal camp spots for Pedro and other White Mountain Apache; so Cooley knew he would have good Indian neighbors. This assured protection to the ranching project undoubtedly had its added attractiveness to Clark, as well as Cooley's connections at the military camp for sale of products.

"It is known that Clark and he raised barley, corn and vegetables on the favorable open places along the creeks," the biography says. "The farm helpers, as needed and available, were a few Mexican wanderers from the Springerville direction and perhaps for short periods some ambitious members of Pedro's band, who chanced to be camped in the vicinity. The farm products were traded to the Apache for labor. Whatever silver was paid for other workers had to come from sales to the army at Camp Apache."

Mrs. Summerhayes, the wife of a young cavalry officer, wrote about staying with the Cooleys: "Towards night we made camp at Cooley's ranch, and slept inside on the floor. ... There seemed to be two Indian girls at his ranch; they were both tidy and good-looking, and they prepared us a most appetizing supper. The ranch had spaces for windows covered with thin unbleached muslin ... glass windows being then too great a luxury in that remote place. There were some partitions inside, but no doors, and of course, no floors except adobe. Several children nearly naked, stood and gazed at us as we prepared for rest."

Jim Bark, a visitor from Phoenix, described a domestic scene involving Molly and Cora. "The army scout was somewhat of a practical joker. It appears that something like putting salt in the sugar jar or lizards down the back of their dresses aroused them to anger. ... They had some quarrel with Cooley, and to escape their vengeance he climbed upon the roof of the building. One of the women threw rocks at him for awhile. Coming down after the storm had ceased, he gave me quite a dissertation upon the advantages and disadvantages of polygamy."

Ironically, it was Chief Joseph's Rebellion on the Canadian border that produced the first historical reference to "Show Low." Nathan Bibo, the New Mexico trader, was visiting Fort Apache in 1873, according to an account published in the *Albuquerque Sunday Herald*. When orders arrived for all troops to head to the nearest railroad for transportation to the conflict, the post commander asked Bibo to take those orders west to Camp Verde and Camp Whipple at present-day Prescott.

"I started with my trustworthy old servant Quate who hailed from San Mateo, New Mexico, on this trip on horseback," Bibo wrote. "There was no wagon road yet.

"I took with me two Apache Indians because the Cibiqui Apaches near whose country we would pass, were not as peaceable as the balance of the White Mountain tribe. After following the road up the White Mountains to nearly the divide, we turned to the trail leading from the summit of the White Mountains west to the source of two rivers, Sholoh and Sho-luh — following the course west through the beautiful pine forest, was known only to the Apache Indians in 1873 and had not been traveled by foreigners (Americanos.) The two Indians serving as guides were [later] the locators of the regularly traveled road between [Fort] Apache and Holbrook. The present road follows the trail that we then followed for the first time. I understand that one of them is now called Silver Creek."

They followed the river to where Holbrook now stands, and stopped there for a few hours to help Mandaloso Calderon build the town's first house.

Bibo told about returning from Prescott in the company of Henry Huning and said, "He and Coriden E. Cooley were the first settlers to take up that fine country called the Sho-Lowh; which I mentioned above."

Bibo's account of the origin of the name Show Low, published in 1922, is of course at variance with the more colorful story that Cooley liked to tell.

Though there is no truth to Cooley's tale, the card game story remains, if not an urban legend, then a forest legend.

Cooley's biographer believed the story. Wharfield wrote, "The crucial day of decision finally arrived, and they decided to terminate the partnership in an amicable manner. It could have been on a stormy miserable day near the end of 1876 that the two were sitting around Cooley's cabin, somewhat disgusted with the hard work on the ranch, disgruntled with each other and 'sick and tired' of the whole deal. Whatever were the immediate reasons, they decided to end the partnership by a Seven-Up card game; winner to get the ranch.

"When the last hand was dealt and the top card turned to determine the trump, the game progressed to the deciding point. Clark is accredited with the statement, 'Show low and take the ranch.' Cooley laid down the low card and won the land."

In spinning this wonderful tale, Cooley was merely practicing the craft that had been refined by the Mountain Men for generations. With no television or movies, storytelling was a preferred entertainment on the frontier, and Cooley was a renowned host. He once told the story of his initial contact with the Apaches, saying he had been tied to a stake and was about to be burned alive when Molly, in Pocahontas fashion, threw her body between the Apaches and Cooley to save his life. Though the story was also nonsense when first told 250 years earlier, Cooley was able to make people believe he had re-enacted the role of Capt. John Smith.

The card game story was a myth, yet it did make the Apache place name for Show Low accessible to the non-Apache speaking world. Cooley's tall tale, perhaps inadvertently, ensured that the central town of the White Mountains would keep a name that would have been recognized by the natives who farmed the creek banks hundreds of years ago.

There is other evidence that the card game story is not true. The game is often said to have occurred in 1876, but an important visitor found that Cooley and Clark were still in partnership in the latter part of that year. Territorial Governor A. P. K. Safford's trip was written up in *The Arizona Citizen* of November 11, 1876. "Messrs. Cooley and Clark have one of the best ranches in Arizona. ... The grazing is superb and extensive and their stock are fat the year through. They raise a large surplus of grain and vegetables which they dispose of at the Post at fair prices. The hearty welcome they give to strangers and travelers makes one feel at home, and the excellent food Mrs. Cooley prepares makes you strong to encounter again a tramp in the wilderness."

Two years later, Cooley and Clark were still working together when they simultaneously filed for water rights for land along the creek. The 1878 filing was recorded in Prescott, then the county seat. A number of things about those legal documents cast the card game legend into further doubt. The filing mentions "Showlow stream." If the name came from the card game, the game would have had to have occurred before the filing on April 23, 1878. But on this date Cooley and Clark were simultaneously filing for water rights — Cooley for one and one-fourth mile above the Cooley Ranch, and Clark for five miles south of it. If their partnership had been already dissolved, why would they have simultaneously filed for water rights?

Also, both of their legal filings mention "Showlow stream" and "Cooley Ranch." If the card game story were true, the ranch would have been named first, and the creek would have derived its name from the ranch at a later date. But it is clear from the legal documents that they both considered the name Showlow

127

more firmly associated with the creek.

Finally, the partners wouldn't have both written Showlow as one word if the name had so recently been derived from the famous sentence, "Show low and take the ranch." A verb and noun would have only become one word after a period of usage, not within 18 months. In fact, it has gone the other way, with Showlow being the older spelling and Show Low only becoming universally accepted many years after the myth was made.

Cooley would no doubt be delighted with the popularity of his tale. While movie actors only get a small statue of "Oscar" for an exceptional performance, Cooley has a life-sized bronze statue of himself in Show Low to honor his mastery of storytelling. People who believe the card game story are generally not aware that Cooley was such a powerful yarn spinner. In a single 1899 *Holbrook Argus* article, Cooley convinced a reporter that he was putting a "hydraulic ram" in a spring near his house to provide the residence with 4,000 gallons of water per minute, that he was sick and hoarse for several days because of an attempt to outtalk a sergeant visiting from Fort Apache and that he had recently received a cane carved by Geronimo.

Cooley's wife Molly gave birth to a daughter in 1875. The baby was named Cora for her aunt, who passed away the following year after giving birth to Cooley's second daughter, Lillie.

Mormons Alfred Cluff and David Adams first worked for Cooley and then in 1877 made an arrangement to rent part of the Show Low ranch on the upper creeks. Herbert Dalton, who settled above Cooley's land claims, rented some cows, according to Wharfield. Adams soon brought his wife to the area. She gave birth to a son, Lind, on Feb. 3, 1877. He was the first child born to a white woman at Show Low. Wharfield quotes Adams as saying, "Our midwife was an Apache squaw, Mrs. Cooley; and as it was a critical case — my wife, Caroline, must have died without her aid."

"A forage station was established at the ranch," Wharfield writes. "Due to the increased army traffic through the region this stop developed a need for accommodations of the officers and soldiers, and stables and feed for the animals. Cooley soon took advantage of the business opportunities and provided good facilities for service to the military and other travelers. With this place available, the military road along Crook's Trail took a bend down to the ranch. Also the road from the post to Camp Supply [a tent city set up near the present site of Holbrook by Kit Carson in 1863 for his campaign against the Navajos] was routed that way. This fork in the roads became a popular stopping place for all journeying through the lonely wilderness country. Here it was that the congenial host and the bountiful table provided by Molly became known throughout the army and to other wayfarers."

In April 1878, Cooley visited Fort Whipple in Prescott and obtained a contract to grow barley and deliver it to Fort Apache. Wharfield said Cooley was to be paid four and a half cents a pound for all the barley he could produce. "Also on this trip, Sheriff Ed F. Bowers appointed him deputy assessor and collector of taxes for the Little Colorado section of Yavapai County. … This area took in the settlements, ranches, and cattle in the St. Johns and Springerville regions. There is no record as to Cooley's efficiency in this county position; but it can be surmised that he accepted the lists as rendered by the property owners. An official did not want trouble with his acquaintances over taxes. In those times you never asked a person how many cattle he was running; not unless you were a county assessor."

In 1879, Cooley was chosen as one of three supervisors for newly created Apache County, giving him responsibilities over a vast stretch of northeast Arizona.

"Some time about 1880 or perhaps 1881 Henry Huning of Los Lunas, New Mexico and Cooley entered into a partnership deal on the Show Low ranch," the biography says. "Huning had made money on various projects and as a supplier to government posts around the Albuquerque country. The deal included most of the land claimed by Cooley, excepting the Show Low place, and involved the cattle and the brand C C, devised from his initials."

"They dug ditches, irrigated and farmed most of the valley," the Show Low Stake history says. "They installed a sawmill near the creek." The Cooley biography notes that the sawmill was horse-powered.

"Henry Mitchell operated it for them," the stake history says. "They launched quite an extensive building program. Several large barns, a black smith shop, a bridge across the creek, and other small buildings were erected.

"They constructed what would be called in that day, palatial homes. Cooley's home, located on the hill where the [Mormon] church building stands, was a two-story frame building. It came to be known as the White House" [because it was large like the president's mansion, not because it was painted white.]

"The place had a big main part with a wing for a kitchen and sleeping rooms upstairs," Cooley's biography says. "There were four chimneys for the fireplaces, a long covered porch across one side, and glass windows."

Huning built a house on the east side of the creek and married a woman who had operated a restaurant in Holbrook. There was some friction because she was already married to Holbrook founder Berardo Freyes. The Cooley biography says the outraged Freyes headed for Show Low, but was turned back by Cooley ranch hands. Cooley most likely embellished this story a bit. Anyway, Huning raised the Freyes children as his own and sent one of the sons to medical school.

Huning "operated the Post Office and store," the Show Low Stake history says. "A long lumber building for the employees, called the men's quarters, was constructed on a prominent hill south of and between the two partners' homes. Their business increased to such proportions that they advertised in an eastern newspaper for a foreman. A Mr. Solette came to take the job. Then Cooley moved his family to Silver Creek and his house was turned into a hotel for the public, and a boarding house for the employees. Mrs. Solette was given the management of this enterprise. The Solettes stayed on the ranch about three years, then returned to the East."

Molly gave birth to two sons before her husband moved the family to Fort Apache, where Cooley again worked for General Crook during an Indian uprising.

"The Cooley family came back to their home," the biography continues. "On July 20, 1888, the United States government issued a deed to C. E. Cooley for the land on which his home stood. This homestead included the present townsite of Show Low."

The *Apache Review* wrote on Aug. 22, 1888, "Henry Huning awarded Show Low Ranch in arbitration in Albuquerque." On

October 3, the paper further reported, "C. E. Cooley in court in St. Johns on dissolving Huning & Cooley. Rumor said he didn't get a tenth."

Then Cooley moved south, building a magnificent house just below the Reservation boundary — near present-day Hon-Dah.

"The location was close to the forks of the east route to Springerville and the north road for Holbrook," the biography says. "Crook's Trail from Camp Verde was changed to come in there and by-pass Show Low. These road junctions afforded him the trade of wayfarers through the country, and also the place was good ranch land. The main house plan was for a large two-storied place with a huge living room and adjoining rooms, and upstairs were bedrooms to accommodate guests. The big fire-place for the living room was an afterthought, and constructed some years later."

Cooley raised his large family, entertained travelers and ranched. He declined a suggestion in the 1880s that he serve again as a county supervisor. The *Apache Critic* quoted him as saying: "That the pay is too little, and the notoriety too great ... that the income of Queen Victoria together with the salary of Grover Cleveland would never compensate a man for the cussin' he gets from the people in general while serving as a member of the honorable board."

Cooley's old house on the hill in Show Low became a fort and a church before burning down. The brave old soldier, pros-pector, Indian scout and master storyteller lived into his 80s and passed away in 1917.

Joseph Holister, an early day school teacher who homesteaded the land in the lower part of Show Low valley, sold out to Huning, who continued to extend his holdings. Huning "fenced a pasture ten miles square adjoining his home, east of the ranch," the bi-ography says. "He raised blooded horses, and his cattle and sheep roamed the range in every direction."

"In due time the government requested [Huning] to aban-don the pasture and move the fence which enclosed both gov-ernment and railroad land," the Show Low Stake history says.

Local newspaper accounts indicate the decision to give up the fence came in the mid-1880s, while Huning and Cooley were still partners. An ad in the *St. Johns Herald* says: "Have for sale at their ranches at or near Show Low, barbed and plain Fence Wire, at the low price of five cents per pound. ... Purchasers will be required to remove the wire from the fence posts at their own expense. This is a rare opportunity to obtain wire fencing at half its value. — Huning's & Cooley, Show Low, Ariz."

Geronimo Becomes Leader

The Chiricahua and Mimbrenos from southern Arizona and New Mexico were the Apaches most dissatisfied with the reservation at San Carlos, possibly because they were the farthest from home. Their anger created the climate for Geronimo to come to the fore and become the most famous Apache of all time. He was born just southeast of the White Mountains in what was then Mexico. The Arizona-New Mexico line now runs through the area where his band lived. Though history has linked him to the Chiricahuas because he was the leader of their warriors, he was born a Bedonkohe, a sub-tribe closely associated with the Chiricahuas. Geronimo said he was living south of the present U.S. border when an attack by Mexican solders killed his wife, mother and children.

"Late one afternoon when returning from town we were met by a few women and children who told us that Mexican troops from some other town had attacked our camp, killed all the warriors of the guard, captured all our ponies, secured our arms, destroyed our supplies and killed many of our women and children," Geronimo said in dictating an account of his life to S. M. Barrett in 1906. "Quickly we separated, concealing ourselves as best we could until nightfall, when we assembled to our appointed place of rendezvous — a thicket by the river. Silently we stole in one by one, sentinels were placed, and when all were counted, I found that my aged mother, my young wife, and my three small children were among the slain." The book *Geronimo: His Own Story* continues, "I had no weapon, nor did I hardly wish to fight, neither did I contemplate recovering the bodies of my loved ones, for that was forbidden."

Discussing Geronimo's statement in a book called *Women of*

Carol Sletten
© 2010

Lozen, the sister of Victorio, was a legendary Apache warrior and healer. She often served as the rear guard as Geronimo's band escaped the cavalry. She died in a prisoner of war camp in Alabama.

the Apache Nation, H. Henrietta Stockel says: "A contemporary author, Edwin R. Sweeney, believes that the older Geronimo's recollections can be trusted 'only in part ... He lost his family but not, it would seem, at the time and place, or under the circumstances he described when he dictated his autobiography ... and in his desire to present himself as an innocent victim, he ignored the long series of raids and reprisals which preceded (the) attack. It is hard to believe that he was not involved in them.' "

Whatever the source of his hatred for Mexicans, it was intense and stayed with him throughout life.

Though Geronimo was not primarily a chief, he was considered to be a powerful medicine man and became an important war leader under Cochise's son Naiche, who followed his father as chief.

Another famous Chiricahua was Lozen, "the Woman Warrior." She was the sister of the legendary Chief Victorio. As a young woman, she was beautiful and able to outrun the men. As a warrior, she was skilled and fearless, often taking upon herself the role of covering the rear guard as it fled. Lozen was a good shot and an expert at stealing horses. She was esteemed for her Power to dress and heal wounds. In *Once They Moved Like the Wind,* David Roberts said Lozen could determine if the enemy was near by praying to Ussen with her arms outstretched. "When her hands began to tingle and her palms changed color, she knew."

Hemmed in on the Apache Reservation at San Carlos, Geronimo started to plan a new campaign to recover lost Apache territory and freedom. He planned well. Some Apaches say he spent up to two years hiding food and supplies in caches to use later when he was on the run. In 1876, Geronimo made his break. From that time on, he was frequently called the war chief of the Chiricahua.

Mickey Free went to Tombstone to round up Tom Horn and Al Sieber to take them back into government service in October 1877.

"Some of the Indians were making whiskey; all of them were drinking it, and they were robbing and raiding and killing, and the soldiers could never come up with them," Horn said.

"I was sent to old Pedro's camp to get some Indians Sieber wanted as scouts and police, and as it took a week to get the ones I was sent after, I had a good visit with my old friends," Horn said. "Many of the young bucks of about 20 years of age wanted to go and fight their own people, but Sieber and Pedro were of one mind about them, for it was the work of able and experienced warriors to get the Indians back where they were eight months before. The tamest and best of the Indians needed a strong hand to control them, like Pedro, for instance, and the wild and bad ones were as Pedro had previously said to Major Chaffee — uncontrollable."

"You will have years of hard work, and many, many of them will have to be killed," Horn quoted Pedro as saying.

One day an old woman arrived with word that Nana and Geronimo, who were living in Mexico, wanted to come back to the Reservation. They wanted to talk to Sieber about it. Horn, Sieber and a Mexican scout set off to meet the Indians at an appointed time and place in Mexico.

The three scouts went to the meeting place "at the full of the May moon" and met an Indian who told them how to find Nana and Geronimo. Apache women made the visitors comfortable until the talk started at dawn the next day. Horn saw Geronimo for the first time.

"Certainly a grand looking war chief he was that morning as he stood there talking to Sieber; six feet high and magnificently proportioned, and his motions as easy and graceful as a panther's,"

134

Horn said. "He had an intelligent looking face, but when he turned and looked at a person, his eyes were so sharp and piercing that they seemed fairly to stick into him. Anyhow, that was how they looked to me; but I was a little shaky, anyhow."

Since Sieber could not speak Apache well enough to conduct a formal conference with Geronimo, he decided to have Horn interpret.

"I speak very fast, sometimes," Geronimo said. "Can you undertake to interpret as fast as I talk?"

"I told him he had but one mouth and tongue, that I could see, and for him to let loose."

"Well spoken," said Geronimo.

"Well, the big talk was on; and how that old renegade did talk," Horn said. "Of the wrongs done him by the agent, and by the soldiers, and by the White Mountain Apaches, and by the Mexicans and settlers, and he had more grievances than a railroad switchman, and he wanted to go back to live on the Reservation. He wanted to be allowed to have a couple of Mexicans to make muscal for him, and he wanted the Government to give him new guns and all the ammunition he could use. He wanted calico for the women, and shoes for the children when there was snow on the ground, and any and everything he ever saw or heard of he wanted. Geronimo was the biggest chief, the best talker and the biggest liar in the world, I guess, and no one knew this better than Sieber.

"Geronimo must have talked an hour or two, and Sieber never said a word in reply. At last Geronimo stopped talking, for he had asked for everything he could think of, and he was a natural born genius at thinking of things."

Sieber looked around at the mountains and then said, "You have asked for everything that I know anything about, except to have these mountains moved up into the American country for you to live in, and I will give you till sundown to talk to your people and see if you don't want these mountains moved up there to live in. If you are entitled, by your former conduct, to what you have asked for, then you should have these mountains too."

Sieber walked out of the council and Geronimo said they would meet again at sundown.

Geronimo, the most famous Indian of all time, lived in the White Mountains, frequently leading his followers on outbreaks and raids into Mexico.

Carol Sletten
© 2010

When the talk resumed, Sieber said: "This morning you asked for many things, and you knew I could not give you many of the things you asked for, and I do think that you asked for the most of them because you love to talk, and not because I could or would do as you asked me. Anything I do promise, you know full well you will get; for you have ever found me as I said I would be. ... Go to the Reservation, and do as you will be advised to do by the Government, and you will get all that the Government can give you. You know what the Government can give you, for you have lived there and drawn your rations, as many Indians are doing now. ...

"Geronimo, I have no idea you will do as I say, for you do not love peace. You are a man of war and battle, else you would not be war chief of the Chiricahua tribe. You could go to the Reservation and stay maybe one season, and maybe only one moon. But within this camp may be some who do really want to come up and settle down to a peaceful life. Any and all such I will take back safely, and most of your people know what you will get. Twice already have I taken you there, and twice have you become uneasy and left."

Sieber continued, "There are hundreds and hundreds of white men to every Apache. It is true many and many of the white men cannot protect themselves from such warriors as there are here, for it is my opinion in the world there are none better. Still, all the Chiricahua and Agua Caliente in existence, or nearly all, are within hearing of the words I am saying now, and they cannot stay on the

136

war path and not be exterminated."

He told Geronimo that he knew the Chiricahua felt safe in Mexico because they did not fear the Mexican troops. But Sieber said that soon Americans would be allowed to pursue the Apache into Mexico.

"When we were ready to start to San Carlos, at the time set by Sieber," Horn said, "62 Indians were ready to go with us, among them being the chiefs Nana and old Loco, a once famous chief, but at this time he must have been eighty years old, or maybe more."

"Geronimo told me to come to his camp at any time that I had any word to bring him from the government officials, and not to be afraid, as I would always be well treated and perfectly safe," Horn said.

"You are a young man," Geronimo said, "and will always be at war with me and mine; but war is one thing, and talking business is another; and I will be just as pleased to meet you in battle as in council."

They brought their Indians back to the reservation and soon received word from another woman walking up from Mexico that there were more who wanted to surrender.

Horn went down to Mexico to pick up the band of 49 renegades. "I then saw what their game was — that is, to raid and kill in Mexico and bring the stock to San Carlos," Horn said.

He brought the Indians and stock back to San Carlos despite threatened trouble with Mexican troops and the U.S. Customs officers who wanted to collect duty on the stolen livestock.

"All that year I was going back and forth between the Mexican line and San Carlos bringing in bunches of Indians and big bunches of stock," Horn said. "The Mexican Government was just raising Cain because we were doing as we did. There was no mistake but that it was wrong, and very wrong; but we were powerless, and it did look to the Mexicans as though our troops were upholding the Apaches and protecting them in their raiding."

Not all of the raiding was one way. Horn relates a later incident when the White Mountain Apaches were soon complaining about Mexicans stealing their horses. Mexicans had made two successful raids and Horn prepared for the third. Apache women camped in the hills gathering muscal alerted Horn to the dawn raid and he was on the trail in 10 minutes. The raiders were headed toward the Hispanic settlements on the Little Colorado east of the reservation on their route back to Mexico. Horn and the Indians caught them near Turkey Springs and shot them dead. The Indians wanted to leave the bodies by the road as a warning to others, and Horn complied, which caused some trouble when a general happened upon the scene.

But it was bringing all the stolen stock back from Mexico that bothered Horn. After a number of trips back and forth to the border he left government employment to herd for a beef contractor.

"It did not take a very wise man to see that the Indians were running the mill to suit themselves," Horn said. "Major Chaffee had been relieved and sent to Fort McDowell and a man named Tiffany, a civilian, was agent. There were no troops at the Agency and things looked a good deal more like a hostile Indian camp than did the camp of Geronimo when we had gone to have the talk with him the year before in Mexico."

Tiffany was charged with stealing $54,000 worth of Indian rations in only six or eight months on the job. But Horn said he did not believe he was ever punished.

A man named Stirling was chief of police and had only 11 men to keep the peace among 5,000 or 6,000 Indians.

In the spring of 1880, Ju came up from Mexico with 100 renegades to take Loco and his band back to Mexico. Horn was living five miles above the agency, a few miles from the Chiricahua camp.

"At daylight, or a very little after, I heard a lot of firing at the Chiricahua camp," Horn said. The former scout and his friendly Indians withdrew to a steep mountain to protect themselves from the Bronks, as they called the Chiricahua. At daylight they started passing Horn's position, strung out for about a mile and a half with 5,000 head of horses and mules.

The police chief, Stirling, also heard the outbreak. "He jumped on his horse, and with one Indian policeman, a captive called Navajo Bill, he rode right into the Chiricahua camp," Horn said. "He never smiled again, as he was killed just as he came up the bank of the San Carlos River. A squaw cut his head off. He was shot about 75 or 100 times. Navajo Bill escaped, but how, one can scarcely tell, for he was right with Stirling.

"Navajo Bill swung back toward the Agency and the rest of the police came to him, and again they rode at the Chiricahuas, and one more policeman was killed. There were at least two hundred Chiricahua warriors, and these police, (there were only seven of them when they came up to where I was) kept right up with the Broncos, and killed one of them just below and in plain sight of myself and the party with me."

The Chiricahua started to fan out and the police broke off the engagement. The renegades eyed Horn's group from about 300 yards and then moved on.

The agency was in confusion and the telegraph line had been cut. Horn rode to Camp Thomas, the next fort, 32 miles away on the Gila River.

"Sieber was there talking to some Indians, and all those Indians knew was that the Indians down the river had signaled that there was trouble from the Chiricahuas," Horn said. "Apaches can signal for a long ways when there is trouble, but they cannot give details by their signals."

Horn and Sieber set off ahead of the cavalry. The soldiers followed under Lieutenant Gatewood, who would gain fame in the final surrender of Geronimo.

"We may not be able to lick them, but we will try if we can find them," Gatewood said.

"So we did," recalled Horn. "We struck them and got six men killed in a minute. Sieber told Gatewood that the warriors we were trying to whip were better men than his soldiers in any place that we could strike them." In addition to the soldiers killed, 11 more were wounded.

Gatewood, who was shot in the shoulder, initially refused to go back to the fort. But later, when the renegades had abandoned more than 1200 head of stock, he and the soldiers took the animals back to the fort.

The Indians had split up into small bands and were heading for Mexico.

Horn and the soldiers found one group, but did not have enough men to force them into battle. After trailing the Indians for miles, Horn heard shots. The renegades, soldiers and scouts headed for the sound of the guns. Sieber, Free and some other soldiers had engaged another band. There were two dead soldiers and five wounded ones. Horn did not list the Chiricahua casualties.

Horn and Free soon fell into an exhausted sleep.

"About 11 or 12 o'clock Sieber came and woke us up, and

told us to get our horses and be ready to go with him after the Indians," Horn recalled. "I asked Sieber what was the use to go monkeying along after those Indians by ourselves when all the soldiers could not handle them. Sieber spoke to me in a language that was more liable to be called forcible than elegant, and told me that the action or scarcity of soldiers was no concern of mine."

The three scouts were soon on high ground, watching the Indians cross into Mexico.

A Major Tupper came up with 40 soldiers and a well-supplied pack train. Tupper said he wanted to follow the Indians into Mexico. Sieber at first thought he was bluffing, but about three o'clock in the morning they pulled out toward the south.

Horn thought the 40 soldiers and 25 scouts were no match for 300 Chiricahua braves.

"We must be very careful and not let him get too many of his men killed," said Sieber.

The scouts were charged with keeping the soldiers out of sight as they moved toward the unsuspecting Chiricahuas.

They found the hostiles camped around a spring, dancing for a wedding celebration. At dawn the soldiers and scouts struck, killing five hostiles. One soldier was killed and another wounded.

As they headed back to the line, they met a larger group of soldiers under a Colonel Forsythe and decided to join forces to attack the Indians again. While the combined force was trailing the renegades, the hostiles were attacked by the Fifth Regiment of Chihuahua Cavalry. The Mexican soldiers under Justo Garcia struck the rear of the Indian group and killed 167 women and children, and captured 52 more.

The Americans went up to the battlefield where the Mexicans were piling up the dead Indians.

"Colonel Garcia immediately told Colonel Forsythe that we were an armed force of Americans on Mexican territory and that we must consider ourselves under arrest," Horn reports.

Garcia invited the Americans to breakfast, but since the Mexicans had no food, the Americans fed them. After breakfast, Forsythe said, "I am going to mount my command and go back. ... I will not submit to go anywhere with you and your command. I will now bid you good day."

The soldiers and scouts went back to their posts.

———————————

Mormons Arrive in Arizona

The first Mormons to arrive in the White Mountains were communists — not in the despised sense of the subversives of the early 1900s, or the hated adversaries of the Cold War — but in the hopeful sense of many failed American experimental communes of the 1800s.

It's hard to know exactly why the Church of Jesus Christ of Latter-day Saints chose this form of economic organization for its early Arizona colonists. Certainly they found justification in the organization of the primitive Christian Church described in the Bible. The Mormons had been driven 2,000 miles across the continent, repeatedly establishing communities, only to be driven out when settlers with more traditional religions became aggressively intolerant of the Mormon faith. Now established in Utah, the Mormons knew they could not pull up stakes and move farther west if they lost their land this time, as California already had a substantial non-Mormon population.

The Mormons wanted to expand their settlements from Utah north to Canada and south to Mexico, not only to spread their faith, but also to control so much territory that they could not be pushed out again. Since most of the irrigable farmland in Utah had already been put under the plow, the Mormons looked south to Arizona.

They had plenty of converts, from the East Coast and even from Europe, to populate new settlements. But not all of the religious novices had the pioneering skills of Daniel Boone, so some were put under the communal "United Order" to give them the confidence to go out into the wilderness.

"A branch of the United Order called the Gospel Plan was completely communal in structure," the *Historical Atlas of Arizona* says. "All property was held in common; the members of the settlement ate at a common table and dressed from the same bolt of cloth. The work of all was directed to the common good, and all activities were begun and ended by bugle calls."

As in every other experiment, human nature defeated communism. People are willing to work to help others to an extent, but real prosperity requires that individuals who work the hardest get greater rewards. In a paper published by Arizona State University, Kent Lightfoot argues that the leadership structure helped doom

141

the United Order. Each community reported directly to Salt Lake City, which, because of the distance, was slow to respond. Later Mormon settlements farther south had the advantage of a regional "stake" structure — something like a Catholic diocese — that directed inter-community cooperation, particularly on irrigation projects.

The Mormon advance into Arizona had been preceded by an ill-fated expedition in 1858, which sought to confirm the existence of the Hopi tribe and perhaps convert the Navajos. Brigham Young was interested in a tale that a lost nobleman, Prince Madoc of Wales, had taught civilization and some Welsh words to the Hopi. The adventurers included Jacob Hamblin, Andrew S. Gibbons, Ira Hatch, Frederick Hamblin, William Hamblin and Ammon Tenney — all with family names that resonate throughout the White Mountains today. The men made it back to Utah – without Indian converts — by living on horsemeat, according to the account in the St. Johns Stake history. For this excursion and many others he made into unsettled areas of Arizona, Jacob Hamblin was named Apostle to the Indians by Brigham Young. He is buried in Alpine.

The Colorado River, running through a deep canyon, was a 300-mile barrier to Brigham Young's plans to settle Arizona. So the Mormons were interested in an ancient trail called the Ute Ford where the Paria River joins the Colorado, according to *Arizona's Honeymoon Trail,* edited by Norma Baldwin Ricketts. Spanish Friars had visited the site nearly 100 years earlier and successfully crossed. But Mormons needed to get wagons across the river. Hamblin, led to the crossing by a Ute guide, realized a wagon road could be constructed by making switchbacks down the slopes on the north side. Then after crossing the river on a ferryboat, the wagons would be able to wind up the treacherous slope on the south side. John D. Lee, who had a ranch in the canyon, was selected by the church to operate the ferryboat.

Lee is a character of tremendous historical interest in his own right. He was a local leader in Mormon Utah, and had played a significant role in what came to be known as the Mountain Meadows Massacre. As the United States and the Mormons engaged in saber rattling in the 1850s, a rich wagon train from Arkansas was plundered in southern Utah. Historians say the Mormons disarmed the settlers under promise of safe conduct through Indian territory, then slaughtered all the adults. The small children — the only survivors — were at first taken by the Mormons, then taken away from them and returned to their relatives. Lee, a leader of the attack, claimed to be acting on orders from Brigham Young. But after the Civil War, and as the victims' relatives continued to agitate for justice, LDS church leaders, now reconciled with the United States, pointed to Lee as the guilty party. He was executed, the only one punished for the massacre. The Mormon Church bought the ferry from Lee's widow Emma for 100 head of cattle, but she only was able to collect 14 head, according to *Emma Lee* by Juanita Brooks. She married a man named French and brought her children to Snowflake and later to Winslow. Emma's children were shunned even though she served her new community as a healer. A teenage daughter, unable to face the ostracism, poisoned herself. Despite the stigma that followed the family, Emma earned the respect of the townspeople and was known as "Doc French." There are many descendants of Lee and his 19 wives in the White Mountains.

The establishment of Lee's Ferry was key to opening up the Little Colorado valley for Mormon settlement. The church hauled in supplies to build the ferry. "The boat, which measured eighty-one and one half feet, fore and aft with a twenty-six foot beam, was a sturdy craft designed to haul one wagon and several head of stock at a time," the St. Johns Stake history says. Building the wagon roads into and out of the canyon was difficult, especially on the south side where the winding road was called Lee's Backbone. Mormons met with little success when they again tried to convert the Hopi. The settlers headed farther south to the Little Colorado.

"In 1876 Brigham Young sent 200 Mormon families into northern Arizona to establish four colonies on the Little Colorado River," Leora Peterson Schuck wrote in *A Tribute to Lakeside Pioneers*. Only one of these settlements, Joseph City, survived.

Brigham Young assigned a quota to each Utah bishop, who in turn selected the families who were ordered to join the expedition.

"The first company ... arrived [on the Little Colorado] in March of the centennial year of America," Schuck wrote. "March is the worst of all the months and one wonders why they didn't just keep going. They coped daily with winds, sometimes being enveloped in clouds of sand, other times in driving blizzards."

The St. Johns Stake history tells the story of the four companies that came in to settle the area. "It was decided that the William C. Allen group would settle at a place 20 miles upstream from Sunset Crossing [which was near present-day Winslow]. To honor their leader they named the place Allen, which was later changed to Joseph City. The George Lake company settled across the river from Allen and about two miles downstream. They elected to call their settlement Obed. Lot Smith took his people back downstream to a point near where the city of Winslow now stands. Because of its nearness to the crossing of the same name they called the place Sunset. The Jesse O. Ballenger company settled across the river and downstream about four miles from Sunset. They first named it Ballenger, but later changed it to Brigham City to honor President Young. There was no time to lose. The first order of business was to clear the land of brush and build dams to divert water from the river. During that first summer many of the settlers returned to Utah. Some brought back their families, but all too many chose to abandon the mission and stay in Utah. That first year the crops were not enough to sustain them until another harvest, so other trips had to be made for seed grain and food supplies."

Army officer John Bourke described these Mormon communities, which he visited in 1881. " 'Sunset' consists of a long building, one story high, built around a hollow square, to which there are two entrances, — open spaces in the line of palisade buildings, — each wide enough for the passage of farm vehicles," he wrote in *Snake-Dance of the Moquis*. "It is constructed of upright cottonwood trunks, chinked with mud, and covered with an inclined roof of pine planking. The square is fifty yards on a side, and amply commodious for all the present needs of the community. All windows and doors face upon this square, a feature in the construction induced by fear of roving bands of hostile Apaches or Navajos.

"In this one building over two hundred men, women and children reside, although at that time numbers were absent for various reasons," he continued. "Families were separated by partition walls, but messing was communal, all the inhabitants eating together in the large dining-hall in the centre of the square."

He went on to praise the produce raised by the Mormons, especially the melons. But he said the wells along the Little Colorado were salty. He noted that the children were dressed in identical church-issued clothing.

"The fort at Ballenger was 200 feet square with rocky walls seven feet high," according to *History of Holbrook and the Little Colorado Country* by Harold C. Wayte Jr. "Thirty six houses were built inside the structure, each one fifteen by thirteen feet. ... The main industry at Ballenger was the farming of 274 acres of land, more than half of it planted in wheat. The settlement of Obed built a strong fort 12 rods [200 feet] square. The walls in certain places were 10 feet high. The fort also contained bastions and portholes for defense."

"For many years the valiant group struggled to harness the Little Colorado for irrigation," Mrs. Schuck wrote. "It was a river of extremes; either too much water or not enough. ... They built and lost dam after dam."

Additional settlements were added along the river, including Taylor near Joseph City. The abandoned town is often called Old Taylor to distinguish it from the existing town south of Snowflake, which is sometimes called New Taylor.

"Dam washouts were a common event along the Little Colorado River," wrote Lightfoot. "For example: five dams were lost in five months at Old Taylor in 1878...; eight dams were destroyed at Joseph City between 1878 and 1894...; two dams washed out at Sunset between 1878 and 1882...; two dams were swept away at Brigham City between 1876 and 1878 ... and eight dams were lost at Woodruff between 1878 and 1886. ... One example indicates that 800 man-days of work were necessary to reconstruct the Joseph City dam in 1878. Unfortunately, this dam was swept away during a flood a few months after it was completed." Often, there was not enough labor available to repair the dam in time to save the summer's crop.

The communities along the Little Colorado River (with alternate names in parenthesis) from north to south were: Brigham City (Ballenger's Camp), Sunset (near Winslow), Obed, [Old] Taylor, Joseph City (Allen's Camp & St. Joseph), Holbrook

(Horsehead Crossing), Woodruff (Tenney's Crossing), Hunt, St. Johns (El Vadito & San Juan), Nero (Richey), Springerville (Omer), Eagar (Amity), Nutrioso and Alpine (Bush Valley and Frisco). Along Silver Creek were Snowflake, [New] Taylor and Shumway, with Show Low and Lakeside (Woodland) along Show Low Creek. To the west were Heber, Wilford, Overgaard (Oklahoma Flats), Aripine (Joppa), Pinedale (Snowflake Camp, Mortenson, Percheron), Linden (Juniper), Ellsworth (Chaffs) and Forestdale. The Mormon settlement in the Concho area was called Erastus.

Most of the Mormon settlements to the north along the Little Colorado failed. "Brigham City and Sunset were abandoned because of poor soil and uncertain irrigation," says the *Historical Atlas of Arizona*.

"The first to arrive stopped at Sunset Crossing, near what is now Joseph City," says Jennings in *Arizona Was the West*. "Of the five or six settlements first established, Joseph City is the only one surviving today."

Beyond the early Little Colorado settlements, the Mormons bought the area where Woodruff now stands from a non-Mormon, Luther Martin. When Ammon Tenney brought several families into the area, it was called Tenney's Camp for about a year before taking the name of the Mormon president, Wilford Woodruff. "The settlers ate in a common dining room, typical of the United Order to which Woodruff belonged for a short time," according Wayte's Holbrook history.

Mormons Move Farther South

In 1877, the Mormon settlement "of Round Valley began with the first wagon train of determined and courageous Mormon families," according to a 1965 article in *Arizona Highways*. "A. V. Greer and Harris Phelps brought their wagons, cattle, household goods and families from Texas.

"Americus Vespucious Greer (who survived a twin brother, Christopher Columbus) was known as Uncle 'H' after serving as captain of Company H during the Civil War," according to *On the Road to Nowhere*. "Also renowned as a Texas Ranger, A. V.

Greer was remembered as a picturesque figure, with white hair standing up on his head, a great white beard, and deep-set eyes."

A. V. Greer's brother Thomas Lacy Greer later started a cattle operation at Hunt, north of Concho.

The first pioneers from Utah arrived in Round Valley in 1878. They were led by Jacob Hamblin, who had been one of the first Mormon explorers in Arizona.

"When they arrived, the settlers would often live in their wagon boxes until forts (usually a self-contained clustering of cabins around a community building of some sort) were built and they could move in," *On the Road to Nowhere* says. "Sometimes the wagon boxes were taken off the running gears, set on rocks or logs; while the gears were used for hauling logs from the nearby forest to put up the typical one or two room log cabin that was home. It would usually have a hardened dirt floor and door and window openings covered with the wagon cover."

The Mormons built dams and dug ditches to support their farms, gardens and orchards. Becker Lake, which was constructed by damming the Little Colorado in 1880, is said to be the oldest man-made lake in Arizona. "The first Mormons in Round Valley settled east of present Springerville along Nutrioso Creek," *Road to Nowhere* says. "As their need for more land increased, they scraped irrigation ditches 'up on the bench,' and moved their settlements to the southwest, in the upper end of the valley."

The Mormons organized their first ward in Round Valley on September 26, 1880, and called it Omer. Soon, it was divided with Omer in the lower part of the valley near present-day Springerville and the Amity ward in the southern and higher part of the valley near present-day Eagar. In 1883, there were 155 people in Omer and 119 in Amity, according to the St. Johns Stake history. In 1886, the two wards were combined to form the Union Ward.

The St. Johns Stake history says a post office was established in Springerville on October 29, 1880, with Albert Franklin Banta as the first postmaster.

"Most of the early locations (of the Mormons) along the Little Colorado were based on squatters' rights, since prior to 1879 none of the land had been surveyed or officially opened to homesteading," says *On the Road to Nowhere*. "Various means were devised to show one's claims, especially for sites seasonally occupied. Being present was the most persuasive means of 'ownership,' but other methods were controlling the water, building cabins, and sheep troughs; laying out logs in a square to show intent of building; planting peach or plum pits on the perimeter of the land (As they first blossomed, they became a sign of occupancy.); or piling rocks along the corners. For a stockman, 'the unwritten law of the range was he who first watered his stock at a stream, spring or water hole had the prior and exclusive right to use thereafter, together with such adjoining range lands as he could use.' "

"The White Mountain land was soon opened to homesteading privileges which essentially meant a single citizen could take up to 160 acres outside government land, or up to 80 acres within limits of a railroad grant or government area," the book continues. "After continuous residence and cultivation for five years, and upon payment of a small fee, [the homesteader would] gain absolute title." Another law allowed individuals to claim land if they planted trees on a quarter of an 80- or 40-acre parcel.

William J. Flake had been taken by his converted Southern, slave-owning parents to Nauvoo, Illinois, as a child of seven, only days before the Prophet Joseph Smith was lynched. They soon fled across Iowa in the dead of winter. "William, with three other small boys ... walked through the snow and drove the loose stock, mostly milk cows" according to his biography, *William J. Flake, Pioneer — Colonizer*, by Osmer D. Flake. They wintered over in Council Bluffs, Iowa, then Flake's father served as a captain of 100 wagons on a train that followed after Brigham Young to Utah. The family was sent to California, but called back to Utah when trouble with the United States began to build. After building up a successful farm of his own in Utah, William Flake was told by Brigham Young to sell everything and head to Arizona. "Leave nothing to come back to," the Prophet said. "On November 19, 1877, he started for Arizona with six wagons, pulled by nine yoke of oxen and seven span of horses," the biography says. "There were also two hundred head of cattle and forty loose horses." After a hard winter journey they arrived on the Little Colorado at the settlement later to be called Sunset. They pushed on to the settlement called [Old] Taylor, six miles east of what is now Joseph City. The Little Colorado settlements were all in the United Order, which did not sit well with

William Flake, who served time in Yuma prison for polygamy, was the founder of Snowflake and played important roles in many of the other communities, including St. Johns, Nutrioso and Show Low.

Flake. When the ox of a traveler died, Flake gave him a replacement animal, causing a fuss. The man who had donated the animal to the commune objected, saying a board meeting should have been called. So Flake saddled up and began looking for another place to settle.

James Stinson was willing to sell his property in the Silver Creek valley, but he wanted $12,000, an enormous sum in those days. Flake couldn't find a partner to help him raise the money, and Stinson would not lower the price. But Mrs. Flake was anxious to leave the Old Taylor commune after one of their sons had died in the Little Colorado valley. She said, "Go buy the place. I will do his washing, sewing, anything to help pay the bill, but I can't stay here."

Next morning a deal was struck. Stinson agreed to take Flake's first corn crop as initial payment and Flake agreed to deliver 150 head of Utah-grade cattle each fall for three years.

Flake's move was not condoned by the church, but he was soon to have many other Mormon settlers in his valley. "In 1876, a large company of converts from Georgia, Alabama, and Arkansas came West. ... They were poor people to start with and were on the road nearly a year," facing outbreaks of smallpox before reaching the Little Colorado settlements where there was no work. Many chafed under the United Order, and many headed to join Flake on his ranch. "They did not care, that he was branded as an apostate; they had also heard that he was a friend to men," the Flake biography says.

Ben Hansen, in his manuscript *Background History of Lakeside-Pinetop*, quotes Stinson as telling Flake that the Silver Creek valley was hardly big enough for "one spread, let alone 50 families. The Mormon philosophy and manner of doing things was much different from those of cattle or sheep ranchers. They began carving out a new way of life on this frontier, following pretty much the same pattern as that established by Brigham Young and the Mormons upon entering the Salt Lake Valley."

The Snowflake land was divided up into 10-acre plots of first-class farmland, 10-acre plots of second-class land and town lots. Each man was entitled to draw for one plot of first-class land ($110), one plot of second-class land ($60) and a town lot ($30), according to the Snowflake Stake history. If a man had multiple wives, he could have a town lot for each of them. Flake drew along with the others and took no profit from subdividing the land.

"Prior to Flake's buying the place a few families had received permission from Stinson to locate above the Stinson place on Silver Creek and use the water that he did not want," the history says. "After the purchase Bill Flake told these families that they could continue to live there as there was plenty of water for all. This caused others to move in and soon quite a number of families moved in about three miles south of Snowflake to the place now called Taylor."

Intense, but friendly rivals of their co-religionists in Snowflake, the residents of Taylor have their own story about how the Silver Creek valley was settled. Their hero was James Pearce, a Mississippi man converted to the Mormon faith in 1847. He came to Utah and fought in the wars with the Utes, helped explore a road to the California Coast, participated in the early explorations of Arizona with Hamblin, and negotiated with the Indians for the purchase of water rights for St. George, Utah. In 1877, he took his family to Arizona, visiting the Little Colorado settlements and stopping at Woodruff.

"On January 23, 1878, James (Jim) Pearce and his lovely young wife Mary Jane Meeks arrived at the present site of the town of Taylor, ... settling on the hillside which is the Joseph Neff property," says the Taylor Stake history. "Here they and their children ... camped and set-up a temporary shelter by digging into the side of the hill for protection. This was the first Mormon family to settle on the Silver Creek."

In another section of the Taylor Stake history, descendants of the Pearce family give an account of the hard life their mother faced in the dugout cave: "During the day, they used the wagon-box, turned upside-down for a table, and for a relaxing area to rest for a few minutes. At night, the wagon box was turned up against the opening of the cave for protection from howling wolves and coyotes. Their provisions were stored in the cave for protection from storms as well as animals. They made their beds from cedar posts tied together at the corners. Strips of rawhide were interwoven across the frame for springs."

The Taylor history points out that the arrival of the Pearce family "was nearly six months before the Flake Party located at Snowflake." The book quotes Pearce as saying, "This land was not surveyed and I simply had a squatters claim. The same right to land and water that James N. Stinson had to his claim down on the stream. When I went there, Stinson offered me all his holdings for $18,000. A few months later, William J. Flake paid him $11,000 for the same claim." The Taylor settlers were soon joined by John Henry Standifird, Lorenzo Hill Hatch and William H. Solomon.

Life in Taylor was difficult in the beginning. "Things were rough that first winter," says Jennings in *Arizona Was the West*. "There was no flour, but John (Standifird) did manage to get some barley meal. One day, while John was away, some range cows came down to the creek for water. Mother Standifird said to the teenage daughters, 'Here is our chance for some milk. Lets go see if we can drive them into the corral.' They were wild Texas cattle and had probably never before seen a woman. The women mounted the ponies and soon had three of them in the corral. Then with their lasso ropes they soon tied the cows down and milked them. The cows belonged to Mr. Cooley, of Indian scout fame. Mr. Standifird sent word that they were milking some of his cows to see the babies through the winter. Cooley sent a message to keep the cows, 'but do not starve the calves.' "

In 1883 a water dispute erupted after Flake purchased R. J. Bailey's place near Shumway, and planned to take out the water from Silver Creek above Taylor.

The matter was settled through arbitration and the Snowflake and Taylor Irrigation Company was eventually set up to administer the water, according to the Snowflake Stake history.

Flake, when he was heading back to Utah with a load of wool to get the cattle for the Stinson's first payment, met Apostle Erastus Snow on the trail near the Little Colorado. Flake told the Mormon leader that he was worried about his reputation as an apostate. Snow reassured Flake by telling him that Brigham Young approved of his actions. After that, Snow continued on to the Silver Creek valley, where he named the new settlement Snowflake.

"The people he had left at (Old) Taylor, who had called him an apostate, and were glad to get rid of him, now followed him up and begged to get homes in the Valley," Flake's biography says. "Of course he took them in, and let them have the one fourth of the valley on the south, even though some of them could not pay for their land, and never did." Flake organized the impoverished townspeople to deliver coal to Fort Apache, and broke big Texas steers to set up people in the business of hauling freight to the fort.

"Classes were held in one of the adobe rooms that Mr. Stinson had used as a stable," says the Snowflake Stake history. "Annie Hunt (Kartchner) was chosen to be school mistress, although she was only 17 years old. There were at least 21 known pupils and although some of the students were unruly this didn't seem to deter her as the parents were good to her. She was paid by them but wherein they failed Mr. Flake paid. The following fall, arrangements were made to construct a log building to be used as a schoolhouse as well as a meeting place for religious, civic and social functions. ... Men donated their labor and hauled logs, laid them up and put on a shingle roof and laid the floor. This building was 23 x 33 feet in size and was completed in time for the Christmas festivities in December 1879."

The community of Shumway, just south of Taylor, boasted a four-story flour mill, powered by a large water wheel on Silver

Creek, according to Jennings who wrote another book called *The Freight Rolled.*

Charles Shumway was at Nauvoo, Ill., when Joseph Smith was killed, and he was among the first Mormons to reach Salt Lake City, arriving two days before Brigham Young. While working in communities throughout Utah, he gained experience constructing gristmills.

Shumway first came to Arizona in 1880 with two of his many wives in an attempt to settle Concho for the Mormon church. "Concho was not a very inviting place and troubles soon developed between the Mormon settlers and the Mexican and Indian people who were already living in the area," his biography says. "Charles began to search for a better place to live and he found a place which was called Spring Valley." After he obtained water rights and built the mill, the small town was named for him.

Struggle for St. Johns

Sol Barth and his Hispanic allies took some of the best farmland in the entire area when they settled St. Johns.

And when Jesse N. Smith, president of the newly created Eastern Arizona Stake, rode to St. Johns in 1879 to see Barth about buying the community for the Mormons, Barth was not overly courteous. He left town before the stake president got there, apparently expecting Smith to follow him or wait for his return. "As I did not like the place, I did not wish to do either," said Smith, who returned to Snowflake without making an offer.

But Ammon Tenney, who had been called by the Mormon Church to settle Woodruff, was interested in St. Johns. He discussed it with Apostle Wilford Woodruff, who was living in Sunset under an assumed name to avoid prosecution for polygamy, according to the St. Johns Stake history.

"On November 18, 1879, Tenney made contact with Solomon Barth to buy the Barth holdings in the St. Johns valley. Tenney successfully contracted for all the land that was under cultivation. ... Their agreement was that the Barth brothers would let the Mormons have the land and water plus three claims at the

153

Meadows, for which the Mormons would pay 750 head of average American cattle, ranging in age from two to six years. The Mormons could take possession upon making the first payment of 320 cows. The Church-owned cattle in the area totaled only 220, but Brother William J. Flake personally loaned the 100 head to make up the shortage," the stake history says. Barth kept his hotel, store, sheep and political career. "Brother Woodruff, desiring to gain Mormon domination of the area, instructed Tenney to occupy the surrounding lands before the deal became public knowledge and thus avoid an inrush of non-Mormon speculators. Mormon settlers were sent immediately to St. Johns, some from other Mormon settlements, and some recently arrived from Utah, to locate on these lands as Tenney saw fit. The settlement, called Salem, was a short distance down river from San Juan. ... Members who were financially able were encouraged to make deals for the land owned by individual Mexicans. ... Eventually, over a period of years, all the Mexican holdings, except a few small places up the river, were purchased."

"At first, the Mexican people were friendly," the stake history says. "Don Asiano Gurule loaned the use of his home to Apostle Snow for the first religious meeting held by the Mormons in St. Johns, but the spirit of cooperation did not last. Little misunderstandings began to build; little things became big things; and eventually the situation in St. Johns became a veritable powder keg."

In another section, the stake history says the Gurule house was on land purchased by the Mormons, and that Gurule was one of a small group of Hispanics who converted to the Latter-day Saint faith.

The Hispanics began to get the idea the Mormons wanted to run an exclusively Mormon community, and they were not entirely mistaken in the impression. There was a dispute over whether the post office would be in the new community of Salem, or in the old part of St. Johns. Apostle Erastus Snow sent David King Udall from Kanab, Utah, to be the bishop. As a step toward sorting things out, he told Udall to live in old San Juan, rather than Salem. After a meeting with the local Mormons, they all agreed to call the community St. Johns and move into the old part of town. This was not popular with the Mexicans. "I, the

undersigned, justice of the peace of this precinct, and the undersigned thirty neighbors here, are writing you with the object of
notifying you that you are endangering our townsite," wrote
Marcus Baca. "We have seen members of the Mormon sect, surveying, driving stakes, and even people living under their wagon
covers, making preparations that indicate that members of your
said sect, of which you are director, are transferring themselves
to the surroundings of our town. ... We will not feel it inconve-
nient to show that we will place all the means in our power and
within our reach to impede the establishment of the Mormons
in the surroundings of this town."

Barth, who saw the approach of the railroad as a threat to
his overland freighting business, had apparently been anxious to
sell. He had assumed that the Hispanics who worked for him
were working his land, but some of them felt they were themselves squatters who would obtain property rights. Bishop Udall
had some sympathy for the Hispanics, "They looked upon us as
enemies, who had come to encroach upon their old San Juan
settled by them in 1873. The Mexicans resented us and we did
not blame them very much."

"Lot jumping" was a problem. "A large group of strangers
were laughing and tearing down a Mormon fence and trying to
move a small frame house onto the lot," Helen Bay Gibbons
records in *Saint and Savage*. "Angry Mormons were storming out
of their houses and running toward the lot. ... The trespassers
brought out their guns and fired several shots, but the Mormons
advanced in face of the threat, shouting angrily. In the melee, the
house was overturned, and a near-riot condition existed." Bishop
Udall eventually urged the Mormons to return to their homes
and the intruders retreated to restore an uneasy peace.

The *Deseret News*, the Mormon paper in Salt Lake City, covered the event and said two more lot jumping incidents followed
in St. Johns. Bishop Udall was arrested for trespass, but freed by
a Hispanic justice of the peace. The *Apache Chief*, published by
George A. McCarter, was a viciously anti-Mormon newspaper
and in fact praised itself for being the only anti-Mormon journal
in the Territory. The *Chief* took exception to the story, calling its
author, Miles P. Romney, also the editor of the local pro-Mormon *Orion Era*, "a mass of putrid pus and rotten goose pimples;

155

a skunk, with the face of a baboon, the character of a louse, the breath of a buzzard and the record of a perjurer and common drunkard." His great-grandson Mitt Romney would find presidential politics a little more genteel in the 21st century.

"Shortly after the 1884 lot jumping incident, the Board of Supervisors, ... decided to have the last word in that controversy and at the same time show their total disregard for the Mormons and their rights," the St. Johns Stake history recounts. "They condemned the land for a right-of-way and forced the opening of a new street which ran at a rakish angle through the center of a tier of Mormon blocks. Today we know this unconventional strip as Commercial Street, which has hosted the principle business establishments of St. Johns."

The Mormons petitioned the county supervisors to start their own school. "The board granted the petition briefly, and then rescinded it, thus requiring that all children in the town – Mormon and Mexican – attend the same school," the stake history says. "This was first deplored by both sides, but proved to be a blessing. It helped the children and their parents understand each other better, and resulted in greater community peace."

The anti-Mormon sentiment was strong, not just from the Hispanics. "How did Missouri and Illinois get rid of the Mormons?" the *Apache Chief* wrote in 1884. "By the use of the shotgun and rope. Apache County can rid herself of them also. In a year from now the Mormons will have the power here and the Gentiles had better leave. Don't let them get it. Desperate diseases need desperate remedies."

Another article in the *Chief* sought to whip up anti-Mormon sentiment even further: "A Mormon recently, in conversation with a party who he supposed to be a brother, said that they had enough Mormons now in St. Johns to control all of the water and that next year they did not intend to let the Gentiles have any water for irrigation purposes, and that by next April there would be enough Mormons in the county to run the Gentiles out, and that they intended to do it."

The reports of plots for mass slaughter came from both sides. "We are informed that Lorenzo Hubbell has been telling the Mexicans ... that the Americans had already formed a vigilance committee and intended to hang all the Mexicans as soon as the election was over," wrote the *St. Johns Herald*. "Such malicious, barefaced romancing was never heard of in the literature of fables or falsehoods. It is too ridiculous to contradict and we only mention the matter to show the desperate, despicable tricks to which they are driven."

Like all good lies, that one contained a nugget of truth. Mormons had formed a militia in Apache County in September 1881.

At about the same time, Stake President Jesse N. Smith was visiting St. Johns, and held a meeting where the faithful were told: "We expect this difficulty here to be settled by the steady growth of our people. The better element will predominate. We will hold a large country by righteousness."

The Mormons believed they saw divine intervention as the anti-Mormon leadership collapsed. "Within two years ... five of the six ringleaders, one by one, met with violent deaths, and none of them at the hands of their Mormon neighbors," *Saints and Savages* said. "The sixth man had a change of heart and became a true friend to the Mormon people. He was none other than Don Lorenzo Hubbell."

As the second payment of cattle for St. Johns was coming due, the Mormons were not certain of what they were buying so Udall negotiated a new deed with Sol Barth, which detailed the tracts held by the Hispanics. Udall then went to Salt Lake City where church President John Taylor confirmed the deal and authorized the payment of cattle from a church herd near Pipe Springs, Arizona.

William Flake helped many communities in northeast Arizona make their payments. The Flake biography says he paid 80 cows to help buy the finest ranch in Round Valley (including 80 acres of standing corn) for the Mormons, and also helped in the purchase of Concho and Nutrioso. On the evening of the same day that Apostle Wilford Woodruff promised Flake and his wife that they would not be asked again, they had a visitor. "Bishop D. K. Udall came in from St. Johns, saying that they were about to lose the place and all they had paid on it," Flake's biography says. Flake lent the cattle, and he and Tom Greer signed a note for the next payment.

The Mormon Church brought in 102 additional families from Utah to bolster its claim to the St. Johns area, according to the stake history. "After several years, when it became evident that the resources in and around St. Johns wouldn't support these extra families, they were released." Mark Hall, who was one of the extra settlers, tried to make a living hauling water to town from McIntosh Spring for 5 cents a bucket. He also used two old Civil War-era pistols, which required loading with loose black powder, to hunt lions for the $10 bounty. Despite all his efforts, and a two-year sabbatical in Utah to replenish his resources, he left with the other temporary St. Johns residents when they were released from their obligation by the church.

The anti-Mormon side also sought to bring in more settlers. In an article that was perhaps an attempt at satire, the *Apache Chief* said, "There is a movement on foot to bring to Arizona, immediately, a large colony of Dunkards. These people on account of their thrift, industry, intelligence and purity are always welcome immigrants to any county and for the good of our Territory they cannot get here any too soon. The immigration plan is one way of solving the Mormon problem, because if there is anything which 'the Saints' do abhor, it is contact with civilization, refinement and purity." The ultra-conservative Dunkard sect remained largely in Pennsylvania and nearby states with Mennonites and other groups that oppose modernity.

In another string of invective, the newspaper sought to stoke flames even higher. "There is now no question but what the Mormons and Navajo Indians have formed a coalition. We have it from reliable sources, and further the Mormons are getting in a large supply of arms and ammunition. Every Mormon is now armed. The first move the Mormons make looking toward a breakout will be their last, as there will not be enough men left to dig graves for the balance."

Though the *Chief* bemoaned Mormon electoral practices in Idaho, it published the following notice of the upcoming political campaign with brazen honesty: "The caucuses to send delegates to the county convention will be held in accordance with the wishes of the anti-Mormons in the different precincts, but it is suggested that they be held on or before the 20th day of July, 1884. A compliance with this notice will harmonize the party more."

Polygamy

As with many religious leaders before and since, Joseph Smith had critics who accused him of using power as a potent aphrodisiac. Smith, who was married, approached Helen Kimball, the 15-year-old daughter of Apostle Heber C. Kimball, with these words: "If you will take this step, it will insure your eternal salvation and exaltation and that of your father's household and all of your kindred," according to *Mormon Polygamy, a History* by Richard S. Van Wagoner. In the last years of the Mormon settlement in Nauvoo, Ill., Smith allegedly made similar approaches to a large number of women, some of them the wives of his friends or wards in his household.

In an earlier age, such indiscretions would have been hushed up, or repented. But with a new religion in a time of newspapers and rapid communication, the outcome was very different. The news media picked up on the accounts of "spiritual wifery" and Mormons and non-Mormons alike became outraged. Smith, as the self-proclaimed Prophet of God, couldn't repent, but he could reveal new doctrines that more-or-less covered his behavior. They were initially met with skepticism, especially from his first wife. The fact that Smith was lynched by a mob in 1844 made him a martyr to his followers and eliminated criticism of his conduct.

Brigham Young took over the leadership of the Latter-day Saints after Smith was killed. When he began to lead the faithful west he had to decide whether to bring polygamy to the new land or leave it behind. His prior involvement in Smith's secret practices pulled him toward acceptance of polygamy.

Plus history and cultural practices around the world seemed to be on the side of plural marriage. Mormons often said four-fifths of the world practiced polygamy. It was true that affluent Moslems had up to four wives, upper-class Chinese had concubines and primitive societies in Africa, the South Pacific and Native Americans practiced polygamy.

Jessie L. Embry in *Mormon Polygamous Families* wrote that the Catholic Church did not consider polygamy a sin until after 600 A.D. Luther was willing to sanction multiple marriages for Henry VIII. The Catholic Church even encouraged polygamy in 1650 after the devastation of the Thirty Years War. Also, the Old Testament tells about patriarchs living with multiple wives in the pastoral society of the ancient Middle East.

Young believed he was free to make his own laws because the Mormons were headed to the remote West, an area only nominally administered by Mexico in those days.

He miscalculated. The U.S. won the vast territories of the West in the Mexican War only one year after the Mormons arrived. And polygamy was anathema in the societies of Europe and their extensions into the Americas. Marx and Engels said monogamy grew up in early Greek societies as men sought to ensure paternity of the children who would inherit their property. Others have pointed to the importance of monogamy in upholding the status of the woman and the status of her kin who had contracted the first marriage. Monogamy had been sanctified for more than a millennium before the advent of Christianity and, with few exceptions, had been enforced during 2000 years of Christian culture in Europe. Monogamy was so well established in America that anything else was treated with revulsion.

Before polygamy brought Mormonism into another conflict with the United States, it was to have some positive effects on the expansion of Mormon settlements. Nearly all Mormon women found themselves involved in a productive role in a family, having children and working to increase the family wealth. Of course, all the family's assets were controlled by the husband, which gave men with multiple wives control over many people and resources. So Polygamy tended to strengthen the extremely patriarchal nature of Mormonism, which says women cannot get into heaven unless they are married to a man who has obtained the priesthood, and is willing to pull them into heaven after death.

Still, most Mormons – approximately 80 percent — remained monogamous. The practice of polygamy was usually limited to the affluent. Awarding additional wives became a method of binding prosperous men into the church hierarchy. In its classic form, a man rising within the church would take a wife in her late teens once every five to ten years, until he had accumulated five or more.

Polygamy was not universally condemned by the non-Mormon world. In *Elijah Was a Valiant Man,* Arvin Palmer says George

Bernard Shaw approved because there were more Mormon women than men, and a frontier society could not cope with a large number of single women.

It took awhile for the idea of polygamy to germinate in the heart of one man who would later settle in the White Mountains. *The Life of Delbert L. Penrod* recreates the words of the pioneer. "Polygamy was being practiced at this time and leaders of the church and others often approached me with the subject, but for some reason I was not interested. One day, a family moved to Escalante (Utah) from Panguitch. The oldest girl in this family was a beautiful, dark haired maiden with very black eyes. For some time I spent considerable time trying to meet her. Without seeming too bold, but from that time on, I thought that a second wife was what all men should have.

"When I began to show an interest in her, I found that the interest was mutual and after getting her father's consent, I spent many happy times with her without seeming to neglect Sarah and children, as they knew my intentions and were willing for me to take this step. We were married in the St. George Temple the 14th of March, 1888. That same summer we received a call to go to Arizona to help settle new country and to build new homes. We were very skeptical about this trip as we had heard some very unfavorable reports about Arizona from some that had been out here and come back." Penrod pushed aside his doubts and took his two wives and children to Taylor.

Polygamy left some young Mormon men without brides while a few older men accumulated many wives. Palmer tells the unhappy story of Joe Thomas and Rhoda Perkins who had recently migrated to Taylor from Utah. "For Joe the situation was different. Rhoda's father had made it clear that he wanted his daughter to marry an apostle, and she apparently concurred, so the young Thomas lad could not measure up. With disappointment in love added to extremely difficult times, Joe got on his horse one day and retraced his path to Utah where he would remain a bachelor throughout his lifetime." Palmer added in a footnote: "Rhoda later became a wife of Brigham Young Jr. and had one child by him. She was to spend most of her married life alone." Rhoda was the fourth of Young's six wives. He acquired the fifth only 10 months after his marriage to Rhoda.

Kent Lightfoot, the anthropologist, writes that polygamy was part of a marriage practice that stratified the communities. While as many as 80 percent of Mormons married within their communities, the more prominent men would marry women from other Mormon towns. "A man of sufficient status and wealth to obtain a wife from a powerful family would augment his own political position and, at the same time, strengthen his inter-community connections," he wrote. "This process of political development was enhanced by [polygamy], which allowed influential men to cultivate social ties with several powerful families. However, the means to support several wives and their respective children was an important factor limiting the rate of [polygamy]. It is clear that poorer men were often hardly able to support one wife, let alone several spouses and numerous children."

The biography of William Flake, written by a son, explains his decision to take a second wife. "William thought it was his duty to obey the principle. (This was before there was any law against it.) Mother thought it right, so with her full and free consent, he sought the hand of Prudence J. Kartchner, who lived on the Muddy (southwest Utah). On October 10, 1868, they were sealed husband and wife in the endowment house, Salt Lake City. Mother was present. Eliza R. Snow asked her if she was willing. She said, 'Yes.' 'Do you think you can live it?' [the wife of the Apostle then asked Mother.] She said that she was willing to try. Sister Snow then gave her a blessing, and said that she would retain her beauty and never grow old. Up until she passed away more than thirty years later, she was an exceptionally fine looking woman. The two women lived in the same house, or in close proximity and often helped each other when their work permitted. Later in life, 'Aunt' Prudence's (we called her) helping days were over. A number of years before she died, she suffered with asthma until life was a burden to her. She rarely left the house for months at a time, because of that disease. I remember her suffering from the time we came to Arizona; for months she could not leave her bed. She was the mother of four girls living and one girl and two boys had passed away in infancy. The girls did a noble part by their mother."

Many accounts of polygamy from the participants are positive. Mary Serena Davis, on March 14, 1888, married Jacob N. Butler as his plural wife. Her story is told by one of the children in the

Emma Batchelor Lee French came to the White Mountains after her husband John D. Lee was executed for his role in the Mountain Meadows massacre. She was the 17th of his 19 wives and once operated the famous Lee's Ferry.

Penrod manuscripts. "I have often looked back down the years, and marveled at the love and companionship that existed in our home, between mother and aunty and we children. We always felt bad when someone would say, your half brother or sister; to us there was no half. I can see mother and aunty at the ranch at Greer, especially on wash days, two big wooden tubs, set on a bench and two washboards. One would wash the clothes and put them in the other tub ... on the fire to boil them. Then they would take them out and put them through two clear waters, then starch them and hang them out. (The starch was made out of flour and water.) Both of them would hang out. Not only did they wash together, but anything that had to be done was done in unity, no arguing or waiting for the other one to do it. They always worked together. Aunty did most of the sewing for both families, mother did the cooking and ... made butter. Daddy always worked hard to support his big family and our mothers were very saving and took care of all that was fetched in, so we always had plenty. ...

"Strangers coming in would never know who our mother was. If any of us needed correcting, they didn't wait for the real mother to do it. We were corrected by the one that was with us. We thought it was what should be done and took it for granted without complaining. If we were to say, 'Aunty slapped me', we would be apt to get another one, so we never tattled. Mother never could milk, but when we girls had to milk alone, aunty would say, 'come on, girls, I will help you milk.' ... We all felt fortunate to have two mothers to care for us."

Some accounts of polygamy, though positive, were given through gritted teeth. David King Udall, the founder of a political dynasty that stretches from Arizona to New Mexico, Colorado and Washington, D.C., came to St. Johns with his wife Eliza (Ella) Stewart. He became bishop and ran the church co-op where he became interested in Ida Hunt, the store's bookkeeper. After Udall proposed to her, Ida returned to Snowflake and wrote to Ella. Her letter is quoted in *Arizona's Honeymoon Trail*. "I feel that I cannot allow another day to pass by without writing you to ascertain if possible your true feelings upon a subject which is, no doubt, one painful to us both, but one which, I realize, must be disposed of sooner or later – the possibility or probability of my becoming at some future day a member of your family. ... I cannot allow the matter to go farther, without first having received some assurance of your willingness to such a step being taken. ... I promise you I shall not be offended, but on the contrary shall thank you for it all my life, and I believe you will not have written in vain, for, unless it meets with your approval, I shall never listen to another word on the subject."

The answer came: "The subject in question has caused me a great amount of pain and sorrow, more perhaps than you could imagine, yet I feel as I have from the beginning, that if it is the Lord's will I am perfectly willing to try to endure it and trust it will be overruled for the best good of all." Ida took that answer for a yes and David, Ida and Ella went to the temple in St. George for the wedding.

Some Mormons remember that polygamy did not always result in perfect harmony. In *Elijah Was a Valiant Man*, Palmer wrote about friction among his ancestors. "His father's home had been rather unsettled by the petty jealousies that one wife had borne for another and to the end of his days it was a subject he refused to discuss."

Congress first made polygamy illegal in the territories in 1862 with the Morrill Act, but there were no resources in the midst of the Civil War to enforce compliance. Latter-day Saints considered the law unconstitutional, and fought it until the U.S. Supreme Court upheld the law in 1879. Then in 1882, Congress passed the Edmunds Act, making polygamy a felony punishable by five years in prison. Unlawful cohabitation remained a misdemeanor, punishable by six months in jail and a $300 fine.

Polygamy was a convenient club for opponents of the Mormons. "In the United States, whatever is unlawful is no part of religion," wrote the *Apache Chief* newspaper in St. Johns. "So long as we fight the Mormons for disobeying the laws we are not fighting any religion, and our warfare, instead of being persecution, as is charged, is merely self-preservation."

"Something must be done by which the Territory can be kept pure and unsullied. ... If some means are not resorted to then Arizona will take its stand by the side of Utah in the great calamity of Mormon domination," the *Apache Chief* said in an article quoted in *On the Road to Nowhere*. In another editorial, the paper said, "It is the elders who keep houses full of wives, the rich old bishops that have accumulated large fortunes out of the church tithes, and who can afford this luxury."

"Persecutions were in full swing and United States Marshals were all over the place," the St. Johns Stake history says. "The Polygamists were busy, too, taking steps to insure their own safety. Some followed the lead of Bishop Udall and sent their extra families back to Utah to live with relatives and some took their families with them and moved to Mexico. A few decided to stay and ride it out by playing a kind of cat and mouse game with ... the Marshals, but in general it was a time of exodus, especially for the people in positions of leadership.

"A roster of leaders who made the Mexico move would include two Stake Presidents, Jesse N. Smith of the Eastern Arizona Stake and Lot Smith of the Little Colorado Stake, and many Bishops, Branch Presidents, and Priesthood leaders. So many of these substantial citizens left that their hurried withdrawals of capital from the co-op store system left it on the verge of collapse."

"A piece of territorial legislation briefly took the vote away from polygamists and anyone who believed in the doctrine," the

Road to Nowhere says. "Hundreds of Mormons fled to Mexico to avoid prosecution, or moved families to other locales to maintain the appearance of monogamy. One early settler in Round Valley who was a polygamist left by foot for Old Mexico, where his family later joined him."

Mormons continued to flee to Mexico for nearly 20 years as the battle with the government over their "principle" continued.

William Flake's wife Lucy gave this account published in *Arizona Memories*: "One of our neighbors came one night and asked for help to go to Mexico. He only had one team and his boys would need that to harvest their crop and haul wood for the family. He had no money to buy another outfit so could William lend him one. Well, a wagon, cover, water barrels and a span of our best horses were rigged up for him. The horses were harnessed up, hitched to the wagon and driven up to his door after nightfall. He and his plural wives slipped away. In about a year he returned the outfit, with thanks. That was all that was necessary. If he had never brought them back, it would have been the same."

She told another story about giving their best horse and a saddle to help a man make a run for the border. "It was always the same, if anyone needed anything and we had it, they knew it was theirs."

The Snowflake Stake history recounts: "In January and February of 1885 most of the polygamist men left for Mexico, with a few going to Utah and elsewhere. Some of those from Snowflake who left were Jesse N. Smith, Joseph Fish, John Hunt, Jesse N. Smith Jr., Samuel H. Rogers, John Kartchner, Isaac Turley, W. W. Roundy and James Palmer. A few others who were not polygamists joined them. This sudden flight of so many of the principle men of the community left things in quite a bad spiritual and temporal condition. ... Many sold property at reduced prices.

"After reaching Mexico John Hunt received word that on his birthday March 8, 1885 his wife Lois, who had remained in Snowflake, had accidentally burned to death. He immediately returned to Snowflake."

In 1886, church property was being confiscated in Utah, so the Mormons sent a herd of sheep south and asked that William Flake get the animals to Mexico, which he did.

A Tribute to the Lakeside Pioneers tells about the flight of the Jonathan Henry Webb family from Pinedale: "In June 1898 the families moved to the Mormon Colonies in Mexico. Edward Milo, Henry's father, didn't want his family separated. He had two other wives, Aunt Ellen and Aunt Lottie. Seven weeks in four covered wagons moved them all 'body and britches.' They had horses stolen, had rough roads, floods, and a whole week at the border with 'Customs.' Henry drove his mother's wagon. He was 12 years old. The excited children sang:

"Eeny, meeny, miny, mo
"On the road to Mexico
"To Mexico we'll go or bust
"When we start, Just watch our dust.

"And there was plenty of dust. They arrived in Colonia Dublan the last week in August. It was very hot, but crops were lush and at their peak. There were plenty of ripe watermelons."

To whip up sentiment against the Mormons, or perhaps to boost circulation, the *Apache Chief* sent an undercover reporter to Utah to learn the secrets of the Mormons. The secret correspondent says he was able to enter the Mormon Endowment House where he learned various secret handshakes and breathlessly told of the Mormon "garment" he was given. The newspaper story, making some obvious comparisons to Masons, lamented that its agent had only one wife and might have gotten more good stuff if he had been able to work into higher degrees through the attainment of more wives. "I was then taken into what they call 'Anointing Room' where I was stripped perfectly nude and every member of my body touched with what I supposed from its smell, was olive oil. A part of the body which I do not care to mention was specially anointed ... to typify and symbolize fecundity." The article published a picture of the Mormon under-garment, but modestly showed it only from the waist up. The graphic looks a little like the base of a lamp, but probably helped sell papers.

The U.S. government's push against polygamy started in Utah. "The other day Judge O. W. Powers, of Michigan, one of Mr. Cleveland's appointees to the bench in Utah, had a two hours' conversation with the President," the *St. Johns Herald* reported in 1885. "The subject was the enforcement of the laws against polygamy in Utah. Judge Powers says the President is determined to wage as fierce a war as possible against the Mormons, and has instructed the judicial officers to carry out the law most vigorously. A large number of leading Mormons are now under indictment, among them being John Taylor and George Q. Cannon, the two being at the present fugitives from justice. Judge Powers says the Mormons generally are rapidly recognizing the fact that the Government is in dead earnest, and that they only preach and practice polygamy when they are out of sight of the officers of the law."

Apostle Wilford Woodruff, who had five wives, was in hiding near the White Mountains because of the ongoing prosecutions in Utah. He was living in Sunset near present-day Winslow under an assumed name, according to the St. Johns Stake history. He later became church president and eventually abolished the doctrine of polygamy.

The crackdown soon came to Arizona, according to this account in the Snowflake Stake history: "After the (St. Johns) Ring had succeeded in the election of 1882 they commenced to agitate on the subject of prosecuting the polygamists and attempted to drive the Mormons out of Apache County. From this time on they began to be aggressive in their actions, encroaching on the rights of the people, taking away their water rights, entering vexatious lawsuits and bringing them before a Mexican Justice who was their tool.

"In March 1882 the Congress of the United States passed the Edmunds Act which provided heavy penalties for the practice of polygamy, including imprisonment, fines, disfranchisement of voting rights or the holding of public office. This was enforced even though most of the plural marriages had taken place prior to the enactment of this law."

"Persecution of Polygamists was more or less a universal thing; nowhere was it pursued more viciously than along the Little Colorado," the St. Johns Stake history says. "The Mormons were blocked at every turn. They were refused the right to vote and barred from jury duty. The extent to which the courts had been prejudiced against them can best be judged by the tone of this excerpt from a supposedly patriotic Fourth of July speech that was delivered by Judge Sumner Howard, Chief Justice of the

Territorial Courts in Prescott:

" 'There is no danger which menaces this beautiful Territory equal to that black cloud that follows the blasting approach to a polygamous priesthood, and which has already cast its withering influence over the most beautiful portion of your Territory. ... I say to you, fellow citizens that it is not only the design of the foul and unscrupulous priesthood to seize upon this Territory and those adjoining it but that it will be an accomplished fact unless there is a rising of the people of this Territory ... to free themselves from the impending danger.'

"With Judge Howard as Chief Justice; George McCarter, the United States Court Commissioner, stationed in St. Johns and moonlighting as the leader of the St. Johns Ring; and United States Attorney Zabriskie (the same who had been prosecutor at the trial of John D. Lee) as Chief Prosecutor at the Mormon trials in Prescott, it is hard to say whether the Ring was corrupting the courts or the courts corrupting the Ring."

McCarter was assisted by Sol Barth, J. Lorenzo Hubbell and others in starting the St. Johns anti-Mormon newspaper *Apache Chief*.

"The Polygamy issue which erupted in 1883 was a perfect opportunity for the St. Johns Ring to further harass the Mormons," the St. Johns Stake history says. "It was with great anticipation that they set about playing the role of stool pigeon for the anti-Mormon territorial courts. Consequently, seven prominent Mormons, including such leaders as D. K. Udall, Ammon Tenney, and William J. Flake, were hauled into the 1884 fall session of the Territorial District Court in Prescott, with Judge Sumner Howard presiding."

Flake's biography expresses anger at the administration of Chester Arthur as it turned up the heat on polygamy: "A weak President and a subservient Congress, influenced by a hireling ministry egged on by a low class of people, such as always follows a carpetbag Government, passed laws that were unconstitutional and retroactive, and had their dupes shove them to the limit. In Utah, many of the leading citizens had gone to jail, others were in hiding, largely in adjoining States. That same lawless element started the persecution in Arizona which, like Utah was a territory and not allowed self Government.

"Early in September 1884, the United States Marshal sent word to Father that he would be at Snowflake on the 15th, at noon, to arrest him for polygamy, thus giving him plenty of time to get away, for he did not want to arrest him," according to Flake's biography. "They had never met, but the Marshal knew his reputation and that almost every man was his friend, and that he was a good honorable citizen, and not to be compared with the rif-raff that were causing the trouble. About noon on the 15th, he drove up to Flake's home, introduced himself as Marshal Donovan, and was much surprised when the reply came, 'Well Marshal, I am your man.' He served the paper and put him under arrest. Flake said, 'Unhitch the team and put them in the stable and feed them, my wife will have dinner for us soon, and I will be getting ready to go with you.' Mr. Donovan said, 'I want to go back to Holbrook to-night, but the train we take does not leave until 2 p.m. tomorrow. You can stay here tonight, and meet me at the train tomorrow, if you like.' That suited William much better. So, after dinner the Marshal returned to Holbrook, where they met the following day. The Marshal took out a roll of bills and offered him some money, and said, 'Take this and pay your own way, buy your own ticket, no one needs to know that you are a prisoner.' He said, 'No, Marshal, I am your prisoner, treat me as one, I am not ashamed of it. I have broken no law, I am a victim of persecution.' "

At Prescott, William Flake was released on bond. John D. Schone had signed the complaint. "Schone came to him and begged him to jump the bonds saying he would pay them. He cried and said that he did not want to see him go, and that he would never have signed the complaint, but they had gotten him drunk and forced it on him."

The trials started in November 1884. Ammon Tenney was convicted first and thrown into the local jail with the common criminals. Flake received help from the non-Mormon who had sold him the ranch to create Snowflake. "James Stinson was living at Tempe, and it was a hard trip to Prescott, but when he learned that his friend Flake was in trouble, he went at once to his aid. Father started at once to hunt for some of his friends, and did not stop until he had Tenney out of the filthy prison."

A plea deal was offered in which Flake would not serve time,

170

but the others would serve eight and a half years at the House of Correction in Detroit. Flake says he went to the judge and objected to the deal. The judge then gave him six months in prison, but cut the sentences of the others by three years.

"His old friend Jim Stinson ... was his main help all the way and he really took it hardest of the two," the biography says. "Next morning he was at the Station to see him take the stage. Just before it was time to leave, Miles P. Romney of St. Johns, under the charge of an officer, came and asked him to go a bond."

Romney was the editor of a Mormon newspaper in St. Johns. He was to become the grandfather of a future governor of Michigan, and great-grandfather of Mitt Romney, who sought the Republican presidential nomination in 2008.

The Flake biography recounts the conversation: "Father said, 'I am a convict just starting for the penitentiary, I can't go on a bond.' Romney said, 'You have friends who would, if you asked them. I haven't a friend in this city and will have to lie in that jail for six months awaiting trial unless you help me.' Always lending a helping hand, he turned to Stinson and asked him to go the bond; he said that he would, but that it would take another. So he asked Bagnall to sign with Stinson. Bagnall said, 'I will, if you guarantee me against loss.' So it was arranged and he bid his friends good-bye, stepped on the waiting stage and off to prison."

In her account, Flake's wife said they wound up paying off $2,000 when Romney skipped bail. "Money was scarce and interest high," she wrote. "It took us seven years to square that two thousand dollars."

In subsequent trials Mormon bishops C. I. Kempe and Peter J. Christopherson were tried, convicted and sentenced in Prescott to a fine of $500 and three and a half years in the House of Correction in Detroit.

The polygamy charge against Bishop Udall was dropped for lack of evidence. "Having failed to bring Bishop Udall to trial on the polygamy charge the previous year, the Ring decided to haul him in on a charge of perjury," the St. Johns Stake history says. "At his trial he was not allowed to testify in his own behalf, nor to present witnesses who would testify in his favor. By dubious means they secured a conviction and on October 10, 1885 he was sentenced to serve a three-year term in the Detroit House of Correction in Michigan."

The *St. Johns Herald* gloatingly reported: "David K. Udall, high priest and counselor of this stake of Zion, and also the leading Mormon bishop of Arizona has been convicted in the United States Court at Prescott, of perjury and sentenced to imprisonment for three years in the House of Correction at Detroit, Michigan. The bishop was found guilty of falsely swearing to the land entry of Miles P. Romney, late editor of the *Orion Era*. Romney is also under indictment for the same offense, but has skipped to Mexico leaving his bondsmen in the lurch to the tune of several thousand dollars." The paper, however, was pleased that Joseph Crosby was acquitted of the same perjury charge, explaining that Crosby "is a business man, a hard working citizen, and undoubtedly made the affidavit in the land entry of Miles P. Romney on the representation of that fugitive and the polygamous bishop that the requirements of the law had been complied with."

In another article on the conviction of Udall, the St. Johns paper said: "We commented on this case for the purpose of enlightening the blind followers of the wicked promulgators of the false and pernicious doctrine of polygamy, and to show the deluded dupes the insincerity and wickedness of their cruel masters."

In yet another article, the *Apache Chief* said: "The late convictions for polygamy at Prescott are a grand victory of intelligence and morality over ignorance, bigotry and degradation. It is a victory for women and decency. It is a step toward releasing from bondage thousands of poor ignorant slaves, who are under worse masters than those freed by the late rebellion. It is a victory for the Gentiles of Apache County and Arizona."

Flake became a champion for prisoners' rights while he was at Yuma. When they were served spoiled meat, he told the warden: "I am a citizen of this state and a heavy taxpayer. I am in your power, now, but you cannot keep me here very long. I have plenty of friends and when I get out of here we will turn this place upside down. We pay for decent food for our prisoners and they are going to have it or we will find out the reason why." Food improved. Flake and the other Mormons counseled inmates, re-organized the kitchen and prison industries, took the warden's children fishing and were beyond model prisoners. "Because of the delay in the mails, the money to pay William's fine had not arrived when his sentence was up," his wife wrote. "Some of the prisoners found this out. They had money of varying amounts deposited with the warden. They drew it out and presented it to him. He only accepted it as a loan and returned it as soon as he got to Mesa."

When Flake reached Snowflake, there was a full celebration of the entire community. "A program of songs, music, readings and sentiments, all written for the occasion, took up the afternoon," Mrs. Flake wrote.

"Upon his release he was asked which one of his wives he would give up," the Snowflake Stake history reports. "His answer was neither – he had married both in good faith and intended to support both of them. He had served his sentence and could not be retried on the same charge."

"As a pendulum reaches the end of its travel and then reverses its motion, so it was with the political fortunes of the Mormon settlers along the Little Colorado," the St. Johns Stake history says. "Almost before the prison doors were closed behind Bishop Udall a spontaneous movement was launched to effect his release. It was a natural thing for the Mormons to do, but it is almost unbelievable that Judge Howard and Chief Prosecutor Zabriskie independently wrote to President Cleveland asking him to consider the granting of a pardon for Bishop Udall. Zabriskie stated that in reviewing the evidence he had formed a doubt in his mind as to Udall's guilt. Even the county officials of Apache County, all of whom were members of the St. Johns Ring, decided to get into the act.

"It is almost certain to have been President Cleveland's appointment of the Honorable Conrad Meyer Zulick to take over the reins of government in the Territory of Arizona that prompted them to make that paradoxical about-face. Arizona had been in the grip of a succession of Republican governors. The first order of business for the new Governor was to start building and strengthening the Democratic Party. The Mormons, comprising one-fifth of the Territory's non-Indian population, and over half of Apache County's Anglos, were a ready made base for which to build his Democratic organization.

"To start cultivating political relations with the Mormons Zulick granted pardons to all polygamists who were serving time in the Territorial Penitentiary. The Governor's appointments to the courts were, if not pro-Mormon, at least men with open minds. To further cement these relations the Governor took steps to make Mormon problems a political issue and ultimately, through his efforts, the Democratic Legislature ... wiped the slate clean of the anti-Mormon legislation that had been railroaded through by E. S. Stover, representative from Apache County, who was a wheel horse of the St. Johns Ring."

The St. Johns Stake history says that John D. Young, who had been brushing shoulders with several railroad magnates, helped Bishop Udall get a pardon from President Cleveland, on Dec. 12, 1885.

"William J. Flake and P. N. Skousen had already returned home after serving a six-month sentence in Yuma," the St. Johns Stake history says. "Ammon Tenney, Charles Kempe, and Peter J. Christopherson, who had been sent to the Detroit House of Correction on Polygamy charges, were soon pardoned for good conduct."

The St. Johns papers, so triumphant in announcing the convictions, were sheepish in telling their readers about the subsequent pardons. In a story barely more than a line, the *Herald* said: "According to a recent decision of Attorney General Garland, it appears their trial was illegal and today President Cleveland pardoned them."

When Udall returned to St. Johns, he had no money, but his former enemy Sol Barth sold him 8,000 head of sheep, and allowed him to pay for them over time. Udall considered the change of heart more or less miraculous, but perhaps Barth was making preparations for his own visit to prison, which was not far in the future.

"The people who had taken refuge in Mexico began returning, some almost immediately," the St. Johns Stake history says. "Jesse N. Smith was there for ten months and returned just in time to forestall the installation of another Stake President in his place. It is estimated that about 50 percent of those who moved to Mexico returned within two years.

"Under the administration of Governor Zulick the Mormon

strategy of domination of the issues by superior numbers was paying off. The political climate was fast becoming somewhat bearable. Though the St. Johns Ring was softening its campaign, its influence lingered on into the Twentieth Century. That lawless element so embittered the people of old St. Johns that even today we occasionally detect traces of those old animosities.

"The Mormons were trading one set of problems for another, as this excerpt from the diary of Jesse N. Smith indicates: 'December 10, (1885) On the road early. Saw a number of acquaintances. Reached home at 1 p.m. after an absence of about 10 months, during which I had earned but very little. My expenses and losses were considerable and my family were a good deal in debt.' "

Meanwhile in Utah, hard pressed by the government and consistently losing in court, Mormon President Wilford Woodruff was backing away from polygamy. On October 20, 1889, he said, "I have refused to give any recommendation for the performance of plural marriages since I have been President." In 1890, he gathered his advisers. In an account in *Mormon Polygamy, a History*, Van Wagoner says, Woodruff told them their last legal defense had fallen and that he came to them "with broken and contrite spirit." Woodruff said he "had sought the will of the Lord, and the Holy Spirit had revealed that it was necessary for the church to relinquish the practice of that 'principle' for which the brethren had been willing to lay down their lives."

"I have arrived at a point in the history of the Church of Jesus Christ of Latter-day Saints where I am under the necessity of acting for the temporal salvation of the Church," he is quoted as saying.

Woodruff's decision applied only to polygamy within the United States, allowing it to continue in Mexico.

Osmer D. Flake, in the biography of his father William Flake, explains the thinking of local leaders as Mormons changed course on polygamy. "The principle of polygamy was taught at that time. It was done away with in 1890, by a revelation to Wilford Woodruff, President of the Church. We, who live fifty years later can see how it was a saving principle. Even at that time, many of the leading men of the World defended the principle. It was being practiced by at least seventy-five percent of the Nations of the

Earth. There were laws passed against plural wives. We, as a people, are taught to obey the laws of the country in which we live, and when prohibitory laws were passed, God relieved His people from the requirement."

Some Mormons, particularly those who had taken multiple wives when it was still legal, persisted in polygamy and the prosecutions against them continued into the 20th century. While opposing new plural marriages, church leaders encouraged members to continue to support all of their wives. In 1904, a new president of the church and nephew of the Prophet, Joseph F. Smith, gave a Second Manifesto, prohibiting church leaders from performing plural marriages and threatening excommunication.

Jake Butler, whose wives and children got along so well in Greer, took his second wife in the late 1880s, six years after it became a felony and only two years before the church abandoned the practice. He maintained his two families well into the 20th century. Butler's story is told by one of his children in the Penrod manuscripts. "The one great sadness for him and his families who had always lived under the same roof, came about 1905 when polygamists were being persecuted, hounded and chased out of the country. He moved his second family to Concho. It seemed very hard, indeed, for the families to be separated after living together for so many years.

"In September of 1906, he was on his way to Old Mexico. He left his second family at the sawmill six miles from Greer and went into Greer to bid his other family goodbye before he left, not knowing when they would meet again. On returning to the mill, just before arriving there, he was overtaken by officers of the law and took to St. Johns to stand trial. He was fined $100 or one year in jail or penitentiary at Florence. Having very little money, it looked like our dear father would have to go to jail as $100 in those days was a lot of money. But thanks to Solomon Barth, a non-Mormon, but a very good friend in times of need, came to his relief and let him have the money to pay his fine."

Barth had come full circle, traveling west with the Mormons, creating a viciously anti-Mormon political machine in St. Johns and then paying a fine to keep a latter-day polygamist out of prison.

Mormons Move
Deeper into Mountains

While the polygamy controversy played out, Mormons kept coming across Lee's Ferry, and moving farther south, deeper into the White Mountains. Louis Elias Johnson, born in 1872 in Monroe, Utah, gave this account of crossing the Colorado in about 1879. "When we got to the Colorado River one evening we camped near a canyon. We could see the water far below and we would light sticks and watch them whirling lighted down the long deep canyon to the water. It seemed at first we could reach across the narrow gorge but of course we couldn't. Next day we drove to Lee's Ferry and crossed the river, ferried one wagon at a time over on a boat just big enough for two horses and a yoke of oxen. It took a good one and a half days to cross. We swam most of the cattle."

The account in *A Tribute to Lakeside Pioneers* says the family continued on through Snowflake and then south again. "First of May Father moved Mother to what is now Pinedale, settled on a piece of land on the Cottonwood Wash below Martensen's and Petersen's. To build a house we went into the woods and cut down trees – there were no sawmills – carried them on sides of wagon, built a wall and made a roof out of shakes. We had no floor but we had a rock fireplace. We covered the windows with factory (a kind of cloth). Mother cooked on the fireplace with very few utensils."

Annise A. Bybee, who married Nathan Oscar Robinson, gave this account of her family's struggle in crossing the Little Colorado. She drove the wagon all the way from Utah while her husband herded cattle. "We were one or two hours behind the others and the river had risen so we could hardly tell where the crossing was. But we ventured in and were almost across when we felt the wagon sinking in the quicksand and the horses just had their feet on the bank and could go no farther. My husband asked what we were to do. I quickly took Laura, my baby was in long clothes, and handed her to him. He climbed over the horses and laid her on the ground, then returned and took the two little boys." After rescuing their three sacks of flour and crate of chickens she got out and they unhitched the horses. Eventually, they attached a long chain to the wagon and used the horses to pull it out. They went on to Snowflake and then to Lone Pine "where we tried to make us a

177

little house about ten by twelve feet, made of logs." Her husband's struggle in the new land would soon be ended by a run-in with Apaches.

"Early in 1879 Abraham Winsor, Frederick Hamblin, William B. Maxwell, with his daughter and son-in-law, William Grant Black, along with other Latter-day Saints arrived in" Alpine, according to the St. Johns Stake history. "William Grant Black was driving a yoke of red bulls, Deb and Curley, and leading two milk cows and two head of horses, Dick and Barney. Anderson Bush was willing to sell to these people and part of the payment to him consisted of a good span of mules, a saddle horse, and a wagon." The Mormons moved the houses built by previous owners onto their chosen home sites, and constructed a fort to guard against Indian attack. The fort was never attacked, but Victorio's band did steal 25 horses. Will Maxwell and Duane Hamblin had been watching the settlers' grazing horses before they rode back to the fort for their noon meal. "As they were returning to the herd, about 15 Apaches rode between them and the herd, swinging their guns about their heads, but making no attempt to shoot," the stake history says. "The boys raced back to the fort, firing their pistols to give alarm." Will and Duane wanted to attack the Indians, but the older men decided a battle with Victorio would be unwise. So the Apaches kept the horses.

About the same time, Mormons were settling in the Greer area. "In 1879 Richard Lee and sons, Lehi Smithson, and others, all Latter-day Saints, took up claims in the little valley lying along the upper Little Colorado River, which subsequently became known as Lee's Valley," according to the St. Johns Stake history. *On the Road to Nowhere* adds Peter Jens Jensen, James Hale and Heber Dalton to the list of early settlers.

E. T. Wiltbank and family, who initially tried to settle in Nutrioso in 1882, came to Greer and set up a sawmill, according to the Little House tape. He also planted a large potato field.

Life in early Greer was very hard. The beautiful valley was far from transportation and had a short growing season because of the high altitude. *On the Road to Nowhere* quotes Mae Wiltbank describing one family, "They were so poor they never had anything. ... They lived on nothing; they didn't have nothing. Everybody was poor and they didn't know it."

Settlers raised crops of oats, barley, potatoes, and a large variety of garden vegetables, the book says. "The season was too short for fruit. … Great wagon expeditions went out in late summer and fall to gather wild thorny gooseberries and raspberries for the winter's jams and jellies. The 'jars' for fruit products were often transformed from pint liquor bottles, cracked to the right size by burning a string tied around the bottles that had been dipped in coal oil."

The Mormons in Greer were successful in taming the Little Colorado where their downstream brethren often failed. Their secret was to capture the river while it was young, before it became a raging torrent. Bunch and Tunnel reservoirs were created in 1887, and River Reservoir followed in 1896. According to *On the Road to Nowhere*, the first dynamite used in the area blasted the tunnel necessary to fill Tunnel Reservoir. "Tunneling from both ends without surveying instruments, this tunnel met almost perfectly," the book says, quoting a dedicatory booklet from the Eagar Ward.

By 1894, Greer boasted a school made of sawed logs with a shingle roof. There were 25-30 children. "Who and when they attended was flexible – the only rule being that the child be smaller than the teacher so as not to cause much trouble," the book says. "The boys were often off with the harvest or cattle and if the parents didn't have anything else for them to do, they were sent to school."

The town was renamed from Lee Valley to Greer in 1898 as part of the process of getting a post office. The Greer book says that E. W. Wiltbank applied for the postmaster job, but didn't get it. President William McKinley gave it instead to E.W.'s wife because she was a Republican.

Meanwhile, Mormons were moving into Concho, Hunt and Vernon as well. William Flake said he gave 40 cows to help buy half of Concho.

One of the early Mormon settlers in the Vernon area was John Smith Harris, who was sent to Arizona in 1880 at the age of 52, according to a manuscript entitled *John Smith Harris in Arizona* by John V. Wilhelm. He built his cabin in the Green's Peak area at a spot known today as Harris Lake. In addition to beginning farming operations, he diverted Mineral Creek to es-

179

tablish a shingle mill. His children found a cave that had been inhabited by prehistoric Indians. Harris, who sold pots from the cave to pay off a $300 debt, believed the cave was a miraculous discovery related to a dream that he had.

The Show Low Creek valley was also filling up with Mormon settlements north of Cooley's Ranch.

"The first recorded use of Pinedale was in 1878, when settlers from the nearby Mormon communities of Taylor and Snowflake logged timber from the area to build their homes," says anthropologist Lightfoot, in a Forest Service document, *An archaeological Survey of the Nicks Camp Timber Sale*. "Pinedale, then known as Snowflake Camp, was selected as a base for logging operations because of its close proximity to these towns. A small sawmill was established in Snowflake Camp by Willis and Jessup. ... Neil Mortensen and Neil Peterson settled on a wash, about one mile east of the modern town of Pinedale" that same year. (Though Mortensen may have spelled his name with a Danish "sen," the wash is usually known to us today as Mortenson Wash.) "Over the next two years other Mormon settlers established permanent homes in Snowflake Camp and a second sawmill was established by Jacob and Charles Brewer." The Mortenson settlement was also known as Percheron and later East Pinedale.

James Rush set up another sawmill, and marked out the four-block town center of Pinedale, according to *Elijah Was a Valiant Man*.

Pinedale, like the other Mormon communities, was isolated from markets in Utah and New Mexico, so the families tried to get by on subsistence agriculture. Sometimes it wasn't enough. "There were three methods of distributing food to needy people," according to Lightfoot. "Individual families who produced successful harvests shared their surplus with less fortunate families. The local Mormon church, organized and directed by the bishop, collected a tithe from the community in the form of various fruits, vegetables and livestock. While some foodstuffs were converted into cash and sent to Salt Lake City, other goods were retained in local tithing barns and distributed to the needy people of the community. People from a failing community could collectively ask for food from a more prosperous one. In 1880 supplies ran short in Snowflake and food was obtained from Sunset."

The Lakeside Barn, long a link to the community's agricultural roots, was built by Ed Reidhead around the turn of the 20th century. Charles L. Rhoton added the distinctive stone silo, which is all that now remains.

While Snowflake and Taylor eventually relied on irrigation, Pinedale had enough rain for dryland farming, raising corn, beans, squash, wheat, barley, potatoes, cane and fruit.

"The construction of dams and irrigation canals along Silver Creek began in 1878 and required several years to complete," Lightfoot writes. "During these years people from Taylor established small dry farms around Clay Springs and Pinedale. Until the irrigation system was in full production, these farms provided a supplemental, but necessary, source of food for the Taylor community."

Lightfoot says the non-irrigated or dry farms higher up the mountain required less work than the irrigated lands below, but were more often affected by killer frosts. "While crop failures occasionally occurred among both upland and lowland farmers, dry and wet years affected yields in each zone differentially, and failures rarely occurred in both areas in the same year," he wrote. "During those wet years when floods destroyed lowland irrigation works and fields, dry farmers in the upland zone often reported their highest yields. For example, after the destructive floods of 1890 and 1891 that swept away dams, canals and fields along Silver Creek and the Little Colorado River, only a handful of crops were planted by the irrigation communities. However, upland dry farmers reported excellent yields for both these years. ... Conversely, when dry years seriously reduced the yields of upland farmers, lowland communities produced very good crops." With all farmers giving a tenth of their crops to church tithing barns, the stake authorities could redistribute food to those in need. But it still didn't make the White Mountains a great agricultural area. Other parts of the country offered farmers the promise of a crop every year, while the White Mountains had droughts in 1885-1887, 1891-1894, 1899-1900 and 1902-1905. Meanwhile destructive frosts were reported in 1880, 1882, 1884, 1885, 1886, 1893, 1895, 1896, 1897, 1898, 1899, 1901, 1903, 1904 and 1905.

Although the tithing system helped many, it also increased the power of Mormon leaders. "Those individuals who were in poor standing with the church or were creating problems for local leaders often did not receive loans of food," Lightfoot wrote.

The archaeologist, who examined the development of the Mormon communities closely in hopes of understanding population shifts of pre-historic Indian inhabitants of the area, said upland farmers were treated as second class citizens while the irrigated lands became concentrated in the hands of a few prominent Mormon families.

The settlers also raised cattle, sheep and chickens. "A few enterprising people, such as Neils Mortensen and Neils Peterson, did earn some cash by transporting butter, cheese, eggs and vegetables to Fort Apache and Albuquerque," Lightfoot wrote. But he added that it took five days to freight goods to even the closest market, Fort Apache, so the number of trips a farmer could make was limited.

"The population of Pinedale increased from a few families in 1880 to 34 families (202 people) in 1900," about the maximum the agricultural land in the area could support, Lightfoot said.

Palmer seems to agree that Pinedale was full, noting the Reuben Perkins family left Pinedale and homesteaded in the vicinity of present-day Clay Springs.

A small party of Utah Mormons arrived in the White Mountains on the last day of 1878. They founded the community of Adair, three miles northwest of Cooley's ranch. (It is under Fool Hollow Lake today, according to a television program created by Richard Lynch.) "For Thomas [Jefferson Adair] and his wife, both over 60 years old, the trip proved to be a long one," according to *Adair, Arizona – A Brief History* by Kay L. Read. They traveled with the family of William L. Penrod and were soon joined by 12 other families.

"The community was comprised of dry farmers who raised corn, sugar cane and vegetables," the book says. "Some men also freighted supplies from the nearest train depot in Holbrook to the soldiers in Fort Apache." While the men were away, the women "would take care of the livestock and the crops in addition to their daily chores."

A building measuring 16 ½ feet by 20 feet served as the school, community center and church. Read said the early settlers did the teaching until 1892 when a school district was formed which brought in outside teachers, who boarded with the settlers. "Most of the settlers had built one or two room log cabins for their families," Read said. She quoted Lydia Emma Whipple Hansen: "It was a humble home and just the necessary furnishings such as beds, chair, tables, cupboards."

The settlers often feared Indian uprisings. In 1881, they built a temporary fort on the hill in Show Low by Cooley's home.

"We kept our families and supplies behind this fort for two months, someone on guard day and night," Hans Hansen Jr. is recorded as saying. "For amusement at the fort we danced most every night. John Whitton played the violin and a couple of boys played the accordion. Cooley's men did scouting and saw Geronimo's men occasionally but we were never molested."

"In 1882, Edson Whipple and his family built a large block building [in Adair] with port holes for future protection against the Indians and white desperados," Read said. "People began to call this Fort Whipple and used it during Indian scares."

Adair was a stopping point for Hans Hansen Jr., later one of the founders of Lakeside. At age 17, he was left in Arizona to care for the cattle while his father returned to Utah on business.

"We took our corn down to Willis Ranch on Show Low Creek and used their little mill to grind it into meal," he told his niece Anna Jackson, in a taped interview published in *A Tribute to the Lakeside Pioneers*. "This we used for bread and cereals. For dessert we had a piece of white bread and molasses or preserves with a pan of milk with the cream stirred in. We had very little fruit. Johnny Fipps peddled it occasionally, an apple or an orange for ten cents apiece. Our supplies came from Albuquerque by ox team. Flour was scarce, impossible to get here for years. I well remember the first white flour that came in. Once I went to St. Johns by team and wagon for flour, but could find none … so I went on to Springerville and was able to buy flour for $14 a hundred and cornmeal for $8 a hundred. I got a hundred pounds of each. Although I had money enough, there was no more to be had."

The Hansens made do with what they could find. "We used 'oose' (yucca) for soap," he said in a recorded interview published in *A Tribute to the Lakeside Pioneers.* "With oose and sand our floors were kept polished and our cupboards clean. We had factory (cloth) over the windows and this gave us very little light."

The Hansens were masons. They built most of the brick buildings in Snowflake, and some of the first in Mesa. "We were the originators of the native cement. We took native clay and burned it. Our first experiment was unsuccessful. It would set so quick that we couldn't use it. By continuing to experiment we made a cement that would stand. After forty years you can hardly get it off with a pick. Our kiln still stands in Fool Hollow." They later ground and burned rock from ledges to make plaster, which they used on the walls of the officer's quarters at Fort Apache.

Adair, or Fool Hollow as it was also called, was a big enough settlement to have a post office and government mail route from Holbrook. Locy Rogers had the contract, and according to *Arizona Was the West* by Jennings, Rogers would sometimes have to lead his team through the snow in the dark, feeling for the ruts of the road with his feet. "He would arrive at the station chilled to the bone, then lie down for an hour, in a cold bed, before starting back for Holbrook." Trying to live up to the spirit of the poem about rain, sleet nor snow was hard on Rogers and his sons, Alvirus (Bige) and Chase, who helped him. When 13-year-old Bige "came to the Lone Pine crossing on Show Low Creek, Bige found it at flood stage. But the mail must go. He unhitched one of the horses and rode it across the stream to see if it was safe for the buckboard. It seemed safe enough and he hitched up the team and started across. However, he overlooked one thing. The stream was rising rapidly. The team, buckboard and mail went with the flood and the horses were drowned. He barely escaped with his life. The mail was later retrieved." His brother, Chase, had a similar experience at Bagnal Hollow, losing the horses but saving the mail.

The community of Lone Pine, just south of the present dam, has a longer history, according to an account by Emma Hansen Adams. It was first settled by Hispanics, who had a dam and an irrigated farm before Cooley settled Show Low. After a flood washed the dam away and the Hispanic settlers abandoned the area, the site was owned by a man named Wolf. In 1878, he sold it to John Reidhead, who settled the area with nine families. It was also called Reidhead or Wolf's Ranch. The Willis Ranch was south of Lone Pine on the creek. Bagnal Hollow was about a mile northwest of Adair. It was settled by George Bagnal in 1880. He had a store and shoe repair shop, bringing in goods by mule from Albuquerque until the railroad was built to Holbrook, according to the Adams account.

"Pinetop's first resident was one Johnny Fipps (or Phipps) who is mentioned in diaries and sketches," wrote Leora Peterson Schuck in *A Tribute to the Lakeside Pioneers.* "Mrs. Annie Penrod states in her account of William Penrod's life that Fipps was the only person living at what is now Pinetop when Penrod arrived there in 1887." Fipps owned a saloon that catered to the soldiers from Fort Apache.

William L. Penrod and his family moved from Adair to Juniper (Linden), and then back to Utah. Returning to Arizona, he began to look higher up in the White Mountains. "This is when he discovered the beautiful meadow at Pinetop with streams running through it," said Schuck. In 1887, they moved to the new home, living in a wagon box and camping out. ... [They] cut logs and built a one-room cabin which took about 10 days." Soon, seven of Penrod's married children had homes close to their father in the new community near the boundary of the reservation.

"A part of the homestead of William Lewis Penrod alongside the traveled road was developed into a settlement," the Cooley biography says. "The name Pinetop became a designation used by the Negro troopers at the fort who requested passes to go to the top of the pines (mountain summit); also the troopers called the red-headed bartender at the saloon 'Pinetop.'"

A manuscript from the Penrod family gives a little more detail. "A man by the name of Johnny Phipps (a bachelor) had a

185

little two room log house where he sold whiskey to the soldiers from Fort Apache, which was the colored troops at that time. In the summer of 1890, Johnny Phipps died and is buried under a peach tree by his home. A man by the name of Walt Rigney, an Irishman, took over the saloon which Phipps left and the colored boys got to calling the place Pinetop, and the owner of the saloon (Walt Rigney) was also called Pinetop, which name he went by until he left there. And when the little burg got a Post Office, it was given the name Pinetop."

In *Top O' The Pines*, Gene Luptak said the town was briefly called "Mal Pai," but renamed Pinetop when the Mormons objected to establishing the first post office in Phipps' saloon.

"After the Penrods came, someone suggested they name the town Penrod, but Grandfather William said no, he liked the name of Pinetop and that is what they would continue to call it," Mrs. Schuck wrote.

"The first merchant was Sylvester McCoy," the Penrod manuscript says. "He had a small one room building which was a Post Office, dry goods and grocery store all in one."

Another unsigned manuscript from the Larson Memorial Library in Lakeside says Rhone Adair had holdings at the spring, which bears his name.

Early Mormons moved often. "Although land comprised an important element in the Mormon value system and was the basis of a colony's existence, its hold upon individuals was generally not great," wrote author Charles S. Peterson. In *Take Up Your Mission*, he said, "As newcomers to the region their sentimental attachments were not yet deeply seated, and allegiance could be and was, shifted with surprising frequency. ... Unfettered by large investment or success, it was easy to look beyond the next hill."

In the late 1880s, Mormons were settling in the Lakeside area. In 1888, "Niels Hansen, John L. Fish with Dick Hansen, Phile Kay and at least one boy, Karl J. Fish, sat beside a bubbling spring located just west of where the old ranger station later stood, ate lunch and rested," says a document from the Lakeside Library. The unknown author adds, "While they rested, they discussed pro and con the locality's possibilities. It was at this time Niels S. Hansen proposed out the town's name and five tin cups were dipped into the clear cold spring water and each drank from the cup. The rest of the water was splattered upon the ground and a town was christened. ... The settlement of Milltown (located across Billy Creek behind the present Blue Ridge school) was also a fast growing community as was Woodland where the Hansen and West families were living."

To the west, Mormons, having given up on the original Little Colorado settlements, were taking up farming just above the Mogollon Rim. "Each group from the Little Colorado had their own place in the Black Canyon," says *The Crooked Trail to Holbrook* by Hanchett. "Brigham City's was at Adam's Valley, Sunset's was at the Forks and St. Joseph's was at what is now Heber. In addition, Sunset had a camp at Ajelon in Chevelon Canyon. ... Adams's Valley was set aside as a ward with Heber as a branch. The ward was to be called Wilford."

John Bushman, a settler from the Little Colorado, headed south on November 4, 1882, and found the valley where Heber is now located. "I made a location here by writing on a newspaper and fastening it to a tree," says his journal, quoted in *The Crooked Trail to Holbrook*. He returned to the site on December 6, 1882, bringing with him six other Mormon men, who began to dig wells. Lot Smith, president of the Little Colorado Stake, encouraged settlers to move from the Little Colorado to the Mogollon Rim. "I think most of the folks will move there," he said.

During the summer, the settlers built homes, cleared land, planted crops and constructed corrals. They had some success with their crops despite the frost that can come as late as June and begin again in September. Though Bushman never actually lived in Heber, some of the other families stayed. The *Crooked Trail* book gives much credit to James and Margaret Shelley as being early pioneers who stayed in the community. Ironically, in the Heber area, the Penrods were among the anti-Mormon faction, while a Mormon family with the same name founded Pinetop.

Living near the Tonto Basin put residents of Heber near outlaws and their violence. The Mormons tell a story about several cowboys being denied entrance to a Heber dance. Jennings in *Arizona Was the West* said, "Three days later, and well filled with John Barleycorn, the party passed through Heber again, on

187

the return trip from Holbrook to Pleasant Valley. But this time, their interest was not social. The hour was midnight, and all lights were out. With glee, they riddled the public building with bullets until it was almost in shambles."

The large number of Saints settling in Arizona created a backflow of Mormons headed to Utah. Some had given up. Others sought to trade with more established towns farther north. And many took to the "Honeymoon Trial" to be married in the temple in St. George, constructed in 1877 just north of the Utah territorial line.

The route, as described in *Arizona's Honeymoon Trail and Mormon Wagon Roads*, had branches originating in Phoenix, New Mexico and Old Mexico. All the branches wound through communities of the White Mountains before fording the Little Colorado at Sunset Crossing near present-day Winslow. From there, they headed up to Lee's Ferry and St. George, Utah.

Not only was the southwest Utah temple "convenient" to Arizona, but it was the only Latter-day Saints temple at the time. The one in Salt Lake City was not dedicated until 1893. And Arizona didn't get a temple until 1927 when one was built in Mesa.

Mormons traveling the Honeymoon Trail usually used "farm wagons that could be spared from farm or ranch work, pulled by a team of strong horses or oxen," the book says. "Wagons were loaded with food in grub boxes, consisting of dried beef, hard biscuits, dried fruit, tins of molasses, wheat flour, and beans. Water barrels were placed on the outside of the wagon. They also carried grain and hay for the animals." Holding a civil ceremony before taking to the trail lightened the load by one or more chaperones.

"Alof Larson and May Louise Hunt, daughter of Bishop John Hunt, were the first young couple from Snowflake to go north to the Utah temple as far as can be determined," the book says. He was elected captain of a company of five wagons making the trip. They were joined near Winslow by Stake President Jesse N. Smith, who wrote that he asked his son "to bring my team along and a young woman named Emma Larson." She was Alof's sister and was to become Smith's fifth wife. Alof and May Louise got soaked in the hard rain because the wagon cover was not tight, and slept little. It took them 20 days to get to St. George, with Smith noting in his diary that it was a very pleasant and successful journey without special incident. The young couple had a few days to enjoy civilization before their wedding day, taking the opportunity to bathe in a big porcelain tub for the first time.

Mormon Conflict With Apaches

When hostile Apaches were brought to the nearby reservation conflicts arose with the pacified White Mountain bands. Whites became fearful and violence occasionally broke out.

In *Arizona Was the West*, Jennings recounts how early settler John Hatch discovered a massacre while driving cattle from the White Mountains to Graham County. "Two or three families, men, women and children, driving their teams and wagons over the mountains, had been set upon by Apaches and killed," the book says. Hatch buried the victims.

But it was the Robinson incident that most clearly brought the horrors home to the White Mountains. The Snowflake Stake history puts the date at June 1, 1882.

"Nathan Robinson had a ranch a short distance below Lone Pine, sometimes referred to as Reidhead Crossing, about half-way between Taylor and Show Low," Jennings wrote.

The Robinsons were having hard times. "My husband got a contract with John A. West to work on the railroad in the San Francisco mountains," Annise Robinson is quoted as saying. "I went along and cooked for fifty men for six months, doing all the work except washing the dishes. I took suddenly ill and was in danger of losing my baby, so my husband took me home to his sister (Mary Jane West) in Snowflake. Then he went back to work. I was expecting my baby in a month when I became very ill, so his sister sent for him. I started flowing: they got a blind woman (Abbie Thayne) to help me and finally stopped the blood. ... Two weeks later my husband, feeling worried, returned home. He went out to find a cow, and as he rode down over the hill and down to Show Low Creek to find the cow's tracks as she came to water, he saw some Indians killing a beef."

An account by Ann Lewis in the Taylor Stake history says the cow had just calved and he wanted the milk for his family.

Mrs. Robinson's account says the Indians "were hidden in a clump of cedars and saw [him] pass by on his way down to the creek. They shot him, fearing he would go and tell on them. Five shots were fired into his body. The Indians stripped him of all his clothes except his [special Mormon under] garments, and then they felt very sorry because he was a Mormon. They threw his body in the creek and threw rocks as big as they could carry on him."

"When he did not return we were much alarmed," Mrs. Robinson said. "I walked the dooryard until late at night with my little children. At midnight I heard the whinny of a horse. It was Nathan's horse with an Indian's lariat on him. I awakened my boy Nathan to help me hook the horses to the wagon. I put the children in the wagon and we went" to John Reidhead's barn in Lone Pine where other settlers were gathered to protect against Indian attack.

The Taylor Stake history says, "Sister Robinson just knew he had been killed by the Indians. Sister Lucinda Reidhead stood all night with a gun stuck through a knothole in the barn while Jane (Standifird) sat and held her baby, Charlie, on her lap. The next day a little old blind lady [Abbie Thayne] they had all forgotten about, who lived down Show Low Creek some distance, found her way to the gathering and declared that Indians had made a crossing not too far from her cabin during the night."

Ann Adams Watts remembered forting up as a child in Edson Whipple's barn. "This fort was a large log hall big enough to dance eight sets of quadrille in. There were eight government stoves in it and when our beds were made out they almost touched each other. ... We stayed at the fort a week."

"Merlin Plumb was shot at by Indians while looking along Silver Creek for stray oxen," the Snowflake Stake history says. "Although his horse was wounded he managed to escape to his home at Walnut Springs (Lovelake) and then sent word to Taylor. Immediately the word was relayed to Snowflake and men were sent out to warn the settlers in the surrounding areas, the sheep camps, lumber mills and small ranches."

Joe Kay, a member of the Taylor militia, initially rode out with the men, but volunteered to go back to town with 17-year-old Edwin Solomon to tell the citizens where the militia would be camped for the night. Along the way, Kay stopped for a drink at Show Low Creek. "He started to drink but quickly raised up saying, 'For Heaven's sake, Ed, come and see what's in the water!'" according to an account by Bert Solomon published in the Taylor Stake history. "My father walked over to the edge of the pool and looking into the clear deep water he could see the bare leg of a man sticking out from under a huge rock. Brother Kay took off his clothes and waded into the pool, removed the rock from the man's body and it floated to the surface. They didn't know that anyone had been killed so had merely stumbled onto the body."

Kay and Solomon were joined a short time later by a man who had been looking for the missing Robinson. Other accounts say the searchers found Robinson's body.

Mrs. Robinson never got to see her home again after she fled with her children. The Indians burned it before she returned.

The Snowflake Stake history gives the Robinson murder as a cause for the Mormons' decision to withdraw from Forestdale on the reservation.

The Cibecue Uprising created panic when the killing of an important medicine man was followed by a battle between Apaches and soldiers, and a breakout by many renegades. After a telegram about the uprising reached Globe, George Turner left on horseback to warn the Middleton family at the Q Ranch, just west of the reservation, according to *The Crooked Trail to Holbrook*. Turner spent the first night at a ranch along the way where he was joined by another young man, Henry Moody. They reached the Middleton ranch, about 30 miles from Cibecue Creek, the next day. Hattie Middleton Allison, then about 16, remembered that frightening time. She is quoted in the book as saying, "Some of this same band of Apaches who were in the fight came on over to our ranch reaching there about noon on the day Turner and Moody came."

At first, the Indians pretended to be friendly, asking for food, and hanging around until 3 p.m. when they began shooting. "Moody and Turner were killed instantly, each being shot twice.

The bullet that struck Moody in the temple first cut off a lock of hair on my forehead just grazing my head," she said.

Her brother shot two Indians and was wounded in the shoulder. As the family barricaded themselves in the house, the Apaches stole all 75 of the ranch's horses. When the Indians were gone, the family hid in the woods while Mr. Middleton started to walk to Pleasant Valley to get help. When he met Indians on the way, he was forced to turn back after enlisting only one old man. The two men avoided using trails. They headed overland toward Sombrero Butte, which they could see 20 miles in the distance. Eventually, they met a rescue party led by Hattie's brother Eugene.

Many settlers had stories about encounters with the Indians, but few topped the one told by Anna Christina Hansen and written by her son, Sanford Warren Jaques. "The McNeils moved to the Ellsworth Ranch on Show Low Creek. The Indians had a drunken brawl and gun fight. Their war Chief Petone was killed, his brother Alchesay was shot through the lung and their peace chief Pedro was shot through the knee while lying in his wickiup. … Alchesay recovered and was Chief of the tribe for many years. A squaw came down the hill and left her baby in the McNeil house. During the fracas some stray bullets came near the homes of the white settlers. As one whizzed near Little Eph McNeil's head he ran into the house screaming, 'I'm shot, I'm shot.' When the fight was over some of the Indians came and asked Edmund Ellsworth and John McNeil if they would come up to the camp and bring 'Mormon medicine.' "

H. B. Wharfield wrote about the same incident in *Apache Indian Scouts*. "During a tulapai drinking spree at Petone's camp south of Show Low the two got into a drunken brawl over a card game of monte. They started pummeling each other and tearing out hair, which caused intoxicated followers of both men to join the melee. It ended in a general gun fight with the two principals shooting each other through the body. Petone was killed as well as several others, but Alchesay was only badly wounded."

The account of David Adams, a Mormon settler who passed the camp, is included in Wharfield's book: "From a distance he noticed that the Indians were behind rocks and armed; some were reeling around drunk. The appearances showed that a tulapai drinking affair had taken place; and a drunken brawl was in progress. Around the wickiups the brush and grass were tramped down, hair scattered around as though mules had been roached, some bodies lay on the ground.

"Pedro, Molly's father, in trying to stop the drunken brawl, was shot in the knee. Using good judgment, Adams withdrew from the place and lit out on a run for his cabin."

Mrs. Hansen told about another scare in the Show Low Stake history.

"Rumors came to the settlers at Show Low that Geronimo and his renegade band was coming to that area. They made a lumber enclosure around Corydon E. Cooley's home on the hill and moved their families inside."

The book says, "The Indians failed to appear at this particular time and at no time did Show Low suffer an all out raid, but the stockade provided refuge and comfort for the surrounding settlers for a long time."

The Cibecue Uprising

People stressed by changes beyond their control, as Native Americans were after European contact, often turn to religion. "When the race lies crushed and groaning beneath an alien yoke, how natural is the dream of a redeemer, an Arthur, who shall return from exile or awake from some long sleep to drive out the usurper and win back for his people what they have lost," wrote James Mooney in *The Ghost Dance*.

Revival movements have repeatedly swept through Indian societies. At least four of them began with Western Apaches. The first preceded the famous Sun Dance, which swept throughout the Native American world. That first Apache movement was started by Noche'Del'Klinne, who predicted that the whites would soon be driven from the land. He held his unique dances near the village of Cibecue on the western edge of the reservation. The "performers were ranged like the spokes of a wheel, all facing inward, while he, standing in the center, sprinkled them with the sacred [pollen] as they circled around him," Mooney wrote.

193

The Cibecue medicine man promised to bring Apache chiefs Diablo and Eskiole back from the dead if his followers gave him horses and blankets. The growing influence of Noche'Del'Klinne among the already dissatisfied reservation Indians worried the whites. Scouts Sieber, Horn and Free went to talk to Pedro, the old White Mountain Apache chief, about the trouble they were expecting to have from the prophet's followers.

"I will give you 150 warriors, all good, picked men," Pedro said, "and you can go over there and kill a good many of them, and then come back and rest up a while, then go back and kill some more, and keep that up the rest of the summer. By winter time there will still be trouble, but there will not be so many mean Indians to help out with it."

"Both of you are well acquainted with both soldiers and renegade Indians, and you know that while your white soldiers are without fear, they can never meet the Apaches in battle where the white soldiers will have a chance," Pedro continued. "Brave though your soldiers may be, you must remember that while the Indians are renegades and outlaws, they also are brave as any, and perfectly well acquainted with all the country, and can live like the wolf and evade the white soldier, who has never had such training as the Indians. ... I have fought the white soldiers many a times, and I know just how they act in battle and on the trail, and I am better able to give you truth than any other man you can find, be he white or red. I cannot read in books, and I cannot write on paper, but I can look at the forest, and the mountains, and on the ground, and I can read every sign there. I can look at the action of a bad Indian, and can tell how he feels and what he will do. ... There is going to be a great lot of war, of which this last outbreak is the starter, and it will continue for many years. Apache soldiers you will have to use, for, as brave as your white soldiers are, they can not endure the hardships necessary to overcome the bad Apaches.

"Those Cibecue Indians will break out soon and they will have to go north to the Mogollons, as they are not Mexico Indians. So it will be war on the south from the Chiricahuas, and war in the north from the Cibecues, and many a white settler and traveler will be killed. Take my advice and my warriors and go at it at once."

Those, of course, were not Pedro's exact words because Horn wasn't taking notes at the time and wrote his autobiography many years later while sitting in a Wyoming jail waiting to be hanged. And, of course, even then ghost writers were available to add a little polish to an Indian chief's speech before it got into print. But Horn knew Pedro and had undoubtedly talked to him about the feelings the White Mountain Apache chief had toward the Chiricahua and Cibecues.

Sieber and Horn returned to the fort.

Bad feelings between the Chiricahua and White Mountain Apaches were running high in 1881. As Wharfield explained: "A band of San Carlos Indians moved into the upper Forestdale Creek area and caused trouble with the White Mountain Apache. They were of the Chiricahua people, somewhat distrusted by the local Apache, and started to encroach on the planted tracts of corn. Soon the peace of the area was disturbed and bloodshed threatened. Word reached Fort Apache and troops hurried to the scene. They rounded up the intruders and removed them back to their own regions."

Noche'Del'Klinne was familiar with white people. He had been an enlisted scout in early campaigns. Wharfield said the medicine man had been to Washington for a visit with President Grant and briefly attended an Indian school at Santa Fe.

As Noche'Del'Klinne led his dances in 1881, scouts reported on developments at the dances and soldiers were sent to ask the medicine man to come to Fort Apache.

"Though angered by the message, the old man agreed to come in two days," Edward S. Curtis said in his Twenty Volume *North American Indian* published only 25 years after the event.

Accounts differ on how the medicine man changed his prophecy after that interruption. Wharfield said Noche'Del'Klinne announced that the dead chiefs would not return until after the whites left, but predicted the intruders would be gone before the corn harvest. Curtis said Noche'Del'Klinne "then explained to his people that, owing to the interruption by the whites, it was probable that the bones would not come to life at the end of four days, as predicted, but that he would make a new dance later and prove the efficacy of his creed."

The medicine man headed to the Fort with his entire band

195

of 62 dancers, stopping to dance along the way. They camped near the fort, waiting to be interviewed by the agent. When he did not send for them, the Indians spent several days walking back to Cibecue, stopping to dance along the way.

"As soon as the band had reached its destination, another summons was delivered ... to appear before the agent at the fort," Curtis said. "This time the old man sent back word that he would not come; he had gone once, and if any had wished to see him, they had had their chance." That was not acceptable to the army. After the adjutant sent for Sieber to go to Cibecue, the head scout found Horn and Free.

Horn quoted Sieber as saying: "I am ordered to take you two boys and go with a detachment of soldiers to Canyon Creek, and from there to Cibecue and see these Indians and arrest five of them who are making all this trouble, as the adjutant says, and we are to take a lot of those same Indians with us to show us who these Indians are. We are to arrest them and confine them here in the guard house."

"Dead Shot and Dandy Jim are both sergeants of the scouts and they will show us the men we are to arrest," Sieber said. "There will be a detachment of about twenty men to go with us. Now, those are my instructions."

Horn and Free thought that was a bad plan. "Dead Shot and Dandy Jim were two of the worst of all the bad men, they were capable of doing anything bad and nothing good," Horn said.

"There will be men [who] leave this post in the morning who will either be brought back dead, or else will be left dead in the mountains," said Free, "for this is a trap that we are going into, and they will try hardest to kill us three, for they think we have no business to come up here and interfere with them."

"Mickey suggested that after we got started he would look after Dead Shot, and for me to look after Dandy Jim," Horn recalled.

"We will civilize them," said Mickey.

"Those Indians are not bad, and are not renegades," Horn quoted Dead Shot as telling the adjutant. "They will all help the soldiers to arrest these bad men, and it is a good thing to send the white scouts, for they tell lies on all of us; and when they see how things are out there, they will have nothing to say."

The soldiers headed out and camped the first night at Canyon Creek. A young girl, the daughter of a Mexican who had lived with the Apaches since being captured as a child, came to Horn during the night to warn him.

"She told me she was sent by her father, who was Suneriano, to tell me that we would all be killed on Cibecue Creek; that there was a trap laid for us, and that Dead Shot was going to lead us into it," Horn said. "She said all the women and children were up in the mountains, and we would find only warriors."

Sieber warned the leader of the group, but Captain Edmund C. "Hentig told Sieber that if he was afraid he could take his two men, meaning Mickey and me, and go back to Camp Apache," Horn said. Sieber decided the scouts would accompany the soldiers.

When they arrived at Cibecue and found no Indians, Dead Shot suggested they continue down the creek. Remembering that Dead Shot was once accused of stealing moccasins from a woman, Mickey told him: "Dead Shot, we are on to your game and I am going to stay close to you all the time, and if anything goes wrong you will be stealing moccasins in the camp of the Great Spirit just as soon as the fight comes off."

A battle looks different to people who see it from different locations, not only because they see different things, but because their view is colored by whom they were trying to kill and who was trying to kill them. As Horn was indifferent to spiritual practices of anyone he considered a bad Indian, he didn't understand the religious reasons for the Cibecue Uprising. Dead Shot and Dandy Jim are considered to be heroes by many Apaches, including their descendants.

Curtis gave this account: "Early in the morning the soldiers reached the Cibecue at a point about two miles above (the medicine man's) camp, whence a detachment was dispatched to arrest the medicine-man and bring him to the place where headquarters were being established. It was the intention merely to arrest and hold him while the troops rested for the day, preparatory to taking him back to the fort; but it was deemed necessary to send a force sufficiently large to cope with the Indians should they attempt resistance."

In Apache stories of the uprising, the bodies of the dead

chiefs were beginning to move under a blanket just as the soldiers arrested the medicine man.

"(The old man) yielded without hesitation to the demands of the soldiers, and forthwith rode up to headquarters," Curtis wrote. "Everything seemed very quiet. There was no demonstration against the soldiers, who stacked their arms and unloaded their pack-trains. The mules were hobbled and turned loose, and the cavalry horses tethered and fed.

"While this apparently peaceful condition prevailed, a brother of the medicine-man, angered because of the arrest, dashed into camp on a pony and shot and killed the captain in command. Instantly, hardly realizing whence the shot had come, one of the troopers struck (the old man) on the head with a cudgel, killing him. Assured that a fight was imminent, the soldiers receded to higher ground, a short distance back, where they hurriedly made preparations for defense.

"On learning that (the medicine man) had been killed, and deeming the soldiers wholly to blame, a small party of Apache attacked the troopers ... . Six of the soldiers were killed, the mules stampeded, and the provisions burned, all within a short space of time. The hostiles made their escape, practically all of them leaving the valley."

"Dead Shot and Dandy Jim being in front of the soldiers while Mickey and I were behind, they both made a run and got away as soon as the firing started," Horn reported. "About 10 minutes after the fight started, Captain Hentig was killed. There were eleven men wounded in the fight, but none badly." Horn went on to claim that he had saved the command by beating the renegades to the high ground overlooking the area.

Indians remembered the Cibecue fight differently. They said that the Apaches who were at the dance followed the soldiers and surrounded them as they made camp for the night. "Suddenly a shot was fired — then many," said Asa Daklugie in an interview quoted by Eve Ball in *An Apache Odyssey: Indeh.* "My father did not know who fired the first shot, but once the fight started, the Apaches got into it. Men were killed on both sides ... when the wounded Noche'Del'Klinne got up on hands and knees and tried to crawl to his wife's body, a solder killed him with an ax."

Mike Burns, the Indian boy raised by a cavalry officer, gave this account:

"When the soldiers reached the camp they went right through to the great wigwam where the medicine man and the singer were seated. This great wigwam had four entrances or doors where the dancers came through, and went out, until they had come through all the four entrances. The medicine man was dressed in eagle feathers, and his body was painted with all kinds of paints, and as was also the man who sang for the dancers. Most of the Indian men left the wigwam, and got their guns, and went up on the foothills, the women and children having gone up farther on the tops of the hills. No one was left in the medicine lodge but the great medicine man, and when the soldiers came there they took him over to the camp. He had warned the young men not to shoot any of the soldiers, saying that if they took him away they would only put him in the guardhouse for a few months or a year, and he would not be killed because he had not done any wrong. He was taken by the soldiers and a guard put over him, and while he was seated on a rock some of the young Indians tried to get close enough to him to speak to him, but the soldiers pulled out their guns and pistols and drove the young men back three times. The fourth time the Indians were mad, and came right down, not minding the threats of the soldiers, and shot down all the soldiers who were there and then they ran off to the hills. The medicine man was still sitting on the rock with his wife and child, but when his wife tried to get him to go away over the hills to where the rest had gone, he told her to go alone; that there was no use for him to go anywhere after there had been so much killing on his account, as they would kill him no matter where he went, and it was just as well for him to meet his fate where he was. Just then one of the soldiers who had hidden among some saddles came out, pulled out his pistol and shot the medicine man through the head while his wife had her arm around him."

There was trouble at the fort on the following day. Daklugie said, "My father learned later that (Col. Eugene) Carr reported an attack on Fort Apache the next day. If so, it was done by somebody other than our forces. Any sniper could have fired into that fort because it was not walled."

199

A historic trading post in Forestdale where Mormons tried to settle on the Apache Reservation.

Horn said the hostiles fired into the Fort for about an hour before the soldiers drove them off, but others remember a shorter attack.

In the confusion of the Cibecue Uprising, Apaches under Nana, Loco, Naiche, Chato and Geronimo left the reservation to raid on both sides of the Mexican border.

The outbreak sent shivers through Show Low. "The settlers heard rumors of an outbreak among the hitherto peaceful bands and that Geronimo was coming into the Show Low area on a raid," Wharfield wrote in his Cooley biography. "The Indians disappeared from their usual haunts, scattering into the mountains. Even Cooley became concerned, and likely lost contact with Molly's people. He gathered the few local settlers to camp at his home, and had a log fort built around some of the buildings. Also a few miles up the mountain at the Penrod settlement (Pinetop), the Mormons constructed a fort around the Hansen home for protection. The Indian scare lasted for some time, and not until word arrived that Geronimo had gone south did the settlers regain confidence. Talk that the Arizona authorities were demanding the return of General Crook was a deciding factor in quieting the fears of the whites."

The Cibecue Uprising ended Mormon attempts to settle Forestdale. Though the original settlers left after being told that they were on the reservation, a second group from the failing Little Colorado colony of Brigham City had decided to settle there any-

200

way. The Indians were displeased when they returned to their summer farms and found whites settling on reservation land in the Forestdale Valley. And "in the inevitable conflict — hostility between Anglos and Apache had recently increased during the Cibecue outbreak of 1881 — several Mormons were put to death on their ranches," McGuire said. Taking the advice of the Church hierarchy and the army command at Fort Apache, the Mormons left the area.

Telegrams were sent to other forts, and Horn went to get 60 volunteers from Pedro's band. Soon the scouts were sent after a group of Cibecue hostiles, who, just as Pedro had predicted, headed west and north rather than to Mexico.

Horn tracked the Indians toward the Tonto Basin. "I found they had taken a lot of horses from old man Tewksbury and a lot from Al Rose," he said. "About 10 miles farther on I found they had killed Louie Huron and Charley Sigsbee. All of the settlers thereabout had joined me. I left them to bury the dead men and look after one of the Sigsbee boys who had been wounded, and who had killed one of the renegades after he was shot."

Horn and his men camped and were joined by Sieber, Major Chaffee, some soldiers and another man named Pat Kehoe.

The next morning they had gone only 10 miles before they discovered the place where the hostiles had spent the previous night. When the men came to the Meadows Ranch on the east fork of the Verde, they found "old man Meadows killed, Hank shot all to pieces, and John also badly shot up." They left some soldiers and civilians to help the wounded, and rode on after the hostiles.

When Horn's group reached the Mogollon Rim they ran into a rear guard and killed one Indian and wounded another, chasing him to a place called Crook's Springs. "He soon died," Horn said.

A man named Tul-pi, who was leading the White Mountain Apache volunteers, said they would probably be able to catch the hostiles as they crossed Chevelon Canyon, which "could be crossed in but a few places on account of its depth and the precipitous nature of its walls."

"As we came to the banks of the canyon the renegades were just starting up on the opposite side," Horn said. "We opened fire on them, of course. About half way up the side of the canyon, on the opposite side, the trail would have to run around on a wide bench for a ways to find an opening in the bench to allow them to pass through. Then there would be a place in the trail leading straight away from us. The distance was just about six hundred yards, and when they came to a place that led straight away from us it made fine shooting. Going up over the last rim was a place about sixty feet long, and no one could get out of the canyon without going through this place. ...

"Not a horse ever did get up that place. There were three started up at first, and the one in the lead was a gray. I suppose we all thought the same thing, and that was if we could hit the lead horse he would fall back on the others and knock them down like tenpins. We all fired at the gray horse and down he came, struggling, and back he knocked the two behind him.

" 'Go to work, men!' cried Major Chaffee. 'Keep that hole stopped and we have got 'em.' He did not use just those words, for Chaffee, in a fight, can beat any man swearing I ever heard. He swears by ear, and by note in a common way, and by everything else in a general way."

The hostiles turned their attention to the dead gray horse. "Several renegades tried to get him out of the way, but it was an awful place to work to much advantage, for we were all good shots, and while the distance was close to six hundred yards, we had the range down so fine, and we were perhaps 50 feet above them, so that for that distance the spot for us was ideal. After they saw they could not get the gray horse away from the place where he had fallen, another tried to lead his horse over the gray one, and down that horse went; not on top of the gray, but nearly so, and that blocked the trail completely. No more horses tried to go through, but several Indians ran up on foot."

A sudden rain and hail storm ended the engagement.

The next day the soldiers crossed the canyon. The soldiers and scouts had killed or wounded nearly 80 of the hostiles' 100 horses. "We found 21 dead Indians, and one wounded squaw," Horn said. "Some of the soldiers afterwards said there were a couple of wounded bucks, but that Mickey had stuck his knife into them. ... I don't know if Mickey did this deed or not; but I am afraid he did.

"A squaw had been shot on the shin bone by a Springfield rifle ball, and the bone was of course shattered in a thousand pieces. The soldiers, some of them, ran onto her, and were getting ready to carry her back to camp, under the direction of the army surgeon; when they were all ready to start with her she began to scream and motion, and kept pointing to a pile of rocks and brush, and one of the soldiers looked to see what there was there that she was making so much fuss about, as they could not understand what she was saying. The soldier found a little old papoose, about 10 months or a year old, concealed under that rubbish. One of the men carried it along over to camp. There the surgeons cut her leg off, and she was sent into Camp Verde along with a few wounded soldiers we had."

"The wounded squaw told Tul-pi that there had been about 45 warriors in the party, and she thought most of them were killed," Horn said. "She said they all knew that a lot of Pedro's warriors were with the soldiers, and they were all very mad because Pedro would send his men out after them."

The hail storm had washed out all tracks and after staying in the area for a while, the soldiers went back to their posts and Horn disbanded his volunteers. "The scattered renegades had all returned to Cibecue and Canyon Creek and were hiding among the other Indians," Horn said.

"A few of the outlaw Apache during the next month camped in the mountains near the fort," Wharfield wrote. "Signs of them were discovered, and on August 15 a detachment of scouts had a skirmish with the hostiles. All scattered and left the country."

"The commanding officer at Camp Apache wanted to get the rest of the Indians who had mutinied when Hentig was killed, and asked me to go and see if I could do anything toward catching them," Horn said. "I sent a man to Jon Dazen, a bad man and a big chief on Canyon Creek, to say that if he did not bring in these four Indians right away I would go to Pedro and get a lot of his warriors and go down there and look for them." The bluff worked and soon Dead Shot, Dandy Jim, Loco and another man were brought in. They were hanged in 1882.

Geronimo, who had broken for Mexico during the Cibecue Uprising, gave different reasons for the outbreak. "A rumor was current that the officers were again planning to imprison our leaders. This rumor served to revive the memory of all our past wrongs — the massacre in the tent at Apache Pass, the fate of Mangus Coloradas, and my own unjust imprisonment (he had

203

been locked up after taking his people from southern Arizona to New Mexico without permission), which might easily have been death to me. Just at this time we were told that the officers wanted us to come up the river above Geronimo (the name of the reservation village where they were then settled) to a fort to hold a council with them. We do not believe that any good could come of this conference, or that there was any need of it; so we held a council ourselves, and fearing treachery, decided to leave the reservation. We thought it more manly to die on the warpath than to be killed in prison."

"We went on toward Old Mexico, but on the second day after this United States soldiers overtook us about three o'clock in the afternoon and we fought until dark," Geronimo said. "The ground where we were attacked was very rough, which was to our advantage, for the troops were compelled to dismount in order to fight us. I do not know how many soldiers we killed, but we lost only one warrior and three children. We had plenty of guns and ammunition at this time. Many of the guns and much ammunition we had accumulated while living in the reservation, and the remainder we had obtained from the White Mountain Apaches when we left the reservation."

Horn related that things quieted down during the summer of 1882, but Charley Colvig or "Cibecue Charley" as he was called, the new chief of police at the San Carlos Agency, was killed at a place called the Ten Mile Pole. "His killing had not created much trouble, as the Indian police with him had killed the man who shot him, and that was all there was to it," Horn said.

But Geronimo and the other renegades were still out. Though little had been heard about their activities in Mexico, reports began to filter in. "A bunch of raiders had come back up from Mexico, killed a man close to Stein Peak, crossed over within 10 miles of Fort Bowie, killed a man and his son, and stolen a lot of horses at Theo White's Ranch, then had gone down through Rucker Mountains and into Mexico again," Horn said. Another group of raiders from Mexico came up to within two miles of Deming, New Mexico, and headed to the upper Gila River. "The first man they killed was at the old Yorke Ranch."

Pursuit was ineffective and the Indians were again in Mexico before Sieber and Horn were close to them. "We ran upon them at the Hot Springs, just across the line," Horn said. "Sieber killed a buck, and I ran up and captured his squaw."

They took the woman back to the U.S., but were soon subject to protests from Mexico about "armed bodies of men" from the United States entering Mexico. They swore they had not been in Mexico, but the investigation continued in ever higher circles. Finally, an officer called them in to inform them of the results of the investigation. After reading them the entire report on the investigation, he said, "The order of the commission that made this investigation is, that you be censured for the violation. That is all." He then invited them to go down to the post store for a drink and invited them to his home for dinner.

General Crook was ordered back to Arizona in the late summer of 1882 to deal with the situation. He came to Fort Apache for a big talk.

Crook held conferences with Apache leaders to hear their grievances, determining that the Apaches "had displayed remarkable forbearance in remaining at peace." He started removing squatters and crooked traders and agents from the reservations.

"One of the fundamental principles of the military character is justice to all — Indians as well as white men," Crook wrote. "In all their dealings with the Indians, officers must be careful not only to observe the strictest fidelity, but to make no promises not in their power to carry out."

Previously, the Indians had been forced to live close to the government agencies so they could be counted at regular intervals. This prevented them from farming fertile areas that were not close to the government posts. Crook ended the counting practice and allowed the Indians to resume farming.

During 1883, White Mountain Apaches raised 2.5 million pounds of corn, 180,000 pounds of beans, 135,000 pounds of potatoes and 200,000 pounds of barley, in addition to wheat, pumpkins, watermelons, muskmelons and cantaloupes.

With the reservation itself pacified, Crook was ready to turn his attention to the renegades, now mostly Chiricahuas.

On March 31, 1883, he received a telegram: "Instructions just received from the General of the Army authorize you under existing order to destroy hostile Apaches to pursue them regardless of the department or national lines, and to proceed to such points as you deem advisable."

With all the authority he could possibly ask for, Crook had to deliver. He sent his men to Willcox to start the campaign and went to Guaymas and Hermosillo to coordinate with Mexican officials.

"General Crook wanted to enlist Indian scouts to go after the Chiricahuas, and he wanted the support of the Indian chiefs to do so," Horn said. "The Indians, on their part, wanted to be started in the cattle business, and they knew that if they could get General Crook interested he would do it for them, or take the proper steps to have it done." With arrangements made for scouts, Sieber and Horn took the Apache woman they had brought from Mexico back down to the border and told her to set up a talk between the hostiles and Crook.

After the woman reached the hostiles in Mexico, they sent back Pee-chee, a Chiricahua warrior who the whites called Peaches. He said Geronimo wanted to talk.

Others say Peaches came to the Reservation with a group under Chato when they came back to the United States to get ammunition for their stolen Winchester repeating rifles. The Account in *Geronimo!* by E. M. Halliday says that Peaches stayed behind on the reservation when the band returned to Mexico. When Peaches was discovered by the army, he told the soldiers that many of the Apaches in Mexico were willing to give up and offered to lead them to the Apache stronghold in the Sierra Madres of Mexico.

In any event, on May 1, 1883, nine officers, 42 non-Indian enlisted men and 193 Apache Scouts headed for Mexico.

After the soldiers crossed into Mexico, the local population cheered their efforts and told them of the depredations of the hostiles, particularly Geronimo.

"The trail of the renegades was hot on the twelfth," says Martin F. Schmitt, who completed Crook's autobiography post-humously. "The expedition was now in the wildest part of the Sierras. The trail was so rough that several pack mules were lost, falling over high precipices from the narrow paths."

Peaches led the group farther and farther into the Sierra, finally reaching a spot 8,000 feet up in the mountains that Peaches said was a favorite campsite of Geronimo.

According to the Schmitt account, a few days later, Capt. Emmett Crawford and a party of scouts surprised a hostile camp and killed several of the hostiles and captured a young woman and four children. The woman said many of the hostiles were ready to give up. They were shocked that Crook had made it into the Sierras. The soldiers sent her to offer the followers of Chato and Geronimo a chance to surrender. Horn does not mention this clash, saying the soldiers and Scouts simply followed Peaches to meet Geronimo.

At first only old men, women and children appeared, but on May 18 a small band of warriors gave up. Eventually, Chato and Geronimo came in, Schmitt says.

"Crook treated the incoming Indians with his usual astute diplomacy," said Schmitt. "He was not really interested in taking them prisoners, he said. They had committed so many crimes, had killed so many people, and depredated so often that he would rather fight it out with them until they were all beaten into the ground and could give trouble no more. He told them, too, that the Mexican troops were moving in on both sides, and that in a few days they would be completely surrounded."

The two leaders begged to surrender and Crook gave them a month to gather their scattered followers and report to Crook to resume life on the reservation, according to Schmitt.

Horn gives a different version of the talks: "Geronimo was one of the greatest and most eloquent talkers in the entire Indian tribe, and when he sent in word that he wanted to talk, he always said he wanted to talk peace," Horn said. "When there was war to be made he never had anything to say, but just went to war; but he would get all filled up with talk, and he would send to the Government to get someone to talk to. This is what the rest of the Indians always said of him."

Crook said he had pacified the area 11 years before and left it in peace. "He told Geronimo that the Chiricahuas had committed many depredations which laid them liable to arrest and prosecution by the Government, but that if they all went back that he would see that none of them were taken away and tried by the civil courts, and that if they would go back to the Reservation and be counted regularly and draw their rations he would locate them on any part of the Reservation (that was not occupied by any other Indians) that Geronimo might choose," Horn wrote.

Crook assigned Lieutenant Gatewood to make sure there was no trouble in the Chiricahua camp. Though Gatewood has been played by many handsome Hollywood actors, Horn took pleasure in revealing the lieutenant's Apache name as "the Long-Nosed, Ugly Soldier."

Crook said, "I have just come back from the place called Washington, which, you know is the head of our Government and there I met officers high in rank belonging to the Mexican Government, and I made arrangements with them to permit my crossing the line in pursuit of Indians committing depredations in the United States. I have come to you as a brother and as a personal friend, to tell you all this and to conduct any and all who want to go back in safety. When I leave here, I must be informed by you if you want war or if you want peace.

"I will then organize a war party and send it to this country and will make several divisions of it, so as to be able to operate all over the mountains at once," Crook continued. "Then will the Chiricahuas be doomed, and I, an old man, will go with a heavy heart to my grave, for the war will be long and bitter, and my days will be passed in restlessness, and my nights without sleep."

In Horn's account, Sieber also spoke to Geronimo: "Now I say to you in all faith and honor that the Chiricahuas cannot resist the white man successfully since we can come to this country. If you continue to war with the white man now and under these circumstances, you and all your people will be exterminated. It takes you 10 years to make a warrior out of a 10-year-old boy. General Crook can make many hundreds of soldiers in a single day. The white man cannot be exterminated."

"I listened to your talk yesterday," Geronimo says in Horn's account of the meetings, "and it made me feel that I had done some great wrong. Perhaps I have done wrong, as a white man looks at my actions. I know that a white man does not see as an Apache sees, and I know that what is life to a white man is death to an Apache. ...

"You complain of my people raiding and killing up in the Americans' country. Do you not think I should complain of your war chief (Sieber) killing my warriors? Well, I make no complaint of that kind, for so, and in the fashion, do many of my young men want to die. I know, and my men know, that sooner or later all will get killed who keep up such a life; and now I am going to tell you that a life of this kind no longer pleases me. I have grown old on the war path, and what have I accomplished? Only this: today I stand before you as a supplicant. Today I am going to ask of you what I, the proud war chief of the Chiricahua tribe, never thought to ask of any white man. I ask you to take me to the Reservation, and there to do with me as you see fit, and as your judgment says is right for you to do."

Geronimo promised to go with Crook, but again, according to Horn, decided it would be a good trick to have the U.S. Army escort a large amount of stolen stock from Mexico. He sent out his warriors to get herds of horses and mules.

After Crook came back to the U.S. with 200 hostiles, Naiche and Chato showed up near their appointed time. And even Geronimo kept his promise eventually, showing up in the spring of 1884, according to Schmitt.

Horn said Mexican lawyers were soon pouring across the border, demanding the return of the livestock. The Indians would not give the animals up so the U.S. government eventually paid for all the ones that could be identified, Horn said.

Lt. Britton Davis met Geronimo's band near the border. On the way back to their reservation, two men in civilian clothes appeared with legal paperwork intent on taking the hostiles back to Tucson for trial. Davis was able to pour liquor into the parched would-be lawmen and sent the Indians north while he waited for his guests to come back to life.

Geronimo and his 51 men and 273 women and children were sent to Turkey Creek, just east of Fort Apache, where his band took up farming.

But while Crook had been gone, the Indian agent back at San Carlos, P. P. Wilcox, had been urging the peaceful Apaches to protest the return of the hostiles to the reservation.

Crook went to a conference with the Secretary of the Interior, the Commissioner of Indian Affairs and the Secretary of War. "The memorandum gave the general the measure of control he had so long advocated for the military and offered him the opportunity to exercise his theories of Indian policy," Schmitt said.

"In view of the difficulties encountered in making satisfactory disposition of the Apache Indians recently captured by General Crook under existing methods of administration, it is determined by the Secretary of War and the Secretary of the Interior, after consideration, that the Apache Indians recently captured by General Crook, and all such as many be hereafter captured or may surrender themselves to him, shall be kept under the control of the War Department at such points on the San Carlos Reservation as may be determined by the War Department. ... The War Department shall be entrusted with the entire police control of all the Indians on the San Carlos Reservation, ... and preventing the Indians from leaving it, except with the consent of General Crook. ..."

Although Crook had won the bureaucratic battle, he was beginning to lose the war. Someone in Washington — Crook blamed the Interior Department — fed lies about Crook to newspaper reporters. The papers printed stories saying Crook had been captured by the hostile Apaches in Mexico and forced to grant excessively favorable terms. The secretary of the Interior wrote to the Indian agent at San Carlos, admitting the department did not really support the agreement, and shifted the blame to Crook.

While Crook fought the bureaucratic battles, he also kept the peace between the whites and the Apaches. For two years there was "not an outrage or depredation of any kind."

Although Crook was blocked in his attempts to obtain farm implements for the Indians, build a mill at Fort Apache and institute competitive bidding among Indian traders, progress was made. The former renegades "generally behaved in a way to warrant the most hopeful anticipations," Schmitt wrote.

The civil authorities continued to try to regain control of the Apache reservation. They appointed their own police chief and head farmer, who worked at cross purposes with the military.

The Chiricahuas, sensing the division in control, saw an opportunity to resume making trouble. Horn said he was sent to the Chiricahua camp when counts started to show Indians were missing from the rolls. The San Francisco papers began to carry reports that the Apaches were continuing to raid into Mexico.

Horn set out with his scouts toward the Mexican border. He

left his men scattered along the line and went himself into Mexico. While camped in the Terras Mountains, he saw a signal on another mountain. "Presently the signals were repeated, and they plainly said to me: 'Answer!' After an hour they were repeated, 'Answer!'

"About 10 o'clock the man doing the signal act had received an answer, but I could not see the point his answer came from," Horn wrote. "He signaled, one long flash and four or five small or short ones, then two flashes and two again. The signals meant to me that they 'were all right and would wait there two days.'"

From the contents of the signals he had intercepted, Horn assumed the hostiles would be heading up into the United States.

"I knew now that it was time for me to be moving to get my scouts together and try to intercept the renegades in Arizona," Horn said. "I traveled all night, and after sunup next morning rode into Slaughter's Ranch on the line at the head of the San Bernardino Creek."

John Slaughter, second cousin to Pete Slaughter of Alpine, was a famed cattleman and sheriff in southeast Arizona. The rancher fed Horn and offered him a fresh horse. As he rode towards Camp Rucker, Horn met up with one of his scouts. Soon men were riding in all directions to contact the others and head them toward Tex Spring.

A Lieutenant Wilder, who had been sent south by General Crook to keep Horn out of trouble with the Mexicans, arrived with 20 troopers. Joined by six cowboys, the party set out the next day to intercept the Indians.

Figuring the hostiles would be passing a place called Dry Creek, the groups camped there for several days waiting for the Indians.

"I arranged for Lieutenant Wilder and his troops to strike them in the lead, and the cowboys, led by Mickey, were to take them in the rear," Horn said. "I would keep my Indian scouts with me, as I had misgivings about the wild soldiers and about the cowboys, wilder still; and as it was to be a fight on horseback, I knew everybody would be more or less excited."

The hostiles were in sight and moving closer to the ambush.

"Just when they got to where I wanted to strike them, one of the renegades gave a yell. 'Un-Dah!' he yelled. (That meant

'White men.') ... He checked up his horse an instant and I blazed away at him. That was the signal, and few men ever saw such a sight as I saw there. Soldiers rode at them from the front, Wilder at their head. Cowboys charged them from the rear. ... In a good deal less than a minute after I fired the first shot, soldiers, and cowboys and renegades were all mixed up and most of my scouts were away and left me. I had got soldier blouses from Wilder's men and put them on my scouts, so that if they did all get mixed up, my scouts would be easy to distinguish from the renegades."

Ten hostile braves were killed along with two women. One woman was captured. Horn said he believed the 14th member of the hostile party, a warrior, went off into the mountains and died of wounds.

"We, on our side, had one dead cowboy, a Mexican from San Bernardino Ranch, and two wounded cowboys. Mickey Free had a big slash in his left arm and one soldier was shot in the neck, and one in the stomach."

"We buried the San Bernardino Mexican," Horn wrote. "He had tried to rope an Indian and did rope him and pulled him off his horse; then the Indian got up and killed him."

The Chiricahua Break Out Again

Though the army had successes against raiding parties, the entire bunch of Chiricahuas on the reservation were getting restless. They had resumed making homemade liquor and mutilating wives by cutting off their noses.

"Gatewood told me he was having an awful time," Horn said. "The Chiricahuas were usually mean; were trading off all their horses for ammunition and whiskey, and that they were raising Cain with all the other Indians; in fact, that he could do nothing with them."

Lt. Britton Davis told the Indians to quit beating their wives and having tiswin drunks. The hostiles said they had never agreed to give up these practices.

They showed up at dawn one day outside Davis' tent, and Chihuahua addressed Davis through an interpreter. "Tell the Stout

Chief, that he can't advise me how to treat my women," Halliday wrote. "He is only a boy. I killed men before he was born.

"The other chiefs were muttering their approval, and Chihuahua was launching into a more defiant speech, the gist of which was that there was no army guardhouse big enough to hold all five hundred of the Apaches assigned to the Turkey Creek part of the reservation. Almost more disturbing than Chihuahua's open defiance was the glowering look on the eagle face of Geronimo, whom Davis regarded as 'thoroughly vicious, intractable, and treacherous' — the worst of the Apache leaders."

Davis sent word to Crook at Camp Verde, asking for advice and assistance. The message had to go through Capt. Pierce at San Carlos and he failed to relay it to Crook. "As Davis tells the story, Pierce took the telegram to Sieber, who was suffering from a hangover at the time," said Crook's biographer Schmitt. "Sieber dismissed the message as 'another tiswin drunk' and let it go at that."

Davis was at Fort Apache waiting for a response from Crook that never came when Mickey Free and Chato, a top sergeant of the Apache Scouts who had once been a famous leader of the hostiles, galloped in to report that Geronimo, Nana and about 100 followers were headed for Mexico. In his account, Geronimo tells the story of the renegade outbreak with some simplicity: "In Arizona we had trouble with the United States soldiers and returned to Mexico."

Horn was down on the border where his group intercepted a band near the head of Skeleton Canyon. The soldiers were only able to kill two warriors and capture three women and five children. The rest of the group of about 26 got away and headed into Mexico.

Having sewed the wind with his love of publicity, Crook was about to reap the whirlwind.

It was a different era. America, which had boasted a wide open frontier for more than a hundred years, now considered itself a settled nation. America was taking its place in the affairs of the world. Men and boys who would die in World War I were confidently looking forward to the 20th century. And suddenly, America was being pulled back to its past by something as old-fashioned as an Indian war. The eastern papers went wild.

213

"By the autumn of 1885 the whole country was aware that large segments of the United States and Mexican armies were unable to catch one fugitive remnant of Apache desperadoes, and the pursuit began to take on the fascination of a particularly dangerous fox hunt," Halliday wrote.

Crook's scouts chased the lightly equipped raiders, sometimes finding a camp only to capture a few ponies and some supplies. Geronimo always designated a rendezvous so that his followers could flee in groups of two or three and get back together days later dozens of miles away.

The soldiers had to return to the fort for supplies and Crook sent his captains to San Carlos and Fort Apache to recruit another 200 scouts. They again enlisted Chato.

"General Crook went to work to establish heliograph stations and started a school in Bowie to teach men the art of heliography," Horn said. Mirrors were used to catch sunlight and flash signals over long distances. "He ordered cavalry stationed at all the principal watering places anywhere near the line, and started out just as though he intended to make good his word with Geronimo in the Sierra Madres.

It was during this time that the Buffalo Soldiers joined the fight. The Apaches called them "black white men." Black cavalry units had been created nearly 20 years earlier just after the close of the Civil War, but the 10th Cavalry had been occupied in Texas until it was assigned to the Geronimo Wars in 1885. The tough veteran horse soldiers of the 10th were ideally suited for guarding water holes, tracking the renegade Apaches across the wastes of the Southwest and bringing them to battle. A Medal of Honor citation for Sgt. William McBryer typified the qualities that the men brought to the conflict. It said that McBryer "distinguished himself for coolness, bravery and marksmanship while his troop was in pursuit of hostile Apache Indians."

During this period a man who would become infamous as the Apache Kid first came into the picture. Though his story is so obscured in myth and legend that very little can be said as absolute fact, he was one of the most famous Apaches after Geronimo. In a 1926 book called *The Apache Kid,* William Sparks said the Kid, Ski-Be-Nan-Ted, learned English while running errands for miners around Globe. When Geronimo fled to Mexico,

Capt. Crawford recruited him to scout for the army.

"On one occasion several American soldiers, packers, and scouts, got drunk in the Mexican town of Huasavas," Sparks said. "There was a Mexican major there with a battalion of Mexican infantry. Some of the Mexican soldiers were called out to stop a small riot, that was said to have been precipitated by an attack three Apache Scouts had made on a Mexican woman.

"When the soldiers appeared on the scene the scouts tried to run away. The Mexicans fired on them, killing one, and wounding another. The third man was captured. It was the Kid. The Mexican major wanted to take him out and execute him, according to Mexican custom, but the alcalde (mayor) of the town said he was afraid it would cause trouble between the two governments; so he fined the Kid twenty dollars; which was paid, and the Kid was sent back to Sieber at San Carlos."

After the incident in the mid-1880s, the Kid dropped back into nameless obscurity for a number of years while Geronimo's raiding continued to command the world stage.

"All the news was bad," Schmitt said. "Horses were stolen, citizens were killed, or there was a general Indian scare over a large area. Gen. (Phil) Sheridan telegraphed Crook on Dec. 29, saying the president himself was getting disturbed over the progress of events and asked whether some good news might not soon be expected."

The heliograph sent messages that a band of hostiles had headed north across the border. This was not a raiding party, but a war party intent on punishing the White Mountain Apaches for helping the soldiers. "Our helio was doing its work well," Horn said. "They were not seen again until they got to the Reservation and there they ran into old Nad-is-ki's band in the White Mountains. The men were nearly all away, so they struck a camp mostly of women and children and killed 21 of them. One of the raiders was also killed, and they cut his head off and took it into Camp Apache. It proved to be Hal-zay, the Indian Sieber and I met on the Bavispe River, when I first went with Sieber to the Chiricahua camp."

"Now, one thing we knew, and that was that they were going to try to do so much damage to the Indians on the Reservation that the Indian men on the Reservation would not go to Mexico

215

to hunt them," Horn said.

The 10 surviving members of the war party went back toward Mexico and Horn and his scouts tried to pick up their trail. "They made remarkable rides while up in Arizona, and the troops were within sight of them several times."

"Well, I struck their trail in the Sierra Madres, and as it was 10 days old when I struck it I knew we would have to be very careful or we would not get up to them," Horn said. "I made arrangements for Crawford to wait two days where we were camped and then follow on down. ... I kept on the trail of the 10 knowing they would go to the main band to tell of their raid on the Reservation. ...

"I left the trail and took up a course parallel with that of the renegades, for I well knew their custom of leaving a few men behind the main party to give warning if any one was in the track of them. I traveled all day, and then at evening began to cut across to see if I could strike their trail. I sent a couple of men to two different mountain tops to see if they could see any sign or shadows of camp fires. Two of the scouts who went up on one of the hills came back about midnight and said they had seen the shadow of camp fires reflected on the clouds in the sky and that the Indians must be camped a long way up the river."

About noon the next day when the trackers began to smell smoke from pits where the hostiles were cooking mescal, they realized they were close.

"We lay off and slept the rest of the day after we began to smell Indians, and we calculated to do the most of our work from that point on, after night," Horn said. "When night came we were all on the highest point around there, and as it began to get dark we began to see shadows of fires and they were not ten miles from us."

"We were all night getting to a place that suited me, and so when we did get where we thought we would be all right we all sat down and went to sleep. As it began to get light, we could see some fifty camp fires, and some of them were not a mile away from us," Horn said.

Horn had been sending scouts back to keep Crawford informed and keep him heading in the right direction. Since he now had only two men left, they headed back toward the main body of troops to bring them up. When the cavalry arrived, Horn divided the command into four groups and surrounded the hostile camp.

Horn said he talked to his scouts "and warned them to try to keep from starting the fight as long as possible, to give us better light, but they were all mad because of the raid that the renegades had made on the Reservation, and the killing of the women and children. They all knew that we would capture some women and children, and I had instructed them that they must not kill any women or children, but to go at the bucks and kill all the bucks they could."

Just as it started to grow light, two warriors walked toward Horn. The scouts aimed their rifles at the hostiles. "They got up within twenty yards of where I was, and had not yet seen one of my men," Horn said. "No one spoke, but everybody seemed to fire at once, and those two bucks never smiled again. ...

"Geronimo jumped up on a rock and yelled: 'Look out for the horses!' And a minute afterwards he yelled: 'Let the horses go and break towards the river on foot! There are soldiers and Apache Scouts on both sides and above us. Let the women and children break for the river and the men stay behind!' "

They all ran to the river and the men on that side held their fire until the hostiles were within 10 feet. "Instructions to the scouts did not amount to anything. They shot everything in sight. Women and children and everything else!"

"Scatter and go as you can!" Geronimo yelled.

Horn tried to stop the slaughter of the women and children and managed to save 16. Then he saw a limping warrior running away from camp and took off after him. The warrior was running down one gully and Horn took off down another gully that intersected the one with the fugitive.

"I beat him to the forks, or met him there," Horn said. "When I came in sight of him I threw up my gun. He stopped dead still and turned towards me. He was old Nana, a formerly noted chief in war and council, but at this time about 90 years old. He said to me as calmly as though we were going to draw his rations: 'I surrender.' "

"Now the best warriors are the ones who start to run first, and their ability as warriors depends on the length of time they can run after they do get started," Nana said, adding that Sieber taught the scouts "to fight anyhow, no matter which is the superior body of men, the ones you are with or the ones you are fighting. Once the Apaches were so, but now they sit around the fires and tell what they will do and what they can do, and they won't do, and can't do anything. We had men enough to make you a good fight, and we could get away in the dark after we did fight you, but no, these braves must run, run, run!"

Nana continued to growl in Horn's account after he was taken back to the women captives: "Did you hear your great chief, Geronimo? 'To the river, to the river! Run to the river!' Why did he not say: Fight, make the scouts go to the river!"

The victors ate and slept and soon a woman came in and said Chihuahua wanted to talk. Horn told her that he and his men were leaving early the next day so Chihuahua should come in if he wanted to talk.

Schmitt wrote this about the battle: "On the tenth of January, [1886] after a very difficult night march, Crawford's command attacked the main camp of the hostiles about sixty miles below Nacori. The battle did not trap or annihilate the Chiricahua renegades, but did capture their entire stock, camp equipment, food, and supplies. Geronimo, Nachez and Chihuahua were demoralized to the extent that they asked for a peace talk."

Crawford began negotiations with the hostiles, but his command, consisting mostly of Apache Scouts, was mistaken for hostiles by Mexican soldiers. The Mexicans prepared to attack.

"Follow me, valientes!" the Mexican captain cried, according to Horn. Crawford asked Horn to try to stop the Mexicans. "These scouts will kill them all!" Crawford said.

"I ran out towards them, and Crawford jumped up higher still, on a big prominent rock, and had a white handkerchief in his hands," Horn recalled. "When they reached the middle of the basin the Mexicans began to shoot. Some would stop and shoot, and then come on towards us on a trot, and others would do the same, so that some were coming on a trot and some were firing all the time.

Crawford fell mortally wounded and Horn was shot in the arm, but the scouts shot up the Mexicans, killing 36 and badly wounding 13, according to Horn. There were lengthy negotiations and threats of executions.

In Horn's account, he has Geronimo appearing on the scene, offering to help kill the Mexicans. "He shouted to me to give the word, and we would all strike the Mexicans at once and kill them all and get their pinole," Horn wrote. "Mexicans, when they go upon a campaign or trip, take only pinole, a kind of parched meal, and the Indians all like it — would do anything to get it."

Horn also recalled that he armed the captive Apache Chief Nana to help fight the Mexicans. Finally, the Mexicans decided to leave and the Americans gave them some captured horses to help move their wounded.

Horn may have exaggerated Geronimo's role in the incident, but he was certainly in the area and Crawford was certainly mortally wounded by Mexican soldiers, dying three days later on the road back to the American base.

Horn made arrangements for Chihuahua to meet General Crook "in the full of the March moon, at the San Bernardino Peak." He urged him to bring Natchez with him.

Crook, accompanied by Alchesay, a scout who was later to become the White Mountain Apache chief, went to Mexico to resume negotiations.

"When the appointed day came along, all parties were on hand and Chihuahua said that he did not have any more talk to make, but that he was willing to go to the guard house and stay there till Geronimo came in, for he said Geronimo would not stay out long now, as many of the men with him were much dissatisfied," Horn said. "There were about 25 men and a good many more women and children with Chihuahua.

"All at once there was some commotion up on the peak and a big bunch of renegades came into sight coming to our talk. Geronimo was at their head. The desire to make a peace talk was too strong in him to miss the chance. ...

"General Crook told him if he wanted to go along as a prisoner to come on, and if he did not, to go on back to the mountains and he would send more scouts there to find him.

"He said: 'Geronimo, you are so much of a liar that I do not want to trust you any more, and if you go with me you will have to go to the guard house till the authorities at Washington decide what to do with you.' "

According to the general's autobiography, Crook asked Alchesay to try to talk the hostiles into agreeing to go away from the Southwest until "this thing was forgotten and the excitement was allayed."

In his journal, Crook says: "March 26. Had private interview with Geronimo, Nachez, Chihuahua and a couple of others with reference to their leaving this country for the East to remain there until they change their ideas, and the feeling against them here dies out."

Finally, the terms were all worked out. All the hostiles but old Nana would spend two years in the East.

Crook left a small number of soldiers and scouts to take the still-armed prisoners back to Arizona.

When he returned to the U.S., Crook found himself caught in the middle. The president demanded unconditional surrender. Crook told his bosses: "To inform the Indians that the terms on which they surrendered are disapproved would, in my judgment, not only make it impossible for me to negotiate with them, but result in their scattering to the mountains, and I can't at present see any way to prevent it." He didn't tell the hostile Apaches that the terms of surrender had been vetoed in Washington.

Geronimo's Last Breakout

While being taken back to the reservation, Geronimo purchased liquor from a trader, got drunk and headed to Mexico with half his band. This 1886 escape was his sixth and last.

Having elevated the pursuit of Geronimo to a national imperative in the press, Crook and his superiors couldn't withstand this setback.

Horn gave it a slightly different spin: "I could plainly see that Geronimo was only with us to try and get some of the men belonging to Chihuahua's band to desert and go with him on the war path." Horn said that at Chihuahua's request, he placed Chihuahua's men under guard. The next morning Geronimo and his followers were gone.

The local press took the news in stride. In those days, papers didn't put important stories on the front page with headlines in huge type. Still, it does seem odd that the story in the *St. Johns Herald* on the final Apache insurrection would appear on an inside page below an item on five-year-old cattle production statistics. "It is rumored that the White Mountain Apaches have broken out, but we have not been able to trace the report to any reliable source. It seems to be the general impression that the hostiles now ravaging the country will use every effort to influence all malcontents to join them. It is believed that the various bands into which Geronimo's forces are dividing are all making for the San Carlos Reservation, but the military are said to be guarding every approach, with instructions to capture or kill the marauders whenever found."

Perhaps local businesses frowned on their local newspaper giving much publicity to difficulty with the Native Americans.

Phil Sheridan had begun his rise to commanding general of the army by setting off to destroy J. E. B. Stuart's legendary Confederate cavalry. Though Sheridan had not feared the rebel raider who terrified the nation's capital, he could not face the public disappointment over the escape of 50 Apaches in northern Mexico.

He berated Crook severely, ordering him to quit following the renegades, and instead deploy his infantry and cavalry in defensive positions to protect the Arizona settlers.

"Troops cannot protect property beyond a radius of one-half mile from their camp," Crook told his boss. "If offensive movements against the Indians are not resumed, they may remain quietly in the mountains for an indefinite time without crossing the line, and yet their very presence there will be a constant menace, and require the troops in this department to be at all times in position to repel sudden raids; and so long as any remain out they will form a nucleus for disaffected Indians from the different agencies in Arizona and New Mexico to join."

Crook also asked to be relieved of command. Sheridan did not allow the telegram to cool before transferring Crook out of the area.

Miles Takes Command

Gen. Nelson A. Miles, who pursued fame with a passion and had chafed with each measure of Crook's success, now got his chance. By May 1886, there were 21 men and 13 women opposing the militaries of the United States and Mexico. Miles discharged nearly all of the Apache Scouts and spread his troops across Arizona and New Mexico.

Horn, who was mustered out when Miles came, took a dim view of the new general's efforts. "Well, two companies of the 10th Cavalry, under Captain Leebo, ran onto a camp of renegades down towards Calabasas, and got whipped, and never saw one Indian. Two days later the same thing happened to a troop of the 4th Cavalry."

Geronimo gives this account. "Troops trailed us continually. They were led by Captain Lawton, who had good scouts. The Mexican soldiers also became more active and more numerous. We had skirmishes almost every day, and so we finally decided to break up into small bands. With six men and four women I made for the range of mountains near Hot Springs, New Mexico. We passed many cattle ranches, but had no trouble with the cowboys. We killed cattle to eat whenever we were in need of food, but we frequently suffered greatly for water. At one time we had no water for two days and nights and our horses almost died from thirst. We ranged in the mountains of New Mexico for some time. ..."

Horn says, "A big bunch of renegades came up by Fort Bowie and across by the Dragoons. They killed a man in the Dragoons, and turned back on their route and killed two men and a boy in Pinery Canyon, in the Chiricahua Mountains."

In all, the hostiles committed 14 murders during this rampage into the U.S.

In his book, *The Buffalo Soldiers,* William H. Leckie says the hostiles "sought refuge in the Dragoon Mountains. There was no respite. Detachments of Buffalo Soldiers under Captain Norvell and Lieutenants Read, Hunt, Hughes, and Shipp pursued without letup, and in desperation the Indians fled toward Fort Apache to seek aid from their kinsmen on the reservation. As they came near, however, they were intercepted by Captain J. T. Morrison and (Troop) A of the Tenth, stripped of all their horses, and driven back."

"Sorely beset, the hostiles turned toward Mexico and were has-

*Buffalo Soldiers were known to the Apaches as "black white men."
They played an important role in the later years of the Apache wars.
Detail of a 1889 sketch by Frederic Remington.*

tened in their flight by troopers working in relays."

Geronimo says, "Then thinking that perhaps the troops had left Mexico, we returned. On our return through Old Mexico we attacked every Mexican found, even if for no other reason than to kill. We believed they had asked the United States troops to come down to Mexico to fight us."

The activities of the hostiles were followed by the local newspapers in the White Mountains.

"There is a rumor of the effect that a band of … Apaches have started out on a marauding expedition," the *St. Johns Herald* wrote. "They have already stolen considerable stock, it is said, but so far have done no killing; and were headed when last seen toward Tonto Basin. When they come to a camp or ranch, they make no ceremony in helping themselves to whatever strikes their fancy, and proceed on their way, apparently perfectly satisfied with the situation of affairs."

"The Apaches have inaugurated a reign of terror in Pima County," the *Herald* wrote. "During the last week in April they killed seventeen persons. The amount of property destroyed and the number of stock driven off cannot be estimated. … The Apaches divided in two bands of from fifteen to eighteen each soon after passing Calabasas Tuesday morning, and each of these bands appear to have subsequently subdivided into smaller parties for raiding purposes, occasionally concentrating at understood points. One of the main bands struck southwest and the other northeast, and from their subsequent movements, it is not improbable that they intend forming a junction in the Santa Rita Mountains, between Nogales and Tucson.

"Geronimo's band attacked ranches near Imuris, completely destroying all the buildings at Casita, a small way station near Imuris, on the Sonora Railroad, killing fifteen persons, all Mexicans. A company of soldiers were sent after them. Two soldiers were killed. The Indians were moving in the direction of Nacora, in the Sierra Madre Mountains. A reign of terror prevails throughout the district."

"They then went into Mexico and killed four Mexicans, just on the line, at a vinataria, or muscal still. ...," Horn says. "Four or five squaws got lost from this bunch that came through last, or else they deserted and came into Fort Bowie, and they said that Ju, a Warm Springs chief, and a half-brother to Nana, had been killed by the Mexicans over in Janos, in Chihuahua. The way we afterwards got the story was that 26 bucks went into this town of Janos and got drunk; the Mexicans gave them all the muscal they could drink, and killed nearly all of them. Ju, in trying to get away, was running his pony at the top of its speed, and it fell down a bank and killed him."

Horn was hired again after the Americans were unsuccessful in catching the renegades.

He said that when he and 25 Apache Scouts took up the chase, "Geronimo was from 10 hours to four days ahead of us for five weeks, and his rear guard saw us many times, so they afterwards said. It was a great race, and I knew the renegades could not stand it much longer. They had no time to raid and get fresh horses, except as they could pick them up, and when they would gain a few days on us we would hear of them by the helio, and we could drop the trail where we were and cut in ahead."

"Four or five times they surprised our camp," Geronimo said. "One time they surprised us about nine o'clock in the morning, and captured all our horses (nineteen in number) and secured our store of dried meats. We also lost three Indians in this encounter. About the middle of the afternoon of the same day

224

we attacked them from the rear as they were passing through a prairie — killed one soldier, but lost none ourselves."

Lieutenant Charles Gatewood and a group of Chiricahuas from the reservation were sent down to try to reopen peace talks. At this point in the story, Horn discusses the slights he suffered at the hands of Miles and his own importance to the process. He probably does not overstate his petulance, but may have overstated his importance as Geronimo does not mention Horn in his account.

Finally, the chase of more than 2,000 miles came to an end and a parley between Miles and Geronimo was arranged. The hostile leader agreed to surrender once again and the group marched to meet Miles at Skeleton Canyon near Douglas on the Arizona-Mexico border.

"General Miles is your friend," the interpreter told Geronimo in Halliday's account. "The Indian gave Miles a defoliating look 'I never saw him,' he said. 'I have been in need of friends. Why has he not been with me?' "

"I want to surrender with all my people," Geronimo says in Horn's account. "I will do as you say, and go where you tell me to go or send me. I am tired of the war path, and my people are all worn out."

Geronimo remembered General Miles giving these promises. "I will build you a house; I will fence you much land; I will give you cattle, horses, mules, and farming implements. You will be furnished with men to work the farm, for you yourself will not have to work. In the fall I will send you blankets and clothing so that you will not suffer from cold in the winter time.

"There is plenty of timber, water, and grass in the land to which I will send you. You will live with your tribe and with your family within five days."

Geronimo said to General Miles: "All the officers that have been in charge of the Indians have talked that way, and it sounds like a story to me; I hardly believe you."

Geronimo remembers Miles replying, "This time it is the truth."

Writing to his wife, Miles said, "If you had been here you would have seen me riding in over the mountains with Geronimo and Natchez as you saw me ride over the hills and down to the

Yellowstone with Chief Joseph. It is a brilliant ending of a difficult problem."

The government had to decide what to do with the Apaches. Some suggested shipping them to Florida to make sure they could never escape and return to Arizona and Mexico. The *St. Johns Herald* wanted a final solution. "Don't ship rattlesnakes to Florida. … Kill 'em."

The 10th Cavalry was in charge of loading the prisoners onto wagons and taking them to the railroad in Holbrook. The hostiles were taken in the first two trips, but the government had plans to include other passengers on the third trip.

Halliday says, "400 Chiricahuas at Fort Apache, who had remained loyal all through Geronimo's last rampage, were summarily rounded up and sent off to Fort Marion also. Not exempted were many Apache Scouts who had served Crook with absolute fidelity, and to the end of his days the General never lost his smoldering indignation at this treatment."

"We didn't know where we were to be taken from Holbrook," Samuel Kenoi, was quoted as saying in *Geronimo and the End of the Indian Wars* by C. L. Sonnichsen. "Some thought we were going to be taken to the ocean and thrown in. Some thought we were going to be killed in some other way."

"It was the first time most of us had seen a train," said Kenoi. "When that train was coming along the river and it whistled, many said it was run by lightning, and they began to pray to the train."

Children ran away, but the train was eventually loaded.

"Left behind as the train slowly rolled along were the tribe's livestock, dogs, and several piles of belongings that could not be fitted into the two baggage cars," according to an Apache account of the scene in *Survival of the Spirit* by H. Henrietta Stockel. "The personal belongings were quickly picked over by souvenir hunters. The horses were rounded up by the soldiers and later sold at auction at Fort Union, New Mexico. The camp dogs, which had faithfully followed the tribe from Fort Apache, were distraught at being separated from their masters and ran pitifully, howling and yapping, beside the train. Some kept up for almost 20 miles."

The men were placed at Fort Pickens in Florida while their

families were kept at Fort Marion, 200 miles away.

While many saw this as treachery to the Chiricahua — especially those who had served as scouts for the army and were also hauled away on the prison train — Horn, with fixed ideas about "bad Indians," saw it as a "fine act."

Author William Sparks reports that an Indian named Massey jumped off the train in Missouri and estimated that it took the fugitive two months to get back to Turkey Creek near Fort Apache. There Sparks said Massey hid in the grass as a woman and her daughter came by to cut grass to make hay. He killed the mother and kidnapped the daughter, then headed for Mexico.

Horn also recalled the escape of an Indian from the train. Perhaps having a better ear for the Apache language than others, he called him Wasse.

"A Chiricahua named Wasse jumped off the train down in Texas while the train was running at full speed," Horn said. "He turned up in the Sierra Madres later, having made all the distance on foot, through the settlements of Texas, and the Texas marshals were after him all the time. He spoke Mexican like a native, and could pass for one anywhere in Texas. He was an outlaw for many years, living around in the mountains, and coming in to the Reservation once in a while to get a fresh squaw. Any kind was good enough for him. He would take a Yuma squaw as soon as any other kind, and he could not speak a word of the Yuma language."

Horn said Jose Maria, a Mexican captive who had been in Geronimo's band, and five other Indians joined Wasse in the Sierra Madre.

Without Geronimo's ability to capture international attention, those renegades lived out their lives in relative obscurity.

"The President has examined carefully the cases of the Apache captives, and has come to the conclusion that life confinement in Florida, where they can do no harm, will be the most thorough punishment which can be visited upon these Indians," the *St. Johns Herald* reported in 1887. "A military commission would have no authority to try them, and if they were turned over to the civil authorities in the Territories, it is believed the prejudice is so great they could not have a fair trial, and the families and survivors would be left to cherish vengeance and keep up constant turmoil on the borders. As a matter of fact the transfer of the savages to Florida, means a lingering death and experienced army officers do not think there will be one of them alive at the end of five years."

"Geronimo and his band are said to be surrendering to the climate of Florida at the rate of four a day," the paper later reported. "There are 454 bucks, squaws and papooses at Fort Marion, while Geronimo and twelve or fifteen others are at Fort Pickens."

More Outlaws Than A Thousand Movies

Many of the most notorious desperados of the Old West haunted the White Mountains and gave Springerville the reputation of being the wildest outlaw town in America for a brief period in the late 19th century. Some, like Butch Cassidy, passed through peacefully, while others like Ike Clanton shot it out and died in the pine forest. The mountains were a fertile field for cattle rustlers, but outlaws interested in more concentrated forms of wealth stole it elsewhere and used the lonely mountains as a hiding place. In addition to Cassidy's Wild Bunch, the area saw gunslingers from the Shootout at the OK Corral, the Black Jack Ketchum and Hole In The Wall gangs, and the fabled Hashknife outfit. The sheriff from St. Johns settled the Pleasant Valley War by single-handedly gunning down many of the perpetrators. One of the famous Flakes of Snowflake was shot and killed by a passing bank robber.

In a purely local matter, cattleman Pat Slaughter was accused of shooting a former lawman to death after the ex-officer killed his brother. But it was the murder of two young men from St. Johns by hardened criminals that shocked the territory and contributed to the formation of the Arizona Rangers.

The "Outlaw Trail" wound through the White Mountains. Though the Census Bureau determined that there was no more frontier after 1890, there were still long stretches of lightly settled land throughout the West. Some of these spots became havens for criminal gangs.

"The topography of the intermountain country was ideal for the operation of such an organization; their activities extended from Canada to Mexico within certain well defined limits which came to be known as the Outlaw Trail," wrote Charles Kelly in a book called *The Outlaw Trail: A History of Butch Cassidy and his Wild Bunch.* "The outlaws who used it operated on an immense scale; their hideouts were practically impregnable. ...

"In Arizona, just south of the Utah line, the trail crossed the Colorado River at Lee's Ferry, continued across dangerous deserts, penetrated deep red sandstone canyons of Arizona, touched the western edge of New Mexico near the Mogollon mountains and continued south into Old Mexico." The trail went through what was then and still is the most isolated part of the U.S. "Valleys east and west of the trail, occupied by cattle ranchers, were constantly raided by gangs of rustlers and bandits, who then withdrew into the back country where waterholes and hiding places were known only to the rustlers."

With few railroads to bring in marshals or Pinkerton detectives, outlaws could ride from the Hole in the Wall in Wyoming down to Springerville and follow the Blue River, then continue south for an easy crossing into Mexico. If they didn't have time to make it to the international border, a good hiding place could usually be found a few miles into the forest.

Law enforcement was an economic good that usually came only to areas where people were willing to pay for it. Robbers who held up trains in distant states were not a priority for people in the White Mountains unless the bad men caused trouble locally. But tolerance for lawbreakers disappeared when local cattle or local citizens became victims.

Early Apache County Troubles

In at least one incident, the army helped with law and order in the White Mountains. "It was in the fall of 1877 that Deputy U.S. Marshal [Corydon] Cooley accompanied a detachment of the 6th Cavalry under Captain Adam Kraemer to Springerville," Wharfield wrote in his biography of the famous Indian scout.

"The responsible settlers there were in distress because of the antics of a bunch of white desperados. Some of the outlaws had been killed in local fights, but two were threatening to take over the settlement. The Camp Apache party arrested an outlaw named Wilson, alias Bill Cavaness, and his companion, E. M. Overstreet, turning them over to a deputy sheriff. The *Weekly Arizona Miner* of November 16, 1877, reported, "Governor Hoyt last evening received a telegram from C. E. Cooley, Deputy U.S. Marshal at Camp Apache, informing him of the hanging of two desperados on the Little Colorado. ... After Cooley and the soldiers left Springerville a mob arose, and in the language of the telegram, disposed of them according to frontier law. ..." The account doesn't explain how Cooley knew the men were hanged after he left town.

Marshal Cooley had to seek advice when a black former soldier killed an Indian on the reservation. According to Cooley's biography, the sheriff told Cooley to keep the suspect in the guardhouse until the next term of the U.S. District Court at Prescott.

James Hale had been unlucky since coming to Arizona from Monroe, Utah, in 1878. He was one of the Mormons who had been forced to leave their homesteads in Forestdale because the idyllic valley was part of the Apache Reservation. Then when his wife died, Hale took his children to homestead on the South Fork of the Little Colorado. His cabin burned one day when Hale was out working with the older children. His small children got out of the cabin but had to track through the snow to a neighboring ranch.

"In the course of his work James Hale became aware of a cattle stealing operation which he reported to the authorities," the stake history says.

In *On the Road To Nowhere*, Applewhite wrote that Hale "and Lehi Smithson had been working for the old Twenty-Four and caught rustlers – the Clantons it is thought – having already stolen two herds and in the process of taking the third. Hale and Smithson reported them to the cattle company, and Smith and Carson got their cattle back. The rustlers, however, had it in for Hale after that."

Tom Tolbert, the leader of the rustlers, was holed up in a Springerville saloon on Christmas Day in 1886. When he saw

Hale passing by on the other side of the street, Tolbert stepped out, drew his gun, and shot the family man dead.

Outraged young Mormon men formed a vigilance committee and trailed Tolbert. "When the vigilantes returned none of them would talk," the St. Johns Stake history says. "Eventually, when pressed, one of them put an end to further speculation with this statement, 'Tom Tolbert will never shoot another Mormon.'"

The *St. Johns Herald*, perhaps given a story that Springerville residents wanted people to believe at the county seat 40 miles away, gave this account of the treatment of Hale's killer. "It seems that a cowboy known as Diamond or 'Ace of Diamonds,' was suspected as the man who shot old man Hale, and a crowd undertook to arrest him, but Diamond refusing to submit, jumped on his horse and attempted to escape, when he was fired upon, his horse killed and a serious, if not fatal wound inflicted about his groin. A messenger left hastily for Dr. Dalby to attend the wounded man. It is feared that additional trouble will arise from the complication of affairs. Springerville seems to be afflicted with a homicidal epidemic latterly. We hope the trouble is all ended."

The paper reported another incident in which the "Graham boys" gave fresh horses to rustlers to help them evade a posse. The brothers were arrested and bailed out of jail. "We are informed that the Grahams and their friends are now walking the streets of that town, threatening vengeance on all who took an active part in following the thieves, and afterward in having them arrested."

Famed Navajo Trader J. Lorenzo Hubbell, who served as county sheriff in 1885 and opened a store in St. Johns in 1887, once said, "When I came to St. Johns I asked the storekeepers why they allowed the thieves to rob them. I sent for guns and ammunition and the fight started in St. Johns, and the first week 17 of them were killed, and eight of our boys," according to an account in *O. K. Corral Postscript: The Death of Ike Clanton* by Rita K. W. Ackerman. "It was a rough fight and lasted a long time."

A brief 1887 lull in Round Valley outlaw troubles was cause for a newspaper story. The *St. Johns Herald* reported, "Undersheriff McKinney reports Springerville as one of the most quiet and orderly places in Arizona. Indiscriminate shooting is indulged in no longer — people are not awakened every night by such a fusillade of fire arms, as would lead one to suppose, who was unacquainted with the customs of the place, that the town had been attacked by a roving band of Apaches — saloon keepers do not have to close their places of business, as they did a short time back, when a gang of the would-be bad men rode into town."

Pleasant Valley War
Comes to the White Mountains

Bad guys from two of the world's most famous outlaw battles, the Shootout at the O. K. Corral and the Pleasant Valley War, made it to the White Mountains where they met their fate at the hands of lawmen. The Pleasant Valley War raged near Young, Arizona, southwest of the White Mountains. That bitter conflict was later immortalized in Zane Grey's *To the Last Man*.

It was the prototypical range war with Anglo cattlemen — the Graham and Blevins families — fighting Hispanic sheepherders — the Tewksburys. In the most famous passage from Grey's book, the Graham/Blevins faction attacked the Tewksbury house, leaving John Tewksbury and a friend dead in the yard. As the gun battle blazed and hogs began to eat the bodies, Mrs. Tewksbury emerged with a shovel to bury them. The firing stopped until she returned to the house. That is the legend. The *St. Johns Herald* had a different version of the story. It said Mrs. Tewksbury found the bodies a half mile from the house and covered them with a blanket and wagon cover until an inquest could be held. While the Blevins faction dominated the early battles in the Tonto Basin, they did not fare well when they ventured above the Mogollon Rim into the White Mountains.

The impact of Pleasant Valley rustlers on the White Mountains was documented in the biography of William Flake. "By 1886, they were well organized, and were stealing hundreds of cattle and horses from our range. We knew they were being stolen, but could not find where they were being taken. We learned that the Blevins and Grahams had begun working together. Both had been stealing for a long time, and in fact it was largely the Grahams who had stolen Stinson's [the pre-Mormon homesteader of Snowflake who had moved to Pleasant Valley] stock and driven him out of his range.

"They grew more bold; the Blevins family just moved into Canyon Creek, where a man named Adams had built a house, and had a small bunch of cattle. They stole nearly all of his stock and ordered him to leave or they would kill him. They were gun men, and he was not; there were six of them and he was alone, so he left the country."

The Crooked Trail to Holbrook by Hanchett tells it differently. Andy Cooper, a half brother to the Blevins boys, found the Canyon Creek ranch unoccupied in 1886 and moved in. The owners, John and Will Adams, were in Utah on Mormon church business, but collected $200 from Cooper for the ranch on their return. The ranch was an ideal location for Cooper because it was just outside of Apache County, where he was a wanted man.

An advertisement in the St. Johns paper read: "Last February we lost Seven Hundred head of Merino Sheep, from a point near Pleasant Valley, in Tonto Basin, Arizona. Said sheep were STOLEN from the range, and supposed to have been driven toward ST. JOHNS, ARIZONA." The victims offered a $1,500 reward for the arrest and conviction of the thieves and return of the sheep.

One of the most spectacular raids by the Blevins gang involved the theft of 75 horses from the Navajos, who sent 40 warriors into the Heber area to recover their stock. Race apparently trumped legality when Mormons hid a rustler from the Navajos. *The Crooked Trail to Holbrook* recounts a family story about one of the Blevins boys being chased down the trail by a band of Navajo. "He ran into their house asking to be hidden. James Shelley quickly covered him up with potatoes in the vegetable cellar and put his horse in the pasture with their other horses. Margaret Shelley handed out loaves of freshly baked bread with butter to the Indians as soon as they arrived at her home. When asked which way the rider had gone, she pointed down the trail."

It wasn't as if the Blevins-Graham faction were the bad guys and the Tewksburys wore white hats. *The Crooked Trail* details the theft of six mares and a stallion from the tiny community of Wilford. The horses were recovered by tracking them to the Tewksburys' holdings below the Mogollon Rim. Hanchett also named James Tewksbury as a suspect in the robbery of the Mormon store in Woodruff.

In 1887, some of the best horses and cattle in Snowflake were stolen out of their barns. A posse tracked them to the Canyon Creek country, but lost them there. William Flake searched for 10 days before finding the horns and hide of one of his oxen along the trail. He gained the confidence of some local homesteaders, who named the rustlers and told him the horses had been taken to a stable in Phoenix. Flake rode hard for Phoenix and identified 35 stolen horses, which he recovered despite objections from the stable owner and difficulty with the local sheriff.

"On the way home across the trail, Father was riding out on the hills looking for more stolen stock, when he met three men," the biography says. "He only knew one of them, Louie Parker, a nephew of the Grahams. They asked him what he was doing. He said, 'I am looking for more of my horses that were stolen.' Parker asked if he had found any more. He replied, 'Yes, you are riding one of them.' They laughed and asked, 'Do you think you will take him?' To this Father replied, 'I guess not, you are all armed, and I am not, (looking at Parker) but we may meet again.'"

Z. B. Decker, who ran sheep on Decker Wash 16 miles west of Taylor, reported a run-in about that same time with the Blevins gang. Cooper had a spread called Longmore Ranch only one and a half miles west of Decker's place. The Blevins gang told Decker to leave the area, but the sheep man responded by practicing with his gun.

"Upon returning to the ranch from a day on the range he found the ranch house burned to the ground," wrote Jennings in *Arizona Was the West*. "With his rifle he started for the Longmore Ranch, feeling certain that the neighbors were trying to make good on their threat. Along the way he came upon Andy Cooper riding his mount. While greetings were exchanged, both were alert and tense. A squirrel ran up a tree and, without aim, Decker brought the little animal tumbling to the ground. With this action, Cooper moved on."

Sheriff Commodore Perry Owens was the quintessential Western hero -- a crack shot, braver than anyone, who single-handedly gunned down one of Arizona's most notorious gangs.

Carol Sletten
© 2010

The same no-aim killing of a distant squirrel was attributed to Sheriff Commodore Perry Owens. The Holbrook history claims the squirrel was shot "at a distance of about one mile." Squirrels in the White Mountains must be glad modern-day lawmen have less to prove.

Decker continued to the Longmore Ranch and drew his rifle on two men who came to the door. "He asked if they were going to leave him alone or must he kill both of them now," Jennings wrote. "They looked as if they were seeing a ghost. They had heard the earlier shot, and since Cooper had told them that morning that he was going to get Decker, they asked Z. B. if he had seen Cooper; the answer was that he had. They assumed that Cooper had become the victim of his own threat."

The two members of the gang vowed to cause no more trouble.

In *Elijah Was a Valiant Man*, Palmer wrote about John Payne, another member of the Blevins gang abusing local Mormons. "In the course of a few months he had physically assaulted George Lewis, Spence Shumway and Emanuel Cardon. He had threatened to kill John Oscar Reidhead of Juniper if Reidhead would not leave his [Reidhead's] land, and had evicted James Pearce from a homestead claim west of Taylor. In May he caught Niels Petersen several miles from home riding a partially broken and near un-manageable horse. Payne proceeded to savagely beat him with a loaded quirt [a whip with lead in the lash]. Because of the fright-ened and wildly thrashing horse Niels was unable to defend him-self. He was also unarmed." Petersen wanted to kill Payne, but Stake President Jesse N. Smith convinced him to let Sheriff Com-modore Perry Owens take care of it. Payne, already arrested once by Owens, left for the Tonto Basin, where he soon became a casualty of the Pleasant Valley War.

About that time, the *Apache Review* reprinted an article from the Arizona Silver Belt in Globe, declaring the "Ranch of Tom Graham in Tonto Basin to be the rendezvous of thieves. Re-cently the Tonto post office has been robbed, the Watkins store burglarized and cattle and horses stolen from various points in the basin."

Legendary White Mountain Sheriff Commodore Perry Owens was named for his father, Oliver H. Perry Owens, who in turn was named for the American hero Commodore Oliver Haz-ard Perry — the famous victor over the British on Lake Erie in the War of 1812. The unusual name added luster to the legend of the eccentric sheriff, whose wavy hair fell nearly to his waist in an out-of-date style worn by the Mountain Men of the previous generation. Owens, who came to the White Mountains as a cow-boy, caught the attention of the county's political elite when he was running the remount station at Navajo Springs. Although Navajo Springs was the first territorial capital, it had been so for only one day. By the mid-1880s it was just a stopping point for express riders passing along what would eventually become In-terstate 40. The remote station was much harassed by Navajos, who felt entitled to the horses there. Owens' aggressive action (some exaggerated reports said he killed as many as 50 Indians) led to charges of murder, but he was acquitted. The horse steal-ing dwindled as Owens gained a reputation with his rifle.

Owens shot down his adversaries without raising the Win-chester to his shoulder to aim through the sights. He fired from the hip with deadly accuracy. For longer-range action, he used a

Sharp's rifle, carrying both guns in a single scabbard on his saddle.

Citizens suffering from rampant lawlessness drafted Owens to run for sheriff of Apache County, which then also included all of present-day Navajo County. The new sheriff was given a warrant to arrest Andy Cooper. Reports said the suspect was in Holbrook.

The St. Johns Stake history says Owens carried the Cooper warrant around without taking action for almost two months. "Some thought he was afraid of Cooper; some said he was waging a war of nerves; others maintained that they were old range pals and knowing that Cooper would resist arrest, Owens did not relish the prospect of a shoot-out between them." Since the delay had spawned whispering, Owens knew the time for action had arrived.

It was known that the Blevins women had a house in Holbrook where their menfolk rested between skirmishes. On September 4, 1887, the sheriff rode into town to arrest Cooper.

Two days before, Cooper and other members of the gang had killed John Tewksbury and William Jacobs in the Tonto Basin. Holbrook-based Deputy Frank Wattron offered to go to the house with Owens, but the sheriff declined. "If I take a posse down there it is almost sure that several men will be killed, but if I go alone they can only kill one man," the sheriff is quoted as saying.

Owens cleaned and oiled his Winchester and headed to the house.

"Before I got there, I saw someone looking out at the door," Owens said in his report. "When I got close to the house, they shut the door. I stepped up on the porch, looked through the window and also looked in the room to my left. I see Cooper and his brother (John) and others in that room. I called to Cooper to come out. Cooper took out his pistol and also his brother took out his pistol. Then Cooper went from that room into the east room. His brother came to the door on my left, took the knob in his hand and held the door open a little. Cooper came to the door facing me from the east room. Cooper held this door partly open with his head out. I says, 'Cooper, I want you.' Cooper says, 'What do you want with me?' I told him the same warrant that I spoke to him about some time ago that I left in Taylor, for horse

237

stealing. Cooper says, 'Wait.' I says, 'Cooper, no wait.' Cooper says, 'I won't go.' I shot him. This brother of his to my left behind me jerked open the door and shot at me, missing me and shot the horse which was standing [be]side and little behind me. I whirled my gun and shot at him, and then ran out in the street where I could see all parts of the house. I could see Cooper through the window on his elbow with his head towards the window. He disappeared to the right of the window. I fired through the house expecting to hit him between the shoulders. I stopped a few moments. Some man (Mote Roberts) jumped out of the house on the northeast corner out of a door or window, I can't say, with a six shooter in his right hand and his hat off. There was a wagon or buckboard between he and I. I jumped on one side of the wagon and fired at him. Did not see him any more. I stood there a few moments when there was a boy [Sam Blevins] jumped out of the front of the house with a six shooter in his hands. I shot him. I stayed for a few moments longer. I see no other man so I left the house. When passing by the house I see no one but somebody's feet and legs sticking out the door. I then left and came on up town."

The *Apache County Critic*, quoted in the James Madison Flake biography, gives a more detailed account of the killing of young Sam Blevins: "The sheriff had stood in his last position perhaps ten seconds, when Sam H. Blevins, (a youth of 15 or 16 years) rushed out, his mother after him, through the same door in which Andy Cooper was killed, with Cooper's six-shooter in his hand. The boy and his mother were about four feet from the door; seeing the sheriff, she screamed, grabbed hold of her son and rushed for the door, but too late to save the life of the foolish boy, as Owens' unerring rifle belched forth its fifth shot and the boy fell face down-wards at his mother's feet, head and shoulders inside the door; the door through which he had stepped but a few moments before, but now a lifeless corpse ... ."

The fight lasted less than a minute, according to most accounts. Sam Blevins was killed instantly. Cooper died that night. Mote Roberts lived about 10 days, and John Blevins recovered. Unhurt in the house were Mary Blevins, the mother; John's wife, Eva; two young girls and two babies.

The *Critic* gave this account of the aftermath: "Dead and

wounded in every room, and blood over the floors, doors and walls. One little child, seven years of age, was literally bespattered with clots of human gore. The agonizing groans of the wounded, the death-rattle of the dying, mingled with the hysterical screams of the females made a sight that no one would care to see the second time."

A coroner's jury upheld Owens, saying he was discharging his duty when he killed the gang members.

Back in Pleasant Valley, gunmen killed Hamp Blevins, the father, and his other son, Charles, on September 22.

James Flake gave a slightly different account of the final battle in Pleasant Valley: "In October of the same year, I went into the Valley with Deputy Sheriff Joe McKinney following three men who had robbed a train near Navajo Springs. We met Sheriff Mulvernon from Prescott, John Francis from Flagstaff, and Glen Reynolds from Globe. We did not know they were coming in, but met Jim Houck on the trail and he took us to the camp. They had come to clean up the Valley. The next day, John Graham and Charley Blevins were killed. Tom Graham, Louie Parker and Adams, who were watching from the Block House, jumped on their horses and left the Valley. About 18 others were arrested."

The *St. Johns Herald* reported that Bill Graham was stopped on the trail by Houck, who had been hiding in the bushes, waiting for one of Graham's brothers. "Mr. Houck then discovered that it was Bill Graham, and told him to go on, that he did not want him. Instead of moving, however, he took a shot at Mr. Houck, which was returned by the latter with fatal effect. Graham succeeded in reaching his home, but died next day." At least that was Houck's account. Bill Graham had no opportunity to tell his side of the story.

The *St. Johns Herald* reported that the Blevins family had previous experience with the Texas prison system and added, "John Blevins, we believe, is the only one of six that is now alive, and he is at present confined in our county jail on a charge that will undoubtedly send him to the Territorial prison for quite a number of years. ... Now four of them fill untimely graves, without coffins. ... The father's bones are, perhaps, bleaching in some wild and unfrequented spot, the flesh having been torn from them by wild animals, as his body has never been found. Verily, the way of the transgressor is hard."

Even then, scores from the Pleasant Valley War were not entirely settled. One of the Tewksburys killed one of the Grahams in Phoenix five years later. Eventually, the case against the killer was dropped "at the suggestion of the Board of Supervisors," according to a newspaper account. But law and order had won a major victory against cattle rustling on the western edge of the White Mountains.

John Blevins, wounded in the Holbrook shootout, was convicted for his role in the gunfight during a jury trial in St. Johns and sentenced to five years in prison. He was pardoned by the governor, according to *The Crooked Trail*. He later homesteaded a tract of land near Heber south of what is now Highway 260 where it crosses Phoenix Park Wash. He became an exemplary citizen and well-known fiddle player. This last survivor of the Pleasant Valley War died in 1929 in a one-car accident on the way to Tucson.

Owens became a local hero. The *Apache Review* doted on his pistols, saying, "Commodore Owens has two of the handsomest colts in the county." Though he was worshipped for his Holbrook exploits, the cattlemen who had supported his election felt he was not doing enough to solve the rustler problem. They withdrew the bonds they had posted to guarantee his performance in office. Also, Owens had a great deal of trouble holding onto prisoners. In one case, Kid Swingle jumped off a train in New Mexico to escape him. In another incident, two prisoners sawed their way through the bars of the St. Johns jail. And on March 19, 1887, a Saturday night jail break created much excitement. All the prisoners fled, except Sol Barth, who refused to go. "Sheriff Owens says he was not away from the jail a great while, but when he returned, found the front door and the door leading into the hall both standing open," the *St. Johns Herald* reported. "He hurried into the hall and was completely dumb-founded by finding the cell doors all standing wide open, and the occupants all 'vamoosed the ranch.' ... That there were five doors unlocked — all having different locks and requiring different keys — to be unlocked in the dark and all done in the course of a very few minutes — shows, as well as proves, that they were unlocked by someone who had frequently locked and unlocked them before."

The paper reported on the roundup of the escapees throughout the Southwest. John Brown was arrested in Socorro County, New Mexico. Red Murphy was captured in Cochise County, leaving George West at large.

Kid Swingle was found hanged after leaving Clifton with someone else's horse, according to Rita Ackerman's *O. K. Corral Postscript*.

Despite the recovery of most of the escapees, Owens did not run for re-election. He served as a guard on the railroad, and then, for a brief time, became sheriff and assessor of the newly created Navajo County. He had particular trouble with a red-headed robber-poet named W. R. McNeil. After the outlaw was wounded holding up the Schuster Brothers store in Holbrook, McNeil left this poem tacked to a tree for the pursuing sheriff:

I am king of the outlaws
I am perfection at robbing a store
I have a stake left me by Wells Fargo
And before long, I will have more.

They are my kind friends, the Schusters,
For whom I carry so much lead
In the future to kill this young rooster
They will have to aim at his head.

Commodore Owens says he would like to kill me
To me that sounds like chaff
'Tis strange he would thus try to kill me
The red headed son-of-a-gun.

He handles the six shooter mighty neat
And kills a jack-rabbit every pop
But should he and I happen to meet
There will be a regular old Arkansas hop.

Owens continued to chase him. Once, according to *History of Holbrook*, Owens came upon a group of friendly cowboys while searching late into the evening for McNeil near the New Mexico line. The sheriff spent the night with the group, but woke up all alone with only this poem for company.

Pardon me, sheriff
I'm in a hurry;
You'll never catch me,
But don't worry.

The outlaw poet had a successful career until overconfidence led him to try to single-handedly rob a train in Utah. He was wounded in the leg by the conductor and sent to prison, where he studied engineering. Legend says he later sought out his former victims and even made restitution.

Owens soon drifted on to Seligman where he married 23-year-old Elizabeth Barrett when he was nearly 50. In a report published in the Holbrook history, J. H. McClintock said he saw Owens "in Seligman only a few months before he died [in 1919 at age 66]. He seemed a fish out of water, and I think his decease mainly was due to the fact that he didn't have a saloon to loaf in."

O. K. Corral Outlaws
Come to the Mountain

Meanwhile, another famous Arizona feud was working to-wards its conclusion in the eastern White Mountains.

In October 1881, Wyatt Earp and his brothers shot it out with the Clanton gang at the O. K. Corral in Tombstone. The four Earp brothers, all with varying full-time and part-time law enforcement posts, had made enemies of two prominent families in the cattle business, the McLaurys and Clantons. The Earps, like many of the townspeople who had come to Arizona from the northern states, demonized those cattlemen who had southern sympathies.

The more-or-less respectable cattlemen trafficked in livestock of questionable origin and had friends such as "Curly Bill" Brocius who were out-and-out outlaws. The Earp's associates were not all lily white either. The brothers were close friends with Doc Holliday, who was under suspicion for stage robbery. In conspiracy theories that would confound the Warren Commission, some enthusiasts believe the real trouble was based on fallout from a joint Earp-Clanton plot to rob Mexican smugglers. For whatever reason, shootings and beatings boiled over into open conflict when the Earps and Holliday went to a lot near Fly's photography studio to disarm the McLaurys and Clantons on October 26, 1881. Three cowboys, including Billy Clanton, were killed instantly or mortally wounded. On the other side, Holliday and all of the Earps but Wyatt were wounded. Ike Clanton was apparently unarmed. He fled through the photography studio. The Earps were charged in the killings, but acquitted. Not long after the gunfight, Marshal Virgil Earp was badly wounded in an ambush. Ike Clanton was acquitted of that attack.

Next Morgan Earp was killed by a shotgun blast fired through the window of a saloon. Wyatt hunted down and killed Frank Stilwell and "Indian Charley," two suspects in his brother's murder. Wyatt said he also killed Curly Bill, though some consider that claim doubtful. By this time, Tombstone was tired of gunfights and ambushes. Wyatt Earp headed for Colorado. Ike Clanton and brother Phin headed north to the White Mountain area.

"After the widely publicized Earp-Clanton shoot-out at the O. K. Corral in Tombstone, what was left of the notorious Clanton gang came to Apache County, where law men were only conspicuous by their absence," says an *Arizona Highways* article published in 1965. "Old man Ike Clanton and Phineas claimed a homestead on Coyote Creek east of Springerville."

In *O. K. Corral Postscript,* Ackerman says the ranch was 20 miles from Springerville, north of Escudilla mountain, near the New Mexico line.

"In the relative safety of their own ranch, they continued in the pursuits for which their previous experience had prepared them ... trading horses and cattle of questionable ownership and generally stirring up trouble wherever they went," the *Arizona Highways* article says.

P. F. Clanton advertised his brand prominently in the *St. Johns Herald*: "Cattle branded JU on left ribs. Ears cropped and slit." However, the Clantons are not remembered for keeping the ownership of cattle straight.

A videotape produced by the Little House Museum says the Clantons also registered the "74" brand so they could easily convert the brand of the "24" ranch to their own.

In the videotape, a story is told about the Clantons' frequent visits to Springerville, where they bought supplies. One day Ike was causing trouble in Gustav Becker's store. Becker slapped him to the ground and lived to tell, the story says.

The *Apache Chief* reports that in 1884 Cub Langley, a Clanton gang member, was shot during a store robbery in the area.

Ike Clanton was involved in a shooting in Springerville in May 1886, the *St. Johns Herald* reported. "We have a rumor from Springerville that there was a little shooting affair in that usually quiet and peaceable town a few days since. The parties engaged in this interchange of civil ties were Ike Clanton and Pablo Romero, and the immediate cause of the ceremonial display was a game of cards. Romero got a bullet through the left hip, and Clanton received a slight wound in one of his legs from a splintered ball. Neither of the wounds, we are informed, are of a very serious nature. Romero was brought to St. Johns and Dr. Dalby extracted the ball."

Though low-level violence was tolerated in the area, it was the killing of Isaac Ellinger, a rich young man from the East, that began to bring things to a head for the Clanton gang.

"Quite a serious shooting affray took place at the Cienega Maria [Amarilla], about 20 miles southeast of Springerville, on last Saturday, at noon," the *St. Johns Herald* reported on November 11, 1886. ". . . it seems that Ike Ellinger claims to have had a ranch jumped by a man named Craig recently. It appears that Lee Renfro had learned that Ellinger had connected his name in a disparaging manner with the transaction. . . . Ellinger and Renfro were both at the ranch of Phin Clanton, and the subject was brought up, when Renfro, after using insulting epithets, succeeded in getting a pistol, and before the bystanders could prevent him, shot Ellinger through the breast and lungs."

Ike Clanton admitted to being present during the shooting, which he said was unjustified murder, but his associate Renfro fled and remained in hiding.

The next issue of the paper reported that Ellinger had died of his wounds. "This is but another of those deplorable homicides resulting from the reckless, indiscriminate use of firearms, and the baneful custom of the constant wear and use of pistols," the editor said. The newspaper went on to report that Renfro had left the country, and to decry the fact that justice would probably never be done.

Ellinger's family had extensive ranching and other business interests. His brother came to claim the body, and may have hastened the undoing of the Clanton gang. A detective, J. V. Brighton, later described the Ellinger killing this way: "A tenderfoot from the States came into that part of the country and bought 200,000 head of cattle and started a ranch. The leaders of the Clanton gang applied to the tenderfoot for positions with his outfit to look after the cattle, but he refused to have anything to do with them. One day they sent him a note, asking him to call at their ranch, and when he arrived they deliberately shot the man dead."

It is not clear who put detective Brighton on the case. Such secrets have a long shelf-life. At first, arrangements were kept secret to allow the spy to infiltrate the gang. Of course, there was an understanding that the detective would kill the suspects when he had the opportunity. Then, after public opinion turned against lynch law, nobody wanted to be tied to the killing. Finally, when the event had passed into the safe territory of history, old timers were happy to brag about their involvement. Will C. Barnes, an accomplished yarn spinner and onetime secretary of the Apache County Stock Growers Association, said he had a role in hiring Brighton. It is also known that Ellinger's brother, William, offered a reward, but withdrew the public offering shortly before Ike Clanton was killed. In 1900, Brighton said he was sent to Apache County by the Continental Cattle Company of Illinois. At times, he identified himself as a county deputy, a U.S. marshal, a detective for the cattlemen and a Pinkerton. A detractor says Brighton once showed him a badge he received from a mail-order detective school.

Brighton spent time setting up his cover in Springerville, establishing several businesses, including a blacksmith's shop and a saloon. He had a long history of working in desperate situations. Brighton was born in 1845 in Indiana, joined the Union Army in 1863, and claimed to have spent time in the notorious Southern prisoner of war camp at Andersonville. He said his wife was killed in a Kansas tornado, but Ackerman found census records that indicate his wife and children continued to live in Kansas after he left.

He was reported to have served time in the Kansas Penitentiary for cattle theft, but it is not clear whether that was a real conviction, or part of his cover, or both. Brighton and a woman he identified as his wife were hired to go undercover and investigate the shooting of a doctor in Missouri. They helped to bring charges against two of the victim's sons, the victim's wife and a hired hand. Although they won convictions and the young sons were hanged, the detectives got in trouble for their investigative techniques, which included opening U.S. mail. Brighton claimed that he infiltrated a rump faction of the James Gang on behalf of the railroad after he solved the Missouri murder.

Ike Clanton was apparently his next big project. In a *Los Angeles Times* article, Brighton explained the gang's business this way: "Their system of operating was to steal from the stock people, who were mostly Mormon, and then run the cattle down into Mexico where they would be disposed of."

Ackerman writes that Anthony Harris, apparently a friend of the Clantons, was at Brighton's home in Springerville when a killing took place. Harris shot and killed Charles Lewis, a man who had been threatening him. It is not clear if, or how, this killing tied into the Clanton gang's operations, but it does show that Brighton was associating with the outlaws.

"I got in with the gang without their knowing who I was and assisted in all their work, keeping in touch all the time with the proper authorities, but they finally got suspicious and laid plans to 'do me up'," Brighton said. "They held me up one day at the muzzle of several guns, and asked me very emphatically if I was 'one of those —— detectives.' Of course I told them I was not, and they came to the conclusion that they had been a little hasty.

"All this time I was forming my plans to kill or capture the whole outfit, and an opportunity to partly carry out my plan came. … The gang fled to the mountains, and wanted me to go along, too, but I excused myself by saying I was going 'hunting.' I meant it, too, for I jumped on my horse and rode to the county seat [St. Johns], where I talked up my plans to the sheriff. He wanted to send out a posse, but I said I could do better alone. I did, however, take one deputy along [Albert Miller]. I had been over the trail, of course, and also knew every member of the gang by sight.

"We rode posthaste to Willcox, and were told there that the gang had fled to Mexico. I knew this was untrue, and on the way back to Solomonville I learned that they were hiding in the hills near there. I went to the sheriff of the town and notified him that the gang were there, and to arrest any of them who came to town.

"While I was saddling my horse in the corral the hostler told me he had seen one of the Clanton boys in town that very morning at the sheriff's office, getting some checks cashed. I also learned that the sheriff himself was as tough a nut as any of the Clantons, and was told that he wanted me 'done up,' and that several of his own deputies were cattle thieves and murderers of the toughest type.

"Miller and I saddled up and rode across the Gila River and laid in the hills all day. The next morning we struck the camp of a cowboy named 'Peg-Leg' Wilson, and here we stopped for breakfast. As we were kindling a fire we heard the clatter of horse's hoofs along the trail and glancing up we saw Ike Clanton approaching. Miller straightened up and Clanton saw and recognized him immediately. He wheeled his horse and unslung his Winchester, starting to ride around us. I grabbed my rifle and covered him, shouting at the same time to hold up his hands and to halt. Miller yelled: 'Shoot the —— —— ——!' Clanton refused to halt and I fired at him, hitting him under the arm. He reeled in the saddle and I gave him another which struck the cantle of the saddle and went up through his body. He dropped and when we ran up we found him as dead as a mackerel. One of the gang had been wiped out and one of its worst members."

In an account Brighton gave to the *St. Johns Herald* only days after the killing, he described Wilson's place as a cabin at the head of the Blue River and Eagle Creek, rather than a camp. Ackerman told the story of a man named Jim McCarthy, who said he heard Peg Leg Wilson's account of the killing. In this version, Wilson said Ike Clanton was in Wilson's cabin alone when Brighton sneaked up and shot him in the back. No matter how it actually happened, it is unlikely that Brighton, facing a desperate killer in the wilderness, called out to Clanton, showed his badge and started to read him his rights.

William Flake's autobiography gives Sheriff Commodore Perry Owens a role in handling the Clanton gang, though Owens was reported to be in New Mexico capturing a prisoner at the time. Ackerman speculates that linking Sheriff Owens to the killing may have been done to establish the legality of the shooting.

Lee Renfro, hiding out in Graham County near the San Carlos Reservation, was killed by authorities looking for stolen livestock. Brighton later identified himself as Renfro's killer.

Arizona Highways, in 1950, put the shootout and Ike Clanton's grave on the Black River, south of Springerville, while Ed Bartholomew in *The Biographical Album of Western Gunfighters* puts the outlaw's final resting place near Camp Grant.

Ackerman says Phin Clanton was in the St. Johns jail for livestock theft when the law went after Ike, thus missing the fatal confrontation. The *St. Johns Herald* later reported Phin's conviction of grand larceny. He was sentenced to 10 years in prison. Phin received a pardon after a witness against him, A. G. Powell, claimed that he and Brighton testified falsely to get a $250 reward. In 1889, Powell and another man stole some horses near Springerville. As they fled toward Texas, they were hunted down and killed by the aggrieved livestock owners.

After his pardon, Phin moved to Globe to raise goats. He was a model citizen, except for a run-in with a Chinese gardener that resulted in more felony charges. Some accounts say it was the old outlaw's son who got into trouble in Globe. Though published stories say Phin was shot to death in Apache County, they are not true. Phin Clanton died and was buried in Globe in 1905.

Brighton, who could shoot the bull maybe better than he could shoot his guns, gave this account of the burial of Ike Clanton: "Tying the body on the horse, we continued on our way and soon met three cowboys who helped us bury Clanton's body. As we were about to place the body in the grave I happened to think that Clanton had once told me that if I was present whenever he 'turned up his toes' to be sure and pull off his boots before he was buried, as his people had often declared that he would be buried with his boots on, and he wished to show that they were mistaken. I pulled off his footgear, high top boots that cost Clanton $12, and were inlaid with silver stars and had a fine pair of silver spurs at the heels, and put them on my own feet.

"When I got back to Springerville a man who was a friend of Clanton's saw me and recognized the boots and asked me where I got them. I told him a hatched-up yarn, but he refused to believe it, and we came near having a fight over the matter. Clanton was an all-round bad man and had a record of nineteen kills to his discredit. I saw him kill two men myself, just for the mere 'fun of the thing,' as he called it."

Brighton relates that he was later indicted for killing Ike Clanton and had a run-in with the corrupt lawmen in Solomonville before getting the drop on them. Brighton took his bad-boy detective act on to California where he won additional fame for busting up a gang of train robbers.

On July 4, 1888, the St. Johns paper reported that Phin Clanton's Cienega Amarilla Ranch was transferred in a foreclosure sale to Al Pratt.

The Original Ox-Bow Incident

Meanwhile, the *St. Johns Herald* was wound up about rustling along the Mogollon Rim in the western edges of the White Mountain area. The resulting 1880 confrontation was the inspiration for the plot of the classic 1940 western novel *The Ox-Bow Incident* by Walter Van Tilburg Clark, and the 1943 Oscar-nominated movie of the same name. The *Herald* said, "From what information we can gather, these outlaws exercise such a reign of terror over the inhabitants of that section that parties who, have lost stock and who know the parties that have taken them, are afraid to swear out warrants for their arrest. They have driven settlers out of their houses — torn down their place of public worship — driven stolen stock along the public highways in the broad glare of the noonday sun, and if reports be true, added murder to their long catalogue of crimes."

In another article, the newspaper said the rustlers from Canyon Creek "recently left one of the citizens of Snowflake without a team to cultivate his ground. They went to his stable and took therefrom the last span of horses he had. These things have been going on almost as long as human patience can endure it;

and we predict that when the people finally make up their minds they have stood it long enough, their mode of dealing with these outlaws will be as swift and terrible as they have been patient and enduring."

While some of the major gangs were out of the way, rustling was still good business in the western reaches of the White Mountain range.

On July 4, 1888, James Stott, an educated man from a wealthy family who set up a ranch near Heber, wrote a letter to the editor of the *Apache Review*. He denied that he had been run out of the Tonto Basin for rustling. "You would confer a favor on me by rectifying that statement, as I have never been in Tonto Basin in my life, and consequently was never ordered out." The paper commented, "We give space to the above communication from a desire to give every citizen a chance to set himself right before his fellows. We are credibly informed, however, that Tonto Basin is not a healthy section for Mr. Stott to range in now-a-days. Go-betweens for rustlers 'must go' along with their masters."

The Crooked Trail, which quoted the newspaper exchange, speculated that the newspaper's source of information on Stott may have been Deputy J. D. Houck, who "had many gripes with Jamie Stott. First, Jamie was thought to be aligned with the Hashknife cowboys [of the Aztec Land & Cattle Co.] This automatically placed him in opposition with the Tewksburys, compatriots of Houck and feudists from Pleasant Valley. Jamie's youth, coupled with his background as a Texas cowboy, gave him a lot in common with the Hashknives. Additionally, his ranch was completely surrounded by Aztec Company land. Second, his property was coveted by many settlers as it was one of the few locations with adequate water and pasture for significant herds of stock. Third, Houck had spent over thirty years of his life trying to build some prosperity, often at great risk to himself. Jamie, on the other hand, came West with the backing of his already prosperous father and could get financial support at any time. Houck must have resented this young upstart who burst on the scene and purchased one of the best locations in Apache County."

Houck claimed to have a warrant for Stott and two other men based on the wounding of Tewksbury associate Jake Lauffer, according to *The Crooked Trail*. Groups of armed men converged on Stott's ranch from three directions, one from the north, another group from Pleasant Valley to the south and the third led by Houck from the west. The riders found Stott at the ranch, along with employee Jeff Wilson, and two tuberculosis sufferers who were staying with Stott, Lamotte Clymer and Alfred Ingham. Jim Scott had been seized in Pleasant Valley by the group coming up from the south and was brought along with them to the ranch.

Jennings, writing in *Arizona Was the West*, added, "The *St. Johns Herald* reports that James Houck, an acting deputy sheriff arrested Stott at gunpoint at the Stott ranch. When Stott asked to read the warrant, Houck said that it had been left at Bear Spring. … Stott graciously gave breakfast to the crowd."

Jennings, who was born in 1893 and grew up in the area, had a cowboy's gift for storytelling and personally knew many of the legendary outlaws and lawmen of the White Mountains. His dates sometimes conflict with those of later historians, but he is unmatched in the human detail he brought to the stories. Having walked the earth with the survivors of many gunfights, he was careful to tell more than one side of the sometimes complex conflicts.

The posse left Stott's sick visitors at the cabin when they took Stott, Scott and Wilson and headed toward Pleasant Valley.

"Early in the afternoon of August 11, they arrived at the place where the Old Verde Road and the Crooked Trail to Holbrook meet," Hanchett said. "There they stopped. Originally, it may not have been anyone's intention to hang the three young cowboys, maybe all they wanted to do was to make them think that hanging was a possibility. Sufficiently frightened, the cowboys would then make a hasty exit out of the country. Unfortunately for the trio, they didn't scare easily, and the more resolved the prisoners became, the further the abductors carried their intimidation. Jim Houck claimed later that he had left the group at that point and added that his prisoners had been led off by a 'band of forty masked men.' "

Osmer Flake, son of William Flake, reported that Scott and Wilson were killed first: "They put the two men on their horses and threw the rope over a limb above them. With the loop around their necks, they drove the horses out from under each. All this time Stott was sitting there in full view of it all."

251

Stott was not intimidated by the murder of his friends and refused to beg for his life. "In response to Jamie's courage, the vigilantes yanked Jamie off his horse. To mock his gentility, they tied a red handkerchief around his neck. They claimed it was so they wouldn't hurt him. Placing the noose of the rope around his neck and throwing the loose end over the branch of another tree, they pulled him up and lowered him down several times, just to give him a taste of hanging. Finally, they left him hanging too long and when they let him down, he was dead. Then they pulled the rope high, secured it and rode away."

William Flake was headed to Pleasant Valley after being told that one of his mares was over there. The Flake book continues, "At Heber, he learned there had been some men hanged up on the Mountain near the trail. As he rode toward the Valley the next day, he saw James Stott, Jimmie Scott and Wilson all hanging in trees, where a mob had left them." Flake rode on to Pleasant Valley where he came across the members of the mob. "Of course they did not tell him they were the ones who did the hanging, and seemed very much surprised when he told them. He knew a number of the men, but they would not talk about it, but he was determined. ... They finally told him enough, so that he knew they had hanged the other two, and then had tantalized Stott. He cursed them to the end, and tried every way possible to fight them, or give him a break. ... While we were all glad to get rid of Stott, we did not approve of mob law, and worse still was to torture the victim."

The *St. Johns Herald* didn't approve either. It said, "For a body of armed men to be scouring the country, picking up men against whom they have a grudge, and hanging them without the semblance of a trial, or without even letting them or their friends know for what they were hung, is going a little too far, even for a deputy sheriff."

Jennings wrote that the supervisors of Gila County refused to pay for an inquest. "People quickly began to take sides. In a newspaper interview Houck defended the arrest of Stott but insisted that he had nothing to do with the hanging. Houck did admit having warrants for the three on a charge that they were involved in two separate shootings. But he also repeated his claim that a party of about 40 masked men took the prisoners away

252

from the posse.

"John Hunt of Snowflake, with whom we often were on the freight road, knew the victims and believed that Stott was a possible rustler," Jennings wrote. "The other two victims, he felt, were at the wrong place at the right time. It was also John's conviction that the leader of the lynching wanted the Stott ranch and later ran sheep there for many years."

In his book *Elijah Was a Valiant Man*, Palmer identifies Houck as the man who coveted Stott's land.

There was considerable discussion of the guilt or innocence of the parties. The *Apache Review* reported that goods from a store robbery were found in Wilson's cabin. An anonymous letter to the *St. Johns Herald*, said Stott owned a home, ranch, 150 head of horses and some 50 head of cattle. "Does it look reasonable that he should be engaged in stealing horses?"

Jennings also quoted *Arizona's Dark and Bloody Ground* by Earl Forrest. "The evidence points conclusively to Houck as the instigator." Forrest based much of his conclusion on the fact that F. A. Ames, an employee of the Hashknife, implicated Houck in a letter to Stott's father. Ames further states that Stott did not participate in the rustling in that section, but that such stories were circulated by the enemies of Stott — the parties who wanted to get possession of the ranch.

Jennings continues: "Houck was in the office of Dr. Robinson (in Holbrook) when Ed Rogers, boss of the Hashknife outfit, walked in. Rogers faced Houck and accused him of hanging an innocent man when he hanged Stott. Houck declared that he did not do it. Rogers started calling Houck unprintable names and then both grabbed for their six guns, putting them in full cock. Houck did not back down. John A. Hunt, who witnessed this, stated that Dr. Robinson and his drug store partner, Frank J. Wattron, tried to quiet them and seek a better way to settle the matter. But these men paid no attention to anyone, but looked each other straight in the face. Finally, Rogers could face it no longer, threw the cartridges from his gun, shoved the weapon in the scabbard and walked out. You could tell by Houck's face and actions that he expected Rogers to reload and return or shoot through the window. He stood for at least 30 minutes and never took his eyes off the openings. But Rogers did not appear. Two days later Rogers got a letter from the post office and, upon opening it he found a piece of paper that had nothing on it but the word 'Go' written in red ink. Rogers immediately disappeared and no one seemed to know just where or why he had gone."

Houck, who had a contract to carry mail from New Mexico to Prescott, earlier had his detractors. On April 9, 1880, the *Arizona Miner* reported that he was arrested by authorities in St. Johns on a charge of complicity, with a tramp, in the murder of a doctor from Cincinnati who had been traveling with $3,000 in cash.

Houck survived accusations and took his own life at Cave Creek in 1921 by eating strychnine at the age of 74.

Flake, who bought the Stott ranch and its equipment when it was sold by an administrator, said he found detailed records indicating "from whom the stock was stolen." The Flake biography says he shared these records with Stott's wealthy father when the family came to Arizona to determine what had happened.

A Passel of Outlaw Trouble

Brighton, the detective who claimed to have killed Ike Clanton, tells a story about uneven justice in Springerville. He said the justice of the peace was a Confederate sympathizer who rode with Quantrell's raiders when they burned Lawrence, Kansas, and murdered many of the inhabitants. The guerrilla outfit also included the men who would later make up the James Gang. The detective, who had been a Yankee, was involved in a lawsuit over the digging of some ditches. He felt he had a good case, but thought the JP ruled against him because of lingering Civil War hostilities. Later, Brighton saw the JP outside court. "I pulled my gun on him and told him to reconsider that case. . . . The fellow was scared at my bravado and promised to do the square thing. The next day he fixed the matter in my favor."

White Mountain bad men were sometimes arrested when they traveled outside the area. William E. Martin, better known as Kid Miller, was convicted in Socorro, New Mexico, of killing Gustave Fitchell. Bud Wilson and "Loco Tom" Licky were arrested in New Mexico with 14 head of horses from Apache

County.

The *St. Johns Herald* doubted reports from Oji Pueblo about the death of Jesus Valenzuela, who escaped from the Apache County Jail where he was being held on charges of attempted murder. "We have been unable to trace the report to any reliable source, and it may be gotten up to throw the authorities off."

Cute stories are told about Climax Jim, an outlaw active in the White Mountains who had excellent skills in lock picking. He was able to open cell doors, handcuffs and leg irons. In an *Arizona Highways* article, George H. Smalley tells how Climax, also known as Rufus Nephews, escaped from the St. Johns jail. He made the break without his shoes and later, with badly swollen feet, crawled into the camp of Arizona Ranger Joe Pearce of Eagar. "Climax, thinly attired, complained that he was very cold. He got an armful of brush and threw it on the fire which blazed high with a surge of smoke which blinded me. When I recovered Climax had disappeared in the darkness." The outlaw once was accused of altering a check to increase the amount that a mining company in Clifton had paid for some cattle. As the trial progressed, Smalley wrote, Climax was able to slip the check into his mouth and eat the evidence.

An account in the local paper says Climax Jim and William Apperson were arrested in Solomonville for stealing cattle. But when Sheriff Ed Beeler arrived at the jail to bring the pair to St. Johns for trial, he was only able to pick up Apperson. Climax Jim had already escaped.

In September 1885, the *St. Johns Herald* reported that the mail coach from St. Johns had been robbed 12 miles north of town where the road crosses the Zuni River. "The mail pouch containing the Springerville and the entire southern and St. Johns mail was overhauled by these miscreants," the paper said. "Dr. Yarrow of the Smithsonian scientific exploration party, was the only passenger, and it is feared that he may be the loser of a very valuable watch in addition to whatever funds he may have had for traveling expenses." The driver reported that the gunmen rode off toward the Zuni villages and the sheriff sent a posse after them.

In 1887, the *St. Johns Herald* reported that highwaymen wearing masks robbed the mail 20 miles from Fort Apache. "It is

255

generally thought that it is the same gang who robbed the Atlantic and Pacific Railroad train three weeks ago."

A little later, the paper reported that a robber held up the buckboard carrying the mail from Navajo Springs to St. Johns. Then the brazen bandit held the driver for four hours while waiting for another buckboard carrying mail from the opposite direction, so he could rob the northbound mail as well.

During that period, stages headed south from Navajo Springs and north from Springerville every day. They gave passengers a brief rest in St. Johns, and arrived at the opposite end of the line nearly 24 hours later. The rate was 3 cents a pound for freight under 50 pounds, and 2 cents a pound for heavier loads. The route was hazardous, not only because of outlaws. The Holbrook newspaper reported that the driver of the Springerville-St. Johns stage died in a 20-foot fall after the horses got off the road. The paper added, "name not known – Mexican."

Not all crimes were major. The *St. Johns Herald* reported on August 27, 1885, that John Norton, N. Marble, A. N. Holden and John Marble, were in the county jail after being convicted of petty larceny for stealing several tons of hay from John Westbrook, who lived at Amity, a small town about three miles from Springerville. Justice of the Peace Juan Armijo sentenced them to five days and seventy-five dollars, or an additional 15 days if they could not pay the fine. The adamantly anti-Mormon newspaper was happy to report the religious affiliation of the convicted, noting in the headline that they were "Herald Mormons," apparently the kind of people who got their name in the paper for the wrong reasons.

The paper was incensed when the rival pro-Mormon paper, the *Orion Era*, printed a suggestion by a Mormon bishop that a vigilance committee be formed as a more effective way to check crime in the county.

Another gang robbed an express train in 1887 at Navajo Springs. A posse followed them to Canyon Creek above the Mogollon Rim, where the trail was lost, according to Ackerman.

On June 27, 1888, a deputy sheriff left for Clifton trailing Solmon Slayback, an accused horse thief. He followed the four-day-old trail to within a mile of Springerville and up the Blue River to capture the thief. The same edition of the St. Johns paper had a story stating, "Stanley, the explorer, was recently wounded in a fight with African natives."

Deputy J. H. Benbrook reported to the *St. Johns Herald* in 1887 that he had gone to the Canyon Creek area to check on some rustling. "I had occasion to interview Mr. Bagsley on the 1st of August, having a warrant for his arrest from Maricopa County, on a charge of grand larceny. Instead of throwing up when I ordered him, he pulled and turned loose, the ball grazing my left thumb, but breaking no bones. I returned the fire and he died." The paper noted that Bagsley had been arrested two years earlier, but "at that time it was next to impossible to convict a man charged with any crime and he was released."

It was a violent era in the White Mountains. Armed men often killed each other when tempers flared. On July 30, 1888, at George Creaghe's ranch eight miles east of Springerville, a cook named Windy Magee shot and killed Henry Jenkins, also known as Dick Bumgreaser. The two exchanged remarks and Bumgreaser came at him with a loaded gun. Bumgreaser's gun jammed and Magee killed him. Bob Thomas, captain of the outfit, was also wounded in the exchange, and died in St. Johns on June 19. Ackerman reported the dispute was over hauling pack saddles in the grub wagon.

Pat Mullen, who had a ranch between Show Low and Fort Apache, was killed by a bartender when he went to St. Johns for jury duty. The *St. Johns Herald* reported that Frank Clark shot and killed Mullen, the lone patron in the saloon. Clark claimed there had been a dispute over money, and that Mullen threatened him, but Mullen was unarmed. The paper concluded, "The shooting seems to have been uncalled for and unprovoked."

The paper previously had less generous things to say about Mullen. It reported that Mullen was sentenced to a fine of $50 or 30 days in jail for declining to show his hides to the brand inspector of the Apache County Stockgrowers' Association. According to *O. K. Corral Postscript,* Clark was given life in prison.

Traveling was dangerous. In August 1896 the *Argus* reported that the town of Taylor had buried 22-year-old Francis Allen, who had been murdered in New Mexico. Initially, Navajos were blamed, but later evidence implicated two white men – "tramps who had taken dinner with him," the newspaper said.

257

A 1965 *Arizona Highways* article tells more tales about outlaw activities in the White Mountains, though their authenticity is not certified in other sources. "Men of the Snider Gang started a gun-fight among themselves and before the day was over, nine of them were killed, conveniently enough, on the hill behind the Eagar cemetery. ... Billy the Kid and members of his gang from New Mexico rode over until things cooled off."

The Blue River area was most certainly a hideout for bad guys. In 1887 the *St. Johns Herald* reported " 'Long-Hair' and 'Jack of Diamonds' met their fate there. Charlie Thomas, when questioned as to the killing, would neither say yes or no, but remarked that they 'would never steal any more horses from him.' " In another article, the *Herald* reported in some detail how Thomas had gunned down the bad men at the head of Eagle Creek after they stopped at his ranch. Ackerman said Thomas and two friends tracked the bad men down after they had stolen his horses.

In another 1887 case, a gang that tried to wreck and rob a passenger train near Bluewater, New Mexico, was captured in Apache County. Ackerman writes that Nat and Dick Greer, R. C. Blassingame, Charles Jones, Burt Potter and another cowboy captured the outlaws after they tried to take items from their camp.

Love triangles also caused deadly gun fights in the White Mountains. The *St. Johns Herald* reported that Patrick Maher suspected J. G. Berry "of being on too intimate terms with his wife." When Maher confronted Berry, he told the aggrieved husband to "hit the road and to hit it hard." Maher left, but returned the next morning before Berry was out of bed and emptied his six shooter into the supposed lover. Lawmen were unable to find Maher.

Alberto Gomez took the precaution of consulting a justice of the peace after his wife fled with Manuel Fernandez. Gomez "was told to go in pursuit, and if Fernandez resisted, he was authorized to use his weapons," according to the *St. Johns Herald*. "Gomez followed the advice without other authority, and as a sequel, the dead body of Fernandez was brought into town, with a bullet hole in the back. When released from jail the prisoner immediately returned to his runaway wife and carried her with him back to his home."

Even then you could not believe everything you read in the

papers. There was a story in the *Socorro Bulletin* that said, "A Navajo Indian was killed at St. Johns, the other day, by a white man named Bud Wilson, while trying to steal the latter's horse." The *St. Johns Herald*, surprised at being scooped on a killing in its hometown, investigated and found the story lacking. "If a Navajo was killed, Wilson did not do it in St. Johns; if a horse was stolen, it was not a Navajo who did it; as there have been no Navajos in town there has been a failure to kill one; and … Bud Wilson has not been in town for about two months."

Tragedy Strikes Snowflake

A visitor to Snowflake on December 8, 1892, was a suspect in a murder during a bank robbery in Magdalena, New Mexico.

William Flake's biography says, "He had seven notches on his gun, showing the number of men he had killed. The first one was his brother, whom he had killed when he was 13 years old. He was now 19 and the last of an outlaw family, all of whom had been killed."

William's sons Charles and James were deputized to arrest the killer, who was staying at a Snowflake boarding house, according to *The Freight Rolled* by Jennings. "James and Charles stood at the woodpile talking the matter over, when it was decided that Charles should go over and engage the young man in conversation, while James was to follow a few minutes later. When Charles arrived he found the man sitting in the yard cleaning his gun scabbard. In the course of conversation, Charles commented about the nice looking pearl-handled six-shooter being worn by the stranger and it was handed to Charles to look over. While looking at the gun, Jim Flake arrived. Mr. Flake grabbed the outlaw by the right wrist and said: "I have a warrant for your arrest," at the same time pulling out his cumbersome 44. Quick as a flash the outlaw pulled another gun with his left hand and shot at Jim, the bullet grazing his face, leaving unburned powder in the skin and passing through the ear. Quickly he [the outlaw] shot over his shoulder fatally wounding Charles in the neck. At the same time, James shot the young man in the face, and a second shot hit

259

him just under the eye, going through his head and killing him instantly."

When the White Mountain Apache Chief Alchesay and his brother "Mike" arrived at the Flake store not long after the killing and found it closed, they went looking for James Flake. Jennings reported the approximate conversation, as related by James Flake's son Don:

Alchesay: "What the matter. Jim no in store. Today not Sunday."

Flake: "I didn't go to the store today because my brother got killed."

Alchesay: "Well, Jim, you not dead; come open store."

"Then Father explained patiently how Uncle Charlie was shot by an outlaw and he, himself, felt too sad to keep business as usual," the Jennings account continues. "Father evidently entered into the pathos of the situation for by the time Father finished, both Alchesay and Mike had tears streaming down their faces. Alchesay was one of the toughest looking Apaches I ever saw. ... When the story was completed, Alchesay walked over and put his arms around Father and said, 'Jim, I be your brother.'"

Charles Flake was the father of five children, including one who preceded him in death and another who was born after his father had been killed. The youngest son would meet a tragic fate in World War I.

The Flakes had another run-in with outlaws when William went to the Gila River in February 1892 to sell his freight teams and settle up other business. He had collected a large amount of cash during the transactions, which he put in a horse's feedbag and threw in the wagon. On the second day of the trip back to Snowflake, he saw two men riding through the cedars away from the road. "He knew at once, that they were after his money," says the biography. "He drove on, and one of them finally rode up by the wagon and talked. Father told him to tie his horse to the side and get in, which he did. The fellow did some questioning, and he told him everything. He told him that he had been down to Willcox to settle some business and sell his freight teams, and then to Safford, where he had finished up and gotten his money. The fellow said, 'You got a good roll of money out of it then.' 'Yes,' said Father, 'I was going to bring it along with me, but my friends would not consent, and

James Madison Flake, son of William Flake, built a Victorian mansion in Snowflake in 1895, which remains as a monument to the town's first family. It is listed on the National Register.

said that there were too many robbers, and that some of them would know I had collected a lot of money and would follow me, and that I had better send it home by express, and I would be sure of it when I got there, and I thought it was very good advice.' The stranger rode a half mile farther, and then said, 'Well, I guess I will get out and ride on.' So he got on his horse and went ahead down the road, and was not seen by him again."

The Wild Bunch
And the White Mountains

The Wild Bunch, Hole in the Wall, Black Jack Ketchum and Smith gangs spent much of their time in the White Mountains. The four notorious gangs are all associated with the Hole in the Wall hideout near the Big Horn Mountains in Wyoming. And the names Hole in the Wall Gang and Wild Bunch are sometimes used interchangeably. Laughing Sam Carey's outfit was given the name of the outlaw stronghold since he was the first to use the hideout. Robert Leroy Parker, better known as Butch Cassidy, hid out there with his gang of about 10 train robbers, which, of course, included Harry Longbaugh, the Sundance Kid.

261

While the Ketchum outfit concentrated on robbing stage-coaches and the Smith gang spent more time in the mountains rustling cattle, the men moved freely among the outfits. They would split the proceeds of each job among the participants. In 1899 Ketchum killed Clint Wingfield, the storekeeper in Camp Verde, before going to Springerville to buy dynamite at Becker's store, the Little House video says. The explosives were for a train robbery near Holbrook.

Bronco Bill Walters was a member of the Ketchum gang who spent a good deal of time in the White Mountains, according to *Black Jack Ketchum: Last of the Hold-Up Kings* by Ed Bartholomew. A railroad detective named Jeff Milton was after the gang and Bronco Bill was unhappy about it. "Bill sent word to Milton that he was holed up in the White Mountains and that he would appreciate it if he would bring him some blankets, horses and food, as he liked to live in comfort. Taking up the bluff, Milton, with Eugene Thacker and George Scarborough and a man named Martin, went by special train to a point near Holbrook, where it had been expected the gang would attempt the robbery of a train. Nothing happened. Next Milton learned that the small band had robbed the patrons of a dance and had fled across the mountains to the vicinity of the Double Circle Ranch in the White Mountains. The posse trailed them and in a pitched battle, Bronco Bill was badly wounded by Milton and his men." The outlaw was found in bushes the next day and taken to Santa Fe where he recovered from his wounds and was sent to prison.

Butch Cassidy, the Sundance Kid and other members of the Wild Bunch assumed new names to work on the W. S. Ranch near Alma, New Mexico, just southeast of Springerville. The ranch was owned by a non-resident Englishman and managed by Capt. William French. The rustling of W. S. stock stopped immediately when Cassidy and his friends were hired.

Cassidy used the name Jerry Lowe while he was there. French considered him the "best man on the trail" and the best hand he had ever had on the ranch, according to Bartholomew. Apparently, Cassidy was quite a charmer too. French said he was always ready for a joke, and on the long evenings, "his conversation was witty and stimulating." When gang members took French's cattle to market, they seldom lost a head and always returned with all the cattle money.

After a train was stopped near Folsom, New Mexico, and robbers made off with unsigned bank notes, a Pinkerton detective arrived at the W. S. ranch. He claimed some of the stolen money had been used in Alma, New Mexico, by one of French's ranch hands. The W. S. cowboy told the Pinkerton that he had received the money in payment for a horse from another cowboy who had left the area. In some accounts, French was shown pictures of the Wild Bunch and recognized his trusted hands "Jim Lowe" and "Tom Capehart."

Several histories, including Butch Cassidy's biography by Richard Patterson, say the detective, Frank Murray, assistant superintendent of the Pinkerton agency, met Cassidy in a nearby town. The accounts differ on why Murray didn't arrest Cassidy. Some say Murray hadn't recognized the bandit. Others claim that the detective didn't have sufficient force at the time to attempt an arrest. Soon, Cassidy decided to move on.

"When Butch left, one of the W. S. hands, Red Weaver, went with him," the biography says. "According to French, before they left the area they made a stop at the ranch of a neighbor named Ashby. Apparently Butch and the men at the W. S. had been having trouble with Ashby. They suspected him of building his herd at the expense of his neighbors' strays, and when they approached him about the problem he had assumed a virtuous attitude that Butch found particularly annoying. ... But on taking their leave from the W. S., Butch decided to settle the score. He and Weaver dropped by Ashby's ranch and took every one of his saddle horses with them."

Cassidy and his accomplice were arrested when they rode into St. Johns with the horses. The *St. Johns Herald* said in 1900, "Jim Lowe and Red Weaver are in the county bastille here awaiting an investigation."

In his autobiography, *Recollections of a Western Ranchman*, French said the sheriff "held them until he could communicate with me at Magdalena. ... His telegram merely asked if I knew them, and I replied that I did, but it must have been entirely satisfactory, for he allowed Jim to go his way with the horses, but he detained Red – whom, it seemed, Jim claimed, was a stranger he had picked up on the road – on the ground of his suspicious appearance and his not being able to give a more definite account of himself. He was, however, unable to establish any definite charge, and after some further inquiry turned him loose."

It turned out that Butch Cassidy and Red Weaver were lucky to have been arrested. Their jail time gave them an iron-clad alibi when a crime occurred nearby which shocked the territory and led to the formation of the Arizona Rangers.

The Gibbons-LeSueur Murders

The *St. Johns Herald* gave this account of the circumstances leading up to double murders that occurred at the turn of the century: "Someone passing from St. Johns to Springerville observed five men standing near the carcass of a cow freshly killed. On reaching Springerville the traveler related what he had seen. Warrants for the arrest of the five men were sworn out; and a posse organized with Sheriff Beeler at the head, to arrest the lawbreakers. The posse didn't overtake the men until they reached St. Johns, where the alleged renegades were purchasing various supplies. For all of which they paid, much to the surprise of some of the merchants. While the outlaws were yet in town a part of the posse came in but made no attempt to make an arrest. The strangers went a short distance from town where they camped; next morning the posse aided by other men of this town sallied forth to bring in the men. But they opened fire on the posse at long range. A general fight ensued in which the alleged thieves had one horse and probably some of their men wounded, and were so closely pressed that they abandoned part of their bedding. But they soon outstripped the sheriff's posse leaving it in the rear. During the engagement the sheriff had sent a courier for reinforcements. ... "

Ben Crosby rode up to the home of Dick Gibbons in St. Johns and asked for help arresting the five desperados. "At eight o'clock we were on our way," Gibbons said in his diary. "There were eight of us in the posse: Will Harris, Gus Gibbons, Frank LeSueur, Antonio Armijo, Frank Ruiz, Ben Crosby, Murry from Springerville, and myself.

"When we got to the County bridge, we met one of Sheriff Beeler's men and he gave us the directions the outlaws had taken. We saw a wounded horse by the roadside and were told that Beeler's men and the outlaws had exchanged about 50 shots and it was thought that one of the outlaws was wounded. We took the trail and found that they were heading straight towards Cedro or the G Bar Ranch. The Sheriff had left word for us to come as quickly as possible for he intended to follow the outlaws and get them if it took all summer. We followed the trail across the Cariso, over the ridge through a narrow pass, down into the Zuni Wash and out on the other side, and then the trail took an easterly course up the wash, just mentioned. I made the suggestion that four of us follow the trail and four of us strike for the Cedro and head off the renegades there and to lend assistance to Sheriff Beeler's men. Gus, Frank, and the two Mexican boys continued on the trail, while I and the other three headed for Cedro. We arrived there at 11:00 a.m., but found no sign of the outlaws or Beeler's men, so we turned around hastily and cut a sign along the road as we hurried to meet the boys who were still on the trail. The party I was with was composed of George Seath, a cowman from the Coyote, Ben Crosby, Will Harris, and myself. When we reached the place where we were to meet the boys, they were not there. We learned from a sheepherder that the outlaws had turned off at right angles from the course they had been taking and had gone south towards Pine Springs and that the boys were close upon them. Our horses were too played out to follow any farther, so we went home thinking that the boys would be all right as Sheriff Beeler was still on the trail. We got into St. Johns about dusk, and found that Beeler and his posse had returned at 10 a.m. and the four boys were still out on the trail. ...

"J. T. LeSueur called while I was still in bed this morning, wanting to know what to do about the four boys as they had not returned yet," the diary continues. "I told him that someone should go out and see what was the matter and that I would go for one, so I got my breakfast and made ready to go. Pearl Gibbons, Gus' wife, was staying with us during his absence and I tried to make her think that the boys were alright, that their horses had given completely out and they had to lay out all night, but although I tried my best, I could not reconcile her. We got off about eight o'clock; Sheriff Beeler, Will Gibbons, Will Sherwood, and myself, and two Mexicans were to follow later."

The searchers made plans to split up and meet later in the day.

"When we met Will Gibbons and Will Sherwood, they told us they had met Antonio Armijo and Frank Ruiz returning from Cedro, where they had spent the night," the diary says. "The Mexican boys had said they followed the trail of the outlaws until they were near Dick Greer's windmill and that they had stopped for a consultation on what course to pursue. Antonio and Frank had wanted to follow the trail farther and Ruiz and Gus had wanted to return home or else go to Cedro," the elder Gibbons said in his diary quoted in the St. Johns Stake history.

"They discussed the matter pro and con and finally, Antonio decided to go to Cedro with Ruiz, but Frank LeSueur persuaded Gus to follow the trail as far as Joe Carn's ranch and then to spend the night there at Ojo Benito. When the boys had finished reporting this, we glanced back the way Beeler and I had come and saw the two Mexicans coming. We took the trail of the outlaws and followed it toward a narrow ridge that extended out from the tableland. ... I saw an object on the steep hillside that startled me. It looked like the body of a man, but I would not admit it. It was still too far away to be able to identify it and while I was thinking about it, I saw another object that looked like a quilt that had been thrown away by the outlaws and had been rolled up by the wind and lodged in the wash where it now lay, but as we drew nearer, I saw that it was the body of a man and upon closer inspection, I recognized it as the body of my nephew, Gus Gibbons. It was laying in the bottom of a little draw with the head downhill and face upwards with three ghastly bullet holes through his head. One of them had entered his mouth and had come out of the back of his neck; one had went in at the left ear and had come out below the mouth, breaking the lower jaw and disfiguring the face awfully. In addition to these, he had several wounds in the body that we did not examine at the time. We well knew that the other object was that we had noticed laying on the hillside. The sight was horrifying to the senses. To see the two boys lying there, that I had known since they were in the cradle and had watched grow up and were just in the pink of manhood, and for them to be ambushed and shot down like dogs, without even a chance to fight for their lives, made me sick. It was murder in its worst form and there is not another crime beneath the roof of heaven that can stain the soul of man with a more infernal hue than an assassination such as this. They had out-villained villainy ..."

The heartbroken men sent back to St. Johns for a team to recover the bodies. "Will and I sat and talked for awhile ... and then we got up and went about half a mile along the foot of the mesa until we found a place where we could climb the mesa. After we reached the top, we cut out around to see if we could find the trail left by the outlaws after they had left the scene of the killing. We found it and followed it back until we found the spot where they had lain in wait for the unsuspecting boys to come within point blank range. They had left a saddle put away nicely under a tree and a blanket folded near and stuck in the top of a small cedar. We found empty shells at different points where each outlaw had been lying when the killing took place. As we approached the spot where Frank lay, we found where two more of the outlaws had been laying in ambush about twenty feet away from the rest. There were two empty shells laying on the ground [which] were doubtless the ones that killed Frank LeSueur. The boys had been afoot and to all appearances, Frank had been ahead and each was leading his horse.

"Frank had evidently fell at the first volley, but Gus must have only had a body wound for he had turned and ran for some distance. It would have been impossible for him to have lived a moment after any one of the gaping wounds in his head had been made. Frank had been shot through the neck and right between the eyes, and one leg, the right one, had been broken by a shot. He lay face downward with his head pillowed on his arm and his legs were partly doubled under him."

Many blamed members of the Wild Bunch for the killings, though no one had witnessed the ambush. Cassidy, of course, had a convenient alibi, being in the St. Johns jail at the time. He was released a few days later. The initial crime – the slaughtering of a cow – did not seem like something the Wild Bunch would do. French said members of the gang "expressed the greatest contempt for the common cow-thieves, whom they always al-

267

luded to as the 'Petty Larceny' crowd." With tens of thousands
of dollars from their many robberies, and huge rewards on their
heads, it seems unlikely that they would draw attention to themselves by slaughtering a single cow.

Bartholomew quotes Joe Pearce, later an Arizona Ranger,
as saying he met Ketchum and his gang in Springerville the day
before the Gibbons-LeSueur murders and believed they were responsible for the killings.

Beeler trailed the killers into southeast Arizona and had
crossed the line into New Mexico when veteran lawman George
Scarborough was killed in similar circumstances. Scarborough
had been working as a New Mexico stock detective while hoping
to get approval to form the New Mexico Rangers. He and Walter
Birchfield were trailing badmen after a steer was found slaughtered. A rifle shot killed Scarborough's horse and wounded him
in the leg. The leg was amputated in Deming, New Mexico, but
he died a day later on April 6, 1900. The New Mexico Cattle
Raisers Association, which employed the former deputy U.S.
marshal, decided to pay his salary to his widow for the remainder
of the year.

Beeler, convinced the same gang was responsible for both
ambushes, which had occurred only nine days apart, led a combined posse in pursuit of the killers. The St. Johns sheriff reported tracking the group for 1,300 miles through Arizona, New
Mexico, Old Mexico, Utah and Wyoming.

In May, the St. Johns paper reported: "Sheriff Beeler returned
Monday from the southern counties, bringing with him a man
suspected of being one of the murderous gang which passed
through here the latter part of March." The suspect was not
named and apparently never convicted.

"On May 26, Sheriff Jesse Tyler of Grand County, Utah,
and a deputy named Sam Jenkins were shot and killed by outlaws
near Thompson, Utah," according to *George Scarborough, The Life
and Death of a Lawman on the Closing Frontier* by Robert K.
DeArment. "After seeing descriptions of the murderers, Sheriff
Edward Beeler went to Utah and conferred with Sheriff William
Preece of Uintah County. The descriptions of these lawman killers, according to Beeler, matched the Apache fugitives he was
seeking 'in every particular' down to the brands on their horses."

In June, the paper said: "Sheriff Beeler came in from Utah this week, having business here that required his attention. He informs us that at present no posse is in pursuit of the gang he had been following so long."

Though members of the Wild Bunch are often mentioned as suspects in the Gibbons-LeSueur slayings, Sheriff Beeler offered a reward in the newspaper immediately after the shootings for a different group of outlaws:

"John Hunter, who is about 30 years old, dark complexion, black mustache, about 5 ft. 7 in. high, wore a black hat and dark sack coat. This man is also known as Skeet Jones and lived at Ft. Wingate last year.

"Bob Johnson, is supposed to be much like Hunter.

"One Wilson, alias Smith, who worked for Wabash Cattle Company for a short time April 1899, in this county. He is about 5 ft. 10 in. high, weighs about 175 lbs., has slightly dark complexion, dark hair and mustache, had short black beard when last seen, is stoop shouldered but quite well appearing, has blue eyes, and is of very pleasing address, but not over talkative, has a peculiar way of ducking his head from side to side when he talks and he usually smiles a great deal when talking. He is an expert bronc trainer.

"One Coley with right fore finger shot off, also a fifth and unknown man.

"They are a well organized band under a tall, nervy leader; they are armed with 30 - 40 & 30 - 30 Winchester rifles and a full complement of six-shooters. They had 12 head of horses and pack outfit; they have one 10 yr. old, bay mare branded EN on left shoulder. Frank LeSueur was riding this mare at the time he was killed. They have two extra guns and one extra saddle which they took from the murdered boys.

"I will pay $850.00 for the murderers, hold until I get them. Arrest and wire via Holbrook, Navajo Co., Ariz. —Edw. Beeler, Sheriff, Apache Co., St. Johns, Arizona."

As Beeler learned more about the killers, he would substitute different aliases with the descriptions, but apparently was always after essentially the same gang. The reward was never claimed.

Dick Gibbons, the outraged uncle of one of the murdered

boys, was a member of the Territorial Legislature. He introduced a bill the following year that created the Arizona Rangers to crack down on the cowboy outlaws running wild in the territory. In September of that year, Cassidy and the Sundance Kid left for Argentina, eventually, according to most accounts, dying in Bolivia in 1908.

Shootout in St. Johns

One of the celebrated cattle-sheep conflicts in the White Mountains took place in 1882 between the Hispanic residents of St. Johns and the Greers, who had brought cattle into the area from Texas in 1877, according to *Arizona Was the West* by Jennings.

The incident had a long buildup. The Greers, Mormons who had settled in Hunt 15 miles west of St. Johns, felt that the large number of sheep coming in from New Mexico was swamping their holdings and scattering their cattle. They searched for their cattle, but claimed to find less than half. With 30 Texas cowhands, the Greers attacked the Hispanics and scattered sheep in all directions.

In response, the Hispanics laid a trap, according to Jennings. "A three-day fiesta was announced. Dick Greer and his friends were invited. The invitation also stated that they might bring cash and buy cattle at a very reasonable price. Greer came, bringing Joe Woods, later to become Navajo County sheriff, and a small contingent of cowboys."

According to the St. Johns Stake history, the Hispanics had brought in a matador from Mexico for the San Juan Days event. "The Greers had recently cut the Greer earmark on a Mexican fellow who, allegedly, was caught stealing a colt, so they were not too welcome in old St. Johns," the history says. "A Mexican deputy demanded that the cowboys leave their guns with him for the duration of the festivities. The Greers considered this an insult, ignored his demand, and rode on to the bull ring."

"As they sat in the bull ring waiting for the bullfight to start, they observed the paisanos secretly arming and moving toward their horses," Jennings wrote. "In less time than it takes to tell it, both sides were in the street shooting it out with guns. In an all-day skirmish one cowboy was killed; Hi Hatch and a Negro named Jeff were wounded."

The book *Saints and Savages* says, "Eight of the troublemakers [the cowboys] escaped out of town, and four others took shelter in an unfinished adobe house."

The stake history says Greer cowboy Jim Vaughn was killed and Harris Greer was wounded, while Francisco Tafolla was wounded on the Hispanic side.

The stake history continues the story by saying Nathan C. Tenney, from the Mormon side of town, offered to act as peacemaker and persuaded the Greers to surrender. As he was leading the group down the street, a shot from the loft of the Barth Hotel killed Tenney. The shot was supposedly meant for one of the Greers and not for Tenney, who was loved by all. The Greers were freed after a slap on the wrist by a Prescott judge.

Dick Greer later shot a Hispanic sheepherder on the range, but turned himself in at Holbrook and pleaded self-defense. The stake history says that Sheriff Commodore Perry Owens rescued Greer from the jail, despite the presence of 80 deputized Hispanics guarding the prisoner.

Hashknife Outfit Brings Trouble

In the biography of his grandfather, *That Hashknife Kid*, Clarence W. Durham wrote about his ancestor's migration to Arizona in 1884. "Several years earlier the Hashknife brand, then owned by the Continental Cattle Company of Texas, hadn't given much thought to moving their cattle into the Arizona Territory. … The region was considered to be too remote, and was still being bloodied by Apache Indian raids. It wasn't until 1884, after the Atlantic and Pacific had extended its track into the area, that Hughes and Simpson [the owner/managers] negotiated a deal with the railroad to move some of their Texas cattle into Northern Arizona. The Aztec Land and Cattle Company evolved out of that business arrangement."

The grandfather, Walter Durham, remembered some of the

company managers driving up in a buckboard when he was a 16-year-old working at a camp near Pecos, Texas. "We've got an operation started in Arizona," Ben Irby said. "A few cattle have already been trailed in, an' now others will be going by rail. We need people there to take care of them. Would you be willin' to transfer to Northern Arizona Territory with a shipment of beeves?"

The young cowboy was willing, and soon was on his way to the railhead, where the cattle were loaded into stock cars and the cowboys joined their mounts in the horse cars.

"Most of the car was assigned to transporting cow ponies," the book says. "It was sectioned off into small individual stalls just large enough to accommodate one animal. The remainder of the railway car was outfitted with bunks, a table, and a pot-bellied coal burning stove.

"The bunks were comfortable enough when the car was standing still, but when the train was high-balling the horse-car swayed crazily on the uneven track. Between the jostling, and the noise caused from the clickey-clack of iron wheels striking uneven rail joints, it was impossible to sleep. It was only when the cattle train pulled into a siding, to allow passenger or mail trains to pass, that the cowboys got any real rest."

When the train arrived in Holbrook, one cow had been trampled to death, and was given to some local residents for hauling it away. Several with broken legs were sold cheaply.

Walter and the other cowboys set out the next day to survey the Hashknife's Arizona range. They headed east to the Petrified Forest, south to Springerville and then west along the mountains toward what he said was a 100,000-acre area of fenced land enclosed by Cooley and Clark near Show Low. (It is doubtful Cooley really had fenced more than 150 square miles of land, but it would be hard for a Texas cowboy to judge the size of the enclosure looking at one part of the fence. Other accounts mention a fenced area of 100 square miles.)

In Durham's account, the Hashknife cowboys were of the white-hat type, friendly to their neighbors and rarely experiencing problems with rustling. Perhaps the Hashknife's reputation is blacker than it deserves to be, or perhaps the grandfather accentuated the positive a bit as he related the story to the third generation, or both.

The St. Johns Stake history takes a much dimmer view of the Aztec Land and Cattle Company. "The Hashknife's sights were set on driving the Mormons out of the country along with all the other small ranchers. To enforce their policies they imported a gang of outlaws and gunslingers to intimidate, bully, and steal the settlers out of business. By doing this they started something they couldn't stop. The band of cutthroats not only made life miserable for the small outfits, but turned on the Hashknife and almost stole it out of business."

Snowflake's Stake history is only slightly less critical: "The Hashknife cowboys occupied most of the water holes. They even had a cabin at the mouth of Silver Creek canyon north of town. Some of the Hashknife cowboys were wild and unruly and proceeded to drive the settlers and other livestock men and their livestock off the land. This intimidation caused a hardship to the Mormon ranchers and contributed to the troubles of the Church Co-op herd." The stake history goes on to say a badman, later killed in the Pleasant Valley War, whipped Mormon Niels Petersen, and in a separate incident bludgeoned George Lewis with a pistol. Both men were out on the range looking for missing livestock.

The Taylor Stake history gets a bit Biblical about the aftermath of the overgrazing attributed to the influx of Hashknife cattle. "A mild drought (if there is such a phenomenon) hit the area and water holes dried up, forage was scarce and the cattle over ran the fenced farms. The little drought turned into a prolonged drought. There was no grass. Cattle ate brush weeds, cedar and pine boughs and limbs that punctured their paunches and they died like flies around a pot of poisoned liquid. Then came the rains for a day and a night and another day and more. Water ran everywhere in torrents. The animal carcasses lifted and flooded away." Logan Brimhall, the author of the article, said he counted 200 dead cattle float down Silver Creek in an hour.

The Mormon histories are not the only ones that are hard on the Hashknife outfit. In an archaeological survey prepared for the Apache-Sitgreaves National Forest, Kent G. Lightfoot writes: "Numerous Texas cowboys ... manned line camps all across the Mogollon Rim. With the arrival of the cowboys, harassment

273

of the local farmers began. The Texans occasionally stole cattle, threatened lives and in general made life miserable for the Mormons."

Trouble also stalked Will Barnes, a telegrapher who had come to Fort Apache in 1880 and set himself up a few years later as a cattle rancher west of Holbrook. "For a time, he ran his cattle freely across railroad land and public domain," says the *Mixed-Bloods* book. Sheep from New Mexico were his first problem.

"Rumors reached us that these wooly pests were overrunning the ranges up the River to the east," Barnes wrote. "Indeed, they were advancing like an invading army; four separate bands on each side of the River, covering a front about ten miles wide. Several fights had taken place already between the sheep men and the cattlemen; sheep herds had been broken up and scattered all over the range; hundreds of sheep had been killed and injured; camps shot up; cattle killed on the range; herders beaten; and men killed on each side. It was a bitter war. Looking back over it all, one cannot help wondering what these men were thinking of.

"Next year an immense cattle company, the 'Hashknife Outfit' of Western Texas, shipped no less than forty thousand head of half-starved West Texas Longhorns from the Lone Star State, where a drought had taken heavy toll of the range cattle. They were dumped along the Little Colorado for fifty miles. These animals swarmed over the vacant ranges like maggots on a carcass. The cattle belonging to me and other small owners were mixed up and scattered over a range two hundred miles square."

Barnes is a little hard to figure. Even his friends say he was beyond good at spinning a yarn. But he had enough credibility, along with the communication skills and perhaps insight into the military bureaucracy, to win the Medal of Honor for actions at Fort Apache during the Cibecue Uprising — without any specific details about what he actually did.

The *Mixed-Bloods* book says the Aztec Land and Cattle Company was a subsidiary of the struggling railroad, formed by its creditors to take possession of the railroad's million acres of land grants south of the tracks from Holbrook to Flagstaff. The land had been given in alternating sections in a checkerboard pattern to encourage the construction of the railroad. Lightfoot said the Hashknife outfit also paid 50 cents an acre to graze cattle on the intervening sections of government land, but others disagree.

The Hashknife "quickly enforced illegal claims to the intervening even-numbered government sections of the range, thus giving itself an immense stretch of plateau grass," the *Mixed-Blood* book says. "By all accounts, the rough Hashknife cowboys controlled their range with a vengeance, and they grazed the land with reckless abandon."

The Hashknife outfit was huge compared to local ranches. "The Hashknife spring roundup just west of Taylor involved a fifty man crew, one hundred fifty horses, two chuck wagons and a lot of grub and equipment," writes Palmer in *Elijah Was a Valiant Man*. "The men could gather as many as 2,000 cows in a day, and appropriately brand, castrate, earmark and check for any problems. ... The Taylor people would be glad to see them complete their work as the dust became nigh intolerable – especially if the easterly winds were prevailing. When many of these same cowboys were not actively involved with the cattle for the Hashknife they would be using the 'long rope,' branding other peoples' calves with their own brand or stealing horses from local ranchers."

Consistent reports blamed the Hashknife's problems with rustlers on the quality of cowboys they themselves had brought into the territory. In 1887, the *St. Johns Herald* reported this incident involving the Hashknife: "We understand Mr. Simpson, the local manager, had determined to do all in his power to break up the band of horse and cattle thieves who had been preying on the people in the western part of this county for so long a time, and to that end called all the men together in the employ of that company. When they were assembled he told them it was the intention of the company to take an active part in trying to stop so much stealing, and wanted the help of all the employees of the company — that those who were not willing to assist them and the authorities in this work, could call for their time. All agreed to do what they could except five, who took their money and left." Men named Tucker, Gillespie and Payne were among the men who collected their wages and were soon hanged for rustling. "It appears they put their liberty to bad use and enjoyed it but a short time," the newspaper concluded.

275

Sheep men also had problems with the Hashknife outfit. The *St. Johns Herald* had this report on May 20, 1886: "Santos Armijo was sent to St. Johns, from Winslow, on last Wednesday, under a conviction before a Justice of the Peace, for trespassing upon the land of the Aztec Cattle Company, by herding sheep upon the same. His fine was fifty dollars, in default of which twenty-five day's imprisonment. He was released upon habeas corpus before Commissioner Ruiz. This case was appealed to the County Court. On Thursday last Policarpio Armijo was brought in upon similar papers. His case met with a like disposition before Judge Rudd."

At that time, the Hashknife apparently lacked influence with the local elected officials.

Sheep men were being murdered, though the investigations never tied the crimes to the conflict with the cattlemen. On July 15, 1885, Sol Barth found Pablo Rivali, a Hispanic from Concho, shot to death along the St. Johns-Springerville Road. The victim had been seen drinking as he sat beside the road ten miles from St. Johns. The coroner determined he was shot in the face and the wound was not self-inflicted.

In the next edition of the paper, under a headline "Another Murder," the slaying of Jose Lusers was reported. He was a sheepherder on the Don Antonio Gonzales ranch eight or ten miles from St. Johns. He was shot at close range with a pistol as he entered the house on the ranch where he worked. Though the autopsy, reported in the paper, seemed as detailed as the Warren Commission report on the Kennedy Assassination, it added, "Nothing relative to the guilty party could be ascertained."

Burt Mossman, a foreman for the Hashknife outfit who was to become the first captain of the Arizona Rangers, considered renegade Mormons to have been the cattle rustlers. Upon first arriving in Holbrook dressed in city clothes and a derby hat, he heard that some cattle had been taken near Snowflake. He headed south in the 10-degree night, finding three men with rifles around a fire near Snowflake.

"Burt pulled up his horse sideways to the fire and swung down from his saddle," says Frazier Hunt in *Cap Mossman, Last of the Great Cowmen*. "His pony was between him and the fire, with the three men on the opposite side. Behind the screen of

276

his horse he quickly slipped his pistol from the right-hand pocket of his overcoat and shoved it up his left sleeve. Pushing his fingers into his sleeves, Chinese coolie fashion, he walked around the head of his horse and stepped to the fire."

Mossman commented on the cold before pulling out the Colt and ordering the men to drop their rifles.

Mossman found the meat and Hashknife-branded hides, and forced his prisoners to accompany him back to Holbrook, according to Jennings in *Arizona Was the West*. With the help of the bishop in Snowflake, Mossman was able to get a conviction. The book says it was the first rustling conviction the Hashknife had been able to obtain in 14 years in Arizona.

Jennings told of another incident in which Mossman captured five rustlers after being alerted by a telegram from a Mormon bishop.

Jennings, a Mormon, doubted that any of the rustlers were of his faith. He goes on to cite figures to indicate that crime dropped 80% in Holbrook after the Hashknife cowboys left.

So how could these people see the same events and reach such vastly different conclusions? Perhaps everyone saw an opportunity to make a good living grazing cattle on government land. Most were quick to see grazing entitlements for themselves and discredit those claimed by others. People were careless about where their livestock grazed and quick to claim ownership of stock that wandered into their self-described borders. Everyone saw themselves as defenders of the good and the others as aggressors. Also, there was a tendency to distance one's self from any troublemaker and see him as a member of the opposite faction. To a settler, any bad man from Texas was a "Hashknife Cowboy." To a Hashknife foreman, any settler with ill-gotten beef was a "renegade Mormon." With a little racism, a little religious bigotry, some pretty tough characters left over from the Civil War and an absence of any generally recognized legal authority, you have the basis for some strong disagreements. A good supply of hardened killers made the situation even worse.

A more positive memory of the local cattle business is given in the St. Johns Stake history by Bert J. Colter, who remembers a cooperative roundup that moved through the area each year. "There were a number of pretty good size outfits and it took about six weeks to cover and work their ranges. We had an average of twenty cowboys all the time. Some would cut out as we left each range and others came in when we moved onto a new range. There were eight or ten of us that were representing the bigger outfits that worked all the way through as there were some of their cattle everywhere you worked."

In 1886, the *St. Johns Herald* reported something new would be tried. "The general round-up for the northeastern and southern portion of Apache County commences to-day. After driving the country adjacent to the Meadows the round-up will divide into two parties, one going down the Little Colorado river and the other up. By this means they will get through with the work much quicker, and save the cattle considerably."

Hard Times for Cattlemen

Even then, the hard work of the cowboy was considered a spectator sport. "Apache County is again to the front in the cowboy tournament at Albuquerque," the *St. Johns Herald* reported on October 7, 1886. "Our worthy fellow-citizen and gentlemanly cowboy, Mr. Nat Greer was the victor this time. The first trial was to catch, throw down, saddle and ride a bronco, which Nat succeeded in accomplishing in 6 minutes and 32 seconds, taking the first prize; W. D. Barbee got the second premium in 8 minutes. The second contest was to catch and tie a wild steer. Nat Greer got off with the honors in this contest, accomplishing the feat in 1 minute and fifty-seven seconds."

Dick Greer had been the champion the year before, giving Apache County and the Greer family bragging rights all the way from Albuquerque to the White Mountains.

Today, eight seconds can seem like a lifetime to a rodeo cowboy, and an eight-minute event seems incredible, but today's bronc riders don't have to catch and saddle their mounts after the clock starts running.

Paul H. Roberts, a range management specialist quoted in the *Mixed-Bloods* book, said the cattle and sheep business boomed, with 150,000 cattle and 120,000 sheep in what are now Navajo and Apache counties by 1885. Prices were good and everyone wanted in.

But Mother Nature, who had only been toying with the stockmen during the previous decade, had no intention of allowing them to continue that level of resource consumption. The overgrazed rangeland did not recover in good years and deteriorated further in bad ones.

Conflict between sheep men and cattle growers continued, especially when the sheep were from New Mexico. In June 1886, the St. Johns paper reported that New Mexico sheep had passed up the river in the last few days. It said these animals were a "disgrace to the territory," as they were "owned in New Mexico, paid no taxes, owned no water and know no law."

In a tongue-in-cheek article, the *St. Johns Herald* wrote, "We have heard considerable talk and read a great deal about the rain belt marching westward with advancing civilization. From our observation in this section, we should judge that the 'rain belt' has not arrived, or if so, it has gone on without stopping. Perhaps we have not arrived at the proper stage of civilization to warrant us our due allowance of moisture. If our county possessed statistics of the rainfall for the last four years, it would be found that the amount of water granted us by Providence to feed our streams and make our grass grow, has been growing smaller and 'beautifully less,' year by year."

The article concluded with an appeal to bring no more cattle to the area. "Our cattle, carefully trained, can exist on a handful of malpai rocks and a pint of water every three or four days. The supply of malpai is unlimited, but we seriously doubt if even the hardy cattle of our section can endure a further reduction in their allowance of water."

"Although St. Johns folk had good milk cows and numerous beehives, the Colorado plateau has never been a land flowing with milk and honey," wrote former Secretary of the Interior Stewart Udall, native of St. Johns and grandson of a pioneer Mormon bishop. "The high desert area is essentially cow-country; grass and water are its two most important resources. When the first settlers came to this virgin land, there was waist-high grass that initially made the grazing of cattle and sheep a thriving activity. However, nature plays cruel tricks in this part of the world, and it turned out that this lushness was the tail-end of a wet cycle that has not been repeated. Ever since, livestock raising has been a marginal pursuit in northern Arizona." Udall wrote in a 1982 issue of *American West, the Land and its People*.

By 1886, ranchers were unhappy with prices, as reported in this article by the *St. Johns Herald*: "Juan Sepulveda returned from Kansas City Tuesday morning, where he went some two or three weeks ago with a train of cattle for Huning & Cooley. He reports a fortunate trip, all of the cattle going through without loss or accident, but says that the cattle sold at unsatisfactory prices, owing to the depression in the market. Railroad tariff and Chicago sand-baggers are waging merciless warfare on stockmen."

A drought in 1891 forced cattlemen to sell on a depressed market. Northern buyers, however, were still willing to buy underweight Arizona cattle and feed them to market weight.

Rain returned temporarily in early 1892. "The summer of that year we branded 2,500 calves," Barnes said. "A fine crop. It was a dry summer, however. Little or no green grass grew on the range. The cattle went into winter thin and gaunt. By January 15, 1893, 18 inches of crusted snow lay all over the country — a most unusual thing. During the day, the snow melted on top; at night a crust froze on it. The cattle starved by thousands. We trailed many a bunch, wandering around looking for food, by the bloody rings in the snow where the crust which they broke through had cut their legs to the bone. The next year we branded 235 calves, and estimated that we had some 1,800 or 2,000 cattle left out of 7,000."

Meanwhile, the market was falling, according to a videotape produced by the Little House Museum, quoting Forest Service research. The tape says the price for a steer in the White Mountains dropped from $40 in 1879 to $10 in 1892.

Cattlemen wanted out of the business. Rustling increased as owners became indifferent to the practice. When demand increased in Kansas for stock cattle, many Arizona ranchers took the opportunity to sell out. Then the Spanish-American War knocked the bottom out of the cattle market, and stock could not be sold at any price.

Ironically, sheep prospered during some of the lean years for cattle. A protective tariff made wool more profitable. In *Elijah Was a Valiant Man*, Palmer wrote an account of 1897, "At any one time there were about six regular and five transient bands averaging approximately 2,000 sheep each. Although they would begin to take their sheep to the Salt River Valley for the winter in a few years, at this time the winters were spent on the prairies in the vicinity of Dry Lake, moving the sheep to the pines just before lambing season began in the spring."

By the beginning of the new century, there were 200,000 sheep and only 20,000 cattle on the range. Jennings said that Frank Wallace was hired in 1901 to round up the remaining Hashknife cattle and deliver them to Babbitt Brothers Trading Company in Flagstaff.

"Without casting reflections on the memory of anything, some old-timers of today say that their families got their start in the cattle business by rustling from the Hashknife," Jennings writes. He quotes them as saying, "How else could they get their start?"

While the Colorado Plateau was denuded of its grass, the higher ground of the Mogollon Rim country remained lightly settled. "There were, to be sure, some scattered ranchers there," the *Mixed-Blood* book says. "Corydon E. Cooley, the Indian scout, retained some of his stock after he sold his homestead in Show Low. To the southeast, a Mormon community tried to make a go of it around present-day Pinetop. Several sheep ranchers used the high meadows as summer pasture. Additionally, some budding entrepreneurs operated stores and bars, drawing clientele from the few local residents and the soldiers down at Fort Apache. Nonetheless, the Rim remained a backwater through much of the 19th century."

"In the last few years of the century, this isolation vanished," the *Mixed-Blood* book continues. "The sheep men, cattlemen, homesteaders and Mormon colonizers, entrepreneurs and loggers arrived, not really in droves, but in an apparently steady trickle."

Though the plateau suffered drastically in the late 1800s, the "largely untouched" Rim country was "increasingly attractive to stockmen," the book says. "In 1891, Congress authorized the creation of national forest reserves, to be withdrawn from the public domain and placed under federal control. The initial act, however, provided no guidelines for the regulation of these reserves. A full three years passed before the Department of the Interior outlined a policy for using the reserves. The policy shocked stockmen, for it prohibited the driving, feeding, grazing, pasturing or herding of cattle, sheep or other livestock within any of the reserves."

Cattlemen took this new kind of range war to the halls of Congress, where they won the right to have their cattle graze on forest reserves if they did not injure the young trees or jeopardize the rights of others. Sheep were allowed on National Forest land only in Oregon and Washington state. After intense lobbying and investigation by experts, it was determined that sheep were little more destructive than cattle and should be allowed on the National Forest in other states as well. Scientific inquiry and political lobbying settled a question that revolvers and rifles had not been able to resolve.

Palmer wrote that after the turn of the century sheep men began to take their animals to the Salt River Valley for the winter. "A trail called the Pleasant Valley Trail had been marked out by the Forest Rangers. ... It dropped off the rim to the west of Pinedale, went close by the settlement of Young, over to Gisela and then south and west to the Salt River. At that river a narrow hanging bridge had been constructed over which the sheep could be crossed (appropriately called Sheep's Crossing). From this place they trailed over the low-lying foothills to the desert valley several miles east of Mesa."

As the size of the outfits increased, more immigrants came from northern Spain. Most were Basques, who have an ancient language and culture that pre-dates Spanish civilization. They were expert shepherds.

St. Johns
Develops A Political "Ring"

St. Johns was destined to become the major town and seat of government for the area through the late 19th century despite some brief moments of ascendancy for Snowflake and Springerville.

Yavapai County, created during the Civil War, covered approximately half the state, stretching from the Mohave County line to New Mexico and from Utah to the Gila River.

The *Historical Atlas of Arizona* tells the story of the creation of Apache County this way: "The settlers in the farming communities along the Little Colorado River and miners in the recently opened mines around Clifton found themselves facing a 180-mile trip to the seat of Yavapai County at Prescott to conduct legal business. The Tenth Legislature, meeting in 1879, created Apache County from all that part of Yavapai County lying east of [a line just west of Winslow] and a very small piece of eastern Maricopa County. The legislature placed the county seat initially at Snowflake."

The Snowflake Stake history has this account of the town's time as the temporary county seat: "It was probably chosen because James Stinson was a member of the Territorial Legislature at the time of its creation. At this time Stinson was appointed judge; William J. Flake, supervisor; and Edward W. East, county recorder — these positions and the county seat to be held until a special election in June."

On the Road to Nowhere by Applewhite credits James G. H. Colter, founder of Nutrioso and a Round Valley cattleman, with a role in making Springerville the next temporary county seat since he was a member of the Territorial Legislature. But it only had that distinction for part of 1880.

The Snowflake Stake history was critical of the decision to move the county seat to St. Johns. "A political convention was held in Snowflake May 25, 1880. Jesse N. Smith was a delegate for the Mormon people at the convention. He would not designate any one place for the permanent county seat but thought all the people should decide by vote. Therefore Sol Barth and others pressured for St. Johns to be the County Seat. They also proposed an entirely different slate of candidates for office. The election was held June 2 and was accompanied by a great deal of fraud and ballot box stuffing with the final result that St. Johns became the County Seat and these people also voted in their own candidates."

The St. Johns Stake history gives a different version of the events. "Wilford Woodruff instructed Amon Tenney to try making up a compromise ticket with Sol Barth. Tenney spoke of this to Jesse N. Smith who was working up a ticket, himself, to present to an upcoming political meeting at Snowflake. ... Smith told Tenney to go ahead, and let him know the outcome of his meeting with Barth before the Snowflake convention. Tenney was unable to see Barth, but met with his agent, Lorenzo Hubbell. They agreed on a ticket and Tenney pledged the Mormon vote to support it. Unfortunately his report did not reach Smith until after the Snowflake meeting had endorsed Smith's ticket. When Tenney heard of this he felt quite badly and stated that President Smith had gone back on him and had not treated him fairly. Barth branded it a double cross. He broke away from the Tenney-Hubbell ticket and joined forces with the St. Johns Ring."

The St. Johns Stake history says the St. Johns Ring had a gunman behind a curtain in the room where the votes were counted, with instructions to kill Jesse Smith if it didn't go their way.

"The election was contested but took so long to be acted upon that the term of office was over before any action could be taken," the Snowflake Stake history says. "Reconciliation between the factions was attempted but failed. The succeeding elections were also corrupt and the Mormon people denied office, even the right to vote, and they were harassed in other ways. In 1882 John Hunt ran for Supervisor on both party tickets and even though he won overwhelmingly he was denied office on a technicality."

In the early Apache County elections, the winning side would sometimes bring in a stack of ballots from Pueblo, Colorado, where the residents were apparently more aligned with the aspirations of the county leaders than the actual residents of the county. Though the abnormality is reported in historical journals, there is no explanation of why anyone capable of committing such blatant election fraud bothered to bring in the questionable ballots from 300 miles away. Pueblo was an industrial city of more than 10,000 residents and a railroad headquarters. Perhaps some of the residents actually traveled through northeast Arizona while working on the trains, or could make that claim.

There were financial reasons for the creation of the new county and the struggle for control. Settlers were adding to the tax base by building small homes and barns, perhaps valued at

$25 to $100, but investors from the East were pouring money into railroads. The line running through northern Arizona was valued at $5,000 a mile. Carving out 80 miles of that bounty provided the new Apache County with $400,000 in tax base. That was a lot of money in those days – equivalent to 2,000 years wages for many of the residents of the new Apache County.

The power of the county purse and badge was eagerly sought by both the Mormons and non-Mormons. In addition to the county jobs and control of the tax revenue, the ability to arrest opponents, and release friends was an important part of county power. As all of these trappings were concentrated in St. Johns, outsiders began to talk of the "St. Johns Ring." County government in northeast Arizona was a big deal. The *St. Johns Herald* reported in 1887 that Apache County had an assessed valuation of nearly $2.9 million, surpassing the $2.3 million of Maricopa County (Phoenix).

When the county was short of cash, it issued "warrants," which were promises to pay in the future. If the warrant holders needed cash, they often sold this paper at a steep discount, and Sol Barth was one of the men with ready cash who was happy to buy them. Barth, according to court records, increased his profit on the transactions by altering the amount of the warrants.

N. H. Greenwood, in an article about Barth, said Patterson & Co. had received an Apache County warrant for $91.24 for materials and lumber used on a county bridge. Patterson sold the warrant to Barth for $72. But with the stroke of a pen, Barth increased the warrant to $191.24. It was an easy way to make money.

Much of the county's wealth came from the tax assessment of the Santa Fe Railroad. But as the revenue flowed into the county coffers, Barth and other members of the St. Johns Ring began to feel they would like to have more money. They brought in lawyer Harris Baldwin and raised the assessed valuation for the railroad from $5,000 to $9,000 per mile. "The apparent objective was to harass the railroad into nonpayment, thus forcing the county to introduce lawsuits which would provide lucrative fees for Baldwin and his associates," Greenwood wrote in his article on Barth. "The ploy worked," at least to the extent that the railroad stopped paying taxes. Baldwin signed on for a $1,000 retainer and 33% of any money collected.

"The case went from the district court to the territorial supreme court and thence to the United States Supreme Court," Greenwood wrote. "Baldwin was not qualified to argue even at the territorial level, and the county was forced to fork over $2,000 to Daniel P. Baldwin (no kin to Harris Baldwin) to argue the case in Arizona and had to raise another $5,000 for Senator Turpie of Indiana, who argued before the United States Supreme Court."

Greenwood quotes A. F. Banta as explaining the disastrous results of the suit for the St. Johns Ring. "Every one of the grafters pulled their freight and St. Johns knew them no more." District Attorney C. L. Gutterson "headed for Nebraska," Greenwood wrote. "Harris Baldwin departed for 'parts unknown.' The clerk of the board of supervisors 'went to the devil,' and J. F. Wallace (owner of the *St. Johns Herald*), sold out and left." Barth, who remained in St. Johns, led something of a charmed life. He was able to survive the suit, continued to thrive as a leading citizen of the county, and even survived more serious scrapes with the law.

As the investigation into the falsified county warrants developed, "thieves" stole county records and took them into an alley where they burned them. Barth was a suspect, along with a Charles Kinnear, who turned states evidence.

Another witness, Harry Silver, escaped an assassination attempt at the hands of a man named Frederico Jiron, according to *O. K. Corral Postscript*. Jiron, who was charged with killing Rafael Garcia to rob him of $100, was later wounded in a bar fight in Carthage, New Mexico.

On January 19, 1887, the *St. Johns Herald* reported: "Mr. Sol Barth was arrested last Tuesday on a charge of mutilating the county records. On a preliminary examination he was bound over in the sum of $4,000 to answer. There is another charge of forgery resting against him, on which he was to have had a preliminary trial last night. In default of bond on the first charge he was remanded to jail."

The *St. Johns Herald* reported: "Sheriff Owens left St. Johns last Sunday morning with Sol Barth in charge, whom he was taking to Yuma, to serve a sentence of ten years' imprisonment for raising county warrants, imposed on him by Judge Wright. ... The discovery of the crime was made some two years ago, and since that time there has been no stone left unturned to bring the guilty parties to justice. As yet, Mr. Barth is the only one that has been made to pay the penalty of these frauds, though it is thought there are others as guilty as he, who are still enjoying their freedom. Crimes of this nature, like murder, will out, and we trust our authorities will continue their efforts, until all who are implicated shall be convicted, or prove their innocence to the satisfaction of twelve of their fellow-citizens. This is not the only crime that has been perpetrated against the county's finances. The Treasurer's safe of this county was robbed — or reported to have been robbed — of something over $11,600 a little over a year ago, in rather a mysterious manner. It had been raining a good portion of the afternoon and early in the evening of the night on which this act was said to have been committed — the ground was soft — it would have been almost impossible for any number of men, or even one man, to have been around the Treasurer's office on that night without leaving foot-prints. But strange as it may appear, the next morning no such signs could be discovered in that vicinity. The country around St. Johns was circled early the next morning by parties pretty skillful on the trail; nothing could be discovered of any one having left town on that night. Taking all these circumstances into consideration, it is somewhat singular that no trace — not even the faintest — has ever been found to that robbery."

Ackerman gives this account of a fake holdup of county funds in St. Johns: "Just as [Deputy County Treasurer Dionicio] Baca was drifting off to sleep, the front door was shoved open. Masked men entered and stood, with guns drawn, over the sleeping men. One gunman went to the adjoining door and held a gun on the women. When one of the women tried to talk she was gruffly told to shut up. One of the masked men then rummaged around the foot of Baca's bed until he found some pants, and digging through the pockets, came up with a set of keys. Baca was then forced to get up and leave the house. At least two men stayed behind with guns drawn on the remaining occupants. ... With three guns pointed at him Baca was taken barefoot and without pants to the county courthouse. ... Baca was forced to open the safe and then stand in the dark hallway."

Baca initially tried to implicate the Clanton gang as the robbers, but as his story kept changing, his brother, County Treasurer Francisco Baca, lost his job and was eventually arrested in Springerville.

As late as 1975, articles were still being published implicating the Clantons, based on 60-year-old revelations of individuals supposedly involved. In all likelihood, little or no money was taken in the robbery. County officials had probably already pocketed the funds, and needed the robbery to explain the depleted county treasury.

St. Johns Herald reported the outcome of the cases against the St. Johns Ring: "The jury in the case of the Territory vs. Francisco Baca, ... charged with the embezzlement of county funds to the amount of $11,166.54, returned a verdict this morning of 'guilty of embezzlement as charged in the indictment.' " Nathan Barth, in a settlement of criminal and civil suits, paid a fine of $500, gave the widow of Morris Barth $9,000, and agreed to leave Arizona by the first of January 1888. "Charles Gray, charged with grand larceny, was also allowed to leave the Territory," the *Herald* wrote. "One or two more terms of Court like the present, and there will not be many of them left."

The *St. Johns Herald* said that Sol Barth was receiving favorable treatment in the Yuma prison from the warden because of past political and business connections. "If this report be true, Apache County had better send her next convicts to the summer resort of Santa Monica, or to the Fifth Avenue Hotel in New York."

The warden responded angrily with a letter to protect his good name. "I never was a member of the Arizona Legislature. I never was Sol Barth's friend nor boon companion. I have never had even business transactions with him. Sol Barth is locked up every night at the usual hour."

But Barth's time in prison was to be brief. "Mrs. Sol Barth started for Prescott last Saturday morning," the *Apache Review* reported in 1888. "She carried the petition for Sol's pardon which has been signed by several hundred people, among the signers being the names of eight of the jury who sat on the case."

The *Albuquerque Democrat* in 1885, had this to say: "A petition is being extensively circulated in Arizona for the pardon of Sol Barth who is now confined in the Yuma Penitentiary and [his] health is so seriously impaired that his physicians say he will not be able to endure his confinement more than a few months longer. Humane people of all parties are signing the petition, and the only opposition to it that we have noticed comes from the *St. Johns Herald*, which attacks the unfortunate man after the manner of a hyena, but such bloodthirsty arguments as it uses should not be permitted to influence the mind of the governor."

"He was pardoned by Governor Conrad M. Zulick less than two years after his conviction," Greenwood wrote. "Once free, Sol lost no time in moving rapidly to regain whatever wealth, power or influence he might have lost. He was 45 when he left Yuma, and it was an older, more congenial, somewhat subdued Sol who emerged. He was still the same shrewd Sol, however, and shortly after his release he sued Apache County for the 'value of the warrants' which had got him into trouble. He recovered $3,584.93. What he meant by 'the value of the warrants' is not clear to us now and was not clear to his contemporaries. Joseph Fish remarked, 'I do not know the basis for the successful lawsuit.' The point is that Sol Barth came out ahead on his warrant speculations after all." Barth was soon re-elected to the state Legislature. A campaigner for statehood, Barth still had a long career ahead of him as community leader, merchant and rancher.

One of Barth's most unusual scrapes with the law involved the alleged shooting of his friend A. F. Banta. Sol, while drunk, allegedly held Banta while one of Sol's brothers fired a shot through the neck of their pal. "Since there was no vital damage, the only lasting effects were two scars, on each side of Banta's neck, about as big as a quarter," the stake history says. "They were friends before it happened and still friends after, so we can assume that, in their own way, they were just having a little fun." The account improbably says the bullet passed behind Banta's windpipe, and missed his jugular veins.

At his request, Barth's funeral in 1928 was held in the Mormon Church, an ironic end for the man who led the anti-Mormon faction in Apache County for so long.

Expansion
Of White Mountain Towns

Meanwhile, the Mormons had been settling the far southeast corner of the White Mountain area.

In 1879, William Flake, who had been purchasing barley from Nutrioso, bought the community for the Mormons for 300 head of cattle, sending Albert Minnerly, Adam Greenwood, George Peck and John Burk to the property to plant the crop, according to the St. Johns Stake history. Flake later sub-divided the land and sold it to Mormon farmers.

By 1880, some White Mountain towns were growing. St. Johns had 546 people, making it nearly a third the size of Phoenix, and the eighth largest city in the territory. Springerville had 364 people in the 1880 census and Snowflake had 275. Brigham City (across the river from present-day Winslow) had 191 residents and Woodruff boasted 66. Sunset (near present-day Winslow) had 161. No other Northeast Arizona community made the list, which included Arizona towns as small as Casa Grande, with 33 people.

The Mormon population of east central Arizona grew from 664 in 1876 to 2,200 in 1900, according to Lightfoot.

Snowflake's petition for mail service was granted on June 27, 1881. "No mail route had been established to get the mail from Holbrook, so the people of Snowflake volunteered to get the mail one week and the Taylor people the next alternately until official service began September 5, 1881," the Snowflake Stake history says.

Though dancing was a favorite pastime of the settlers, they were under orders to do it right. "At a meeting in Snowflake I spoke on the subject of dancing," said Stake President Jesse N. Smith. "Reprehended the practice of swinging around in a wanton manner and more times than the figure or the music required."

The first government land survey of the area was completed in 1883 by O. D. Wheeler, deputy surveyor, according to Ben Hansen, in his manuscript *Background History of the Lakeside-Pinetop Area.*

The St. Johns Stake history gives a slightly different account, possibly referring to a different area of the White Mountains. "The Government survey wasn't started here until 1882, when A. P. Johnson, a contract surveyor, ran out the township lines. The survey was finished three years later when C. Burton Foster, another contract surveyor, filled in the grid by adding the individual section lines."

Meanwhile, the government set up a commission to resolve the question of Spanish land grants. The *St. Johns Herald* reported: "Congress has passed a bill appointing three commissioners to investigate these claims. They are to serve for four years, and are to be governed in their investigations by the provisions of the [Treaty of] Guadalupe Hidalgo, the Gadsden treaty with Mexico, the law of nations, the law, usages and customs of the Government from which the claim is derived, and the decisions of the United States Supreme Court." Though there were spectacular frauds over Spanish land grant claims in other areas of the Southwest, east-central Arizona was left out of that drama. The fierce resistance of White Mountain Apache bands during the Spanish era apparently convinced favorites of the monarchs to request land elsewhere.

While Mormons were filling up many of the towns in the White Mountains, they were not welcome everywhere. The railroad company moved its telegraph office out of Horsehead Crossing, where a Mormon store and warehouse were located, and placed it a couple of miles away at Barado's ranch, which was re-named Holbrook. "They soon after took up the side track at the old place," wrote Mormon leader Jesse N. Smith. "This left the A.C.M.I. [the Mormon's Arizona Co-operative Mercantile Institution] out in the cold. John W. Young having quarreled with F. W. Smith, the superintendent of the A&P railroad, the latter seemed to extend his enmity to the whole Church, and as he had a controlling interest in the lots of the new town of Holbrook, he would neither sell nor rent any ground for us for our store. As the next best move we located the store at Woodruff and erected some temporary buildings there for its accommodation."

The Woodruff store served as the anchor for a chain that had tiny stores in most communities in the White Mountains. "A major function of the A.C.M.I. was buying local surpluses from families and tithing houses and freighting these goods to non-Mormon settlements for a profit," according to Lightfoot.

After an 1888 fire burned the downtown section of Holbrook, the A.C.M.I. purchased a Holbrook lot and a shipment of goods from merchants Adamson and Burbage, according to *Elijah Was a*

291

Valiant Man. "This put A.C.M.I. into a much better position for securing freight and mail contracts as well as being more conveniently located for shipping wool, cattle and other produce. Some Mormon settlers, rather partial to the institution which was more liberal and understanding in matters of credit, may have seen the fire as a special act of God," Palmer wrote. "Originally founded as a Church cooperative, the company had begun to evolve toward being a private firm. Even though its prices were not very competitive (and it used its influence to discourage competition in the local communities), it nonetheless accommodated the local Mormon population in a variety of important ways. In addition to allowing credit it would often trade with someone when other companies would not and provided such courtesies as a place to stay while away from home or a meeting point to catch a ride up the country."

Mormons were also moving into Lakeside. Hans Hansen and his father settled in Woodland, near present-day Lakeside, in 1893, according to *A Tribute to the Lakeside Pioneers.* "At that time the locality had been called Fairview or Hog Town, and a few squatters already lived there. They were Joe Stock, Albert Crandall, Alex McCleve, John Marvin and Al Young."

There were other families in what is now the Lakeside area. "The Kelleys lived down in the canyon on Porter Creek," one early historical account reads. "He kept a cow to milk, a couple of dogs and had a beautiful pint size garden."

"Hans bought the rights of [Al Young] and immediately set about obtaining a homestead of 160 acres," the *Tribute to the Lakeside Pioneers* says. "It took several years because of disputes in surveying boundaries, but he finally won good title."

"The family of Ezra West arrived in Woodland, Arizona, to make their home sometime in 1896," the book says. "They bought 160 beautiful acres from Abe Amos in Woodland which he had homesteaded. Woodland Creek, fresh and clear, trickled through the land. … Another piece was situated north of the present Homestead Road."

"The two families (Hansen and West) combined to obtain a school district, then built a small one-room log schoolhouse, and acquired a teacher each year," the book says. A television program produced by Richard Lynch, says the Mormons invited the children of the Hispanic sheepherders to attend their school.

"There were several families in that school: the Hansens, the Adairs, the Youngs, the Wests, the Becksteds, the Stevens, and the children from the Eph Penrod family in Pinetop," according to the *Tribute* book. "The log building had one big classroom and was also used for church and community meetings." Pinetop got its first school sometime later. "The first students were taught their three R's in the old Eph Penrod home," the book says. ... In the summer of 1894, a one-room log schoolhouse was built west of the old William Penrod home which was situated on the rise east of the present Baptist church."

The best farming sites were those where irrigation water could be taken directly from a flowing stream and diverted when necessary onto the land. Unfortunately, those were very rare. When the water was needed, the streams were not flowing.

"Between 1883 and 1921, there were 17 dams built in the St. Johns Stake," the stake history recounts. Seven were replacements for dams that were washed out.

Woodruff had its share of problems. "In 1880 a small number of the old pioneers began the work of erecting a dam about 40 feet high and 400 feet long, which looked like a stupendous undertaking for so small a number of people with scarcely any cash capital, but with courage and confidence they went to work, realizing their hopes only to have them blasted by the torrential floods which swept away their labors like straws before the wind," wrote W. H. Clark, Commissioner of Immigration, in a 1910 pamphlet entitled *Navajo County, Arizona, and its Resources.* "The dam was replaced four times when finally the people were compelled to ask aid, and the county and other outside assistance came to their rescue and aid was given so that they put in place a structure that has held." The 1890 dam lasted for 25 years, providing the area with "several hundred acres of land being finely cultivated and ... producing the usual annual crops and the town abounds with orchards, gardens, flowers and neat and comfortable homes."

The *St. Johns Herald* reported in May of 1885 that the local dam gave way. "A force of men were at work on it all night trying to prevent the escape of the water, but up to the time of going to press their efforts were unsuccessful. Water was still flowing through the irrigation ditch near St. Johns and water was also heading down the normally dry channel of the Little Colorado. "We hope the liberated waters will enliven the dry places below, so that the stock along the river may 'eat, drink and be merry.' It may prove a serious misfortune to some, but at the same time illustrates the truth of the old adage, it is an 'ill wind which blows no man good.' "

In the early 1880s, life for the settlers was hard. Additional Mormon settlers were arriving without sufficient food and the carrying capacity of the land was being challenged. "In order to relieve this situation John W. Young, who formerly was 1st Counselor to President Brigham Young, suggested that he and Stake President Jesse N. Smith go to Pueblo, Colorado to try to obtain a grading contract on the Atlantic and Pacific Railroad which was just being started from Albuquerque," the Snowflake Stake history says. About 40 men and 20 teams left to work on a five-mile stretch of the railroad 24 miles east of Fort Wingate, New Mexico. They were able to send flour back to their destitute families, but, "The pioneers continued on this work for only a relatively short time as there was dissatisfaction with John W. Young after he took over additional contracts in his own name."

A cloud over title to their land was a continuing concern for the residents of Snowflake, Taylor and Woodruff. The Aztec Land and Cattle Company, or the railroad, claimed their property. In *Elijah Was a Valiant Man*, Palmer writes that Stake President Jesse N. Smith and Brigham Young Jr. went to New York and settled for $4 per acre for the Hashknife land and $8 an acre for the railroad land, "on which Woodruff had unfortunately been located. To have clear title to their land was a considerable relief, but that did not make the proposition seem any fairer. The settlers had to buy the land, much of which they had already purchased from someone else, that they had claimed before the railroad even knew it existed. Furthermore, they had sacrificed blood, sweat and tears in reclaiming it from the wilderness."

Plagues and Early Medicine

Epidemics frequently spread through the White Mountains in the early days with poor living conditions and the cold climate making the situation even worse. It would be tempting to say a lack of doctors was a problem, but that is debatable. Nineteenth century doctors were a mixed blessing at best. Joseph Smith's pronouncements against the profession may have been a blessing to his Mormon followers. Smith, whose brother died undergoing harsh treatments, embraced the herbal medicine advocated by Samuel Thompson. The treatments with Indian tobacco and other plants might not have done much good, but they were far less harmful than the bleeding and purging that killed many patients under the care of professionals.

Mortality was high. "Peter Wood buried four of his children in one month," says a Mormon history of Show Low, without specifying the illness.

In Adair, "A smallpox house was also constructed a distance from the settlers so as to quarantine such epidemics as smallpox, scarlet fever and diphtheria," according to *Adair, Arizona – A Brief History.* "The children were often responsible for taking the food to the house for the sick." Etta Colvin, who died of smallpox, was the first person to be buried at Adair Cemetery in February, 1883, according to a website established by Edward Holliday.

The McNeil family moved to Adair where an epidemic of scarlet fever killed their baby James in 1886, according to an account by Sanford Warren Jaques. "The McNeil children all took the disease."

Most of the dreaded illnesses that affected those White Mountain settlers are unfamiliar today.

Scarlet fever is caused by a toxin released by strep bacteria. It causes fever, a bright red tongue and rash on the upper body. Complications can lead to death. For pioneers, quarantine of the victims was the best practice. It was not treatable until the discovery of antibiotics in the middle of the 20th century. Scarlatina is another name for scarlet fever.

The process of vaccination for smallpox was discovered before 1800, but few in the West were protected against the disease before the 20th century.

Diphtheria is a highly contagious infection of children that blocks the throat and produces a toxin that can cause heart failure. "Many children recovering from the throat infection died suddenly from an acute inflammation of the heart," wrote Volney Steele in *Bleed, Blister, and Purge, A History of Medicine on the American Frontier.* The bacteria that caused the disease wasn't discovered until 1883 and an effective anti-toxin was not produced until 1895. It was not widely available until much later.

Whooping cough, a disease especially deadly for babies, could kill by blocking breathing or by creating a high fever that could cause brain hemorrhages. The small victims of "croup," as they called whooping cough, also frequently died from pneumonia. A vaccine for whooping cough was not developed until the 1940s.

Typhoid fever is caused by a salmonella bacteria spread when human waste from infected individuals comes in contact with the food or water supply. It usually lasts for four weeks, starting with fever and progressing to diarrhea. It was fatal in up to 30% of cases before antibiotics became available. A U.S. vaccination was created in 1909 but was not widely available to civilians until later.

Though Fort Apache established a hospital in 1885, it was 40 years before similar facilities were constructed for civilians in the area.

Ann Adams Watts told this story about her experience in Snowflake in 1886. "That winter we all had typhoid fever. I got over it first and went to stay with neighbors. I was too weak to go to the main school, which was almost a mile away so I went to a kindergarten. Here I got scarlet fever, but wasn't very sick so I went on to school and all the children got it in the neighborhood. As soon as our family got over it we moved back home [to Adair], but several people around died from the scarlet fever. My sister Lillie was left deaf." Mrs. Watts felt bad all her life about a boy whom she believed had been left unable to hear or speak by the illness. Her grand-daughter determined 100 years later that the child had actually recovered.

Whooping cough and diphtheria hit St. Johns hard in 1888. Brief articles in the local paper tell the story of the epidemic.

• On July 11, it was reported that Carlos Tafolla's 3-year-old daughter died.

• On July 25, the paper said Juan and Francis Baca lost their second child within a week to diphtheria.

• On October 3, the town officials decided not to open school because of the epidemic.

• On November 14, the paper said: "To date over 35 children have died of diphtheria in St. Johns."

296

• On December 5 the paper reported the loss of Anastacia Chaves, Gabriel Armigo's six-year-old daughter, and Rosalio Colomo's daughter, bringing to 40 the number of children who died in the last 10 months.

• By December 19, the paper said at least 100 children had died of diphtheria in the last three to four months in St. Johns.

Meanwhile, in Concho, the paper said, 17 children had died out of a population of 300.

This story comes from the Taylor Stake history: "Grandfather Jesse N. Perkins was the postmaster of Taylor, and Uncle John H., his son, was the mail carrier between Taylor and Holbrook in the early 1880s. John spent the night in Holbrook, and the next morning the landlady informed him that she had forgotten to tell him that a man had died of smallpox just the day before in that same bed he had slept in. This was an alarming thing. Neither young John, his parents, nor family had had this dread disease. This was before vaccinations were given, and the disease was often fatal. There were no modern medicines, either. So it was a sad family when they learned of the news of John's exposure to this disease. What should they do in such a crisis?

"It was decided that the mother, Rhoda Condra McCleland Perkins, and the other family members would move into the little home with their son Reuben and his wife Jane. They took everything they could out of the main house, and prepared for the worst. The father chose to stay with John if he became sick. The family talked of business, of decisions that needed to be made, and of problems that might be faced.

"They did not have long to wait before John came down with the smallpox. Father Jesse cared for John as best he could, and gave him tender loving care. The mother and father would visit each other from opposite sides of the road, and she would bring supplies and medicine, but she never came any closer, for if she did she might carry the sickness to the other family members. John grew steadily worse and then he passed away. His father, with the help of Joe Kay, who had survived the smallpox when it had been about once before, took care of the burial.

"Now, the father, Jesse Perkins Sr., came down with the smallpox and the only one who dared to care for him was Joe Kay. Joe did the best he could for his friend, but soon, Jesse, too, was called home and Joe Kay had to bury his friend."

Disease claimed many children in St. Johns. "Great fatality exists among the children of St. Johns, this Territory," wrote the *Florence Enterprise*. "Doctors seem to be unable to determine whether the disease is diphtheria or spinal meningitis." The *St. Johns Herald* reprinted the report and attempted to add its own explanation: "Physicians report the cause of the great fatality among children of St. Johns, other towns of Apache County, western counties of New Mexico, and other counties of the Territory during the past winter and spring, has been scarlatina in a severe epidemic form. It is said no meningitis has occurred in St. Johns or adjacent localities, neither has diphtheria made its appearance, except in a few reported cases where it co-existed with scarlatina."

Joseph Neal Heywood told the story of a Christmas in an Alpine cabin in the late 1800s. The account, published in *Arizona Memories*, relates that he was about 15 and his sister Mattie was about 11 when they both came down with colds on December 18. "Mattie's cold was also deep-seated but apparently not so severe as mine. I well remember that one night. She slept in the 'front room' where there was a fire. My brother, Spence, and I slept in the northeast room which had no stove or fireplace. It was cold and stormy. As I went to bed … the thought occurred to me, 'This may take one of us. I wonder which one.' I wasn't afraid, but apprehensive. … I was quite miserable and coughed considerable most of the night. Toward morning a change took place and I rapidly improved. During the night the wind howled and whistled as the snow fell. In the morning our bed was covered with a layer of snow that had drifted through the cracks.

"During the night Mattie made a change for the worse. Mother was worried and fearful. I realized that she was real ill, and felt a sort of guilt. It seemed that I was selfish in getting better and letting her get worse. Mattie breathed more rapidly and with each breath a grunt – pneumonia. There were no doctors to call – only the practical nurse and the kindly neighbors. … Christmas Eve Mattie was very low, and passed into unconsciousness. If she was not to recover, why the prolonged suffering? I wondered why. I still wonder. Christmas her breathing became irregular and weaker until it ceased."

298

The White Mountains got its first doctor in 1897 when Joseph Sidney Woolford, who had obtained a degree from the Jefferson Medical College in Philadelphia, arrived in Pinetop. He joined his wife and children, who had come west by train the year before. "To earn a living, Joe drove mail and freight to Fort Apache for a while," says the *History of the Woolford and Hall Families*, compiled by Jacqueline Woolford Solomon. "The following year they moved ... to Snowflake .... Joe taught school in Linden, a small farming community several miles to the southwest of Snowflake, for one school year."

Though his medical work alone would not support his family, "Dr. Joe finally gained a reputation for the fine doctor that he was and built up a profitable practice which included the towns around Snowflake, north to Holbrook and other places in the county," the family history states. The book also quotes the *Holbrook Argus*, which said, "Dr. Woolford came down from the pretty village of Snowflake a few days since and has been spending the time administering to the wants of the afflicted of this community. The Doctor is highly recommended as a physician and we cheerfully advise all sufferers in need of medical attendance to give him a call."

Plagues were still deadly. The whooping cough claimed the daughter of Mr. and Mrs. J. Fish of Woodruff in 1899.

But illnesses didn't prevent young people from teasing. "When May Brimhall was a young girl of about fourteen years, the typhoid fever was raging again in Taylor, and she was one of the many victims," according to a story in the Taylor Stake history. "She had lost her hair because of the fever, and had saved the hair to make a wig. These wigs were a common sight among the fever patients. Her hair was just growing in and was very short and curly. No one, in those days would think of wearing short curly hair in public. May had her wig on, and looked very lovely as she attended her first M.I.A. [Mutual Improvement Association] after her illness. Just as she started to leave the meeting, Gertie Colbath grabbed her wig from her head and exposed May's short hair. May was very embarrassed, and even a little vexed at Gertie. She retaliated with the same prank on Gertie at the first opportunity she got. Gertie had had the typhoid, too."

While residents suffered real illnesses, the newspapers were full of quack cures, which were often printed in the same columns as legitimate news. "I have used Chamberlain's Colic, Cholera and Diarrhea Remedy in my family for 15 years, have recommended it to hundreds of others, and have never known it to fail in a single instance," the Holbrook paper reported in 1900, quoting a newspaper editor from Iowa and noting that the treatment was available at F. J. Wattron's drug store. The paper also reported that the insane asylum for women in Mexico City was killing its patients with the narcotics used to help the women sleep. Researchers found that this could be avoided by using the seed of the white zapote, which put women to sleep without killing them through "brain congestion" as occurred with other narcotics.

Gold In Them Thar Hills, or Not

Arizonans have always savored stories of lost gold mines – really for two reasons. First, a tale which promises hidden treasure is sure to capture the listener's imagination. Second, there actually is gold in Arizona's mountains — certainly enough to keep people interested, though usually not enough to make a lone prospector and his burro fabulously rich. Today, gold is mined from large ore bodies in Arizona as a welcome addition to the copper that pays for those mining operations.

After the Spanish found gold in Mexico and Peru, they sent Coronado to Arizona, expecting the Indians to have treasure houses full of the yellow metal. Later, the Spanish actually did have mines in Arizona, though not in the White Mountains. However, as the area was one of the last to be settled, people hoped to find undiscovered riches in the White Mountain wilderness.

"The literature of Arizona is full of legends and fairy tales of lost mines and buried treasure," *The Historical Atlas of Arizona* says. "Many are purest fiction, but some are based on historical fact." The Atlas places the "Lost Adams Diggings in the White Mountains between the headwaters of the Little Colorado and White River."

The story starts after Adams, a freighter, lost his wagons in an Indian attack near Gila Bend. He set off looking for a new opportunity and found a group of prospectors. They were traveling with a Hispanic youth who was willing to take them to "a canyon where you might load a horse with gold in one day's gathering," wrote Marshall Trimble in *Arizoniana*. The men believed the story about the "pieces as big as acorns, scattered on the ground." The boy naturally offered to trade the secret of this mine for a couple of horses, a red bandana, a rifle and a hundred dollars. The lack of good business sense on the part of the boy is explained – to the satisfaction of the gullible – by the fact that he had a deformed ear.

The book *Lost Mines of the Great Southwest* by John D. Mitchell quotes a letter from a Lt. Robert T. Emmett of the 9th Cavalry, dated March 5, 1882:

"Nearly twenty years ago a man named Adams with seven others came from California into Arizona prospecting. They stopped at Camp Apache for rations and continued east. A few days march from Apache they found a great deal of gold in a small canyon. One of the men, a German, after working about ten days, became alarmed about the Indians and left, carrying about ten or twelve thousand dollars in gold as a result of his labor. This is shown by the books of the Post Trader at Fort Yuma who bought the gold from him.

"The remainder of the party built a cabin and continued work till rations were low, when all but two, Adams and another man, started back to Camp Apache for supplies. The gold they had already mined was buried under the floor of the cabin."

According to the account, Adams and the "Dutchman" left looking for the others, then returned to the area to find Indians killing their comrades and burning the cabin. The two went on a long journey before appearing at a fort in New Mexico. Then they got in trouble with the law, and never found their gold mine again.

The book continues: "The description, by Adams, of the mine should be helpful. The burned cabin was on the side of a narrow gulch, near an old stone corral in which the horses were kept. The sluice boxes were directly in front of the cabin and the flow of water to operate them was large. Pine timber, from which the boxes were made was plentiful, although the area was not heavily timbered."

Though the story is carefully crafted to create interest, there are just a few problems. The Civil War would have occupied the attention of most of the American military in the early 1860s. Certainly, there would be no soldiers lying about in eastern Arizona passing out supplies to prospectors, and certainly not at Fort Apache, which was established much later. The stone corrals are also very interesting. They give the hopeful something durable to look for. But it is hard to imagine Humphrey Bogart in *The Treasure of the Sierra Madre*, crazed by the riches he was gathering, taking time out to build a stone corral for his horse.

The Adams legend is closely tied to the legend of the "Doc Thorne" mine.

A colleague of Cooley, A. F. Banta, said Cooley believed the story. Thorne was supposedly captured by Apaches and released after using natural herbs to cure them from a plague. When he returned to Santa Fe, he supposedly told a story of placer gold in Apache country. "The tribe at that time was somewhere in the White Mountains," Mitchell writes in his book. "In the course of their travel they camped at a little stream that Dr. Thorne afterward said was between thirty and forty miles from the Black River. On the bare flat rock bottom of this stream, Dr. Thorne found a yellow metal which he took to be gold."

But of course the rich stream was lost. "Before leaving Dr. Thorne located the place in his mind by observing landmarks, but suffering badly from snow-blindness his perspective was not so good," Mitchell continues. "The camp was near an old stone corral which was an old structure according to the Indians. From the camp he could see 'Sombrero Butte' and the 'Sierra Pintadas,' and located the camp as being between them. On leaving the camp the journey was south, and the trail crossed Salt River near its junction with the White River."

No one explains why Apaches, who lived in semi-temporary brush structures, would have whipped out their masonry skills to build a stone corral for their horses.

The stories only get better in the re-telling. An Internet site called "LostDutchman.Net" has Cooley leading an expedition of 267 men in search of the Doc Thorne mine. Notice the precision of the size of the group. Included in the group was Jacob

Waltz, the fabled "Lost Dutchman," namesake to the granddaddy of all Arizona legends of hidden riches. It is not known why Cooley, renowned throughout his life for his scouting abilities, would have enlisted someone known as the "Lost Dutchman," but maybe he felt 266 men just wouldn't be enough.

Not everyone who became crazed with the idea of instant riches became famous. Billy Jones, a carpenter who helped build the Shumway schoolhouse, became obsessed with the idea that there was gold west of Shumway along Show Low Creek. "He owned a ranch house there and worked from there on the mine which was located across the creek from the house," wrote Lorenzo D. Rhoton in the Taylor Stake history. "My father worked for Billy as a hired man. Together they set up a drilling rig and drilled. I believe they got the hole down about 80 feet. Billy was running out of money but he still wanted to keep Father helping, so he thought if he could make Father think they were finding traces of gold he would be interested and keep on working on the hope of a strike. Billy dropped some brass shells in the hole and depended on the drill cutting them to powder. His plan didn't work because in cleaning out their cuttings Father found a recognizable piece of the shell. He accused Billy and he owned up to what he had done, and explained why."

"Billy had a beautiful wife, a son, Leo, and two lovely daughters," Rhoton said. "His wife left him and took the children, but Billy wore his life out still seeking the elusive gold."

History books don't mention the Pinetop Gold Rush, probably because it fizzled out almost as soon as it started. The *Holbrook Argus* broke the story on January 6, 1900: "Word comes that Robt. Scott and W. N. Amos have unearthed a four-foot vein of mineral near Pinetop. The vein contains gold and copper. No assay has as yet been made. There is considerable excitement over the find. We hope they have struck it rich." [Scott and Amos were two of the wealthiest sheep men of the area at the time.]

Activities of the hopeful residents in the remote region continued to be reported in the county seat newspaper.

- Saturday, January 13, 1900: *Holbrook Argus*: "Considerable excitement prevails around Pinetop over the discovery of a supposed mineral section. Assays of the ore have not yet been returned. The ore is believed to contain copper and gold. The whole adjacent country is being staked and shafts are being sunk. We hope that a bonanza has been struck out there, as there is plenty of water and timber in that section, and everything favorable to pursue mining successfully."

- Saturday, January 27, 1900: *Holbrook Argus*: "People of this place are doing considerable prospecting for mineral. Some have found some good looking rock and are searching for better. Nephi Packer and D. L. Penrod were the first to start the ball rolling in this direction. ... T. Saul of Linden was in town last week and staked out a mining claim. He returned home Monday, but will be back in ten days to commence work on his claim."

- January 31, 1900: *Holbrook Argus*: "The general occupation of the people here for the past week has been mining. Blast[s] are going off continually. Every one is busy working his claim. Assays have been made by different assayers and some returns are very good. ... C. E. Cooley was down Monday inspecting the mining prospecting of this place. Wm. Amos was in town Sunday. He started for Phoenix Monday and took several ore samples with him to have them thoroughly tested."

- Feb. 7, 1900: Holbrook, Argus: "The miners are still working industriously on their claims and taking out some good ore. Several more samples have been sent off for assaying but no returns have yet been made. Mr. D. I. Penrod and Alva Young have sunk about fifteen feet and are in some good rock. Mr. D. L. Penrod & Co. are driving a tunnel; they have got in about ten feet."

The last report came almost two months later.

- March 31, 1900: *Holbrook Argus*: "D. I. Penrod was down from Pinetop Thursday. He reports that the mining prospects there are getting brighter the deeper down they go. The ore contains silver, gold and copper."

Perhaps having dug the deepest, D. I. Penrod was most hesitant to give up.

Mormons Prosper
At End of 19th Century

As basic needs of food and shelter were met, the White Mountain towns began to pay more attention to education. In 1888, the Snowflake Academy was established. Also that year, the St. Johns paper reported, "Miss Clara V. McCormick will open a select school here on Monday the 11th inst., at the public school building." It is not known what a "select school" was, but the announcement came while schools were closed because many of the children, particularly from Hispanic families, were dying of diphtheria. Another announcement in the paper said a school would be opened in Bush Valley [Alpine] that year. Springerville also had a schoolhouse which burned in January 1889 and was quickly rebuilt, according to the St. Johns paper.

By 1890, some of the hardest pioneering days were behind the settlers. A correspondent of the *St. Louis Globe-Democrat* gave this account of a trip from Holbrook to Fort Apache, which was quoted in *Arizona Was the West* by Jennings. "It is astonishing how these Mormon people, fleeing from contact with the Gentiles, erect comfortable homes for themselves and turn western deserts into garden spots. I found in every settlement through which I passed, fine reservoirs and complete systems of irrigating ditches. Orchards and shade trees had been planted, hundreds of acres of land brought into cultivation, and fine vegetable gardens laid out. ... I could not help noticing the marked difference in the appearance of the cattle and horses of the Mormons from those I had become accustomed to see elsewhere in the Southwest. They were fat and sleek-looking, showing that they had good care. At every farm house there was an abundance of milk, butter, chickens and eggs, things almost unknown to the average Arizona rancher. ... I was surprised to find pianos and organs in most of the houses, and was equally surprised at the hospitable manner in which I was treated."

Local Mormons supported the construction of a new Temple, in Salt Lake City. When William Flake attended the dedication with his wife and son James, President Joseph F. Smith told James he would be listed as the first to do "Temple work" in the new facility.

The political situation, however, was again in flux. Forces in the western portion of Apache County wanted to move the county

The Shumway Schoolhouse was built of locally fired brick in a village settled by Charles Shumway in 1878. The pride of the community, the one-room school is preserved in excellent condition.

seat to Holbrook, so the St. Johns political machine was forced in 1890 to court the Mormon vote. "Better look out you St. Johns chaps, or the 'city of sand' as you derisively call us, will drift you clear out of sight next fall," the Holbrook paper taunted.

"The St. Johns Stake Mormon vote proved to be the deciding factor and the county seat remained," the St. Johns Stake history reports. "However, in that same year the western forces pressed for a division of the county whereupon the western part became Navajo County, with Holbrook as its county seat. The Mormons had at last taken their rightful place in Arizona politics." In *Elijah Was a Valiant Man*, Palmer credited the new county to the efforts of Will Barnes, who had become a representative to the Territorial Legislature. "Some people had wanted to call the new creation Colorado County but Barnes argued for Navajo with the Spanish 'j' and had carried the day," Palmer wrote.

Interestingly, a map published in newspapers would have left Whiteriver and Fort Apache in Apache County, making the southern border of Navajo County a straight east-west line south of Pinetop. However, Navajo County managed to get a panhandle that took in the fort, leaving an ironic situation. The principal towns of the Navajo Reservation are in Apache County and the main town of the Apache Reservation is in Navajo County.

Carrying freight from the Holbrook rail yard to Fort Apache continued to be a source of cash income for the Mormons. "The round trip of one hundred eighty miles took eight days in good weather," writes Jennings in *The Freight Rolled*. "Bad weather meant bad roads and several additional days to make the trip. Under such conditions it was frequently necessary to borrow teams from other 'outfits' and hitch them to 'stuck' wagons to pull them out of mud holes. The Willis brothers from Snowflake were known to hitch twelve horses to two wagons and haul them all the way from the Cooley Ranch, near Pinetop, into Fort Apache and then return to pick up other wagons that had been left behind.

"A freight outfit usually consisted of six horses hitched to two wagons coupled together," with up to 4,000 pounds in the first wagon and up to 3,000 in the second. "Freight ran the entire gamut of human needs on the frontier. One load might be barbed wire, another rock salt, other sacks of flour, sugar, oats, barley, Timothy hay from New York state, boxes of clothing, sacks of walnuts, boxes of canned goods – anything and everything needed in a community."

The campsites from Holbrook south were Five Mile Wash, Washboard, The Cedars, Ten Mile Wash, Seven Mile Wash, Five Mile Wash and Three Mile Wash. From Taylor south they were The Divide, Show Low Creek, Ellsworth Hill, Morgan Draw, Adair Springs, Cooley Draw, Murphy Canyon, Black Canyon, Miner's Flat, Alchesay Field, Natson Field, Big Bend and Whiteriver Cottonwoods, according to Jennings.

Freighting was integral to the economy. To make ends meet, the freighters had to grow their own forage to feed the horses. When townspeople got behind on their accounts at the General Store in Snowflake, they could haul freight to pay off their bill.

Although Fort Apache was the usual destination, trips were also made to Cibecue, Young and even Keams Canyon. On the return trip, wagons were frequently empty, but sometimes carried firewood or wool.

Just before the turn of the 20th century, one last tragedy would strike the Flake family. It occurred in the James Madison Flake house, a Victorian monument which is listed on the National Register of Historic Places. "About 5 o'clock Love came screaming and said little Lois was burnt," wrote Lucy Flake, wife of William Flake and grandmother of the four-year-old victim. "I ran as fast as I could and oh, what a terrible sight. She lived eleven hours, was in dreadful agony about two hours, then went to sleep and never waked up, passed away so quietly, just breathed easier and easier until her breath was gone. She was upstairs with Theresa [her 18-year-old sister]. She said [she] was cold. Theresa told her to go and warm and the poor little baby went into the room where the fireplace was and the next thing Theresa knew she heard her screaming, and ran in and found her all ablaze. Theresa put out the fire with her hands. It seems a miracle that anyone would have the fortitude to keep fighting fire 'til their hands burn off. It was dreadful to think of. The baby died nearly four o'clock in the morning."

The splendid Victorian house, built in 1895, survives today, a monument to the son of William Flake, who himself had 1,200 descendants within 100 years of his birth.

Another landmark surviving from that period of Mormon prosperity is the Shumway schoolhouse. It was built from fired brick and served as a community center and church. Up to 25 students in grades one through eight studied together in the same room. It was completed just after the turn of the century.

The Forests

Mormons settled in or near a huge ponderosa pine forest, and needed sawmills to make lumber. Some of those first mills were turned by water power, or by horses.

Then came the "Mt. Trumbull sawmill." It was a steam-powered behemoth, originally set up by Mormons on Mt. Trumbull in northwest Arizona to create the beams for their temple in St. George, Utah. After the temple was finished, the sawmill was loaded onto seven wagons pulled by 72 oxen, according to *Arizona's Honeymoon Trail.* The two large boilers were placed on timbers stretched between two wagons. When the brakes failed on a steep trail near the Colorado River, the party was saved only by the two "wheeler" oxen, who dropped to their haunches and stopped the runaway load. The sawmill was set up on the western edge of the White Mountain area near Mormon Lake.

"Logs could be used for walls but for window frames, roof

sheeting and flooring, lumber was necessary," the Snowflake Stake history says. "On March 1, 1881, arrangements were made for a Snowflake Sawmill Cooperative headed by William J. Flake to buy the Mount Trumbull Sawmill from the Little Colorado United Order for the sum of $4,000. [The mill] was moved to a site about 22 miles southwest of Snowflake. [To Pinedale, which was then called Snowflake Camp.] Gradually the stock holders pulled out until Flake was the sole owner." The mill was sold and moved to Pinetop from Pinedale in 1890, then taken to Lakeside the next year.

In 1885, the *St. Johns Herald* reported this dispute between the government and residents over timber. "The Land Department is taking active steps to forbid the citizens of Arizona cutting and using timber from the government lands. The prohibition extends to the use of wood for building purposes and all other domestic necessities. Agents of the government are now in the Territory with a view to stopping such so-called depredations, and instituting proceedings wherever the same may seem necessary. ... If the program is carried out it is difficult to see how the citizens of the Territory will live. With purchases being limited to 160 acres, such areas would prove of little practical benefit to the saw mills in the mountains in supplying lumber for home consumption. Many citizens, in fact most of them, are unable to enter 160 acres of the desert land which has no other value than is represented by the scrubby cedars growing upon it. It is impossible for settlers to live without being allowed the privilege of using sufficient timber to supply the ordinary comforts and necessities of life. The government will not sell its timber, and if it is so rigidly forbids its disturbance necessity will force the people to supply themselves as best they may." The paper encouraged residents to petition the government.

In 1888, the St. Johns paper reported that three tree cutters were called to court in Prescott to settle for taking government lumber.

Congress passed legislation in 1891 allowing the president to set aside public lands covered with timber, but it wasn't until 1897 that the Bureau of Forestry officially set aside a portion of the White Mountains as the "Black Mesa Reserve," according to Palmer in *Elijah Was a Valiant Man*. "The local range users would be regulated and restricted increasingly, and most of the time the changes would be beneficial to the forests and its users; occasionally regulations were incomprehensible to anyone but minor bureaucrats in Washington, D.C."

The *Holbrook Argus* reported in 1899 that "Joe Pearce of Snowflake, D. J. Penrod of Pinetop, George Bryan of Pinedale, and a son of George Adams of Show Low have received commissions as forest rangers and would soon enter upon their duties."

According to a Forest Service publication, those first rangers made between $75 and $90 a month, but had to pay for uniforms and maintain a string of at least three horses.

Pearce was the chief ranger and was responsible for the largest expanse of virgin timber in the United States, stretching from Flagstaff to the New Mexico line and from Springerville to Clifton, according to his account in *Arizona Memories*.

"My most important duty as the first forest ranger in Arizona, then the same as now, was fighting fires," Pearce wrote. "But in April 1899, when I was appointed, the chief cause of fires wasn't the stub of a cigarette or a careless campfire, but the intent and purpose of the Apache Indians, whose reservation bordered on the Black Mesa Forest. They set the fires deliberately for the smoke. They had a sincere belief or superstition that smoke would bring rain. And in the driest seasons, when the forest was all ready to burn like tinder, up would pop a big fire near the boundary of the reservation. And you couldn't catch them at all."

"The toughest fire I had to fight was the one at Pinedale," he wrote. "A cowboy came racking along at top speed to my headquarters at Nutrioso to tell me that a fire was blazing away at Baker's Butte and Long Valley, and the cattlemen were unable to check it. That was the spring of '99.

"My horse and pack horse were grain fed and in fine condition, and I had them packed and saddled and ready to go in fifteen minutes. In two and a half days I was in Long Valley, almost two hundred miles away, and much of the trip over mountain trails. I pushed those horses. When I arrived I summoned more help, cattlemen and sheep men anywhere I could get hold of them, putting them on government pay. It took three days for 40 men to get that fire under control. Smoke-blackened and tired, but satisfied, those stockmen returned to their ranches, with an order for two dollars a day wages from the Government in their pockets.

"On my return along the Tonto Rim I bumped into the Pinedale fire … . It had no doubt been started by the Apaches, for it had nothing to do with the Long Valley fire. It was boiling along south of Pinedale, a settlement of 20 families in log houses. A south wind fed it and whipped it, and Pinedale was direct in the path of the fire. What made it worse, the folks at Pinedale, having need of logs for one thing and another, had cut down a great many of the trees surrounding the settlement and had left the dead branches scattered everywhere on the ground. If the fire got to those dead branches nothing could stop it. I didn't have much hope of saving the town."

Pearce hired his crew and arranged for supplies.

"Mounted and on foot we rushed south three miles through the pines to the fighting line," Pearce said. "There was a fire! The smoke had piled up into a thick gray-black mist that made the sun the color of blood. With smoke stinging our eyes, we could see the red flames crawl up a hundred-foot pine tree in half a minute, and then like as not the pine tree would go down with a shivering crash. We saw the fire leap 20, 30, 40 yards from one tree to the next. The fire was so hot we could only face it a minute or two and then had to turn our backs or move away."

They retreated, cut a fire line and tried a backfire, but the wind came up and the fire jumped the line. "The men were tired, back-weary, some of them slightly burned and most of them singed in their beards and hair, faces black from smoke. Leaving the men to fight the fire, Pearce saddled up and rode to Cooley ranch where he could send a telegram to the commander at Fort Apache:

"Forest fire, originating inside reservation, burning north to top of mountain, now moving fast toward Pinedale. Unable to check it. Send all available scouts and Indian police to Pinedale with three days' rations," he wrote.

"Thirty mounted Apaches, riding plumb wore-out ponies, reached Pinedale at dusk of that same day and went immediately south to the fire line, where I put them to work extending the fire

311

barrier, cutting a new barrier where the fire had crossed beyond control on the other side," he wrote. With the additional men, the fire was checked until the wind changed. The blaze then turned back on itself and burned out.

The Forest Service got into the fire-fighting business largely to protect government timber from being lost, but also to protect nearby ranches and communities from wildfire. It was a slippery slope. Initially, firefighting was relatively simple. "When a fire call came to the ranger station, the ranger dropped everything and went," says *Timeless Heritage: A History of the Forest Service in the Southwest.* "Gathering his crew, which included ranch hands and the local cattle outfits, mill workers, Indians from the reservations, and others (most of whom realized the potential danger of unchecked forest fires), the ranger walked or rode to the fire location. Most often they built a fire line to contain the fire and stayed with it until the fire was out." In addition, local residents found work as a "per diem guard." "He was trained as a fire fighter and given a complete set of tools, including rations, first-aid kit, and lantern. He would, on his own initiative, go to and attempt to suppress area fires, and received pay or "per diem" only when engaged in fire work." Unfortunately, the forest needs fire to clear out undergrowth and keep the ecology in balance. The longer the minor fires were suppressed, the more dangerous the threat of major fire became.

Indians at the End of the Century

A late clash in 1887 with some Navajos raised concern among local settlers. Three deputies, named Lockhart, Palmer and King, were killed 25 miles southeast of Navajo Springs, as they investigated what they said were charges of horse stealing. The army was called out, but Indians said the horse stealing allegations were fabricated and none were punished. "If Indians are to be permitted to leave their reservations to steal, plunder and openly defy the civil law and murder civil officers or any one else, we believe they should be turned over to the civil authorities to be held responsible for their depredations and crimes, or the citizens should shoot every Indian found off the reservation," the *St. Johns Herald* wrote. The paper reported that a man named Hostine Chee had been found in possession of a mare belonging to Lockhart, and that the shooting broke out when the three deputies attempted to arrest the suspect.

The Indians in the area of Navajo Springs were again in conflict with the law in 1899 when C. H. Landreth, a gambler, embarked on a scheme to cheat them out of their railroad wages. "As Sunday was pay day, Landreth proceeded to fill some of them up with whiskey in order to induce them to gamble," a newspaper account says. "He succeeded, but during the game a dispute arose and Landreth shot an Indian wounding him severely. The Indians then attacked Landreth, killing him and pounding his body into an almost unrecognizable mass." Deputies were not able to restore order, so troops from Fort Wingate rode to the rescue of the remaining white settlers of Navajo Springs. The incident was reported widely, receiving three paragraphs in the *New York Times.*

The *St. Johns Herald* quoted a government investigation on the Apaches who were with Geronimo in Florida. "The report claims that of the eighty-two Apache men who are now imprisoned at Fort Marion, not more than thirty have been guilty of any recent acts of hostility. The report goes along further and says Chato and a great number of the remainder were employed as scouts by Generals Crook and Miles, and greatly assisted our soldiers in following and securing Geronimo and his hostile band, and that it is a shame that these should be confined as prisoners with the rest."

The *Herald*, however, had no sympathy. "The report and its effect as already manifested, shows a fast increasing sympathy, which is likely, ere long, to be converted into an appeal for the release of more than one-half of these Indians and their return to their native clime, where they can, after becoming rested, again take the war path and fill our country with horror and blood."

Crook, now commander of the department of the Platte in Omaha, launched a campaign for better treatment of the Apaches. By the time Crook died in 1890, he had laid the groundwork for the Apache prisoners to come to Fort Sill, Okla., where the climate was healthier and more like their accustomed Arizona and

New Mexico homeland.

Geronimo's biographer, Halliday, described the war chief's degrading final years. "Though still nominally a prisoner of war, he was allowed to travel to various fairs and exhibitions, where he filled his pockets with change by crudely signing his autograph and looking fierce for snapshot portraits at a quarter or half dollar a snap. As much as possible of his legitimate loot he spent on liquor — and one day in February 1909, riding back to the army post from a spree, he fell off his horse into some weeds, lay there all night, and contracted a mortal case of pneumonia."

Geronimo had been preceded in death by Lozen, the fierce woman warrior, who died of tuberculosis when she was an anonymous prisoner of war in an Alabama camp.

Meanwhile, Back at the Fort

"Through the last decades of the 19th century, Indians of the Fort Apache reservation began their necessary adjustments to this new social landscape," said McGuire in *Mixed-Bloods*. "They faced new landlords – first the U.S. Army at the post along the White River, and in the late 1890s, when the reservation was administratively separated from San Carlos, the first in a series of U.S. Indian agents and their accompanying bureaucrats."

Infighting between military and civilian authorities was extreme, especially involving agent Clum from San Carlos. Richard Perry in his book *Apache Reservation* told how "Clum traveled to Camp Apache to secure the release of some Apache prisoners and take them back to San Carlos. A military detachment pursued him and rearrested the bemused Apache." The military fired Fort Apache Indian Agent James E. Roberts and installed the Rev. J. M. Mickly in his place. Clum was ordered to take charge of Camp Apache. "When Clum arrived, he arrested Mickly for opening Roberts' mail. … The officer of the day arrested Clum for riding his horse too fast across the parade ground. When Clum asserted that he was now in charge of all the Apache, the post commander opened the doors of the guardhouse and released the Apache prisoners."

While Native American problems are usually thought of as the result of their conflicts with "whites," in the late 1800s, most of the soldiers were black. "Two companies of the 24th U.S. Infantry (Colored) have been here en route from the Indian Territory to Camp Apache," stated an item from Holbrook in the *Apache Review* on June 6, 1888. "It is intended to have all the troops at [Fort] Apache of one color hereafter which is a very suitable idea. There are already four troops of the 10th Colored Cavalry at Apache and these two companies will complete the garrison."

Apaches were forced to live near the fort, which made them almost totally dependent on government rations. "Hunting and gathering excursions were discouraged or forbidden," wrote Winfred Buskirk in *The Western Apache*. Anthropologist Goodwin estimated that 35 to 40 percent of all pre-reservation White Mountain Apache food was from wild plants, much of it gathered in areas off limits under the new regulations. Another 35 percent of their former diet was meat, mostly from wild game that could no longer be pursued. While the government encouraged the Indians to farm, it would not allow them to travel to their distant fields. But they were allowed to leave the reservation to find employment in circumstances where the labor was hard and the wages low, such as field work in the burning deserts. Some more fortunate Apaches earned wages as policemen, keeping order on the reservation. But that was dangerous work.

Lt. Britton Davis gave this account, which explains why Apaches were malnourished. The "rations provided for them by the Government were being openly sold to neighboring towns and mining camps. That beef on the hoof, forming the principal part of their rations, was so thin that it was hardly more than skin and bone. That the weekly issue of flour, the other principal portion of the ration, would hardly suffice a family for one day. That other components of the ration were almost negligible when issued and frequently not issued at all."

Part of the government control of the reservation involved administrative identifications that some Apaches came to use as names. "The use of neck tags to assign people to administrative bands also was irksome to many Apache," wrote Perry. "All males over fourteen were given brass military identification tags. They were ordered always to keep [the tags] on their persons. On these tags were letters and numbers indicating the band to which the

Indian belonged and his number in the band."

Goodwin wrote that tag-band identifications were often used as names. In fact, some Apaches were better known by their band tag than by either their Apache or English names. Chief Alchesay was called A-1, which later became the name of a high country lake. *The People Called Apache* says, "Girls used their father's tag-band number until married, then they used their husband's. The boys in a family took successive numbers beyond that of the father, but using the same letter. ... The Apache received their English names in various ways. Missionaries bestowed some names, and children born in hospitals were sometimes given an English name. Parents named children after whites they liked. ... Since the people were often in Mexico, Mexican names became common. Now and then, in utter frustration at trying to pronounce an Apache name, a soldier would give the person an English name."

Officials favored boarding schools over day schools because they wanted to remove the children from the influence of their parents and other relatives. "What this approach to education meant, essentially, was that children were to be de-Indianized – weaned away from an identification with their ethnic background," wrote Perry. The children were taught to fill low-wage jobs. "In this situation, young minds that were self-assured, critical, questioning, and imbued with a strong sense of ethnic validity were not appropriate. Acceptance of discipline, minimal instrumental skills, loyalty to the wider state system, and internalization of its ideology were more consistently the goals of Indian education."

"This is one reason why children in Indian schools were beaten for speaking in their own languages," he wrote. "Discipline usually was very strict. A favorite punishment for children in San Carlos was to make them carry a ball and chain to keep them from escaping and running away. Even so, many did run away from boarding schools, and some died trying to find their way back to their people." It is understandable why parents and grandparents went to great lengths to hide children from the Indian police who served as truant officers.

Toward the end of the century, Apache men began to adopt the garb of cowboys, their cinematic Nemesis. Jeans, boots and western shirts were common. Women adopted "camp dresses."

They were actually loose-fitting blouses over long full skirts, made from eight to ten yards of bright calico. Apache women continued to wear colorful camp dresses, and use cradleboards, into the second half of the 20th century and beyond.

Late 19th century Apaches were fascinated with games, particularly with any that offered the prospect of gambling. They cut playing cards from leather and painted them. Following Spanish models of the time, they had four suits, each having an Ace, two through seven, a king, knight and page. The knight was apparently more important than a queen, and they did without the eight, nine and ten. Decks of Apache playing cards are at the Southwest Museum in Los Angeles and are described in a leaflet written by Virginia Wayland.

Though far from prosperous, the White Mountain Apaches were able to keep more reservation resources than other Native groups. "In contrast to the situation in San Carlos and the Gila River uplands to the south, Mormon and Gentile settlers on the Mogollon Rim did not control the headwaters of the reservation drainage system," McGuire wrote. "Unlike San Carlos, too, Fort Apache was largely devoid of exploitable mineral wealth and, for the most part, did not experience the incursions of prospectors. Finally, by repelling the Mormon colonization efforts in the Forestdale Valley, the Apache had effectively established their readiness to defend the integrity of the reserve."

Communications and transportation were gradually improving in Arizona. By 1877, according to *Arizona as it Was,* a weekly stage line ran from Prescott to the Little Colorado and Santa Fe. Author Hiram C. Hodge adds that a military rider took mail from Camp Goodwin on the Gila River to San Carlos and Camp Apache before continuing on to meet the Prescott to Santa Fe stage along the Little Colorado.

Maintaining the military in Arizona was expensive for the government. A fire reported in 1883 did $100,000 damage at Fort Apache while another in 1885 did $160,000 in damage.

The *Apache Review* reported a Phoenix trial in 1888 that sent a number of Indians to prison in Columbus, Ohio, for murdering settlers. An Apache named Miguel and another named Sayers got 10 years, while Hast-u-du to-dy and Captain Jack received 25 years.

Oddly, the military contingent at Fort Apache increased during the Spanish American War with the arrival of the 9th Cavalry in 1898.

In 1899, agent A. A. Armstrong reported that the Apaches were starving, partly because floods had destroyed their crops and their wood contract with the fort had been reduced. He went on to report that the Indians had sold 850 cords of wood, nearly two million pounds of hay, 120,000 pounds of corn, barley, beans and charcoal to the government. "This is fine grazing country and should be stocked with cattle by the Government in the interest of the Indians," Armstrong wrote. "They can do the work, because they are natural horsemen and take readily to the business, and it can be made profitable if managed by experienced persons. These Indians can be made self-supporting by that method long before it can be reached through any other channel." He urged Congress to ban grazing by white-owned sheep and goats on the reservation. Cattle were already restricted. Armstrong advised Washington that it would be pointless to try to divide the reservation into individual "allotments" for the residents until an irrigation system was built. That, and the lack of mineral resources, saved the Apache reservation from being dismembered based on the government policy of the time. Though Armstrong did much to stimulate Apache farming and ranching, he also eliminated their food rations, which forced them to eat the cattle and crops he had hoped they would use to enter the cash economy.

"By 1900, then, there was potential for a smooth, unmolested, and relatively prosperous adjustment to the new conditions of sedentary life on the reservation," McGuire wrote. "This potential, however, was not to be so quickly realized."

One man who did make the transition was Wallace Altaha, known by his government ration number, R-14. He created a cattle empire on the reservation and was said to be the most successful Native American cattleman ever. The dynasty started with Wallace's father, who was taken prisoner during the Apache Wars of the late 1800s. "The nucleus of his immense cattle herd began when the War Department issued his father an old black cow, intended for his weekly beef ration," *Arizona Highways* wrote in a 1940 article. "Instead of killing the critter, however, the Altahas roped the animal and put their brand number on her. A few months later they put the same distinguishing mark on her heifer calf." The story says whenever the Altahas were issued a steer by the government, they would trade with another family for a heifer or cow. When Wallace, who took over the cattle operation from his father, had 300 cattle, he began selling to the government to feed the soldiers at the fort and supply the beef rations to other Apaches. When he died in 1937, his wealth was estimated at $500,000, which was a fabulous sum for anyone during the Great Depression.

Apache men took to the cowboy life. They found riding the range more in keeping with their traditional ways than tilling the soil. But most Apaches were too poor to build up cattle herds even though the government tried to stop non-Indians from grazing livestock on the reservation. Available animals were quickly butchered and eaten.

The government policy at the time was to prepare Indians for assimilation into Anglo culture with a three-pronged program. "First, the Indians were to be taught to be economically self-supporting through agriculture," wrote William Kessel in a paper about the first missionary to the White Mountain Apaches. "Second, schools were to be opened and children taught to read, write and display proper etiquette. Finally, the Indians were to be converted to Christianity."

In an odd series of events, White Mountain Apaches wound up with conservative Lutherans from the Wisconsin Synod as missionaries. Other denominations had adopted the peaceful tribes. When the Wisconsin Lutherans finally decided to get into Native American missionary work, the "wild Apaches" were the only tribe left. A history describing the synod's late entry into the Indian missionary field, says: "The commission had cast about for Indians that were still without the preaching of the Gospel, having adopted the heathen mission policy that it behooved American citizens to look out for the Indians first, and had been informed about the recently pacified Apaches in Arizona, known ... [for] their last great insurgency leader Geronimo, as the most savage of them all."

In those years the Wisconsin Synod was squabbling with rival Lutherans about the pettiest of doctrinal differences, so the new missionary could easily have been completely intolerant of Apache beliefs and customs. It didn't turn out that way.

When Paul Mayerhoff was a child in Wisconsin, he met Winnebagoes and learned to love Native Americans. On arriving in Arizona, he went to San Carlos, where the Lutherans had established a mission a few years earlier. Mayerhoff spent a month there learning the basics of riding a horse and the rudiments of speaking Apache. He set off in June 1895 to become the first missionary at Fort Apache. When he arrived, Mayerhoff wisely paid his respects to Chief Alchesay at the fort and Chief Cooley at Cibecue. Then he pitched a tent at East Fork, four miles from the fort.

"Soon a line of Apaches on horseback half encircled the missionary," wrote Kessel. "A corpulent chief, Y-1, ordered Mayerhoff to 'get out.' In an unexpected flash of bravado, Mayerhoff retorted in broken Apache, 'Don't tell me to get out.' Y-1 indicated that he would set fire to the missionary's tent and then rode off. That night, tired, sore and frightened, Mayerhoff lay in bed dosing, thinking of home and dreaming of pleasant things far away in Wisconsin. Suddenly, he was aware of someone crawling into his tent. The intruder turned out to be an Apache woman called Christmas, who invited him to an all-night ceremonial dance taking place nearby. Still frightened, but adopting the philosophy, 'It is the bold who win,' Mayerhoff attended. Among the hundreds of Indians in attendance, two men recognized him, Chief Alchesay and Chief Cooley, who he had met only days earlier.

"Mayerhoff returned to his tent for a few hours sleep and then attended the festivities the next day. That evening, Chief Y-1 and his followers again paraded into the missionary's camp. The chief indicated that Mayerhoff was on his land and that for two dollars he could stay for five nights. Mayerhoff paid and eventually stayed for eight years."

Raised on hair-raising stories of the Apache wars, the missionary took special care to travel quickly past the camp of a band that was said to be particularly quarrelsome. "His horse stumbled and the animal and rider fell to the ground," said Kessel. "Immediately, he was surrounded by Apaches. Mayerhoff recalled, 'They helped me to straighten out and I suppose had a gleeful laugh at the tenderfoot afterwards. From then on, the Indian bugaboo departed from me.' "

One time a drunken Apache ran into Mayerhoff's cabin and

hid behind the stove to escape another Indian who was loading a Springfield rifle nearby. Mayerhoff locked the door and sat down to read a magazine, pretending to be alone as the pursuer looked through the window. "The man behind the stove had earlier been at a drinking party where he hit his wife in the head with a rock, apparently killing her," Kessel said. "The man with the rifle was her father, coming to kill his son-in-law. ... Mayerhoff went to the scene of the crime and found the woman alive." After he dressed her wounds, another woman came at the missionary with a knife, but was stopped by the son of a chief. Mayerhoff later wrote, "I was glad to leave with a whole skin. This was the only time I felt myself in danger among my Apache neighbors." He acquired a mastery of the difficult language, speaking both the Cibecue and Fort Apache dialects. He took many notes that eventually turned into an English-Apache/ Apache-English dictionary. This work was helpful when he translated Luther's Small Catechism. He taught Bible classes at the local school, and rode from camp to camp, preaching and aiding the sick when he could.

"On several occasions Mayerhoff watched Apache ceremonies featuring masked dancers," Kessel said. "Not only did he refrain from calling the dancers by the ethno-centric term 'devil' but provided an explanation of their moves." He wrote extensively on Apache beliefs and preferred telling simple Bible stories to disputing theology. He sometimes worked side-by-side with medicine men to help sick patients, including one man who was diagnosed by the native healer as having a toad shot into his abdomen by an evil spirit. Mayerhoff treated the patient with a more conventional gastro-intestinal remedy while the medicine man was providing ritual treatment. "No doubt the toad bethought himself to behave and come out after H-1 and I had joined forces to lay him low," Mayerhoff said.

The Apache Kid

The last Apache warrior to become a famous renegade was Ski-Be-Nan-Ted, or the Apache Kid. Despite his trouble with Mexican authorities during the campaign to capture Geronimo, he rose through the ranks to be the sergeant of scouts at San

Carlos. The chief of scouts, Al Sieber, trusted the Kid enough to leave him in charge when Sieber took a trip to Whiteriver.

The Kid heard that a band of Indians were brewing tulapai about 10 miles from San Carlos and took a small group of scouts to investigate, according to *The Apache Kid* by William Sparks.

"He did not destroy the tulapai, as his standing orders required him to do, but joined ... in their debauch," wrote Sparks. "There was an Indian killed during the festivities. Neither the Kid nor any of his men had anything to do with the killing, but it was their duty to arrest those who were responsible for it, and they were not in condition to do so." Sparks' tale differs from others.

Tom Horn, in his account, says that the Kid's father, a chief named Toga, was murdered as a result of a 40-year-old row over a girl with another old Indian named Rip. Sieber knew that as the oldest son of Toga, the Kid was bound by honor to avenge his death. He warned the Kid, but as soon as Sieber was away from the agency, the Kid and some followers went looking for Rip and shot him.

All agree that when Sieber returned to San Carlos, he sent for the Kid. When the Kid showed up with armed followers, Sieber ordered them all to the guardhouse. "Some of the bucks with the Kid ... said to the Kid to fight, and in a second they were at it — 11 bucks against Sieber alone," Horn said. "It did not make any particular difference to Sieber about being outnumbered. His rifle was in his tent. He jumped back and got it, and at the first shot he killed one Indian. All the other Indians fired at him as he came to the door of his tent, but only one bullet struck him; that hit him on the shin and shattered his leg all to pieces. He fell and the Indian(s) ran away."

While the Kid was at large, he and his band killed a man named Bill Dihl, and later a man named Mike Grace. They also, according to Horn, killed a freighter or whiskey peddler while hiding near the reservation. The Kid and his band eventually surrendered. They were convicted on federal charges and given long prison terms. President Grover Cleveland, however, soon pardoned the Indians.

Local authorities were less than pleased to have them back. The Kid was tried in Globe on state charges of killing the whiskey peddler. The Kid and several others were sentenced to seven years prison in Yuma. Sheriff Glen Reynolds, Deputy Hunkey Dory Holmes and a driver set out with the prisoners by stage for Casa Grande where they planned to catch the train for the Territorial

Once an Apache Scout, the Apache Kid remained a feared outlaw well after the Indian wars were ended. He would occasionally come to the area to kidnap a fresh "wife" and carry the unfortunate woman back to his hideout in Mexico.

Prison in Yuma.

When most of the prisoners were taken off the stage to make it easier to get up a long hill, the Indians jumped the deputy and the sheriff. They took the deputy's gun as he was dying of a heart attack and shot the sheriff to death, according to Sparks. Only the wounded driver survived as the Indian convicts fled into the brush.

"Most were soon killed or captured," Keith Wheeler wrote in *The Scouts.* "But the Kid eluded all pursuers, even the scouts with whom he used to track other outlaws. For years, he remained a renegade with a $5,000 price on his head and his random killings terrorized the Arizona countryside."

Sparks, who combined facts and misinformation in his effort to create a legend, said the Kid joined Apaches still living in Mexico and occasionally raided into the U.S. "It was while he was traveling between the Sierra Madres and the reservation that the Kid killed most of the white men he was known to have murdered."

"If the squaw he had at the time was not strong enough to accompany him, and do the camp work, he would sometimes kill her, and start on the trail to where there were many that were fresh and strong," Sparks said.

"Finally, in 1894, an Apache woman reported that she had recently left the Apache Kid dying, probably from tuberculosis, in the craggy Sierra Madre," Wheeler said in his Time-Life book.

"The Kid had been sick when he captured her, and was rapidly growing worse," Sparks said. "He coughed all the time, and finally got so thin in flesh, and so weak, he could not leave the camp. One day he called her to come where he lay wrapped in his blankets. He was very sick. He told her he was going to die; that he could not live more than a few days; and that because she had been a good girl to him he was going to let her go home. He said that when he had had to leave other women, he had killed them, because they knew where his camps, and the places he frequented, were; and if he let them leave they would tell the whites, and the Mexicans, and he would have no place to go where he could live in peace." She walked back to the United States and reported that the Kid was probably dead.

"That was the last that was ever heard of the Kid," Sparks said. "The U.S. government officials believed the squaw's story to be true; and although several persons were afterward killed by outlaw Indians, the government's attempts to capture the Kid were abandoned."

But legends die hard. In 1900, the *Holbrook Argus* reported that Mexican troops attacking Yaquis near Hermosillo found the Apache Kid and killed him. "Before the execution took place the Apache Kid was positively identified by an American named [Alexander] McDonald, who was an army scout and knew the Kid in Arizona," the paper said.

Lost Children
At Start of 20th Century

On December 31, 1899, residents of the White Mountains gathered in Pinetop at a huge dance hall run by the Penrod Brothers on the site where the Crown Dancer store was later located. They might have paused a moment to ponder what the 20th century would bring. Certainly none of them could have imagined all the changes that would take place in the world and even in their remote part of the American West.

About this time, the *Holbrook Argus* reported that women's suffrage speakers would be coming to the area. The topic was also discussed at a Mormon women's Relief Society in the tiny village of Adair. "Some women were for it and some were against," Read wrote in *Adair, Arizona -- A Brief History.* "However, the issue wasn't resolved." Women, who had more property rights in Arizona than in other states because of the influence of the Spanish legal system, won the right to vote in state elections in 1912, the same year Arizona became a state. But Indians did not get the right to vote in Arizona for another 36 years.

In 1901, two little boys were lost near Pinedale. The *Holbrook Argus* reported that a large party looked for Carl Fish and Charles Cheney for one day and one night. They were found, hungry but safe 10 miles from home. "The little fellows were not even frightened," the newspaper said.

Another incident pulled the diverse people of the White Mountains together in an effort to find a 7-year-old girl who was lost in the forest in 1905.

The Hatch family of Taylor was in the habit of camping each year near the White River on the Apache reservation. It was a big outing with many uncles, aunts and cousins, and they set up camp on June 14 where Paradise Creek comes into the North Fork of the White River, just east of present-day McNary. The horses were taken to graze near a spring and the children went along to play.

"Ez and I went back to camp, telling the older kids to watch the little ones," said Jack Hatch in the Taylor Stake history. His younger sister Katie had turned seven the day before. "The kids back at the spring had, I guess, been kidding Katie about animals and Indians and had her half scared, and she left to come to camp. She didn't find camp but headed down past the road and down into the canyon."

When the children were called to dinner, it was discovered that Katie was missing. "We hunted all afternoon between Gooseberry Creek and where McNary is now," Hatch wrote. An alert went out to Cooley's Ranch, about six miles away, and Col. Cooley's sister-in-law joined the search. "There was no trace of her. We came back to camp in the evening and there was a young Indian woman there and she had found Katie's tracks where she crossed the road and just before she went into the canyon she threw away a big arm full of flowers. We found them. The

Indian woman took Newt Knight and me down the trail and showed us where she had gone into the mud just west of where the fish hatchery is now."

They hunted all night and men on horseback joined the search the next day. Word reached Taylor on Sunday morning and people immediately left to join the search. Hunting dogs couldn't follow her scent, but an Indian scout named "Chicken" picked up her trail on the second day. "There was a malapai formation there that was pretty steep and we could see where she had slid down the rocks into the creek," Hatch wrote. "He followed her trail down to where she tried to cross the creek and then turned back." A hard rain, unusual in mid-June, came up and no more tracks could be found.

"By the second and third day people came from far and near to join the hunt," wrote Jennings in *The Freight Rolled*. "Some came from Show Low, Lakeside, Springerville, St. Johns, Taylor, Snowflake, Pinedale and the surrounding area."

The search area also expanded. "A report came that some-one had seen a little girl down near Lakeside and so we moved down there to search, but nothing came of it," Hatch wrote. The searchers went from Lakeside to Vernon where a Hispanic sheep-herder spent most of the night cooking sopapillas and mutton for the hungry men.

"The Indians were awful good to help the first two or three days, but then they were afraid they would find her dead and they didn't want anything to do with it" because of their taboo against being near dead bodies, Hatch said.

According to Jennings, the search was nearly three weeks old when the father, John Hatch, called the men together. "Gentle-men, because of some rumors which have come in, someone has suggested that we go across the river and hunt," he said. "Now I realize that some of you need to leave and go home, some have been away from home a long time. My boys, family and I all appreciate your faithful efforts in helping to find my lost child. You have not faltered and stumbled; now if any of you feel that you must go, you may be excused, and if any want to stay and hunt a day across the river, it will be appreciated and if we find nothing then tomorrow I will excuse all. My boys and I will stay and hunt the rest of the summer if necessary."

Some left, but the remaining men started searching across the river.

Charlie Savage, a rancher, found one of Katie's shoes. "The next day I was with the group that found her clothes," Katie's brother wrote. "They were piled up in a neat little pile." The clothes were found near where Hawley Lake was later built. The next day, three shots were heard, the signal that she had been found. "My dad found her himself," Hatch wrote. "Andrew Perkins and Andrew Peterson were with him."

In Jennings' account, Perkins was riding next to Katie's father in a heavy rainstorm. "He became horrified to see locks of white hair on the bushes. The rain was coming down fast, but John Hatch dismounted, took a step forward, knelt down. Perkins said he saw a look of agony on the father's face which he would never forget, as the father looked at the remains of his little seven-year-old child."

The body was under a big juniper tree. "There was nothing left but a skeleton," Katie's brother wrote.

The searchers had concentrated on the west side of the White River, not believing the tiny girl could have crossed the raging stream. But Hatch surmised that his sister may have crossed on a log that stretched across the creek about a half mile from the original search site. "Some thought she may have died the first night or early the next morning, but some said she may have lived two or three days," Hatch wrote.

Katie had walked nine miles after crossing the river.

"She went till she was give out and laid down to rest and went to sleep and when she woke up, she was out of her head and just pulled off the rest of her clothes and left them piled up there and took off. Her body was found about two or three miles from her clothes," her brother wrote.

A monument has been erected at the camp site and a bronze marker was placed where the little girl was found.

Ann Lewis, Katie's sister, was two at the time of the disappearance. In a 1986 interview with the *Falcon* newspaper, she said she was glad she was so young when it happened. Her 12-year-old sister never got over it., nor did either of her parents even though they had nine children.

Economy, Agriculture
And Dam Failure

The new century started out very dry. An item in the *Holbrook Argus* in 1900 said most of the wells in Pinetop had dried up. "We get about half enough water to drink by waiting three or four days every week," wrote the Pinetop correspondent on June 6. The editors of the paper did not attempt to clarify her statement.

Agriculture was still a difficult way to make a living, despite much boosterism. Though apple trees would grow at the elevation, they produced a good crop only one year in three, due to drought, late frosts in the spring or early frosts in the fall.

In 1905, there was so little summer rain that the roundup was put off to the fall, according to an excerpt from the biography of Bert Colter published in the St. Johns Stake history.

Even though farmers were having a tough time, the overall economy of the area grew. Fred Colter established the first bank in Snowflake in 1908, according to Richard Lynch.

A brochure published by E. Armijo, Commissioner of Immigration, St. Johns, Arizona, was entitled: "Apache County Arizona U.S.A. The Banner Co. of the Greatest State of the Most Glorious Nation on Earth." It said, "Conditions are now ripe for the making of fortunes in Apache County, but they will not be so long. The many opportunities will soon be snapped up. You should investigate." The pamphlet is in the archives of the Southwest Museum in Los Angeles.

A brochure from the Lyman Land Company boasted irrigated land near the new dam for sale with low down payments. "Under irrigation the sunshine is delivered straight and undiluted with a certainty of results at harvest time that always puts the balance on the right side of the ledger," the brochure promised.

A Works Progress Administration book, *Arizona, a State Guide,* recounts how the first Lyman Lake Dam was washed out early in the century. An *Arizona Highways* article from 1965 says the first dam was at Salado Springs, nearer to St. Johns. The Lyman Lake dam was built at its current location at a cost of $200,000 and completed in 1912.

"The next two years were dry, but in 1915 a record runoff filled the lake," recounts the St. Johns Stake history. "A soft spot developed under the dam; some say there was a small spring under the dam at the time construction started."

"Gordon Parks, a boy on guard at the dam one night in April 1915, had crossed over to the north end on his rounds of inspection, when he heard the roar of flooding water," the stake history says. "In the dim light he could see the flood cutting through the base at the south end of the dam." Parks raced back over the failing dam to get to a telephone and warn the town of St. Johns 12 miles downstream. Most people had been attending the Junior Prom when word reached town of the coming flood. "We heard a terrible roar and as we ran up the side of a little hill by the river, the crest of the flood came like a tidal wave," said John A. Hamblin. "The Palmers, met disaster. Mrs. Palmer taught school right under the dam and their house was close-by. Mr. and Mrs. Palmer came to the dance that night, leaving their three children at home with a baby sitter. The flood drowned the children and the sitter and two of the victims were never found, though we searched for their bodies for days." In all, at least nine people lost their lives that night. "The power of the water swept everything before it. At Holbrook, 68 miles downstream, it was reported that dogs, horses, cattle and some wild animals were seen tumbling along in the first rush of the water."

A woman named Mrs. Ray, three small girls and a 16-year-old boy were travelers who had stopped to rest for a few days along the river below the dam. "When the flood struck, Mrs. Ray told the boy to bring the others and she climbed to higher ground with the youngest girl," the stake history says. "She told the child to stay there and then rushed back into the raging waters to search for the others; she and two other girls were drowned." In addition to the youngest girl, only the 16-year-old was saved. "The boy was washed away and became entangled in the branches of a large tree from which he was rescued the next day." A Mrs. Sevedra, along with her baby, also died when the flood reached their farm a little farther downstream.

"All the homes that were adjacent to the river were swept away," the Stake history says. "Some of the adobe houses a little farther back lost one whole side wall, leaving the interior of the rooms, furniture still in place, exposed to public view. Much of the valuable bottom land along the river was either washed away or buried under a heavy layer of mud and rubble." The irrigation water was gone, along with the dam that had been built with so much labor and tremendous expense. The flood water raged downstream, also taking out the Zion dam and the Woodruff dam, which had held since 1890.

"Over the years St. Johns had survived some staggering lows, but nothing compared to this," the stake history says.

"I cannot forget the gloom and depression that settled over the town for quite a while after that," Hamblin wrote. "Toil, sweat, tears and dreams went with that flood, swept away by the waters of the Little Colorado the night the dam washed out."

The Mormons organized a new dam company in September, and put up another dam at the same location at a cost of $600,000. Since it was felt that the little spring had caused the dam to fail, this time they dug a trench into the bed rock and filled it with material that allowed the spring to seep to the reservoir side of the dam. They also drove wooden timbers into the base of the dam and took other precautions against seepage. The new Lyman Lake dam has lasted nearly a century.

Along Silver Creek, the Mormons created Daggs Reservoir in 1914. It is now known as White Mountain Lake.

Mormons Buy Show Low

William J. Flake bought his last White Mountain town for Mormon settlers in 1903. By this time, Cooley had left Show Low after settling up with his partner Henry Huning. The Show Low Ranch had suffered setbacks. The government had insisted that the operation remove a fence that enclosed extensive government and railroad land. The Forest Department had placed restrictions on range land as well, according to the Show Low Stake history. "William J. Flake heard rumors that Huning wanted to sell. He was a man of great foresight and good judgment. He saw the possibilities of a thriving community on the Huning ranch," according to the stake history. The Snowflake patrician also saw possibilities in Huning's water rights to Show Low Creek and its tributaries. Flake paid the $13,500 price by dividing the property into four and a half shares. He paid for one share himself and arranged for James C. Owens, John Henry Willis, and Abner and Frank Ellsworth to take the other full shares. Niels Hansen took the half share. "W. D. Rencher was hired to survey the holdings," the stake history says. "A townsite was laid out in symmetrical blocks and wide streets. The block on which the Cooley home stood was given to the church. The fields were divided into plots and classified and numbered according to their value. Each man drew a number from each class. After the drawing there began a series of trading so that each owner's land could be fenced in one enclosure. It was discovered that some of the improvements purchased from Huning were on railroad land. Therefore it was necessary to buy this land from the railroad to protect the equity. James Clark Owens and J. H. Willis acted in behalf of the community and made the deal with the railroad officials for 18 sections of land. ... Anyone in possession of any portion of this land was given the first opportunity to buy at the purchase price of $1.50 per acre."

The stake history says Flake occupied the Huning home briefly before moving back to Snowflake while James C. Owens moved into Cooley's palatial house.

Mormons began to settle in. "Many families in town had a flock of turkey that roamed free," says *Firm as the Mountains,* a Mormon history of Show Low. "They sent to Sears and Roebuck for special bells to attach to the turkey necks. Each group of bells had a different ring to help identify and keep track of the various flocks."

The Latter-day Saints used Cooley's old house on the hill as a ward house, but it caught fire and burned. "James Clark Owens let the community use his red barn for classes and church after the White House burned," says the Mormon history of Show Low. Eventually, the Cooley house was replaced on the site by the current Mormon chapel in downtown Show Low.

Along with the Show Low Ranch came the rights to the water in the creeks as far up the mountain as Lakeside, according to *A Tribute to the Lakeside Pioneers.* But there were great difficulties. The drought in 1904 was extreme, and all the springs dried up except for one in Lakeside called Adair Springs, according to a video by Richard Lynch. Food was so scarce during the drought of the early 20th century, that after the wheat harvest, people went through the fields to individually pick up any kernels or shafts that had been missed, according to the Woolford family history.

The Mormons began to improve Huning's irrigation system, which used the natural flow of Show Low Creek, but had no dams. They built their first dam in Lakeside in 1898, according to *Top o' The Pines*, but it washed away. In 1903, William Flake traded Adair Springs to William Amos for a five-acre site to build Rainbow Lake. Leora Peterson Schuck, in the *Tribute* book, recounts how Flake supervised the construction of the dam to create the lake. His granddaughter Theresa Caroline Flake Johnson cooked for the work crews to earn money while her husband completed a mission in his native Denmark. After putting in the dam for Rainbow Lake, Flake and his men moved to Porter Creek to create a second lake, according to Flake's biography.

Since Mormons were expanding their settlements in the Lakeside and Pinetop area as the sheep business collapsed in 1905, they purchased the holdings of pioneer sheep men. James L. Fish bought Billy Scorse's homestead in what is now downtown Lakeside, and opened a small store in what had been Scorse's saloon, according to *Top o' The Pines*.

Alpine obtained its most distinctive landmark that same year. The two-story rock house was created — with help from a mason from St. Johns — by Hubert Burk, who had arrived in the community in 1884. The structure is built of red sandstone with white sandstone corners. Mud and lime were used to chink the stones in the walls, which are 21 inches thick. Burk had engaged in a variety of enterprises in Alpine, including cattle ranching, operating a sawmill, farming, horse raising and running a mercantile store. Burk's house still stands in the center of town.

Forest and Timber Industry In New Century

In 1900, the *Holbrook Argus* published an article written by a man from Alpine, one of the many settlers who were living in the National Forest without legal title to their land. "We have just received orders from Forest Supervisor Rowe to the effect that all squatters must vacate immediately. We hope this order will not be enforced as it will work serious hardships on many of us."

Living in and near the forest even then meant living with the danger of fire, particularly in the summer season. The St. Johns paper reported on July 14, 1900: "Forest fires are still raging in reservations south of us. The air here is still laden with smoke from the fires."

Early forest rangers worked without fire towers, instead they climbed "lag trees" when they wanted to see into the distance. Metal spikes were pounded into the tree to provide rudimentary steps. The branches from the tree itself and neighboring trees partially obscured the view. The rangers had to constantly hang onto the tree, reducing their ability to use their hands for field glasses or other equipment. But old timers recall that the biggest problem was with ants. It was hard to hold on when the swarming ants were biting and crawling inside the climber's clothes.

President Teddy Roosevelt, taking office in 1901, created the Apache National Forest and signed legislation transferring the forests from the Department of the Interior to the Department of Agriculture, where trained foresters were at work.

Eventually regulations on timber cutting by locals were relaxed. The new rules, published in the newspaper, permitted residents to take timber from government land for firewood, fencing and buildings for their personal use, but only if they lived in the area and did not have sufficient timber on their own land.

Competition for grass on public land was still intense. "The grazing lands were stocked far beyond their capacity; vegetation was cropped by hungry animals before it had opportunity to reproduce; valuable forage plants gave way to worthless weeds and the productive capacity of the lands rapidly diminished," according to *Hoofprints on Forest Range* by Paul H. Roberts, as quoted by Hansen. "In the absence of lawful regulation it was quite natural that the period from 1880 to 1900 should become one of spoliation."

It was tough for the first forest ranger, Joe Pearce, to enforce grazing regulations. "Many times I've come on close-packed flocks using forest land and have ordered them off, and more often than not they refused to go, the owners claiming the land had been theirs for 40 years and they'd be damned if they'd give it up now, government or no government," he wrote. After Pearce reported them to his boss in Santa Fe, warrants were issued. "A few arrests and trials, with stiff fines, began to make the stockmen change their minds."

"There was a bearded old-timer, a sheep man and a nester in a little shack on government lands," Pearce wrote. The ranger went up to the door, knocked and went inside. "Just wanted to make a little collection for the Government on your sheep," Pearce said.

"Listen here, young feller," Pearce recalled the old man saying. "I pay the Territory and the County taxes on my sheep and goats. I'd like to see the color of a man's hair that'll make me pay my taxes twice in Arizona. You see that door?"

Pearce used the door, but returned with two other rangers and a warrant. "In the end he paid the fee – about 80 cents a year per sheep – and in addition a stiff fine," the chief ranger wrote. "There wasn't any more trouble collecting from him after that."

Pearce spent much of his time creating trails and improving springs. "Generally in trail blazing over rough country I would follow the backbone of a ridge, as this was usually the safest and best way down off a high place," Pearce said. "One could stay away from the ups and downs of gorges and canyons. ... There were two kinds of lost: being turned around and being stranded." A good horse always remembers the last place he was fed, he noted. "A man never needs to be lost riding a gentle horse. Storm stranded is another matter. I've been in snow so thick with whirlwinds in those mountains I couldn't see 10 feet in front of my nose, and blizzards howling for three days without letting up. In a storm like that there's no use trying to go on; you have to make some kind of shelter for yourself. ... I'd unload my packhorse and unsaddle my horse and leave the stock to shift for themselves. Then I'd stretch my rope from one pine to another, cut branches from the small pines and lean them slantwise on each side of the rope. When I was done, there was a cozy shelter." He would then find dry wood, build a fire and wait out the storm.

When Supervisor Gifford Pinchot visited, Pearce took him down to where the Blue Range breaks off to almost a sheer cliff north of Clifton. Pinchot doubted they could get down the mountain, but Pearce said he had blazed a trail. "To prove it, we went down, leading our horses," he said. "That evening in camp I asked him: 'Do you think there'll ever be a wagon road there, down the Blue Range to the flats?' He got a laugh out of that. 'There'll never even be a good horse trail,' he said. 'The only way a man'll ever get down there easily is to grow wings and fly down.' " Within 40 years, a highway called the "Coronado Trail" provided automobiles a way down the cliff, but it remains one of the most winding roads in the nation.

In 1906, the Black Mesa Reserve, along with part of the Tonto National Forest, was re-created as the Sitgreaves National Forest, and new regulations required that all stock be removed from the forest during the spring months. "The sheep men were stunned by this seemingly arbitrary order that would wreak havoc with their stock production cycle, especially at the crucial time when the lambs were born," Palmer wrote.

"Grazing permits were issued only in accordance with what the range would bear," says Hansen in *Background History of the Lakeside-Pinetop Area*. "After passage of the Forest Homestead Act of 1906, … grazing policies would give special consideration to homesteaders on or near the National Forest. This marked the beginning of the end of sheep ranching on a large scale in this area."

The state politicians, having great sympathy for the stockmen but no authority, passed resolutions favoring uncontrolled grazing.

"Representatives were sent to Washington, D.C. and the Chief Forester, Gifford Pinchot, agreed to come to Arizona the next year to survey the situation," Palmer wrote. "When he did arrive he was disturbed at the poor condition of the forest in the vicinity of the bedding grounds." Will C. Barnes, the old Indian fighter, stockman and father of Navajo County, was appointed as an assistant forester and Chief of Grazing. "He spent the next 22 years trying to protect both the forests and the stock raising industry. With better moisture the forest soon began to recover, allowing the stockmen a reprieve from the more severe regulations. However, a trend was started in which increasingly stringent guidelines and rules were applied to usage of the public land."

In 1909, Aldo Leopold graduated from Yale and joined the Forest Service. The first assignment for the man who would become the nation's most famed naturalist was a timber survey on the Apache National Forest in eastern Arizona. The next year, three other graduates, including Raymond E. Marsh, were assigned to join Leopold. "They took the Santa Fe train to Holbrook, Arizona, where they transferred to a stagecoach (described by Marsh as 'something out of the Wild West') bound for Concho," according to *Timeless Heritage: A History of the Forest Service in the Southwest.* "From there they took a lighter one-horse spring wagon to Springerville, arriving the evening of the second day. ... The next day they boarded a freighter's wagon through the rough country to the reconnaissance camp at the headwaters of the Black River."

They marked off 40-acre parcels and then estimated the board feet of lumber by carefully analyzing a much smaller sample plot.

In Leopold's *Sand County Almanac* he described riding through the White Mountains. "The top of the mountain was a great meadow, half a day's ride across, but do not picture it as a single amphitheater of grass, hedged in by a wall of pines. The edges of that meadow were scrolled, curled and crenulated with an infinity of bays and coves, points and stringers, peninsulas and parks, each one of which differed from all the rest. No man knew them all, and every day's ride offered a gambler's chance of finding a new one. I say 'new' because one often had the feeling, riding into some flower-spangled cove, that if anyone had ever been here before, he must of necessity have sung a song, or written a poem."

Leopold was promoted to a position in New Mexico where he fell very ill after he had been caught in a rainstorm and blizzard while trying to calm a range dispute. During his long convalescence, he read Thoreau and other naturalist authors before returning to duty in Arizona.

"Leopold's enforced inactivity gave him time to contemplate the effects of erosion on the fragile, delicately balanced environment of the Southwest, the consequences of rapidly multiplying deer herds, and the long-range results of the continuing war on predators," says *Timeless Heritage.* "Like most young foresters, he had equated a flourishing deer herd with control or even extermination of wolves, mountain lions, and coyotes. He recalled a cruising expedition (probably in 1910 or 1911 in the Apache National Forest) during which he and his companions saw a she-wolf swim across a river and join her cubs on the near side. At once the foresters seized their rifles and pumped lead into the pack until the old wolf was down and the cubs dispersed into the mountain canyons. What happened next was instructive and important to his developing thought."

"We reached the old wolf in time to watch a fierce green fire dying in her eyes," Leopold wrote. "I realized then, and have known ever since, that there was something new to me in those eyes – something known only to her and to the mountain. I was young then, and full of trigger-itch; I thought that because fewer wolves meant more deer, that no wolves would mean hunters' paradise. But after seeing the green fire die, I sensed that neither the wolf nor the mountain agreed with such a view."

"Leopold slowly came to the conclusion that while the deer lived in fear of wolves, the mountain lived in fear of its deer, which, when uncontrolled and allowed to multiply without restraints, could destroy a range that might not recover for decades or even centuries," *Timeless Heritage* says.

His theories were proved correct when the Kaibab deer population near the Grand Canyon increased from about 4,000 in 1906 to near 100,000 in 1924. "Everything was overgrazed, and thousands of deer died of starvation during the winter, including most of the young fawns," says *Timeless Heritage.*

Leopold is credited with establishing the science of wildlife management. He helped create the Gila Wilderness Area, the world's first designated area without roads or human settlement. The vast tract around Reserve, New Mexico, on the eastern edge of the White Mountain region, is now joined by the Blue Primitive Area on the Arizona side of the line. These stretches of precious protected forest serve as a monument to the famous naturalist who developed his theories while working in the White Mountains.

One of the least-popular parts of the government stewardship program was a decision to shoot unbranded wild horses on the Forest. In *A Tribute to the Lakeside Pioneers*, Hansen recounts the opposition to the program carried out by Lakeside Ranger

Clarence Shumway. This policy brought an end to the Mustang roundups, which had been a popular pastime in the area.

Though the horse killing occurred after he left the Forest Service, Pearce commented on it in his memoir. "A little sense in carrying out this order would have saved a mess of trouble," he wrote. "But the rangers went to killing cowponies as well as mavericks, fine saddle stock worth a hundred dollars and up per head. One ranger named Fears shot several head belonging to a rancher named Trammel, and Trammel filed a criminal complaint against Fears, charging him with wantonly and maliciously destroying his animals. A stockman jury convicted him, but on appeal his case was thrown out of court on grounds that he was merely carrying out orders. In another case the stockmen warned a ranger who had been killing saddle horses that this was a very unhealthy climate for a man that would shoot down horses on an open range. The ranger replied that he represented the U.S. Government and intended to keep on carrying out his orders just the way he had been doing. A few days later he vanished, and no trace of him was ever found."

Grazing regulations were unpopular, but the Forest Service worked to enforce them. "Most ranchers gradually recognized the need for regulations and the limitation of herds on the available pasture," says *Timeless Heritage*.

But the most valuable resource on the forest was the timber. The Whiting Brothers leased their first lumber mill in Springerville in 1907 and set up another one below Green's Peak which operated until 1943, according to *On the Road to Nowhere*.

The Forest Service decided that a large amount of timber on the Apache Reservation and surrounding areas of the National Forest should be opened for bidding as early as 1910. Twice the government failed to get bids from a company with enough resources to build a mill, according to an article in *Arizona and the West* by Robert L. Mathney. On a third attempt during World War I, Thomas Pollock of Flagstaff and A. B. McGaffey of Albuquerque formed the Apache Lumber Company to bid on the sale. Winning the bid, they built a company town on the Apache Reservation. The area already had a post office calling the community "Cluff Cienega," named for a Mormon bishop of Show Low who gathered hay there in the early days. Pollock renamed

his town "Cooley" after the famous Indian scout, according to
Top o' the Pines. The name was eventually changed to McNary by
later owners of the mill. The Santa Fe Railroad agreed to build a
branch line to the mill after being promised a reduced price for
railroad ties.

Much of the work in creating the rail bed was done by horses.
"We had to use 25% to 30% of Apache Indians when we got on
the Apache Reservation and they proved to be very good," wrote
Ed Foster, who was in charge of the construction project. "I
remember I had a cousin of Chief Geronimo who looked after a
group of Apaches and they were very good with the handling of
the work horses."

After the grading was completed, the 120 workers began constructing the log pond. Nearly all were taken down with flu. No
doctors were available, not even from the post at Fort Apache,
because of the war. The men strong enough to take care of the
others did so. Only three died.

Foster then went back to Holbrook and began laying ties
and rails. William Flake himself drove the final spike when the
railroad reached Snowflake in 1918. Don Cooley, son of Indian
scout Corydon Cooley, drove the ceremonial spike when the railroad reached Cooley the next year.

The mill employed 400 men operating three band saws and a
planing mill. The company town included four- and five-room
cottages for the married employees and bunkhouses for single
men, according to Mathney. The uptown included a general store,
bakery and hospital. World War I ended before the mill was completed. Then the downturn following the war wiped out Pollock
and the mill was closed.

Small lumber companies continued to operate, but had their
problems as well. The historic Mount Trumbull sawmill, which
had been taken to Lakeside, blew up and was destroyed by fire in
1928. After that, Mahonri Lazelle Fish, son of Lakeside pioneer
John L. Fish and owner of the ill-fated mill, built a new mill at
Woodland.

"When a forest fire destroyed the Fish Sawmill in 1928,
Lakesiders rebuilt it in a matter of months, the new structure
producing more lumber and employing more mill workers than
its predecessor," Pat Stein says in an archeological study, quoting

the *Snowflake Herald*. *A Tribute to the Lakeside Pioneers* says Fish built two more mills in Lakeside, losing each to fire. He and a son eventually relocated to Ellsworth Hill, near Show Low, where they had fewer disasters.

The Ellsworths themselves had run a sawmill on that hill for nearly 10 years, before selling out to Jonathon Henry Webb, who moved the mill to his nearby ranch before relocating to Vernon, Forestdale and a number of other sites on the Apache Reservation. According to *Tribute,* Webb and his family owned or helped set up 25 sawmills.

The brief-lived community of Standard can be traced to a sawmill set up by early settlers in Water Canyon south and east of Pinedale. A family named Worthington built the mill, but it was later operated by Ed Reidhead. According to Palmer in *Elijah Was a Valiant Man,* the brothers Claude and Tom Quebideaux purchased the mill in 1923. "These people had been in the banking business and were wealthy by Pinedale standards," Palmer said. In 1924, the mill was purchased by John Zolaha, an adopted son of Tom Pollock, who had built large mills in McNary and Flagstaff. Taking in Brandon Smith as a partner, they built housing for employees near the Water Canyon mill.

James G. McNary was a larger-than-life character who left his stamp on lumbering in the White Mountains. He was born in Pennsylvania, and moved to Las Vegas, New Mexico, where he taught languages at a teacher's college and became publisher of a community newspaper. After he beat up the editor of the competing publication in the streets of Las Vegas, he was charged with assault to murder, but the case was dismissed by the district attorney. His family helped him get into the banking business, and he moved to El Paso, Texas. With William Cady, he began investing in Louisiana timber land. They eventually opened a sawmill, which prospered. McNary, a delegate to the Republican convention, was a supporter of Warren G. Harding. After Harding won, McNary became the new president's poker-playing buddy and was offered the position of Comptroller of the Currency. But the appointment was blocked by a threat of a filibuster.

Meanwhile, the Cady Lumber Company of Louisiana had cut all of its timber and was facing liquidation unless it could find a new location. Relocating to northern Mexico seemed unwise because of the Revolution. Timber in the Northwest was deemed to be too expensive. Arizona seemed more promising. When Pollock's banks got into trouble in 1921-22 during the financial downturn after World War I, the First National Bank of Los Angeles took them over, taking his lumber operations as security. McNary, Cady and other partners put up $1.5 million to buy those lumber operations in Flagstaff and "Cooley" as well as the Apache Railroad.

"Mr. Cady could not visualize a lumber operation without the employment of Negro labor, and he decided to import about 500 of our experienced and faithful Louisiana employees to Arizona," McNary wrote in his book, *This is My Life*. "We required two fairly long trains to move the people, with all their household possessions, and great quantities of sawmill and logging equipment of every description. Mr. Cady built a town for the colored people, with a restaurant, a hotel, a couple of churches, and everything to make them comfortable and contended. There was a good deal of indignation in some quarters in Arizona over the importing of 500 colored workers with their families into the state, and there were even threats of mobbing Mr. Cady, which threats, however, didn't materialize."

"Probably the most notable passenger traffic was a train which passed through town Feb. 12, 1924, at 11 p.m.," says the Snowflake Stake history. "It carried six coaches of passengers with black skins, totaling 411 persons, three baggage cars and five freight cars of their baggage and belongings. They were brought to this country to work for the lumber company and the train parked overnight in Snowflake." The history quotes the local newspaper as saying: "On account of an unrest among the people of Holbrook, the officials decided it would be best for them to move the Negroes on and they proceeded to slip them into Snowflake to spend the night."

"McNary segregated its townsfolk," explains *Top o' the Pines*. "Anglo families lived in homes on the hill north of town. African-Americans resided east of the mill, the Hispanics were located across the tracks from them and the Indians lived on the west edge of town [just over the county line in Navajo County]. The Negro quarter and Hispanic quarter each had its own elementary school, church and café. From the early years into the

1950s, Negro teenagers had to go to Flagstaff or Phoenix to attend high school."

Though the blacks faced segregation in housing and discrimination in wages, they knew the lumber business and adapted to living in the mountainous West.

Concern over the black residents of McNary reached a fever pitch when Senator Burton Wheeler of Montana held hearings in Whiteriver to raise concerns about reports of drinking, prostitution and low wages in the logging town. "If it does not stop I am going to take it on to the floor of the Senate and find out why it is that the Indian Bureau permits such a condition as has been reported to us to exist up at McNary, with Negroes being imported on to an Indian reservation when you have Indians right here who want to work and can not get it," Wheeler said in a part of his testimony quoted in the *Mixed-Bloods* book. "It is going to stop or we are going to know the reason why."

Arthur McQuatters, an eastern capitalist who chaired the company's board of directors, said Apaches were being given preference in hiring, but were not qualified for most jobs. "The Indians on the Apache Indian Reservation have not had an opportunity to learn anything about industrial enterprises," he said. The chairman reported attendance statistics for workers at the mill. "When given the opportunity to work full-time, Apache laborers would report to the mill on only 8 of 26 work days per month. In contrast, the blacks worked on the average of 23 ¾ days per month, whites for 21 days, Mexicans 18, and Navajo for 12 days."

Roe Clark testified that Apaches were not being given a fair chance. He said they were only being asked to fill in for others who did not show up for work, and never given a chance to keep a regular position. "We do not learn nothing in such a way as that," he testified. "The white man will not give us a chance and we will never learn nothing."

Charles Pettis Jr. said the Indians were not given warm houses in McNary, like the blacks or Hispanics, and were paid only 25 cents an hour, while others made $2.25 to $2.50 as common laborers.

Memories of McNary, edited by the late Martha McNary Chilcote, daughter of James G. McNary and a leading citizen of the White Mountains for decades, took a more positive look at the racial situation. "Despite the variety of races and cultures, McNary never had any inter-racial trouble. Its high school was integrated long before the U.S. Government got around to ordering integration of schools. The high school football and basketball teams held the State Championship for its class many times through the years and sent many fine young men and women of every color out into the world."

Residents of the remote company town took pride in their houses. "In the summer, there were many pretty flower gardens and the company gave prizes for the most attractive," the book says. There were awards for both "uptown" where the white people live on the hill and also for the "Quarters" down below.

"The old general store ... was known all over the state," Mrs. Chilcote wrote. "It had everything – hardware, fishing and hunting supplies, furniture, toys, men, women and children's clothing, shoes, groceries, meat, a drugstore, and, for many years, a soda fountain." It also served as a lending library for the community.

In the early days, logs in the woods were attached to a pair of big wheels 10-feet high and pulled by draft horses. In the winter, draft horses pulled a large timber down the road to serve as an early version of a snowplow.

"For years, in the South, we had operated under the name of the W. M. Cady Lumber Company, of McNary, Louisiana, had carried a full page advertisement in the American Lumberman continually for a good many years and our company was extremely well and favorably known in the lumber trade," McNary wrote. "Mr. Cady decided to adopt the same name for our Arizona enterprise and he, accordingly, changed the name of the Apache Lumber Company to the W. M. Cady Lumber Company, and changed the name of the town from Cooley to McNary, so that we might maintain our well-established identity with the lumber industry."

When Cady built a home in Pasadena, California, he left the Arizona operations in the hands of men from the Louisiana mill who were not very conscientious. Management of the company suffered further when Cady was injured in a railroad accident. The new business was soon in financial trouble.

So McNary, who had been a banker in El Paso, came to Arizona to run the operation. He arranged for New Yorkers to invest a million dollars and increased the amount of money the company had borrowed for working capital by another million dollars. Cady quarreled with the new owners and was quickly bought out.

The company bought and expanded the Standard mill and surrounding town in 1927. The Apache Railroad built a branch line to the community. "In addition, a complete company town, consisting of a hotel, schoolhouse, guesthouse, commissary, cookhouse, store, hospital, segregated housing for Mexican/Indians and Anglo workers, and 'mansions' for the mill supervisors, was built near the new mill," archaeologist Kent Lightfoot wrote.

Lewis Peterson, who grew up in the community, said that his family had lived in a section reserved for white workers. When he was interviewed by Carol Sletten, he explained how the town was laid out. "Mexicans had a section of about 50 frame houses in rows of 12 houses each. Blacks who didn't arrive until the '30s had a separate section. Indian workers camped by the Mortenson Wash. … They were mostly Navajo men, but there were some Hopis and Apaches as well. A few of the Indians brought their wives but not their children. Then, there was the 'silk stocking section' for families of the white managers. Their houses were bigger and fancier with fireplaces on each end of their living rooms."

"The population of Standard at its peak (1929) was approximately 500, with 175 employed at the mill," Lightfoot said. "Mill employees labored 10 hours a day, six days a week. … Cady Lumber Corp. employed numerous Swedes, Louisiana blacks, Indians (mostly Navajos), Mexicans and local Mormons as loggers. Timber cutters were paid approximately 72 cents for every 1000 feet of sawn timber, and a good worker earned between $7 and $9 a day. Trees were felled with two-man saws, hewed into logs, and dragged by caterpillars or work horses to the railroad tracks. Logs were loaded onto flat cars with mobile cranes and shipped to Standard. … The loggers and their families lived in work camps near the site of the logging operation. Normally between 50 to 60 men were employed within one camp. These camps were moved periodically, as areas were logged out; and most people resided in either converted railroad cars or portable one-room shacks." The Navajos sometimes built traditional hogans.

McNary was the largest town in the White Mountains for a time, featuring a hospital, movie theater and the huge general store.

The company entered into a brief heyday, turning substantial profits in 1927, 1928 and into 1929. Lumber production thrived in the 1920s, but prices fell from about $38 per thousand board feet in 1920 to $24 in 1929.

James McNary was slowed down considerably by an accident which happened while he was going from Arizona to El Paso. The car hit a bump and discharged the chauffeur's Colt .45, sending a bullet through McNary's leg. They drove back through Springerville to Holbrook with the wounded banker, then took a train from Holbrook to Albuquerque, where they met a surgeon dispatched from El Paso. Three operations, 50 pounds lighter and 10 months later, McNary was able to make a trip to New York where he attended a baseball game with future President Herbert Hoover. A deal was negotiated to sell the lumber business to Minneapolis interests for $10 million, a substantial profit, but circumstances continually delayed the signing as the months of 1929 ticked away. The sale never happened.

Arizona Becomes a State, Elk Return

Arizona was the only part of the contiguous United States that was still governed as a territory, so it was inevitable that it would eventually become a state. An enabling act was passed in 1910. After the resolution of an issue involving the Arizona State Constitution's provision for the recall of judges, Arizona became a state on Feb. 14, 1912 — 49 years to the day after becoming a territory. Though the new state expected to attract more residents, few imagined that the first large group of immigrants would be elk.

Native elk were eliminated in the White Mountains about 1900 because of indiscriminate hunting and overgrazing by sheep and cattle. In 1914, the Winslow Elk's Club decided to remedy the situation. They obtained 86 Rocky Mountain elk in Montana and brought them by railcar to Winslow. They loaded them into horse-drawn wagons and carried them through deepening March snows into the higher elevations of the White Mountains. They have thrived ever since, now numbering in the tens of thousands. The native animals were Merriam's elk, with broader and flatter antlers than the Rocky Mountain elk that now populate the area.

Although Leopold wrote of the killing of Bigfoot, a giant grizzly bear on Escudilla in the early 20th century, the species survived in Arizona until 1935.

Wolves disappeared from Arizona in the 1920s, but were re-introduced in wilderness sections of the Apache-Sitgreaves National Forest in 1998.

Pronghorn antelope, mule deer and white tail deer have never left, though their numbers have decreased because of hunting pressure and loss of habitat. Turkeys are plentiful. Black bears still roam through the forest. Sometimes mountain lions appear suddenly where least expected, then move gracefully out of sight. Big horn sheep range into the southern portion of the wilderness areas of the Apache-Sitgreaves National Forest.

Early 20th Century Medicine

The Apache County Board of Supervisors paid the local doctor, Joseph Woolford, $20.25 for "attending" the people of Concho when a diphtheria epidemic struck in 1902. Diphtheria struck Show Low in the winter of 1906, and "visited almost every home in town," according to the Woolford history.

Palmer tells the story of diphtheria coming to Snowflake in 1902. "Because of the widespread nature of the epidemic all schools were closed and church and other meetings were suspended or postponed for several weeks." Even children who did not come down with the disease had to gargle a sulfur and alcohol mixture twice daily.

The White Mountain area lost Dr. Woolford in 1906 after he had moved to St. Johns. "Sixteen-year-old George returned home to find his father very ill and weak," the family history says. "We can imagine his frantic attempts to help his father as the doctor tried to tell him what to do, and the frustration George felt when he could not understand what his father was saying." After his dad died, young George had to ride nearly 50 miles to give the bad news to his mother because she was visiting Show Low.

The Show Low Mormon history says Dr. Junius Neil Heywood came to Snowflake to become the second doctor in the area. The community also had a maternity home.

In 1909, scarlet fever claimed the lives of three children in Greer: Lorenzo Crosby, Mary Lund and Jay Hale. A passage in *On the Road to Nowhere said,* "A cousin of one of them remembered stories of the children having to be lowered into their graves by a parent or close relative for fear the germs would spread."

Scarlet fever came to Pinetop in 1911, according to a manuscript handed down in the Penrod family. "Tucked away in a snug little valley, south of Pinetop, a family of seven lived. The grandfather, the father, mother and four small children, all little girls ranging from the age of one year to five years. In February of that year an epidemic of scarlet fever was going around. These little children all had taken it, which was very much of a worry to their parents. The eldest girl and the third one we thought to be the sickest of the four. ... The father and mother were up for about six weeks, night and day, waiting on sick babies, till they were almost exhausted. The nearest doctor was at that time in Winslow, except for the government doctor in Fort Apache. So we had the Winslow doctor come. He didn't give much encouragement for the two girls that were so sick. The mother prayed so earnestly for the lives of these little girls to be spared.

"She was inspired to use fat bacon cut in slices and warmed on the fire, and applied to the stomach of the little dark girl, Fern," the manuscript says. "The bacon was used on her till about 1 a.m. She had bloated so much that she looked transparent. Her kidneys had not acted for over 48 hours. She had intense fever and when her kidneys did act, it scalded her so badly it blistered her little bottom badly.

The doctor promised the Ralph Penrod family that he would

send oranges from Winslow, at $1.25 a dozen. "We gave them each a half an orange a day," Sarah Penrod is quoted as saying in the manuscript. "Whole families died in our neighborhood. Our neighbor had three little children and lost them all.

"So we were very anxious about our girls, but after six weeks, they commenced to feel better. Then some officers came and brought some formaldehyde and had us fumigate, which we did. We took the children to the meat house below the road and shut all the doors and windows and Ralph set it off.

"You know it burnt like fire and the fumes were terrible. When Ralph got them all set off, he had a tub of water ready for a bath in the kitchen. He got his clothes all off when the fumes came in through the upstairs and four of the rooms and he had a little trouble with the window in the kitchen. I noticed him and came running to see what the trouble was. He was being overcome by fumes. He got out, but oh! No clothes! No blankets or nothing, so he took my apron and covered up his nakedness till he got where he had taken some bedding to sleep that night. Then he covered up with a blanket till I could get in the house the next morning and get his clothes.

"We didn't worry over such trifles. We were so glad that all was alive and well again. We stayed away from the house 24 hours before we opened up the house to air it out. We weren't bothered with any mice, bedbugs and it even killed our cat that had got in somehow."

During World War I, an influenza epidemic struck Show Low. George Woolford, Jr., said, "It 'purtinear' cleaned this town out." The Woolford family history continues, "A doctor came from Albuquerque or some place, but he said there was nothing that could be done. He stayed around for a few days and then left. Eph McNeil and Dad spent night and day making coffins and Mother and several of the women, Nancy Lewis, Aunt Em Whipple and a bunch of them would line them. Almost everyone who was able was helping out."

The flu was worse among the Apaches. An article in the *Falcon* newspaper says, "They spread out into small camps to try to avoid re-infecting each other. But in the camps they had no food. They lay down to starve and die on the cold bare damp earth."

"Almost every family with children had moved to a hiding place

Minnie Guenther with her daughter Wenonah in an Apache cradleboard made by one of the missionary's many Apache friends.

in the foothills to escape whooping cough and pneumonia," wrote the Rev. Edgar Guenther. "Their fears were well founded for these maladies soon swept across the entire Reservation. My wife and I spent many weary days in the saddle from morning till dark trying to find our people so that we might minister to their children. We were led to many a temporary abode by smoke rising from camp fires; others we came upon merely by chance. Having no medicines of any kind I trapped skunks, rendered the fat and mixed it with turpentine and coal-oil. To give the concoction a pleasant odor my wife added some of her precious perfume. … For chest pads we cut up every spare piece of warm cloth on hand and when that was used up our long winter underwear was dedicated to the cause. Humanly speaking we saved the lives of many youngsters; every one of our school children survived, but several hundred others died throughout the Reservation for lack of proper care."

"Of special consequence was his friendship with the important Apache Chief Alchesay, who when he became ill and was not cured by the medicine men, went out to a lonely place to die," says *The People Called Apache*. "Guenther went after him, administered medicine, and brought him back to health."

Minnie Guenther, who rode on horseback with a can of cold milk hanging down on one side and a can of soup on the other, was recognized posthumously for compassionate nursing and other good works by induction into the Arizona Women's Hall of Fame.

Epidemics often swept through the reservation. The Apaches

were hit with flu in 1904 and again in 1914-15, as well as out-breaks of whooping cough, measles and pneumonia.

"Diarrhea, cholera, and pneumonia took their toll on the Apaches" wrote William Kessel. "The major chronic disease was tuberculosis," with one death every month. Of the 563 children in school, 150 were too sick to attend. Epidemics of measles swept across the reservation. "These were mild compared to the ominous presence of tuberculosis, eye diseases and whooping cough. In 1911, 58 percent of the White Mountain Apaches ex-amined by agency physicians had tuberculosis, and an estimated 65 percent were affected by eye disease" — more than half of those with trachoma, which can cause blindness.

Dr. Fred Loe, the government physician, "established friend-ships with the medicine men and tried to learn some of their songs and cures, hoping that they in turn would become eager to learn his techniques," Kessel wrote. "In spite of his efforts, many Apaches remained suspicious and frightened. Numerous indi-viduals were suspicious of pills, believing them to contain poi-son."

Round Valley got a medical professional in the 1920s, one who was home grown. Atella Wiltbank left Springerville in 1918 to attend three years of high school in St. Johns and then moved on to nurse's training. A high school certificate was not necessary to enter nursing school in those days. After her training, Atella was working in Miami, Arizona, when her aunt, Molly Butler, called to tell her that her boyfriend, Carl Haws, had typhoid fe-ver. So the young registered nurse moved back to the White Mountains to care for the man who would become her husband. There was no doctor in the area except one in St. Johns, she said in a 1988 interview. He would come to Springerville "if he hadn't been hitting the bottle too hard." So Atella Haws had to deliver most of the babies. In order to do that, she had to be a midwife. Her RN didn't qualify her. She said, "You didn't need to get any training. All you had to do was send in the money." Atella loved helping others but said the most she had ever been paid for her work was $15. At one graduation ceremony at Round Valley High School, she remembered that she had delivered all of the gradu-ates.

Martha McNary Chilcote wrote about the 1929 typhoid epi-demic in *Memories of McNary*. She said, "Many people died, including the manager."

Another plague hit the company town in the winter of 1936-37 "when the commissary butcher came down with spinal meningitis," she wrote. "Seven people died in a very short time, and since there was an outbreak of intestinal flu at the same time, most of the folks in McNary were sure they had spinal meningitis at some time or another. No Spanish Americans came down with it and Dr. Herbst, who was the sole doctor at the time, attributed this apparent immunity to the chili consumed by these people as the germ was known to enter through the nose or mouth. As a result, there was a run on the Mexican Café in the Quarters with many an Anglo consuming hot chili in the hope of warding off the dreaded disease."

"McNary had the only hospital for many miles around and, thanks to the lumber and logging business, it had excellent doctors almost from the very beginning," Mrs. Chilcote wrote. "Many a badly injured logger or mill hand was saved by the company doctors and many a baby took its first breath within the walls of the McNary Hospital."

In an article in *Memories of McNary,* the late Dr. Arnold Dysterheft says the hospital, built in 1927, had two beds, an examining room and an apartment for a physician. He said the first doctors were itinerant Bureau of Indian Affairs medical practitioners whose primary function was the care of trauma patients. "Meals were brought by the patients' families to the patient," he wrote. "Members of the family stayed with the patient. Nursing help was fragmented." In 1930, the hospital was expanded to six beds and a doctor was hired by the lumber company.

Springerville opened its hospital in 1936, thanks to the federal government's Depression recovery efforts.

Last Hurrah for Sheep

The sheep industry was changing as the 20th century unfolded. Previously, Hispanics had run herds of sheep, often in the lower areas north of the mountain peaks. But the Scott brothers and others who brought their sheep into the area grazed them in the high elevations during summers and transported them to the

351

Phoenix area for the cold months. Arizona was better for the industry than California and Montana because it offered both winter and summer range.

Four Scott brothers — Raleigh, Robert, James and George — arrived from Oregon, according to an interview with the late Marion Elizabeth Menhennet, a daughter of George. Their uncle, Felix Scott, had been an early pioneer of Woodruff, according to Hansen's *Background History of Lakeside-Pinetop Area*. Hansen also said Robert and James, who had come to the area earlier, encouraged their little brother George to join them as the Scott ranches grew around the turn of the century. The Scott boys were forced to become acquainted with hard work in their early youth when their father was killed by Indians on his way to Missouri to purchase purebred horses. George was only five at the time.

Originally setting up near Forestdale, George moved the ranch south of Show Low, where the Home Depot is located today. Mrs. Menhennet cherished a log cabin on the property. She said it was built in Forestdale by Mormons before 1870, and moved log by log to the Show Low site in 1903. Her father numbered the logs so they could be placed in the proper place at their new location.

The Scotts were ambitious, building huge dams with shovels pulled by teams of horses. Scotts Reservoir survives today as part of the irrigation network above Show Low.

Mrs. Menhennet's uncle James Scott had his headquarters near Pinedale.

Another uncle, Robert Scott, owned the land where Scotts Pine Meadow subdivision is today. His third wife, Anna Christina Jaques, had a son from a previous marriage, Sante Jaques. The step-son, who owned the property where the Show Low hospital is located today, built on the family fortune to the extent that his daughter became known as the Cattle Baronness of Northern Arizona. Two chimneys from her burned ranch house can be seen from Porter Mountain Road just outside of Lakeside.

George had 16,000 sheep. Before heading to the valley each fall, he would set the mountain pasture afire to burn off the little trees. The sheep were handled expertly on the trail by shepherds and dogs. "The dogs had to be smarter than the people," Mrs. Menhennet said. George had 320 acres of alfalfa near Mesa on property which was later sold to Dobson Ranch. The Scotts sold railcar loads of lambs to the eastern market each April before heading back up the mountain. One year, they sold 35 carloads.

Bringing the sheep up from the valley took 40 days. "At first, sheep men would take trails of their own choice," Hansen wrote. "But after the Graham-Tewksbury War, a special trail one mile wide was established from east of Mesa, across the Verde River near Blue Point, on up over the Mogollon Rim taking a long circle to the north, then back towards the White Mountains."

One year, it was so dry that the sheep had to be brought up on the railroad, Mrs. Menhennet said. The sheep were taken high up into the White Mountains where George held grazing leases on the Apache Reservation. "You couldn't live there in winter," she said.

For awhile, sheep raising was good business. The Snowflake Stake history quotes the local newspaper as saying 1.5 million pounds of wool were shipped from Holbrook each year, along with 120,000 fat lambs in good years.

To landscape their ranch headquarters, the Scotts transplanted fir trees, bringing them down the mountain on horseback. There were no furniture stores in the area so they bought their furnishings in California and had the goods shipped to Holbrook. The house was well adapted to a dry and sometimes warm climate. They used water from the roof to fill a cistern. There were high ceilings and a milk cupboard with screens designed to keep the contents cool with air flow.

When it was time to distribute the army payroll, the whole cavalry would pass by the ranch on their way to Holbrook. The Scotts had hooks on the outside of the barn for the soldiers to tie up horses when they stopped. There were nose bags to feed the cavalry mounts.

Joseph Sponseller, another sheep man, gave his name to a mountain and a lake, according to Hansen. Morgan Flat was named after William Morgan, another sheep man in the Lakeside area. He had ties to the original sheep men of the area through his marriage to Juana Candelaria from Concho. Will Amos also had a large sheep operation in Lakeside.

"In 1905 the 'bottom fell out,' as the sheep men termed it, and some wanted to sell," says *A Tribute to the Lakeside Pioneers.*

Niels Hansen, along with Robert Scott and others bought the Will Amos property, opening much of Lakeside for Mormon settlement.

Though the sheep business was in decline, Hansen was able to sell ice. He cut it on Rainbow Lake and stored it in sawdust at an ice house.

In the Woolford family history, George Jr. recalls that ice froze 18 inches thick. "It took a lot of work to cut those blocks with an ice saw, load them into the truck backed out onto the ice, then unload them again. They then stacked the blocks on end, put seasoned sawdust between, over and around them so they would not freeze together. The stacks were almost six feet high. Come summer that ice was sure great. George made a wooden pull wagon that would carry two blocks of ice at a time and with this they carted it to the store where it was used in the ice boxes to keep pop cool, and produce they might have – the eggs, butter, milk and cheese, etc. No doubt it was sold for use in home ice boxes. Sometimes, at the end of summer, when the ice house had to be cleaned out, a few blocks had survived the summer heat."

Outlaw Echoes of the Wild West In the 20th Century

Less famous than the Wild Bunch, the Smith Gang also made their mark on the White Mountains. Bill Smith, who had been part of the Dalton Gang in Oklahoma, moved to the Blue River near Harper's Mill to live on a ranch with his mother and brothers.

In *Arizoniana* Marshall Trimble describes Bill Smith. "He stood about six feet tall with a slender, muscular frame with dark eyes and thick, coarse hair. The only flaw in his handsome features was a gap between his two front teeth. He was about 35 years old when he decided to turn outlaw. The ex-cowpuncher gathered around him a band that included three brothers and four other fearless border hombres."

"By the turn of the century, he was Arizona's most notorious cattle rustler," according to *The Arizona Rangers* by Bill O'Neal. Smith was first arrested in 1898 for taking calves from local ranchers Henry Barrett and Bill Phelps. Smith was jailed in St. Johns, but broke out using a .45 caliber revolver smuggled in by his brother Al. Bill Smith locked jailer Tom Berry in a cell and slipped away.

In the St. Johns Stake history, Bert Colter gives this account of the Smith Gang's later activities in the Springerville area: "They were a tough bunch. They had a cattle stealing ring that covered quite an area around their headquarters which was located on the Little Colorado River ... about eight miles south and west [of Springerville] called the Walton place. They were a fearless brazen bunch and all operated as one man, the youngest boy was about sixteen or seventeen and the wildest of the bunch. The Law arrested them on various occasions but didn't seem able to convict them and they kept getting bolder in their operations. One time they arrested the four and put them in jail on a cattle stealing case and they were unable to give bond and in a couple of days they broke out of jail and got out of the country for a year, but it seems the Law didn't try to find them so they felt it pretty safe to come back and start where they left off and had got the word to the sheriff that if he tried to arrest them they would kill him and they were bad enough to do just that. The sheriff got the word and quietly laid for them and one day they came to town thinking everybody was afraid of them. I happened as usual to be around where the most excitement was. The four were seated on the sidewalk in front of the Becker Merc. Co. store and well armed and were where they could see up and down the street but the sheriff, Ed Beeler, had other ideas. The store was a two story brick and some of the windows in the upper story looked directly down on the four men. The sheriff placed the men, five or six, with shotguns in place where they could all shoot the outlaws if it became necessary. Some in the upper floor looking down on them and one in each side of the store door on each side of the men. The sheriff and men all at the same time told them to raise their hands and appeared partly in sight. The outlaws looked the situation over immediately and could see they didn't have a chance to beat them, so surrendered like a bunch of good boys. The sheriff disarmed them and immediately they were rushed to St. John's before the judge, put under heavy bond and hauled to the state penitentiary where they were safely locked up until their trial was held and they were sentenced to prison for a couple of years. . . . The men taking part in the arrest were Ed Beeler, sheriff; Jim Murray, Gus Becker, Tom Phelps and Bob Harper and I, a scared but excited spectator."

The Smiths weren't reformed by their brief incarceration. "In early October (1901), members of the gang were seen around Springerville," says Trimble. "According to informants they had robbed a Union Pacific train in Utah. On the way back to their lair on the Blue River, they stole a bunch of horses."

In *The Arizona Rangers,* O'Neal says, "A couple days later, one of the younger Smith brothers rode to St. Johns to buy supplies and casually asked where Barrett was. The tough old rancher heard of the inquiry and organized a posse. Barrett, Hank Sharp, Pete Peterson and Elijah Holgate rode to Greer where they found Rangers Carlos Tafolla and Duane Hamblin, who had been assigned to search for the Smith Gang. The posse followed the trail three miles south to Sheep Crossing of the Little Colorado River and on to Lorenzo Crosby's ranch on Black River. There the posse enlisted Crosby and brothers Bill and Arch Maxwell, regarded as superb scouts. The Maxwells had been friends with the Smiths until the Smiths stole several horses from the Maxwell ranch."

Mrs. Molly Crosby (later Molly Butler) told what happened then. The gang circled back and spent time with her at Crosby Crossing while her husband was out with the posse looking for them. Her story is on the Little House tape.

The O'Neal account says, "The trail led south to Big Lake and to Dead Man's Crossing on the Black River to Pete Slaughter's ranch, where according to signs, the gang had camped. The posse made camp at the same site, then the next day, October 8, followed the trail six miles down the west bank of the Black River. The difficult but beautiful country was almost impenetrable wilderness and provided a natural hideout." The posse heard a shot and found where the outlaws had killed a bear. A trail of blood led from that site to the outlaw camp at Reservation Creek, in a gorge near the headwaters of the Black River. Some of the bad men were skinning the bear while others were starting supper when the outlaws' dogs barked an alarm at the approach of the lawmen. "The posse tied their horses to a cluster of bushes and crept the last 300 yards through the snow on foot. They moved in from the west as the sun set between Mount Ord and Mount Baldy. The sun rays, highlighting the rim to the east, made it difficult to fire into the rustlers' camp. Most in the posse crawled to positions on the rim but two Rangers boldly advanced. Barrett shouted for the lead man to get down. Hamblin flattened onto the ground, but Tafolla and Maxwell ignored their danger. Maxwell called out an order to surrender. 'All right,' replied Bill Smith. 'Which way do you want us to come out.' 'Come right out this way,' Maxwell said. Smith walked toward the lawmen, dragging a new Savage .303 repeating rifle behind. Suddenly, he opened fire from a distance of 40 feet. Tafolla went down, shot through the torso. Maxwell was hit in the forehead and died on the spot. Smith darted for cover as other outlaws fired from behind the trees. Tafolla emptied his Winchester. Others shot from the rim. Two rustlers were wounded, shot in the foot and leg." One of the dogs was killed as the gang retreated into the timber. "During the shooting, Hamblin had worked his way around to the outlaw mounts — nine saddle horses and a pack mule — and drove them away. On foot, the rustlers escaped into the wilderness and night fell."

Tafolla, who was shot twice through the middle, died at midnight, moaning for water. Bill Maxwell was dead with three bullet holes in the crown of his hat. The posse found the dead hound, saddles, bridles, camp gear and personal belongings of the outlaws. Tree trunks throughout the gorge were scarred with bullet marks. The clearing 40 miles south of St. Johns would become known as the Battle Ground. "Bill Maxwell's hat was left on the ground. Cowboys who later rode through refused to touch it."

O'Neal says Arch Maxwell and Hank Sharp rode east for help in Nutrioso where the Maxwell homestead was located. Henry Huning, a St. Johns merchant, sent a message to Captain Mossman of the Rangers. Tafolla "died of wound send force if possible up Blue to Mrs. Smiths place near Harpers Mill site she is mother of one of the murderers."

357

In a book *Cap Mossman, Last of The Great Cowmen,* Hunt quotes Tafolla's last words: "Give this dollar to my wife. It, and the month's wages coming to me, will be all she'll ever have." It was a hard time for the Ranger's family. Tafolla's three-year-old daughter had died two years earlier of whooping cough.

Mossman sent orders to guard routes to Mexico and rode out with three Rangers and reached the Battle Ground late the next day. Two Apache trackers from San Carlos, Josh and Chicken, joined the search into the White Mountains. The gang had gone through the snow-covered wilderness to Beaver Creek where they got a meal from drovers and heard of the identity of the dead men.

"Well, I'm sure sorry," said the outlaw leader after learning that Bill Maxwell had been slain. O'Neal quotes Smith as saying, "When he stood up that way we thought it was Barrett. He was the man we wanted. We feel mighty sorry over killing Bill Maxwell. He was a good friend of ours. Tell Bill's mother for us that we're very sorry we killed him."

The outlaws walked on into Bear Valley between the Blue River and the New Mexico state line. They arrived at the isolated ranch of Hugh McKean and asked to buy horses. "When he refused, they took his best mounts and saddles, guns and a sack of food and headed toward New Mexico," O'Neal said. The Apaches led the Rangers to the McKean ranch the next day. They pressed on into heavy snow, which obliterated the trail. Then a snowstorm drove Mossman back to the McKean ranch. Again they found a trail but lost it south of Socorro, New Mexico. Other Rangers had made their own sweep into New Mexico, finding stolen Arizona horses, but no one to arrest. Since their favorite haunts had been penetrated, the Smiths never resumed operations in Arizona. The widow Smith later told the Rangers that her sons had taken a boat from Galveston, Texas, to Argentina.

"In 1909, George Smith returned and surrendered to Sheriff Jim Parks of Graham County. However, since the only charges filed were in Apache County, he was released," O'Neal wrote. "George Smith settled at his mother's ranch on the Blue River and handled her little herd of cattle."

Innocent people were sometimes mistaken for outlaws. "A

young lady in this vicinity recently thought she had actually come in contact with one of those desperadoes we read of in the festive dime novel," wrote the Pinetop correspondent for the *Holbrook Argus* in 1900. "She got a gun and marched her man to the nearest neighbor. He turned out to be one of William Amos's sheep herders who had started to move camp, but being unfamiliar with the country, lost his bearings, and pack burro, and wandered off to the young lady's home. It's nice, you know, to be a brave girl. The sheep herder says it's anything but nice to be the unwilling companion of a heroine."

Barrett survived the threat of the Smith gang only to die in a dispute with his neighbor. A fight developed between Prime T. Coleman and Barrett at a roundup camp in the White Mountains in 1903. They were old friends and even business associates. "The trouble started over range rights and as the argument heated up, tempers flared," according to the St. Johns Stake history. "Each went for his Winchester and when the firing ceased both men were riddled with bullets, and presumed dead.

"While taking the bodies on the long, rough trip to St. Johns, it was noticed that Coleman was showing signs of life. The driver changed course and went to the nearest settlement, Walnut Grove (Richville). At the first place, the John Sherwood home, he asked for help. After getting the story of what had happened, Brother Sherwood said that he and his family would do all that they could for the wounded man. This offer to help was not unusual in itself; almost anyone would have done the same. This case was unique because Coleman, the man whose life hung in the balance, had just killed Brother Sherwood's son-in-law, Henry Barrett."

The story continues: "Coleman was to benefit once more from such a gesture when he reached St. Johns. The lady who ran the nursing home where he was taken was another Sherwood, a sister-in-law to John. Charlotte Sherwood was using some of her unmarried daughters to help with the nursing. One of the girls, Verna, became interested and more or less took over the care of Mr. Coleman. Then, as it sometimes happens, the patient fell in love with the nurse, and she with him. As soon as circumstances would permit, they were married," the stake history says.

Coleman was acquitted during a trial in Prescott, partly

through the testimony of an 11-year-old boy who had witnessed the shooting.

A few years later at the roundup, according to Bert Colter, Tod Hilliard and Pat Slaughter were clashing. Hilliard waited until it was Slaughter's turn to cook, then rode into camp and kicked over all the dutch ovens, saying that Slaughter's chow was unfit to eat. Colter wrote, "I was sure this was it, but Pat said only, 'That's a hell of a way to do.' He got on his horse and rode out." Others who got into disputes with Pat Slaughter were not as lucky.

Ed Beeler was one who came into conflict with the Slaughters. The *Argus* of Holbrook reported on January 19, 1901, "News has reached here from St. Johns that ex-Sheriff Beeler had shot and killed Montie Slaughter and wounded Clare Peary. The killing took place in Springerville on last Saturday afternoon about 2 o'clock." Montie was a son of the legendary cattleman Pete Slaughter.

"Beeler and Slaughter have been at enmity for a long time and when they met in Springerville Saturday they engaged in a friendly quarrel which no one thought would have such a bitter ending. But, Mr. Slaughter seemed to tire of quarrelling and departed saying, 'I'll be back in a few minutes and I'll fix you.' Mr. Beeler fixed himself before Mr. Slaughter returned by procuring a shotgun. When Slaughter came back to Sam Saffell's saloon he came in at the door, raised his Winchester and fired at Beeler, but missed, where-upon Beeler seized his shotgun and called out to Mr. Peary, who was standing near the door. 'Get out of the way, Peary, I don't want to have to kill two men.' Then he fired and Slaughter, who was about to fire a second shot, fell dead."

A stray shot wounded Peary. Beeler gave himself up and asked for trial. There was nearly a shootout between the friends of the Slaughters and Sheriff Beeler until Beeler was locked up in St. Johns.

Though Beeler was acquitted, Montie Slaughter's brother Pat showed continued hatred for Beeler. The retired sheriff was gunned down in an ambush at the Cieniga Ranch about 30 miles east of St. Johns. The Holbrook paper quoted a man who observed the scene after the shooting. "I went up to the wagon and saw that one of the horses was dead. I heard a groan nearby and looking around I found Ed Beeler lying on the ground. I questioned the wounded man. Beeler said, 'I am shot all to pieces and am going to die.' He said he had driven his team up to the gate, and was going through when a shot knocked splinters from the gate. Several other shots were fired in rapid succession, one hitting him in the hip, others entering his body. He ran for cover but fell before reaching it. The assassins fired eight shots at him after he fell: he said that he was so blind by the shots that he could not tell who fired." A doctor was called, but could not save Beeler.

Suspicion settled on Pat Slaughter and his friends. Slaughter was arrested and tried, but also acquitted.

Pat Slaughter's father was also suspected of murder. Molly Chick, the mother of Pat and Montie, divorced their dad and re-married a man named Jim Owens, who soon disappeared. Molly feared he had been murdered, according to the Slaughter book. But there was no evidence so Pete Slaughter was never arrested.

The *St. Johns Herald* later reported that William B. Slaughter, a brother of Pete and a New Mexico rancher, had been shot by outlaws named Marion Youngblood and Joe Atkins, and that Youngblood had fled to Mexico. The paper said it was expected that Slaughter would recover. The Slaughter book quotes a newspaper account that says Youngblood was captured in Tombstone. Continuing the family tradition of larger-than-life exploits, William moved to Pueblo, Colorado, where he set up a bank that failed. His son Coney was convicted of embezzlement after many years as a fugitive. The father was acquitted, but returned to Texas a broken man.

Youngblood was later charged with killing Thomas Lang at the headquarters of the Twenty-four Cattle Company in Apache County, but was acquitted in the killing, according to Ackerman in *O. K. Corral Postscript.*

Not everyone was acquitted. Navajo County made worldwide news for a somewhat unusual execution. Sheriff Frank Wattron, in line with an Arizona statute that required a notice of executions to potential witnesses, asked for the printing of 50 cards with this message: "You are hereby cordially invited to attend the hanging of one: George Smiley, Murderer. His soul will swing into eternity on December 8, 1899 at two o'clock P.M. sharp. The latest improved methods in the art of scientific strangulation will be employed and everything possible will be done to make the surroundings cheerful and the execution a success."

The newspaper in Holbrook sent the order to a printer in Albuquerque, where an Associated Press reporter saw it and spread the word as far as London, Berlin and Paris. The U.S. president purportedly, according to Jennings, even called the Cabinet into session to discuss the incident. President McKinley wired a rebuke to Arizona's Territorial governor, who ordered a 30-day stay of execution and told Wattron to curb his sense of humor.

George Woolford, a child at the time, was not sent an invitation. But his dad had to attend because he was the official county physician. George was told to wait outside the fence. An exhibit in the Show Low Museum says, "As young boys usually do, George found a friend, the young son of Sheriff Wattron. Together they found a couple of knotholes in the fence where they watched what was taking place inside. The rope was put around Smiley's neck and the hood over his head, but before the trap door was opened to drop him, the two boys could take no more. They turned and ran."

Arizona Rangers were going after White Mountain bad guys in the new century. According to *Arizona, a State Guide*, Rangers Jeff Kidder, Joe Pearce and Oscar Roundtree heard a report that Indian ponies were stolen from the Fort Apache Reservation in 1905. They took off on a 200-mile ride before surrounding the rustlers' cabin at dawn on the third day.

The Rangers were disbanded in 1909, after less than eight years of operation, partly because they had done such a good job of ridding the state of outlaws. But there were other reasons too. The Rangers' invasion of Mexico to put down a mine strike was not universally popular and sheriffs and district attorneys, particularly in Northern Arizona, felt the Rangers were treading on their turf.

In 1912, Joe Pearce, by this time a former Ranger, and Clay Hunter, an Indian of the Clay Tribe who lived in Springerville, took off after a man named Maris and two of his men who had stolen horses from the Zunis and Navajos. Despite the fact that the trail was two days old, Pearce and Hunter tracked down the bad men and brought them back for trial. They recovered all the horses, except one that had been ridden to death in the chase.

In 1909, when the 5th Cavalry was moved from Fort Apache to Wyoming, two men deserted and returned to the White Mountains, conning their way into running an old stage station between San Carlos and Fort Apache, according to Jennings in *Arizona Was the West*. The deserters, John B. Goodwin and Bill Stewart, offered hospitality to Fred Kibbe, a grocer from Globe, and Albert Hillpot, a produce stand operator, who were in the area for deer hunting. Goodwin and Stewart killed the two hunters, took their valuables and led lawmen on a long chase. The sheriff from Globe decided to use a four-cylinder Cadillac in the pursuit, his first use of an automobile in law enforcement work. A bearing burned out on the rough road. "But the ingenious mechanic made a cast of mud, melted metal in a frying pan and soon had a new bearing," Jennings said, in a story that may have been embellished. The bad guys had ridden their horses to exhaustion so they were walking by the time they came through Taylor. The killers waded in Silver Creek to hide their tracks, and were hiding in a plum orchard when the posse passed nearby. "They were found to have spent one night in the chicken coop at Bert Allen's in Taylor," Jennings reported. "They had dug potatoes and carrots from the Allen garden and eaten them. One had even gone to the Palmer store in Taylor to buy food."

"As boys, in Taylor, we followed with excitement the daily progress of the manhunt," Jennings wrote. "All were familiar with the Bert Allen plum grove. All went fishing and swimming in Silver Creek. We knew the name of every bend in the stream." The killers were captured at a remote train station near Woodruff called Adamana and taken to Globe for trial. The five years of legal wrangling over the case indicates that lawyers had followed settlers into the area by the early 20th century, though the outcome still reflected the values of frontier justice. Goodwin and Stewart were hanged in 1914.

In 1921, a man rode his horse into McNary and robbed the bank, taking off with a sizable amount of money. "John Earl, the deputy sheriff, and Ed Cole, another deputy or posse man under Earl, rode after him," Melba Butler and Ethel Burke wrote in *Memories of McNary*. "They trailed him into the town of Springerville, where he hid out in an old shed or shack. He slipped out and headed for the Blue River. They trailed him into that area

363

and one of them got a bullet into him, making the trail of blood easier to follow."

The outlaw, Oscar Schultz, was killed and his body was packed out on a mule. Allegedly, he had been denied a loan from the bank to bring his mother from Germany. If he had survived, he would have been handcuffed and kept in a barn since McNary had no jail.

The Studebaker Corp. used a White Mountain crime story to advertise its automobiles. They told the tale about two Navajo County deputies chasing a horse thief in their 1925 publication, *The Arizona Sheriff*. When Joe Young stole a horse from the Flying V ranch south of Holbrook, two deputies mounted a trusty Studebaker and set out in pursuit, according to the story. "Part of the way, [one of the deputies] laid out over the front fender, watching tracks in the mesa sand, as [the other] drove the car back and forth across country, regardless of roads, a task which will amaze anyone who has seen the Arizona flats, filed with cactus, mesquite and other brush. As usual, only a Studebaker can do it." The horse thief was captured and sent to prison, it being his fifth offense. One of the deputies was identified as George Willford, but it was probably George Woolford of Show Low. It's possible the misspelled name may not have been the only inaccuracy in the story.

A final echo of the outlaw West, with some hint of Bonnie and Clyde, was heard in 1925-26 when the Sullivan Gang hit a series of trading posts along U.S. 66, taking Indian jewelry, guns, ammunition and cash during nighttime burglaries. "Law enforcement officers in both Arizona and New Mexico were at wits' end," the St. Johns Stake history records. "The break came when someone in the G Lake country discovered car tracks turning off the St. Johns-Sanders road, heading into the high country to the west." Sheriff Andrew Maxwell organized a posse, followed the trail to a well-established camp and waited for the outlaws to return. "Three bandits, two men and a woman, drove into camp in a high powered get-away car," the stake history says. "Catching them completely off guard, the lawmen had no trouble in making the arrest."

They handcuffed the trio, took the spark plug wires off the thieves' car, found a cache of guns and ammunition, and began to warm themselves by a fire. When the young woman said she was cold, they took off her handcuffs so she could put on her overshoes. "Stepping back, she picked up the shoes, then returning to the fire, she passed close behind Jack Sullivan, the leader of the gang. She quickly thrust into his waiting hand a small gun she had hidden in her overshoe. Suddenly, the whole group was in commotion. Sullivan pulled his cuffed hands around by his hip and fired at Maxwell, striking him in the face. The three prisoners raced to Maxwell's waiting car, Sullivan firing wildly as he ran. Letting the others into the back seat, the woman jumped behind the steering wheel and sped away through the trees."

Deputy George Woolford recalled the outlaws "shooting the hatband off his Stetson." He also remembered it being his car that was stolen, rather then the wounded Maxwell's.

"The lawmen were unable to replace the spark wires on the bandit car in their proper order, so they started the long trip to St. Johns on foot. Fortunately, the bandits had ditched the lawmen's car at the main road and took to the hills on foot. ... The bullet had passed through Maxwell's cheek and nicked his ear."

A large posse was formed, and the bandits were again caught and taken to the Apache County jail. After Sullivan died in the Florence prison, a legend grew that he had left jewelry stashed in the wilds of Apache County.

The murder of a Columbia University anthropology student on the Fort Apache Reservation made national headlines in 1931. The outgoing Henrietta Schmerler made friends with the people she had come to study. While she was walking to a social dance, wearing traditional clothes lent to her by a highly respected Apache matron, a drunken man convinced her to ride double with him on his horse. The subsequent rape and murder made the pages of *Time* magazine. Golney Seymour was convicted and served a long prison sentence despite the best efforts of an Apache medicine man, who tried to assist him.

The "Quija Board Killing" was another sensational 20th century White Mountain murder case. James E. Cook told the story of Irene Kelynack of Queens, N.Y., in a 1991 *Arizona Republic* article. "When she was 18, she was chosen 'Miss American Venus' from 51,000 women nationwide who felt their figures matched that of Venus de Milo (except that most presumably had forearms)."

She married Ernest J. Turley, a retired Navy chief gunner's mate in 1933, and they bought the Cross Bar Ranch at Colter, west of Eagar. "While Ernest ranched, his wife idled away the hours in the company of Kent Pearce, her 'handsome cowboy.' " The cowboy was the son of famed pioneer forester and Arizona Ranger Joe Pearce. "The couple traveled around in the Turleys' big Oldsmobile, accompanied by Pearce's friend Pollard Wiltbank and Irene Turley's daughter, Mattie, then 14," Cook wrote. "This caused some loose talk."

"Irene and Mattie consulted a Quija board, which chose Mattie to do the killing," Cook wrote. "Just to be sure, Irene also consulted fortune-telling cards. Mattie testified, 'The ace of spades meant death for Daddy.' Mattie said that on the evening of November 18, 1933, she and her father were alone at the ranch. Irene and son David, 12, had gone to Springerville to shop. Ernest Turley was milking and feeding cattle in the corral. As he walked toward the house with a pail of milk, Mattie knelt and leveled a shotgun.

" 'I lost my nerve momentarily,' she said. 'Then I raised the gun again and fired both barrels, one after the other.' "

Mattie said the shooting was an accident, but later changed her story under questioning. Turley died two months later in a Navy hospital in San Diego. Cook said Mattie pleaded guilty in juvenile court to assault with intent to commit murder and was sentenced to a reform school, but was released when adopted by a Phoenix couple. She testified against her mother at the trial.

"There was little substance to the testimony, aside from Mattie's charges and her mother's denials," Cook wrote. "A visiting judge from Navajo County was not strict about procedure, and Irene Turley lapsed into rambling discourses on her undying love for her husband, the picturesque nature of cowboys and her amusement at local folkways. Pearce, wearing a 'store-bought' brown suit and red necktie, denied that he had ever so much as held Irene Turley's hand." The jury deliberated 14 hours before convicting Irene Turley of "intent to murder."

But the former beauty queen walked when the Arizona Supreme Court found fault with the judge's jury instructions.

———————————

New Communities, the Baptist Migration, Ghost Towns

Other communities were beginning to form near Heber in the early 20th Century. John E. Palmer told the story of moving to the area with his family. "In the spring of 1909, my wife, myself and our two children, Otto and Dorcie, took up a homestead of approximately 160 acres of lovely dark sandy loam at a place called 'Oklahoma Flats' located about four miles east of Heber and across the road northeast of the location that would later become the town of Overgaard. We first lived in a tent, the front of which faced north." His son, Otto, added: "We soon moved from the tent into a one-room log hut with a dirt floor and dirt roof that my father had built. Later my father built a two-room frame cabin with a fireplace in the front room." The town got its name from the Overgaard family, which established a sawmill there.

In 1911, Preston Bushman, son of John Bushman who had helped set up the community of Heber, began the settlement of Zeniff, near Dry Lake, at the confluence of Sheepskin Draw, Heber Road Draw and Hay Hollow Draw. Even after digging a diversion ditch to bring in water from Phoenix Park Wash, he was still not able to establish a profitable farm in the high rocky soil. He made a living providing water for the cattle that were being driven from the Tonto Basin to the railroad in Holbrook, charging 25 cents a head. Other families settled in the area. In the 1930s, Bushman lost his land because he couldn't pay off a mortgage he had taken out to buy cattle. Eventually Southwest Forest Industries bought up all the land and used Dry Lake for waste water from its paper mill.

About 40 years after the Mormons, the Baptists began a wave of migration into the White Mountains in the 1910s and '20s. Maybe it was really more of a ripple.

One of the communities founded by Protestants was called Plenty. It was 10 miles west of Concho and north of Vernon. "Plenty had a school, a blacksmith shop, a small store and even a post office," says a 1989 *Falcon* newspaper article by Carol Sletten. The village was called Plenty instead of its original name, Floy, so the postal service would not confuse the town with Eloy, Arizona.

Ruth Rasmussen, who bought the deserted town with her husband, Charles, said the area was settled in 1912 by a Mr. White.

"He advertised for others to join him. Many came from New Mexico and Texas to homestead the Bureau of Land Management property. But the Depression hit the little settlement so hard that it never recovered.

The irony of the name of Plenty in hard times was poignant. With black humor, the residents would joke that they had "plenty of nothing."

Mrs. Rasmussen found a note in an old house written by one of the pioneer women. "It just makes you want to cry," Mrs. Rasmussen said. "Sometimes all she could buy would be one spool of thread, two pounds of sugar and two stamps."

The demise of the tiny community was hastened when a married man seduced a teen-ager, who then died in childbirth. Her broken-hearted father shot and killed the neighbor, whose widow was left to raise their own young children.

Burton, another Baptist community, was set up near Linden and maintains a number of residents and a church. It was homesteaded by Arthur A. Burton, who took title to 160 acres in 1923. He went back to Louisiana in 1928 and then homesteaded in the area again in the 1930s.

Grace Carlisle, in an interview, recalled sitting in the Burton school as an eighth grader in the 1920s. She looked out the window and saw her future husband, Jason Carlisle, ride by on his horse. "I was already having heart flutters over that young cowboy," she said. Before long, they were riding together. The Carlisles had been married for 56 years and two days when he died.

Mrs. Carlisle's uncle was the traveling pastor who also served Plenty. "Grandfather Rich was one of the first to have water," she recalled. "Everyone came to get water and baptisms here in the creek."

In Burton, the church key could open the doors to almost all of the other buildings in town.

Most of the residents of Burton are now in the cemetery. They include veterans from the Civil War, World War I, World War II, as well as an Overland Stage driver and one mother's four infants.

Meanwhile, all the major towns of southern Navajo County were small but prosperous, according to a 1910 pamphlet entitled *Navajo County, Arizona, and its Resources*. It put the population of Snowflake at 500 and Taylor at 200 people. Three stores and a bank in Snowflake and a store in Taylor are mentioned. The pamphlet doesn't give the population of Show Low, but dwells on the potential of the community. At the time, the Lyman Land Company gave St. Johns a population of 1,500.

Though the White Mountain area does not boast picturesque ghost towns with abandoned saloons, hotels and livery stables, there are quite a few towns that once were and are no more.

The residents of Adair moved into Show Low and the community is now partly covered by Fool Hollow Lake, while the extinct village of Silver Creek is in the White Mountain Lake area.

There were communities near Vernon called Bannon and Pineyon, which disappeared during the Depression. In a 1988 article, Bannon was described as "nothing more than a meadow, a house."

The area along the Little Colorado between Springerville and St. Johns had almost as many early 20th century settlements as pre-historic Indian villages. Craig, which once boasted a post office, was in the Lyman Lake area as late as 1931, while Tule and Walnut Grove disappeared from the maps earlier. A little farther south, a community first called Nero and then called Richville is no more. Northwest of St. Johns, a place called "The Meadow" was listed on an early 20th century Conoco road map, but motorists would not be able to find it today.

Colter, once a separate community just southwest of Eagar, gave up its separate identity. And Mulligans, southeast of Springerville, went missing from the maps in the 19th century.

Farther south near Hannagan Meadow, Sulzberger appeared briefly and then vanished after the highway took a different route. Its neighbor, Espera, suffered the same fate.

Near Pinedale, Standard was deserted after the mill closed during the Depression. Farther west, Joppa showed briefly on a map in 1931 and then disappeared. The residents of Zeniff, northeast of Heber, relocated when the paper mill needed a place to store its waste water.

Modern Contraptions
And Newfangled Ways

Though Snowflake had been connected to the military telegraph in 1891, it wasn't until after the turn of the century that Fred W. Nelson started a telephone system in Holbrook that spread south into the White Mountains.

The first telephone was installed in Pinedale in 1906, connecting a store run by the Thomas family to the outside world, according to Arvin Palmer. The Thomas children made 10 cents each time they had to deliver a message to someone in town and 25 cents for going out to one of the local ranches. The Snowflake Stake history says telephone lines reached Snowflake in 1907 and were extended to Show Low, Pinetop and McNary in 1918. The old crank telephones were monitored by an operator "placing the call and sometimes informing you that the party you were ringing was not home but was visiting so and so."

St. Johns was the first community in the area to get running water, according to the St. Johns Stake history. Joseph Patterson bought pipe that had been used for the St. Louis Worlds Fair in 1904 and hauled it to St. Johns. At the time, even Holbrook residents depended on private wells for their water.

Wall Street millionaire J. E. Thompson arrived in Greer in 1919 and built the first home in the community with running water, according to *On the Road to Nowhere*. His Greer house had running water 20 years before people in Show Low. "Frederickson and Heywood Water Company brought running water to the homes in 1939," says the Show Low Mormon history. "Their system was located in southeast Show Low and was ditch water filtered through cinders. The water was then pumped to a tank on the hill by Charlie Whipple's home. Some families installed pumps on the wells and continued to use them." The Show Low system came six years after the government built a home for the Forest Ranger in Pinedale with running water.

The blazing of a transcontinental route in 1910 brought an automobile to the White Mountains. A. L. Westgard was selected by the National Highway Association as the "pathfinder." He followed trails from Washington to Kansas City and then retraced the Santa Fe Trail into New Mexico before running into a dead end near Grants. "He happened to meet a sheepherder … and he asked him if there wasn't a route that he could take westward," according to the St. Johns Stake history. The sheepherder told him how to get to the Zuni Salt Lake and a route from there to Springerville. "He was driving a car known as the Pathfinder, with a very high clearance, and he arrived in Springerville in due time. From that point Mr. Gustav Becker guided him to Fort Apache over the top of the White Mountains and from there he followed the Government route and the Indian route to Rice and into Globe." Westgard made it to Phoenix, Yuma and Los Angeles, at one point laying out canvas to cross the sands.

Additional motor vehicles began appearing in the area. The Palmer book says David K. Udall began using trucks to deliver the mail from Holbrook to St. Johns and Springerville. In 1912, the first car made it to Pinedale. The strangers, who were named McAlpine, offered rides to local residents.

The automobile sales business came to the White Mountains in 1912 when Bill Parks and Fred Johnson opened a sub-dealership in St. Johns to sell Model T Fords, according to the St. Johns Stake history. One of their first customers was Dick Gibbons, an older gentleman who had trouble understanding the dealership's driving instructions. "Nevertheless, he soloed and was bringing the new Ford home to his family," the stake history says. "He proudly nosed it into the little garage that had been built for it. At that point, he momentarily forgot the main point of his training: Do not panic. Missing the brake pedal, he froze on the controls. Calling, 'Whoa!,' in a loud voice, he took it on through the back wall of the building. Regaining his composure, he cut a large circle and parked what was left of his new car in what was left of his new garage. This was the first recorded auto accident in the St. Johns area."

Joy B. Patterson built the first service station in Apache County in St. Johns in 1922, and opened the first Chevrolet dealership in northeast Arizona, selling 120 new cars in 1929, according to the St. Johns Stake history.

For a time in the 1920s, St. Johns was an auto racing center, even attracting Barney Oldfield, the most famous driver of his generation. The celebrated sportsman came, no doubt expecting to easily collect the $1,500 first prize for the three-day event, according to the St. Johns Stake history. The competition started out with a road race from Gallup to St. Johns. Joy Patterson was just a local but he had a plan. After scouting the course, he knew he could win if he could fix his flats quickly. Patterson's 1924 Chevrolet was one of the first models with detachable rims, so he loaded several spares and his tire changing boy, Roy Tanner, into his vehicle. "When the starting gun fired Oldfield was off in a cloud of flying dirt, leaving the others groping their way through his dust," the stake history says. "Eventually, Patterson passed Oldfield, who was out in the sand trying to jack up his car to remove a flat. This was the last they saw of each other during the race. When Patterson had a flat he, being a giant of a man, lifted the car while Tanner changed the tire." The locals defeated the national champion on the road race. Perhaps Oldfield did better during the next two days, which featured time trials and then a 200-mile race on an oval track near St. Johns.

The automobile craze created demand for oil. Wildcatters drilled around Snowflake in the early 1920s after selling stock to the local residents, according to the Snowflake Stake history. All of the holes came up dry.

In 1936, U.S. 60 was completed to Phoenix, giving White Mountain residents a paved road to reach the state capital.

Some of the new contraptions were small but very useful. A pressure cooker was purchased by the Relief Society of the Mormon Church, giving the ladies of Pinedale a safe way to preserve vegetables and meat for their families.

In 1927, the Lige Thomas home in Pinedale was one of the first in the area to get carbide lamps. "The gas was stored in an outside tank and piped through the house to wherever lights were desired," Palmer wrote. "The fixtures were equipped with flint and steel lighters which ignited the gas when a switch was turned. Later the flints played out and matches would be necessary."

Show Low also boasted a Kohler light plant in the late 1920s, which was owned by Eph Mills and John Willis, and served several families. "The plant burned ... in 1928 or 1929," says the Woolford history. "A bucket brigade was formed but it was no use. Inside the burning building was a barrel of gas used to run the plant. Everyone was waiting for that to explode and when it did there was quite a spectacle."

Electricity made mountain life a lot easier. In 1926, the

Pinedale Mormon church purchased a Kohler Electric Generating Plant. "This unit generated electricity for lights in the church house, and ward and school activities could more easily function at night," Palmer wrote. "There were times when the gas engine would not start or would choke out, but when it was working (and if one could stand the steady din of its noisy engine) it was certainly an improvement. The Forest Service later provided a Kohler Plant for the local ranger and in time other residents of the community purchased units for their personal use."

Lakeside got its first trickle of electricity in the early 1930s, according to *Top o' The Pines*. "Abe Johnson was successful in his attempt to build the first water-powered, electric-light plant on a Lakeside creek. He and a co-worker ran wires into town. Although Abe Johnson didn't have experience or knowledge on how to construct a generating plant, he obtained plans and materials and diligently went to work to bring electricity to town."

A hydro-electric plant was also established in Whiteriver. *Top o' The Pines* says that sawdust was used in McNary to fire a large boiler that produced electricity for the plant and part of the community. Show Low came on the grid in 1938, with power brought in from the Silver Creek Power Company of Snowflake.

Soon after, there was another strange invention. "I'll never forget the first radio I heard," recalled George Woolford, Jr. "This guy brought it in and set it up in the store. He got up on the roof and strung an aerial from one end to the other using broom handles. I think everyone in Show Low was there that night to listen to that radio."

In 1935, butane gas became available in the area and was used for heating, ironing, stoves and to power refrigerators, at least in some of the larger homes.

Girls' softball came to the White Mountains early in the 20th century. In *Background History of the Lakeside-Pinetop Area,* Hansen tells the story of the Lakeside girls forming a team. "Their costumes [were] black bloomers, white middy blouses, and a red tie. Lakeside was well represented when these girls went out onto the baseball field in competition with other girls' teams from surrounding communities, especially Show Low."

McNary had movies in the early 1930s, according to an article in *Memories of McNary* by the late Art Crozier. "A traveling man showed both silent and sound movies one night weekly for the people of the area," he wrote. Then in 1935, the community got a permanent theater.

In 1929, the people of the White Mountains found themselves on the edge of Trans-Continental air service. Tri-motor Fokker planes landed at Holbrook, one each day from opposite directions on their way from coast to coast.

World War I

A selective service act was passed in 1917 when the United States entered World War I. Twenty-four million men between the ages of 18 and 45 had to register. "Three million of these were drafted and approximately two million went overseas," according Palmer. "Taxes were quickly increased, but despite this there was genuine enthusiasm in Pinedale on June 5 when the draft registration took place. These people, so long isolated from the larger world, had deep reservoirs of patriotism and love for their country. An atmosphere of the carnival prevailed as the men were selected, most people underestimating the effect of war on life and limb. Many believed the war would be quickly ended once the Americans got to France. ... About ten Pinedale boys were drafted and all left for training by the first of September. These included Roy Lewis, Parley Petersen, Jim Petersen, Ira McCleve, Wilford Brewer, Bill Dalton, Fred McNeil and Hyrum Hancock. Jim Petersen died three weeks after his departure, stricken by influenza in Camp Funston, Kansas. Wilford Brewer was poisoned with mustard gas in France and returned, but died of complications in 1920. Fred McNeil survived the war but was killed in an accident shortly after he returned home. Roy Lewis was a combat fatality while serving in France."

In Show Low, Fred Adams wanted to join the army, but his father convinced him to work on the family farm until his draft notice arrived. When four of Fred's friends were drafted, he went to see them off. The mail coach arriving to pick up the friends brought a letter for Fred. It was his draft notice. "I was more than a quarter of a mile from home, and on foot," he said in his book, *Memories of Fred Lindsay Adams.* "So I had to hurry home, get ready to go into the army, and I had not much more time than a quarter of an hour. So you see what preparation I could make and bid my folks good-bye and be back to go on the mail." Jesse Brady, one of those Show Low men, died in the war.

John Slaughter, youngest son of legendary cattleman Pete Slaughter, joined the army in Springerville. He was killed in action and is buried in Arlington National Cemetery. The Springerville American Legion Post is named for him.

Tragedy continued to stalk the Snowflake family of Charles Flake, who had been killed by an outlaw in 1892. His son, also named Charles, was the first American to die in his country's failed attempt to intervene in Russia's civil war. The World War I hero never knew his father or his only child. He was born after the robber killed his dad, and he went to war before his daughter was born.

Tourism

In 1899, the *Holbrook Argus* began advertising a stage line that connected Flagstaff with the Grand Canyon. It promised new six-horse stages, which would leave for the Canyon on an 11-hour trip every Monday, Wednesday and Friday. Return stages would leave the canyon on Tuesdays, Thursdays and Saturdays. The trip cost $20, but overnight accommodations at the Rim were an additional $3 and lunch was 75 cents.

The exceptional beauty of Greer attracted tourists, many of them wealthy. Molly Butler, who married John Butler after her first husband died, said she "officially" opened her lodge in 1908, after feeding hunters, fishermen and vacationers for years for free. "Molly's daughter, Hannah, who had worked in the informally run boarding house for some time, finally got up enough nerve to start charging guests – at first only twenty-five cents per meal," according to *On the Road to Nowhere.* Guests included Zane Grey and the Herbert Hoovers.

In the early 1920s, as towns realized the value of having a highway, Gallup and other places lobbied for a more direct route bypassing Springerville and St. Johns and aligning the major east-west highway corridor with the railroad through Holbrook. Still, the people in southern Apache County never gave up, according to the St. Johns Stake history. They lobbied the Bureau of Public Roads for a federal highway number for their route. It was finally James McNary, through his friendship with President Hoover, who secured the designation of U.S. Highway 70 for the route through Springerville. In the late 20s, Oklahoma officials, seeking to bolster their claim to a transcontinental route, obtained the designation of U.S. 60 for the highway beginning in Virginia and running through Springerville, Show Low and Globe to the West Coast. As Springerville appropriated the number 60, it had to give up 70 to a more southerly route through Safford. The old portion of the earlier transcontinental highway that goes from Springerville to St. Johns and Holbrook is now called U.S. 180.

An artifact from Springerville's highway boosterism is the 10-foot high statue "Madonna of the Trail." During an effort in the 1920s to promote a route called the "National Old Trails Highway," future president Harry S Truman and the Daughters of the American Revolution commissioned sculptor August Leimbach to create 12 identical monuments to be placed along the Washington to Los Angeles route. The statues depict a pioneer woman striding forward carrying an infant with another child clinging to her legs. The German-born Leimbach apparently felt that women who walked so much should be sturdy with substantial leg muscles. The route roughly followed the paths of Braddock's and Washington's Road, the National Road, Boone's Lick Road, the Santa Fe Trail and the Old Spanish Trail. It went through Maryland, Pennsylvania, West Virginia, Ohio, Indiana, Illinois, Missouri, Kansas, Colorado, New Mexico, Arizona and California. One statue was erected in each state. Julius Becker, a member of the board of the Old Trails Association, worked to make sure Springerville was the home of Arizona's "Madonna."

In 1924, Hollywood mogul C. J. Brunson bought the O. W. Ranch near the Mogollon Rim and sold it to Ken Jay in 1937. "Ken used it as a retreat for his family and friends including Clark Gable and Carol Lombard," according to *The Crooked Trail to Holbrook*.

Emily Michener came to the White Mountains when her father worked on oil exploration near Winslow. She and five or six other

Bill's Bar was popular with both the locals and tourists. The building once included a café, bus stop, grocery, gas station, post office and tackle shop. Bill Jennings decided to concentrate his efforts on the bar and dance hall.

girls camped in the early 1920s on the Little Colorado, according to the St. Johns Stake history. She rented the Bill Bourdon ranch on Silver Creek for a girls' guest ranch, and then bought the Bernard Whiting ranch near Vernon to create the nationally known Timberline Ranch for teenage girls. In June, 25 to 35 girls would arrive for a summer of trail riding and hiking. They visited ranches during branding, and traveled as far as the Hopi mesas to see the dances. The season ended with a dance in early September, when local boys and guests from the Tapadero boys' ranch got a chance to meet the girls before they were shipped back East.

Lakeside was also beginning to cater to tourists, with the establishment of rental cabins in 1926, and a festival at Rainbow Lake beginning in 1928. According to Richard Lynch's TV presentation, an advertisement promised "Apache Devil Dancers," a rodeo and boxing. The Lake of the Woods resort was established in 1936 as an auto court.

"What is now Charlie Clark's was born during prohibition days when two log cabins were joined together at the present location," according to the official history of Pinetop's iconic restaurant. "When Prohibition was repealed, Jack Renfro opened a legitimate business known as Jake Renfro's Log Cabin Café." After Charlie Clark purchased the business, the emphasis was on steaks, though the former cowboy also peeled potatoes and prepared salads after orders were taken. "Most times the customer would be bartender while Charlie prepared the meal."

Another dude ranch was established near Heber by the Turley family in the 1930s. The Sun Down Dude Ranch was near Aripine.

The remote and lush Hannagan Meadow also became a tourist stop. It was named for Robert Hannagan, a one-time Nevada miner who made it to California. Then he came to Arizona to run cattle in a wide-ranging business that extended from Silver City, New Mexico, to the high country south of Alpine, according to a brochure written by Tessa Waite. For some reason, he owed $1,200 to two brothers in the area, who took him off a stagecoach and chained him to a tree until his son paid. Toles Cosper, an early rancher whose family was involved in building the lodge at the site, said he and Hannagan happened on the meadow one day while riding, and flipped a coin for the naming rights. Improbable as that may seem, it is the best explanation available.

The meadow became something of a wilderness transportation hub with trails extending south to Clifton through the Blue River country and north to Alpine. The area became famous for game when the renowned hunter Ben Lilly killed the largest grizzly bear ever taken in the Southwest in 1911. Lilly was a latter-day Daniel Boone and once served as a guide to Teddy Roosevelt. The story is that Lilly had already shot the bear three times from long range and was approaching for the kill when the enormous animal ambushed him. The celebrated hunter fired twice more before killing the bear with the large knife he kept handy in his belt. The 900-pound bear's chest measured 96 inches.

A ranger station was built at Hannagan Meadow in 1920 and the lodge followed. The Diamond Rock dude ranch was established nearby.

The Coronado Trail from Clifton to Alpine went through the meadow. They started building the road in 1923 and completed it in 1926. "Completed" meant the crews had finished making a winding one-lane gravel road with steep drop-offs. Though primitive even by the standards of the 1920s, Coronado would have been grateful for the improvements — had he followed this route, which he did not. Five thousand people attended the dedication ceremonies in Hannagan Meadow, including Governor George Hunt and Chief Alchesay.

Tourism and recreation became more profitable than ranching in the high mountain meadow. Cabins were built and hunters used to pay $10 each to sleep on the floor of the great log cabin lodge.

An attempt was even made by an entrepreneur to promote what would today be called "Health Tourism." A brochure collected by the Southwest Museum in Los Angeles solicits investment to create a resort for tuberculosis sufferers. "A 14-room house in excellent condition, also at Show Low, is ready at any time to be used as a preliminary receiving place," the brochure says. "Among other assets is a barn which will house 50 head of cattle. It is equipped with a large water tank and within easy reach of 15 acres of well-timbered land with all sorts of lumber. A short distance away are 160 acres covered with Norway Pine and Blackjack Pine. The appeal for $500,000 by Winslow doctor George P. Sampson gets a little carried away. "The resort is not confined to a mere camp site, but it extends 15 miles along the Show Low River, a picturesque stream with crystal clear water, abundant of fish and along which the scenery is second to none." The company said it had obtained the services of a Chicago newspaperman who could find potential residents. "One of his valuable methods of obtaining names of tuberculosis or asthma sufferers is his systematic organization of an army of boarding house and furnished room house keepers, as well as grocery and milk delivery men, newspaper carriers and other persons who call at residences and have a knowledge of the occupants." It is not known how much money the brochure raised. Perhaps the suggestion that a health resort for contagious people would operate a dairy made investors leery.

The original Paint Pony Lodge in Show Low was built in 1937 by Comdr. Walter J. Willis, a New Yorker, who sold it when he was called back into the Navy. He named it for his children's pinto horses, according to records of the Show Low Museum. It was originally a simple lodge, and didn't become an elaborate landmark until purchased by a Wall Street millionaire, who upgraded it with extensive landscaping, huge custom-made Navajo rugs and rustic furniture to please his wealthy Eastern clientele. The historic lodge burned and was replaced by a modern

379

structure, which was later converted into a Mexican restaurant.

Indians were of phenomenal interest to tourists who bought skillfully woven baskets from Apache women in the White Mountains.

World Famous Writers Work in White Mountains

The White Mountains contributed to the romantic notions of the Old West because writers who were most responsible for making Westerns a worldwide sensation spent a great deal of time in the area.

Zane Grey is one of America's best known authors. He was seen throughout east-central Arizona as he hunted, fished and combed the area for plots. According to biographer Candace C. Kant, more than half of Grey's books were based in Arizona. The closest tie to the White Mountains is *Man of the Forest*. The book was written in 1918 and sold more than 200,000 copies, an impossibly large press run in those days. It was a No. 1 best seller and was made into a movie at least four times, in 1921, 1926, 1933 and 1940. Though Shakespeare scored real Hollywood appeal with Macbeth, and children's stories such as Cinderella have proven popular with a number of moviemakers, four versions is perhaps a record for films of a Western novel. The 1921 offering was filmed, as a silent movie, by Zane Grey's own brief-lived production company. The 1933 version by Fox starred Randolph Scott. It was a "talkie" shot in Hollywood, but used Arizona location footage from the earlier silent versions.

"This novel's main character is Milt Dale, who lives at the base of Old Baldy, highest of the White Mountain peaks, rising to over ten thousand feet," Kant wrote in *Zane Grey's Arizona*. "At thirty years old, he resides on the mountain by himself, as he does not care for human society, and accumulates animal companions instead. Occasionally he ventures down into town, where he has a few friends, but his uncouth appearance, aloofness, and propensity for bringing his pet mountain lion with him make him unwelcome in most establishments. His solitude is disturbed when he overhears a plot to kidnap Helen Rayner, a young woman who is coming west to join her uncle." Of course, the hermit takes the heroine to Mount Baldy where they fall in love. In addition to Scott, the 1933 movie featured Verna Hillie with Buster Crabbe in the supporting cast. Candace Kant finds deep themes of Darwinism in the natural settings and human interactions of the book.

The town in the novel is called "Pine." Zane Grey scholars disagree over which White Mountain community was used as a model for that village. Some say Pinetop while others say Pinedale. Like Pinedale, the novel's village is "on the last level of sparsely timbered forest," where Pinetop is higher at 7,000 feet. From the context of the story, Grey's Pine is not a predominantly Mormon community, while Pinedale is an LDS settlement. Perhaps Grey made Pine a composite of several White Mountain towns. There is, however, little doubt where Grey got the idea for the community of Snowdrop that appears in *Man of the Forest*.

Grey had to wait until 1921 to get enough material about the Pleasant Valley War to write *To the Last Man*. He had made two unsuccessful "hunting" trips into Pleasant Valley without learning a thing, before gaining the confidence of the locals on his third try. "In 1920 I went back with a still larger outfit, equipped to stay as long as I liked," he wrote in the introduction. "And this time, without my asking it, different natives of the Tonto came to tell me about the Pleasant Valley War. No two of them agreed on anything concerning it, except that only one of the active participants survived the fighting. Whence comes my title, 'To the Last man.' Thus I was swamped in a mass of material out of which I could only flounder to my own conclusion." It is unclear whether his sources in the Valley were the ones who told him to weave in the plot of Romeo and Juliet, but maybe they did tell him to leave the lovers alive after everyone else was dead.

Other books with White Mountain settings followed those successful novels. A slow-witted cowboy wins the boss's daughter on a ranch near the White Mountains in Grey's 1926 *Under the Tonto Rim*. Springerville is the scene of *The Dude Ranger* of 1934. In that book, an Easterner buys a ranch, only to find that the cattle are being stolen, so he goes to work undercover as a cowboy on his own ranch to solve the crime. Grey may have heard the story of the Isaac Ellinger murder in Apache County, and combined the role of ranch owner with the detective who solved the crime.

Arizona Ames tells the adventures of a cowboy from the Rim Country who never stops loving the Tonto Basin. *Nevada*, published in 1926, is a tale of rustling and love in Arizona. Though set in the Rim Country, it gets its title from an alias of the protagonist.

Grey left behind simple plots when he created *The Hash Knife Outfit* in 1929. It is based on the local cattle operation and local settings. On the fourth page of the novel, he explains how the Cibecue outfit was split up by Hack Jocelyn's interest in Molly, sister to Slinger Dunn:

"Wal, Jocelyn was after her hard, an' he double-crossed the Haverlys an' Slinger Dunn by tryin' to play both ends against the middle. He hatched a low-down deal, if I ever knowed one. But it fell through. He got away with the girl, Molly, however, an' thet precipitated hell. Slinger quit the Cibeque, trailed them to a cabin in the woods. Back of Tobe's Well somewhere. Must have been the very cabin Anderson put up there years ago. Wal, Jocelyn an' the rest of the Cibecue had kidnapped young Jim Taft for ransom. But Jocelyn meant to collect the ransom an' then murder the boy. The Haverlys wasn't in on this, so the story goes. Anyway, things worked to a hot pitch at this cabin. Jocelyn had a drink too many, they say, an' wanted to drag the little girl Molly off 'n the woods. An' she like what you'd expect of Slinger Dunn's sister, raised hell. Jocelyn tried to shoot young Jim. An' she fought him – bit him like a wildcat. Wal, Slinger bobbed up, Injun as he is, an' killed Jocelyn. Then he had it out with the Haverlys, killin' both of them. He was terrible shot up himself. They fetched him to Flag. But he'll live."

After thus launching the plot, Grey takes 150 pages to unravel the details.

A Grey short story called "The Wolf Tracker" is also set in the White Mountains. "Old Gray had terrorized the range from Cibecue Creek to Mt. Wilson for years, always eluding capture; Brink becomes determined to end the wolf's days of slaughter," Kant wrote. "He tracks the animal through the winter, from

October to April, but at every juncture, the wolf evades him. Brink stays on his trail, becoming increasingly impressed with the cunning of the wolf, and a strange relationship develops between the animal and the persistent tracker. Finally, the wolf is walked to death; exhausted, not allowed to rest, he no longer has the strength to survive. When offered reward money in return for Old Gray's pelt, Brink declines and disappears into the forest."

"Much of Grey's appeal lies in his practice of basing stories on his own experiences," Kant wrote. "When he described a particular canyon, desert, forest, or mountain, his descriptions were believable because he was writing of what he had observed. His characterizations of cowboys, homesteaders, prospectors, and even outlaws bore the stamp of authenticity; in them, he was recreating people he had met on his trips to Arizona." Though it is natural for a biographer to fall in love with her subject, Arizona must have been an unusual place indeed when Zane Grey arrived, with two-dimensional characters walking through the breath-taking landscape. But Kant was correct in reporting that Grey bemoaned the passing of the frontier in Arizona. "The old timers, from whom Grey had originally heard the stories of the Old West, were gone, replaced by people who knew little of the old days and were more concerned with the future than the past."

Molly Butler's Lodge in Greer was one of Grey's haunts. Her husband, John Butler, took him hunting and fishing, for a fee of $10 a day. Grey also stayed at the Sunshine Grocery, Hotel and Lunch Room in Show Low, run by Liona Penrod and his wife. When the author signed Sunshine's register, he just signed "Mr. Grey," either hoping to remain anonymous, or assuming he was so famous that everyone already knew his identity.

Many White Mountain families have stories about Zane Grey. In one account, a local Mormon fan saddled up and rode off to see the great man in order to convince him to characterize Mormons more favorably in his novels. Unfortunately, there is no record of a Hispanic making a similar pilgrimage to dissuade Grey from referring to his people as "greasers." Grey's cabin near Christopher Creek was a popular tourist attraction until it was consumed by a forest fire in 1990.

Tarzan's creator was also inspired by his experiences in the

White Mountains. The author, Edgar Rice Burroughs, who was a cavalry soldier in Arizona from 1895 to 1897, later used the area as the setting for the opening of his first commercial success — ironically, a science fiction trilogy called *Under the Moons of Mars*. The first book in the series, *A Princess of Mars*, started out as a Western with the hero involved in the Apache Wars. Perhaps Burroughs decided that after transporting his readers to the wild and unfamiliar landscape of Arizona, it was a short leap to the next planet in our Solar System.

In that book published in 1912, John Carter, a former captain in the Confederate Army, is prospecting for gold in the White Mountains when he is chased into a cave by Apaches. He finds himself leaving his own body, which is left lying on the cave floor when he emerges to see the planet Mars in the sky. "I closed my eyes, stretched out my arms toward the god of my vocation and felt myself drawn with the suddenness of thought through the trackless immensity of space," Burroughs wrote. "There was an instant of extreme cold and utter darkness." A half century before earthlings accomplished the first moon landing, Burroughs had sent Carter soaring to Mars through the power of his imagination. The hero wins the love of the princess of Mars and then saves the planet by restoring its air supply before returning to Arizona.

Carter continues his exploits on the Red Planet in the final two installments of the trilogy, *The Gods of Mars,* and *The Warlord of Mars.*

Though Burroughs' books seem cliché-ridden to contemporary readers, his ideas only became clichés when later writers copied him.

In the prologue to *Swords of Mars*, published in 1936, protagonist Carter visits a friend in a cabin near the headwaters of the Little Colorado to tell another story of swashbuckling on Mars. "I stood upon the little porch of the cabin enjoying the soft beauties of this Arizona night; and as I contemplated the peace and serenity of the scene, it did not seem possible that but a few years before the fierce and terrible Geronimo had stood in this same spot before this self-same cabin, or that generations before that this seemingly deserted canyon had been peopled by a race now extinct." The cave through which Carter traveled back and forth to Mars was nearby. Burroughs later said he based the description of the Mount Baldy cabin on a house he had visited at the Steinberg Ranch.

His Apache books tell the story of Shoz-Dijiji (Black Bear), a white infant taken from a settler's wagon and raised by the Be-don-ko-he Apaches. In *The War Chief,* published in 1927, Shoz-Dijiji gets his name by killing a bear as a child, grows up to be war chief of his tribe, and saves a white woman during an uprising. She goes back to civilization and he disappears into the wilderness. The story has some parallels to Burroughs' smash hit *Tarzan,* published in 1914, but no hint of Cheetah. The book, which contains many Apache words and personalities from the Apache Wars, was one of many popular novels on Burroughs' long string of successes.

He used Black Bear again six years later in *Apache Devil.* "A little to one side, watching the dancers, sat Shoz-Dijiji, the Black Bear, with Gian-nah-tah, friend of boyhood days, companion of the war trail and the raid," Burroughs wrote. The book is set in the final months of the Geronimo wars. Shoz-Dijiji, a war chief of Geronimo's tribe, survives the conflict and wins the love of a white girl. The mix of Apache language and lore, combined with a world class fiction writer at the height of his powers, made the novel an intriguing book.

When Burroughs was involved in Paramount's production of film shorts on "Unusual Occupations," Snow Whiting appeared as the last pony express rider. The White Mountain rider's job was one of many out-of-the-ordinary occupations featured, which included a Mexican woman who dressed fleas.

The noted juvenile author James Willard Schulz and his son, Lone Wolf, had a part-time home in Greer called Buttterfly Lodge. It was built in 1913 by Greer residents John T. Butler and Cleve Wiltbank. The cabin is now a museum and listed on the National Register of Historic Places.

Schulz was born in New York's Adirondack mountains in 1859 and visited Montana at the age of 17. He lived among the Piegan, a tribe of the Blackfoot Nation, marrying a 15-year-old girl named Natahki, or Fine Shield Woman. Their only child was Hart Merriam Schulz, also called Lone Wolf, who was born in 1882.

James Schulz later came to Arizona and lived and worked among the Pima. His first book was *My Life as an Indian* in 1907. After that he wrote novels with titles like *Plumed Snake Dance*, *Questers of the Desert*, and *A Son of the Navahos*.

"Most of his books had national influence through their serialization in juvenile magazines, ... including *Youth's Companion*, *American Boy* and *Boy's Life*," according to the National Register application. "James' appeal to juveniles was his critical undoing, however, as many discounted his work as being little more than adventure stories for boys. Other, presumably more thoughtful, readers have found lasting value in Schulz's work. Some critics consider *My Life as an Indian* a classic in the genre of Western literature." Advertising blurbs rated him higher, with comments like, "The most remarkable work that has ever been done in the western field with the Indian as a character."

In The Great Apache Forest: The Story of a Lone Boy Scout told the tale of local teenagers George and Hannah Crosby and their adventures when George was summer fire lookout on Mount Baldy during World War I. It was serialized in *American Boy* and gained international fame due to its popularity among European children, according to the National Register filing.

The main character, George Crosby, is too young to enlist for World War I, but wants to serve the village of Greer in some way beyond doing chores for the families of boys who have enlisted. In the story, he becomes a remote member of a Phoenix Boy Scout troop, and then is asked by the Forest supervisor to man the fire tower on Mount Baldy.

"Far to the north, across several hundred miles of the great, gray desert, I could see the cliffs of the Hopi Indians, and nearer, to the northeast, the Zuni Buttes," the boy says as he describes the view from the fire tower on the 11,400-foot mountain. "Eastward as far as I could see into New Mexico, a hundred miles and more, loomed up the grim, black-forested Mogollon Range. To the south, across a hundred miles of greener forest, the snaky outline of the Graham Mountains hid the hot country from me, else I could have looked down upon the deserts of Old Mexico, more than three hundred miles away. More to the west, the Sierra Anchas Mountains prevented a view of the great Roosevelt Lake."

When George's sister visits, they are confronted by porcupines, a giant killer grizzly bear, an army deserter and leftist trade union members who start fires. The siblings also meet an Apache hunter and Hopi pilgrims, who are climbing to the summit to plead with their rain god to end a drought. Though it is interesting to read about the White Mountains in the early 20th century, the book is certainly juvenile fiction.

The author kept Butterfly Lodge while maintaining homes in Los Angeles. "Schulz did some writing in Greer, but the White Mountains were used mostly for hunting or other forms of relaxation," the application says. He gave the lodge to his son in 1924, but continued to visit. Lone Wolf spent summers in a tipi in Montana, winters in Tucson and the spring and fall in Greer, working at Butterfly Lodge.

Schulz worked with other famous writers and artists to oppose the government policy of prohibiting Indian ceremonials. In particular, he went to Winslow in 1922 to gather statements from Hopi leaders who had been threatened by a government commissioner intent on forcing them to give up their religion. "Following the meeting with Schulz in Winslow and the assurances of support from individuals and associations from all over the United States, the Hopi stood firm and carried on their religious observances as before," Harry C. James wrote in *Pages from Hopi History*.

Lone Wolf began his artistic endeavors as a child, studying under his grandfather, Yellow Wolf, who taught the youngster how to paint with buffalo bone brushes on stretched animal skins. After heading south because of tuberculosis, he worked as a cowboy and guide at the Grand Canyon, where noted artist Thomas Moran met him and encouraged him to pursue a career as an artist. Lone Wolf attended the Art Students League in Los Angeles and the Chicago Art Institute. He met his wife while working as a bronc rider in Montana. Like Charles Russell and Frederic Remington, he drew on cowboy life for his artistic themes. He had his first one-man show in Los Angeles in 1917, and later got rave reviews in the *New York Times*, which said he had "taken the art world by storm." Patrons included Mrs. Calvin Coolidge, Herbert Hoover and the Santa Fe Railroad. Some of Lone Wolf's sculptures were created at his studio in Greer.

"He would show up at community picnics in full Blackfoot

regalia," says *On the Road to Nowhere*. After having too much to drink, he forced a white friend to "dance" as he fired a six-shooter at his feet. "One time a young mother was so worried about him drinking and galloping through the village vowing to kill all the Mormons, she stuffed her kids in a cupboard."

Lone Wolf died in Tucson in 1970 at age 88.

The Fort Closes, Slowing Economy in the 1920s

There was one more Indian "uprising" in 1905, which Jennings wrote about in *Arizona Was the West*. Apaches were outraged about the rape and murder of a nine-year-old girl and suspected some of the soldiers were responsible. Jennings said the angry Indians appeared at Fort Apache and chanted for two days before scout Mickey Free could convince them that justice would be done. Jennings said the guilty soldiers were apprehended, but could not recall their punishment.

In a 1958 *Arizona Highways* article, Ross Santee tells about wild horses being exterminated on the reservation because of a disease called dourine. Though the venereal disease was most dangerous to domesticated horses, the more resistant wild ponies were thought to be carriers. "Over 10,000 wild horses were shot and killed on the Reservation in the early '30s," he wrote in an account that centers on the nearby San Carlos Apache Reservation. "A tragic and terrifying end. Old saddle horses and pack mules from the white outfits, gone to the wild bunch, were exterminated too. The government paid so much a head for each branded animal killed." He tells in graphic detail how the last bunch was gunned down by hunters as the horses attempted to run across a big flat.

Tom Horn, the faithful scout who did so much to bring the Apaches into reservation life, met a bad end in Wyoming. After leaving the White Mountains, he became a lawman and Pinkerton detective, taking responsibility for killing at least 17 outlaws. He also worked as a "livestock detective" for wealthy cattlemen, killing two dozen suspected rustlers. He was arrested in 1903 and hanged for killing the 14-year-old son of a sheep man. A mock retrial found him innocent, but 90 years too late to save his life.

After the United States emerged from World War I as a world power, it was hard to justify stationing troops on a remote Indian reservation that had been pacified in the last century. The troops were re-assigned and the fort was decommissioned. "Between 1920 and 1925 Pinedale farmers experienced an economic recession primarily caused by the closure of Fort Apache and a drop in meat prices," wrote Lightfoot in an archaeological survey article. "When Fort Apache terminated military operations in 1922, a major source of income for local freighters and farmers was lost. Cattle prices began dropping between 1921 and 1923; and by 1924, the bottom fell out of the cattle market. While most people were still primarily subsistence farmers, they depended on some cash income to purchase goods they could not grow or manufacture themselves. The loss of revenue was severe enough, in several cases, to force families to migrate from the Pinedale area."

During a panic in 1925, some 49 of the 88 banks in Arizona failed, including the Bank of Northern Arizona, which wiped out many local cattlemen, Palmer wrote.

According to Stewart Udall, writing in *American West, The Land and Its People*, the residents of St. Johns were doing OK in the 1920s, largely because they weren't connected much to the national economy. "Machines and manufactured goods and foods took a back seat in St. Johns: each family had an orchard, a garden, and the domesticated animals (cows, pigs, and chickens) needed to provide the majority of its food. For the most part St. Johns was a self-sufficient farm village, apart from the cash economy; we had no railroad to tie us to the nation's economic system, and there were no industries to provide payrolls. The only products which were sold for outside cash were livestock and baled hay, and although St. Johns was a county-seat, there was insufficient cash-flow to support a bank. Some men found work in other places and brought their savings home, but in the main, people were self-employed and got by on their ability to make good use of local resources."

"When the schoolhouse burned in 1927, Lakeside citizens

floated a bond issue and raised money to build a new one by the following year," according to an archeological study by Pat H. Stein, who researched articles in the *Snowflake Herald.* "If one theme dominates the history of Lakeside and its residents it is resilience: the ability to recover quickly from adversity, through community commitment and hard labor."

The fire and reconstruction of the Lakeside school echoed events that had occurred in Snowflake more than a decade earlier. On Thanksgiving Day in 1913, the new Academy building was dedicated at a cost of $35,000. The money had been raised over three years after an earlier, just-completed, Snowflake school was destroyed by fire.

Apaches In the 20th Century

When Rev. Edgar Guenther came to Fort Apache in 1911, people from his Wisconsin Lutheran church had been the exclusive missionaries on that reservation for 15 years without making much headway in converting the Apaches. The caring pastor worked hard to build a school as well as a church. *The People Called Apache* says, "He and Mrs. Guenther traveled constantly to every part of the reservation on foot, horseback, and finally by auto, to bring the Gospel, to advise the people, and to give medical aid to the sick. Of special consequence was his friendship with the important Apache Chief Alchesay, who when he became ill and was not cured by the medicine men went out to a lonely place to die. Guenther went after him, administered medicine, and brought him back to health."

After that, Alchesay, who had blocked construction of a Lutheran church, gave his consent. "When the new Lutheran Church building was dedicated in Whiteriver in 1923, Alchesay officiated . . . and then led one hundred of his followers into the building to be baptized," the book says.

Guenther opened a facility that served both as the first orphanage for Indians in the Southwest and also as a temporary care facility for children of hard-pressed families.

Unlike Mayerhoff, the first missionary, Guenther sometimes

expressed his sincere disapproval of traditional Apache ceremonies.

The German roots of Guenther and his church caused trouble during World War I. The minister, who had a picture of the Kaiser in his house, said it was only there to cover a hole in the plaster. But it aroused suspicions. "In August of 1918, the home of Rev. E. E. Guenther was searched and the missionary arrested and held in the Fort Apache jail on charges of spying and being sympathetic to Germany," says a thesis by Lenard Brown. "He was arraigned before the military authorities at Fort Apache the next day, and being unable to prove anything, they released him."

In 1921, the 25-year Lutheran monopoly on the reservation was threatened by the arrival of Father Justin Deutsch, a man who had befriended many White Mountain Apache children when he was the headmaster at St. Johns Indian School in Phoenix. Apaches remember the reservation being flooded with Lutheran clergymen in response to the Roman threat. The ministers canvassed all the villages and camps, attempting to get the Apaches to sign pledge cards to send their children to the Lutheran schools. "Although by far the greater number of these Apaches are not active members of their church, nor baptized, still they seemed to count all as belonging to them and tried their utmost to induce all not to join our church," Father Deutsch wrote. The priest persevered, eventually finding 17 literate Apaches to sign his petition for a church site. He was able to obtain help from a contractor from the community of St. Johns, who brought a small machine that made concrete blocks. "One of the Apache leaders, Mary Riley, came forward to help," according to Melvin and Mary Wendrick, writing in *The Way of St. Francis*. "Destined one day to be the first woman elected to the Apache Tribal Council and to be named one of Arizona's Living Treasures, she daily drove a buckboard to Fort Apache to bring the sacks of cement to the construction site. She had no trouble lining up helpers." The workers soon completed St. Francis Apache Church, which still survives. At Christmas the sight of a beautiful crèche donated by Chicago Catholics resonated with Apaches accustomed to religious symbolism.

Mary Riley remained a close friend of the Rev. and Mrs.

Guenther despite her strong Catholic faith. The dedicated Lutheran missionaries raised a son, who also served as a pastor to the Apaches, and a daughter who became the principal of the elementary school in Whiteriver.

The early part of the 20th century brought more changes to reservation life. "While many Apaches continued to make their living during this period much as they had in the previous decade, the government recognized the necessity of introducing better herds of cattle," William Kessel wrote in a thesis. "In 1917, 800 head of grade Hereford were brought from Mexico and driven to Fort Apache. This marked the beginnings of the White Mountain Tribal herd."

"By 1918, it appears that an increasing number of Apaches began to perceive the possible advantages of formal education," Kessel wrote. "New road and building construction projects both on and off the reservation were begun and Apaches who could understand and speak English were being hired."

The kindly Father Justin Deutsch, before being sent to another mission in 1923, also noted Apaches adopting a more accepting attitude toward education.

After the patriotic service of many Native Americans in World War I, the Apaches, along with members of other tribes, finally became citizens of the United States with an act of Congress in 1924. In addition to fighting the Germans, Apache warriors had also served the military as scouts searching for Poncho Villa.

It was often necessary for Apaches to travel to distant locations to earn wages in the early part of the 20th century. Eva Watt described her family's many journeys in her book, *Don't Let the Sun Step Over You*. The extended family closed down their homes in Cibecue and Oak Creek. "They camped near springs and seeps, sleeping at night in shelters made out of brush, and seldom had dealings with strangers," wrote Keith Basso, who helped her with the book. They worked as farm laborers, cracked rocks on highway crews building the Apache Trail and worked on roads near Roosevelt Dam. "My father carried rocks," Watt said. "He carried one at a time down the mountain there. But then he got some of those boxes – powder boxes they call them, cause dynamites come in them – and he wired them together and built up the sides a bit. Then he put a long stick across, and he wired it down and then he tied a rope to the ends. He put that rope over his head and down around his shoulders and he packed that thing on his back. He put the rocks in there, three or four at a time, and he carried them down to where they were building the road. Pretty soon, other mens were doing that." Her three brothers carried water to the workers.

The ancient Sunrise ceremony survived the problems of the 20th century. Early on, missionaries "strongly criticized the 'old way religion,' causing younger Apache to doubt that the ceremony will actually assure the pubescent girl ... long life and prosperity," says *The People Called Apache*. Also, the cost of the four-day celebration caused some families to forego or shorten the ritual.

But when the ceremony was held, the girl's sponsor or god mother often helped her family with the cost as well as guiding the initiate through the strenuous puberty rituals.

A 1901 ceremony is described in *The People Called Apache*. The girl was first chased by other young people and then began running by herself to each of the four sacred directions. She was sprinkled with sacred pollen and danced on a blanket throughout the day, attended by singers, drummers and Gan impersonators. "That afternoon a feast was given in her honor. ... About six o'clock in the evening the captain of the ceremonies took a large eagle feather and rolled it in ashes. After holding it toward the sun, he tied it in the girl's hair." As night fell, all the people seated themselves on blankets in a large circle. A medicine man sang as the drums beat time. "The girls danced first. They formed around the central fire in groups of five to seven, like the spokes in a giant wheel, with the central fire and the musicians for the hub." Women sprinkled cattail pollen on the dancers, and the girls chose male partners. "Thus set after set was danced throughout the night, being varied now and then by drinking tiswin and by the old women dancing singly, as clowns to amuse the onlookers. ... At sunrise the dance broke up and the men hurled presents at the feet of the girl – stacks of saddles, blankets and cloth. One man gave her a horse. This act closed the ceremony."

In addition to holding the Sunrise ceremonies, 20th century Apaches continue to make pilgrimages to sacred mountains, particularly Mount Baldy, which they call White Mountain.

Stresses Produce
New Apache Religious Movements

Stress increased for Apaches during the early part of the 20th century. Rations dwindled and droughts and floods destroyed crops. A comet appeared, along with a major earthquake which leveled wickiups; rocks fell from the sky. Children were forcibly removed from their families and suffered harsh treatment in government schools. Continual epidemics contributed to bouts of drinking and fear of witchcraft. White Mountain Apaches believed the world was coming apart.

Government food, never adequate, was denied to families with able-bodied men, then taken away from everyone. Many men were forced to leave their homes and take menial jobs off the reservation where they were mistreated and paid only pennies per hour. White traders got away with overcharging because competitors were far away. Some Apaches, who had resisted selling their sacred objects, were now forced to part with them in order to feed their families. But the money gave them only temporary respite from hunger.

The string of natural disasters started in 1904 when a drought destroyed crops. The dry conditions fueled forest fires, which consumed more than 115 square miles of timber. The next year, heavy flooding washed out irrigation ditches. "In 1910 Halley's Comet appeared in the sky," according to a thesis by William Kessel. "It frightened the Indians, and medicine men were hard put to explain its existence or meaning." A few years later, "meteorites were observed hitting the earth near Canyon Day, Amos Wash, and the North Fork River." Stars were seen shooting across the sky. "Panic spread among the Apaches who were fearful that the earth might blow up like a bomb." Though the spectacular meteorite fall on the reservation was not precisely dated, a similar incident near Holbrook was investigated by scientists in 1912. Three years later, early in the morning of April 17, a major earthquake with epicenter near the north boundary of the reservation flattened wickiups, giving greater credibility to those who warned of the world's imminent destruction. Flooding returned with a vengeance in 1916.

The Apaches, like all people after major disasters, wondered why they had to experience such hardships. Rev. Guenther said the

Christian God had sent the floods for some unexplained reason. Traditional Apaches believed the tribe was being punished because stingy people were unwilling to share their food with the needy. "As a consequence [some thought], a giant snake came down the river bringing flood waters with him," Kessel wrote. "Finally, other Apaches attributed the flood to witchcraft."

Guenther, who had tried not to criticize Apache lifeways, became less tolerant of native religion as the dispute heated up. "In addition, medicine men encouraged the Apaches to wear traditional clothing which was also viewed as non-progressive," Kessel wrote. "It had become obvious to agency personnel that the medicine man was a symbol for the Apaches of their traditional culture. Consequently, the agents began making plans to rid the reservations of medicine men."

The government believed education could break children of their Apache ways and prepare them to be productive adults. "Forced education was regarded with fear and suspicion by the Apaches," Kessel wrote. Tribal members, who were children at the time, remembered being "afraid to go to school because they felt they might be killed by the white people."

"Both parents and medicine men were opposed to sending children to school because they were needed in subsistence pursuits and feared that while in school the youngsters might become too much like white men," Kessel wrote. "The medicine men were also afraid that, removed from the influence of their Apache elders, the children would have no desire to learn to become medicine men."

The missionary's wife, Mrs. Guenther, watched what was happening to her friends and later recalled, "They were forced to change, to live like the white man."

Disease ravaging the reservation undermined both traditional beliefs and Christian teaching.

Apache healers and medicine men treated sick children with herbal remedies and broths. But sacred pollen, rituals and prayers did not seem to work. Medicine men frequently explained their failures by saying "the epidemic originated among the Anglos, and consequently traditional Apache cures were not always efficacious," wrote Kessel.

Apaches, like many people under great stress, looked for a religious solution. Some turned to a series of cults that combined elements of traditional belief with new promises.

Das Lan was a medicine man who came from the same village as Noche'Del'Klinne, the prophet who had died more than 20 years earlier in the Cibecue Uprising. Das Lan's movement promised heaven on earth and agitated the San Carlos and Fort Apache reservations from 1903 to 1907. It was called "daagodigha, the name meaning 'rising upward' or 'they will be raised up,' " wrote Alan Ferg in *Western Apache Material Culture*. "After [the believers were taken into the sky] a great flood or earthquake would purge the earth of its evil, and the followers would then be set back on the rejuvenated earth where they would live in peace and plenty," Ferg said.

But there was a difference between the two Cibecue prophets. Noche'Del'Klinne was a traditional Apache medicine man, while Das Lan was influenced by Christian doctrine. The new prophet "claimed to be able to travel to the realm of the dead, and to come back alive three days later," said Carlo Severi in an article in the *Journal of the Royal Anthropological Institute*.

The prophet began to require believers to don special clothing. An article in the *Southwestern Journal of Anthropology* quoted Neil Buck, one of Das Lan's followers, who said, "All the men had to dress alike. ... They had to wear white drawers, white shirt, white gee-string, and black vest. We dressed just like old-timers. The women the same. From each shoulder hung down four strands of ribbon, about to the ground. These were the colors of the directions. Also on the front of a man's shirt or a woman's blouse they each wore a cross made of silver with a crescent moon over it and from the bottom of the cross hung four or five conchos, made of dimes hammered out and strung on a piece of buckskin by little wire hoops soldered to them, so that they reached the bottom of the shirt or blouse."

"In 1906 Das Lan had his followers cut his head off as a means of proving he could return from the dead," Ferg wrote. "His failure to return to life in three days as he promised, the deep-seated Apache fear of the dead, and the subsequent deaths of two other daagodigha medicine men in 1907 and 1908 brought the movement to a close."

The third religious movement of the Apaches was an apoca-

Das Lan's religious movement on the Apache Reservation ended when he failed to rise from the dead three days after he had followers cut off his head.

Carol Sletten
© 2010

lyptic cult called "It is Going to Happen" started by a man known by his government tag number of P-1. He was assisted by his son P-6. In 1916, they instructed their followers to carry pouches of cattail pollen, which they sold to them. P-1 held dances and told his believers to wear white. He said "followers of the movement would be lifted off the earth by one of several Apache deities or by Jesus Christ," Kessel wrote. "Meanwhile, the earth would be destroyed. Those lifted up would be transported to a happy, heaven-like place." When other medicine men adopted P-1's dances, the cult spread. P-1 announced that the world would end on a certain day in the spring. It didn't happen. Next, he said, "The long-deceased mother of an old scout would come back to earth dressed all in white mounted on a white horse, to carry back the worthy ones to the new world." She didn't arrive. After a third prophecy failed, the cult began to fall apart. Like others who have confidently looked forward to the world ending at a designated time, many Apaches had neglected planting and other practical matters, which left them further impoverished.

The fourth movement, founded by Silas John Edwards in 1920, spread beyond Arizona. It survives today despite the long imprisonment of its leader. He studied under an Apache medicine man and learned Christianity from Guenther, before having a powerful vision and starting his own religion. It is said that he climbed a rainbow to receive sacred instructions directly from Ussen, the Apache Giver of Life. After his vision, the prophet quit using his last name and told his followers to call him "Silas John." He combined Christian and Apache symbols and beliefs with elements of the Hopi Snake Dance to create dramatic new ceremonies. Many distressed Apaches flocked to Holy Grounds set up by the new prophet because they believed in his healing Power. "Before the ceremony Silas John instructed twelve young men to collect snakes," Kessel said. "He told them not to be afraid because, having blessed them by making crosses of [pollen] on their hands, they would be protected. Silas John also showed them how to use forked sticks to pin down the reptiles and how to pick them up behind their heads. Sprinkling [pollen] as he went, Silas John led the twelve young men following him to a location where they could find snakes. After two days the men had collected 18 snakes – the majority of which were rattlesnakes."

Silas John trained nine girls and nine boys to dance with the snakes. The ceremony continued much like a traditional Apache dance until early in the morning when attention focused on a brush and canvas shelter. "Inside, Silas John blessed the [snake] dancers one by one with [pollen] and told them not to be afraid," Kessel wrote. "He then handed each of them a snake telling them to hold it behind its head and near its tail. After gentling the snakes within the enclosure, during which time Silas John chanted, the dancers left the shelter. All persons who were ill lined up facing Silas John who walked before them sprinkling them with [pollen] and praying for them. He passed in front of each person and asked them what their trouble was. Then, applying [pollen] to the location of the ailment, he took one snake at a time from the dancers and placed these on the spot."

He told his followers not to go to traditional Apache crown dance ceremonies. Like the Christian missionaries, he called them devil dances. While those words disturbed quite a few traditional Apaches, who believed crown dancers or Gans were true representatives of their revered mountain spirits, Silas John's new religion still flourished. His followers believed he could raise the dead and make a drum beat without touching it.

The ceremonial use of snakes was a compelling ritual of a highly spiritual nature to his followers, but not to the missionaries

Silas John Edwards created a religion that mixed Christian and Apache beliefs with elements of the Hopi snake dance. He became known as the Apache Jesus.

Carol Sletten
© 2010

and government officials. They considered the snake dances to be a grotesque display of idolatry. And Silas John's growing influence was a dangerous threat to their authority. They were further alarmed when they learned that he was called the "Apache Jesus" because of his identification with Na'ye'ne'zy'ane', one of the twin war gods and the central culture hero of Apache mythology. The preachers preached against him and secular officials found reasons to imprison him.

Even though he was forbidden to visit reservations other than his own, his religion continued to spread. He sent blessings and instructions to followers through the mail. Like Jesus, he selected disciples to carry his religion to distant people. They traveled throughout the Apache world, from Fort McDowell to New Mexico. He created an ingenious symbolic language to preserve his prayers and ritual movements on pieces of buckskin and cardboard so that his disciples could chant his words and perform his ceremonies correctly even when he wasn't with them.

Silas John avoided giving specific predictions like those that failed and ended the second and third cults. But like Noche'Del'Klinne of the first cult, his growing influence generated ever stronger reaction from the white authorities. They prohibited his religious practices. When he hired an attorney to help him legalize his religion, reservation authorities convinced his lawyer to withdraw from the case. So his religion remained illegal.

Silas John's wife was brutally murdered in 1933. She was found strangled with her head smashed in. Someone had used blood to write her husband's initials on a rock near her body. The prophet's trial, held in the Depression-racked mining town of Globe, drew the curious and idle. And even though it was conducted in Globe's elegant courthouse, the trial seemed like a sick sideshow when the prosecution brought the severed head of the victim into the courtroom. The newspaper said the building had to be cleared because of the smell.

Silas John Edwards was found guilty of first-degree murder by the all-male, all-white jury and sent to a federal penitentiary in Washington state. He was in prison more than 20 years, until Earl Stanley Gardner, the Perry Mason author, helped him get a parole.

Believers continued to practice the prophet's teachings during his long incarceration, and still do so many decades after his death. Silas John's revelations have deep meaning for his followers. They conduct ceremonies on the sanctified areas called Holy Grounds, but no longer use live snakes.

The Lost Apaches

An incident in Mexico in 1927 focused world attention on "wild Apaches," who were still living in Mexico's Sierra Madre more than 40 years after the final surrender of Geronimo. Francisco Fimbres, his wife, Maria, and their two children were traveling from Nacori Chico about 100 miles south of the border to a gold mine in the Sierra. Senor Fimbres was walking, carrying his young daughter while Maria and the young son rode. "Apache women rush from hiding," according to an account in the diary of anthropologist Grenville Goodwin. "They grab the reins of Maria's horse and pull her down, stab her with knives, slit her throat, drop her body into the ravine by the trail. They take three-year-old Gerardo with them and disappear."

The Fimbres family was apparently of interest to the wild Apaches because of their adoption of Lupe, a young girl captured years earlier by Mexicans trailing the wild ones. She had at one time tried to go back to her tribe, but they rejected her, saying she was no longer one of them. But with her keen senses

400

trained in the Apache ways, she would often sense the presence of hidden Apaches stalking the family. If she had been with the family on the fateful day, she might have been able to give a warning.

After the murder, Fimbres led a revenge expedition against the Apaches, killing three. In retaliation, his little Gerardo was killed. The boy's body was left on the graves of the slain Apaches.

The prospect of Native Americans living in a completely wild state attracted the attention of many, but especially Grenville Goodwin, a wealthy young man studying anthropology at the University of Arizona. His notes, published by his son Neil, as *The Apache Diaries,* is one of the best accounts of the search for the wild Apaches.

"Many believed that the Sierra Madre Apaches were descended from Ndendaa'i Chiricahuas who were not swept up in the final campaigns of the Apache Wars of the 1880s," the book says. "The Sierra Madre Apaches subsisted in small bands, groups, or family units isolated from one another and from Mexican society. Scattered over a huge area, about seventy-five miles wide and two hundred miles long, directly south of Arizona and New Mexico, there may well have been as many as a hundred people in 1900, but their numbers steadily declined thereafter. They raided ranches for livestock and occasionally robbed and killed people caught alone and unprotected in the mountains, but they were on the brink of extinction, going against the march of time and the odds of survival. Between 1900 and 1920 they seem to have kept a relatively low profile, but in the early 1920s the Sierra Madre Apaches began to make their presence known as increased development in the remote mountains brought them into more frequent contact with loggers, ranchers, and miners. By the end of that decade the Apaches were big news throughout the border region; they had become legends in their own time."

Goodwin, who set off to find the lost Apaches in the early 1930s, began his quest by visiting Arizona Apaches, who knew the wild ones "all too well. During the following summer, while at Fort Apache, [Goodwin] heard that the Sierra Madre Apaches would sometimes roam as far north as the reservation to raid for horses and women."

In a diary entry written in August 1930 in Cibecue, Goodwin

wrote: "Got talking with an Apache Police here, and he said that sometimes in summer some of Geronimo's people come up from Old Mexico and run horses off the reservation. These had been seen in the summer of 1929 by an Apache, a friend of his, but were wild and would not stop to talk. He only saw them from a distance, but they appeared to be dressed in modern clothes."

Goodwin interviewed the old Apache Scout John Rope, who said he knew a couple of the Sierra Madre Apache personally. Visiting the Mescalero Apaches, he learned that a man named Adi-lna'idzi.d was the chief of the wild Apaches in the late 1800s. Sherman Curley, another old scout, confirmed the chief's name, and said he had personally recognized him on an expedition into Mexico. Adi-lna'dzi.d had been a prominent member of Naiche's band and had even served as an army scout before joining the renegades during one of their outbreaks.

Though Goodwin went into the Sierra Madre looking for the band, he never found them. They were experienced Apache warriors and he was a freshman from the University of Arizona. In a sense, he proved the truth of the old cavalry saying, "If you saw them, they weren't Apaches."

But as a budding anthropologist, Goodwin was able to locate their camps and identify their belongings as being definitely Apache. The diary tells of finding caves used by the band for storage. "One or two of these were sealed with mud and rock, which they tore out, finding much Apache material stored. Inside were some moccasins, a pair of buckskin breeches, women's dresses of cloth, several four-strand, twisted, rawhide riatos [ropes] of various sizes, a good many tanned cowhides, some big balls of tallow, a burden basket, a dish basket, and a pitched water bottle." They also found "a buckskin saddle bag, several saddles, one of which bore the brands of all the local ranches cut into it [and] two cowhide shirts. There were "arrows of two kinds, one of mountain willow, and of cane with separate hardwood point, sometimes tipped with a nail. There were also "one or two bows of mountain willow hardened by fire, backed with sinew, shaped in 2 demi-arcs, and strung with sinew, and finally a flat stick about 12 in. long which had on it paintings of horses, cattle, deer, etc., done with great skill."

Though the group was clearly Apache in culture, they were hardly pure from a genetic standpoint. Their leader, Apache Juan, according to the captured woman Lupe, was himself the son of a captive.

Helge Ingstad, the famed Norwegian explorer who proved that the Vikings landed in North America 500 years before Columbus, spent a great deal of time searching for the wild Apaches in the Sierra Madre. He came to the area in the 1930s, and like Goodwin, started his quest by going to the White Mountains and talking to old timers on the reservation. "It turned out that the Mexicans had killed quite a few Apaches during the last several years," Ingstad wrote in his book, *The Apache Indians, In Search of the Missing Tribe.* "The Indians were usually shot when every once in a while they came down from the mountains to steal cattle." In the book, recently translated into English, Ingstad recounts an interview with a local Mexican named Moreni. "All those he had seen had been shot and were dressed in hides. Every once in a while they would find them with some type of old gun dated back to the Apache wars, but otherwise the Indians used bows and arrows. Nothing indicated that they had any contact with civilization."

While he never met any wild Apaches, he believed they were close. Coming upon some Mexican ranchers in the Sierra, he asked if they had seen any Apaches lately. They said, "Only a few weeks ago the Natives had stolen two horses from their corral, one which even had a bell tied around its neck. Furthermore, the Mexicans had also recently seen a campfire way up in the mountains to the northwest."

The romance of the wild Apache legend was stoked by the publication of *The First Hundred Years of Nino Cochise*, an account by a grandson of Cochise who tells of slipping away from the soldiers and living in Mexico.

———————————————

The Udalls,
St. Johns' Political Dynasty

One of the West's most famous political dynasties began when David King Udall was sent from Utah to be the Mormon bishop of St. Johns. His descendants have served Arizona, nearby states and the nation for nearly 150 years. Bishop Udall, a polygamist, had sons by different wives — Levi Stewart Udall and Jesse Addison Udall – who both became chief justice of the Arizona Supreme Court. Levi, like his famous son Morris, was an athlete. George Woolford, who had been the catcher for St. Johns High School, vividly remembered Levi's smoking fastball. The recollection was clear because the boys played without gloves in the early years of the 20th century. Levi's path to the top of Arizona's judiciary was not without at least one setback. His older brother John Hunt Udall defeated him in 1922 in his first bid for the county court clerk's office.

Levi and his wife Louisa, a granddaughter of John D. Lee, had two famous sons, Stewart and Morris. Stewart grew up in St. Johns before serving in World War II, graduating from Law School and becoming a congressman and Secretary of the Interior. Morris's early life in St. Johns presented the first of many challenges he would have to overcome. In 1929, he lost an eye from a knife accident while he and another boy were cutting a piece of twine. Udall said it didn't help that the doctor was a drunk, who wasn't even very good when he was sober. Morris, or Mo as he was called, later contracted a nearly fatal case of spinal meningitis.

"Dad believed, like the old Mormons, that work is the best cure for all your problems, and he deliberately kept a farm," Mo wrote in *This Land, These Voices*. "He was a lawyer and judge, but he wanted his boys to learn to farm. So Stew and I, from the time we were in high school, really, ran dad's farm. It was about 300 acres, and we'd have to irrigate at night when it came our turn in the community to use water out of the ditch. You'd use it solidly for three days, and you'd have to take a blanket and sleep out there and change the water over every three or four hours from one field to the next. And we'd get together a baler crew and bring in the hay. You learned how to bring in the hay and repair harnesses and mowing machines and simple farm equipment. And it was a very exciting life, a very satisfying life."

"Dad was a judge, and we'd go up to the courthouse and watch trials," Mo wrote. "So we set up the kids' court and had elections for prosecutor and defense attorney, and we actually had trials where one of the Greer boys had stolen two dollars from his brother's bank. We put him on trial, had a defense counsel and empanelled a jury. Out in our garage we'd have all these little kids sitting in the jury box, and we'd be arguing to them. Well, we'd have those trials and convict some kid and then confine him in the chicken coop for three hours with the 'sheriff' standing guard to see the sentence was carried out.

"Stew and I always put on a kids' rodeo every year where we'd roundup everybody's calves and have roping ... roping the calves, bulldog them, have cow-milking contests and different kinds of things like that."

Mo overcame adversity to be co-captain of the high school basketball team, quarterback of the football team and play the leading roll in a school play. He led the basketball team from tiny St. Johns on a five-school tour of Mesa, Phoenix and Tempe and won all five games, despite the fact that his team did not even have matching uniforms. He edited the yearbook and served as student body president and valedictorian, according to an article in the *Arizona Republic*. He went to the University of Arizona on a basketball scholarship, served in the army during the war and returned to Tucson to study law. Though he played professional basketball in Denver for a year during his studies, he received the highest score on the bar exam in 1949. When Stewart moved from Congress to become secretary of the interior, Mo won a special election for his brother's House seat. Mo Udall was perhaps the greatest conservationist since Teddy Roosevelt, passing legislation protecting 100 million acres of federal land in national parks, wildlife refuges and national forests. If Mo has a rival for the honor as the greatest conservationist of the latter half of the 20th Century, it would be his brother, Stew, who helped create the Wilderness Act. Mo's run for president in 1976 is chronicled in his book, *Too Funny to be President*. Mo held Tucson's congressional seat for 30 years until ill health forced him to resign in 1991. He struggled with Parkinson's disease until his death in 1998.

The fourth generation has also done well in politics. Stewart's son, Tom, was elected to the U.S. House from New Mexico in 1999 and Mo's son, Mark, was elected from Colorado the same year. They both moved up to the U.S. Senate in 2008. Gordon Smith, who served as a U.S. Senator from Oregon, is also a fourth-generation descendant of the original Bishop Udall. His mother, Jessica Udall Smith is a cousin to Mo and Stewart.

Depression Hits Slowly But Hard

When the stock market crashed in 1929, there was little immediate impact in the White Mountains. It was not even mentioned in the *Snowflake Herald*. Though people knew cattle prices would fall, lumber mills continued to run. The Standard mill did not close until the fall of 1930.

"Banks were closing all around the country, but the locals were not too concerned," wrote Solomon in *A History of the Woolford and Hall Families*. "They personally knew the bank owners and trusted that they would deal honestly with them. Roundup time was over and the cattlemen sold and shipped their cattle. George [Woolford] sold some of his herd and received a large sum of money that would help sustain them through the crisis at hand. He took his money to the bank in Snowflake. The next morning the bank closed its doors — just a couple of days after everyone sold their cattle."

A bank holiday, declared in March of 1933, saved most of Arizona's banks, but not the Round Valley Bank in Springerville, which never reopened.

When Holbrook's two banks folded, their assets were purchased by J. R. McEvoy, who created the First National Bank of Holbrook. Palmer, in *Elijah Was a Valiant Man,* said McEvoy agreed to carry some of the local cattlemen, rather than call their loans.

Even so, the number of foreclosure notices published in the *Snowflake Herald* tripled, as did the notices of land being sold for delinquent taxes.

The national income dropped from $87 billion to $40 billion, and the Depression settled in throughout the country, hitting Arizona hard. According to *The New Deal in Arizona,* by William S. Collins, "The total salaries paid to all Arizona workers declined by nearly half from $253 million in 1929 to only $132 million in 1933, driving down the average income per person from $592 to $321." Tax collections slowed until the total delinquency amounted to more than a full year's taxes for the state. Arizona's warrants, or I.O.U.s, were not accepted by merchants. Strapped for cash, the state gave away commodities to try to help. Hispanics and Indians were expected to survive on a supply of flour, milk, sugar, fresh vegetables, rice, and beans valued at $3.55 per month. Anglos got more. In addition to the basic package, whites received potatoes, lard, baking powder and whole-wheat cereal, bringing the monthly cost of feeding them to $6.69.

A three-day blizzard in November added to the misery and insecurity of people facing a winter without income and provisions. "The snow had piled up to the top wire on fences and was so wet and heavy that many of the juniper trees had their branches stripped by the weight," wrote Palmer. "The heat from indoor fires protected house roofs from caving in but many outbuildings were crushed. Transportation was by way of horseback and the occasional sleigh." Cattle froze to death in the drifts if ranchers could not feed them.

"Life had become bleak for the residents of this mountain community but they were still faring better than many who lived in the cities," Palmer wrote of Pinedale. "Through bartering work and goods, raising a garden and some livestock and getting a few dollars for a job here and there, families could eke out an existence. Consequently, many former residents, and even the offspring of earlier community members, gradually began to filter back to the small Northern Arizona settlements. This phenomenon caused a reverse in the population trend and Pinedale began growing after declining in size for years."

Public employment programs were slow to get started, especially in rural areas. But with vast public lands, the White Mountains were destined to become the temporary home of thousands of young men. Thanks to the government's largess – if a dollar a day can be called largess – the Depression was one of the few times humans earned money in the High Country and used it to support their families elsewhere.

The first New Deal employment program to come to the White Mountains arrived in 1933. A "mobile" camp was set up in Lakeside that employed 43 transients in jobs on the National Forest, including road building and fencing.

But it was the Civilian Conservation Corps that promised to bring massive numbers of young men to work in rural Arizona. State politicians protested against "importing undesirables," *The New Deal in Arizona* says. Also, many unemployed loggers feared that eastern city boys would take their jobs. "Fortunately, the provisions setting up the program called for employment of local experienced men as foremen and section leaders," according to *Timeless Heritage*. The government also made it a practice to place CCC camps where they were wanted, and they were wanted in the White Mountains. The *Snowflake Herald* reported in 1933 that 20 local men had been given jobs with New Deal agencies and the local sawmill was having to run day and night to keep up with orders of lumber for the CCC.

The boys had to qualify to work at the camps. Kathryn Flynn of the National New Deal Preservation Association said recruits had to be from needy families, stand at least 5-foot-6, weigh a minimum of 106 pounds, have no communicable diseases, and possess "at least three good masticating teeth."

The boys were paid $30 a month, but were expected to send $25 of that home to their families. They were initially clothed in surplus World War I uniforms. In the first season of operation, Arizona had 20 regular camps and three camps for veterans. There were approximately 4,000 young men and veterans, and 550 locally employed men. The number of camps peaked at 50 and enrollees at 9,000 in 1935. Most of Pinedale's young men joined, so women were the only young adults left in the community, Palmer said.

Four camps were set up in the Apache-Sitgreaves National Forest in the first year. "These camps typically housed 200 men and were comprised of a few dozen semi-permanent, canvas structures," a Forest Service website says.

One of the first CCC camps was located near Pinetop on land that would later become the White Mountain Country Club. *A Tribute to the Lakeside Pioneers* says the real name for the site was Welch Springs, though the camp was called "Los Burros," creating confusion since there is a public campground and ranger station also called Los Burros about a dozen miles farther east near Lake Mountain.

The camp was originally occupied by a group from Texas, who arrived long before their rations. "When we left El Paso we were given burlap bags full of bread," wrote Marshall Wood. "This was intended to hold us over till the camp was properly supplied. But it took three weeks for the supplies to catch up to us at the camp. In the meantime, the bread got terribly old and hard. We even had to resort to boiling beef bones to make a type of beef gravy broth. By the second week our supplies were down to beans, coffee, flour and the bread from El Paso. By this time it was so hard and dry that a cleaver was required to chop it up into serving size. There must have been about 260 men in camp and I'll bet half of them had diarrhea and were always at the latrine. Of course, that was one of the first things we built at the camp. The story went around camp that our military camp officers ... scoured the nearby towns and with their own funds purchased canned goods, eggs, potatoes and other such foodstuffs as were available to tide us over."

After the first group moved out, the camp was taken over by a mixture of Arizona and Texas boys, who built a fish hatchery in Pinetop, the Ranger Station in Pinedale, a ski run on Springer Mountain and the boundary fence between the White Mountain Apache Reservation and the National Forest. They also worked on a "rodent problem" near Aripine, poisoning prairie dogs. The public campground in Lakeside, built by the CCC boys, claims the distinction of being the first such Forest Service facility in Arizona.

Another of the early CCC camps was Blue, reputed to be the most remote in the United States. Supplies were trucked in 130 miles from Silver City, New Mexico. The men helped solve that problem by building a more direct route. Forest Road 232 was cut through to the east to meet another crew working from New Mexico. They also brought telephone lines to the area and built bridges across the Blue River above and below the camp. They constructed campgrounds for the public in the area. Blue, at 5,800 feet, was their winter quarters. They later built a summer quarters higher up in the White Mountains at Buffalo Crossing.

When the boys were up on top, they were primarily firefighters. "By early summer 1937 they had already fought 15 fires in less than a month," says *The CCC in Arizona's Rim Country by* Robert J. Moore. They also built roads and stocked fish.

"The CCC camp at Buffalo Crossing was in a beautiful setting, a splendid location for a camp site," Moore said. "As an official report noted, however, being in the middle of the White Mountains made recreation opportunities for the young men somewhat of a problem. Nearby towns were small, and trucks were not always available to take the men in on weekends. Desertions by homesick boys from Texas were very high. One young man who decided to go over the hill from Buffalo Crossing was on the road hiking into town when he happened to meet the camp's army commander driving back to the work center on the same road. ... The official record simply states that the boss got him to return after talking to him for some time."

Another early camp was at Hart Canyon, west of Heber. The young men worked on forest roads, particularly the Rim Road. They closed up shop after one season and moved to "Los Burros" near Pinetop. The fourth of the original camps, sometimes called Camp Lawton, was near Alpine. The boys built fire lookouts at KP Cienega and Escudilla Mountain, as well as a public campground at Hannagan Meadow, and the Stone Creek Road, FR 275.

Later camps, in addition to Buffalo Crossing, included Three Forks, Juan Miller, Eagle Creek, Chevelon Canyon and Greer. The Three Forks camp near Big Lake was made up of World War I veterans, who worked on road improvements and telephone lines. Men from Juan Miller and Eagle Creek camps in the far southern portion of the Apache National Forest worked on roads. The boys who set up camp in Chevelon Canyon were from Pennsylvania. In addition to roads, they constructed a steel bridge over Chevelon Creek, and put in a public campground and telephone lines.

The Greer Camp was located at what was previously the town dump, and is now Benny Creek public campground. Nearly 300 people were based at the camp, according to *On the Road to Nowhere.* "The young men from the Benny Creek camp realigned the west fork road, blasted out stumps of big trees, and put in metal cattle guards and gates; put little log spillway dams on creeks clear up to the reservation; built a new ranger station in 1939; cleared trails and improved picnic areas," the book says. "Up on the mountain, an area that had once been just a slough was dammed up in 1934 by the CCC and Big Lake was created." They also made firewood available to local residents.

The work of the young men was hard and required planning and supervision. "To improve the roads, they widened them, installed bridges, and re-surfaced the ground; two significant roads given a dramatic facelift during this time were FR 300, also known as the Rim Road or the General Crook Trail, and Highway 191, also known as the Coronado Scenic Trail Byway," the Forest Service website says.

CCC crews created the ranger station at Water Canyon. "As for fire look-out towers, the Forest Service used prefabricated steel parts so as to construct the structures in less time and in many more locations," the website says. Additional fire towers were constructed at Bear Mountain, Big Lake, Blue, P. S. Knoll, Springer Mountain and Dutch Joe.

While young men were eligible for the CCC, more experienced tradesmen got jobs with the Works Progress Administration and other agencies.

The Taylor Stake history explains that workers on highway projects in the early 1930s were limited to half a day so that more people would have a chance to work.

"In St. Johns, where the old school building had been condemned in 1934, children were forced to take classes in an old, overcrowded house," *The New Deal in Arizona* says. "Using [federal] funding, the community made some 33,000 adobe bricks, then, in 1936, the WPA assembled them into a new six-room school." "In Springerville, where the closest hospital had been in Gallup, the WPA constructed a new 12-room hospital." In addition to the medical building, Springerville also got a fly-proof outhouse courtesy of the American government.

The National Youth Administration, designed to help high school-age children, was involved in building baseball diamonds in St. Johns, Round Valley and Concho. The teenagers also leveled the ground, built retaining walls and put in walks and steps at the WPA hospital in Springerville. They catalogued old Apache

County records and created a library in St. Johns. "In the small community of Concho, girls at the school were cleaning and renovating books," Moore said.

In Burton, the government provided bales of cotton that the residents used to make mattresses and quilts.

The administration also created programs to put artists to work, with some earning as much as $38.25 per week, according to *The New Deal in the Southwest* by Peter Bermingham. A bas relief sculpture was created by Robert Kitteredge for the post office in Springerville. It was called "Apache Chiefs" and depicts Geronimo and Victorio riding into battle on spirited horses. The plaster sculpture, which was installed on August 15, 1939, can still be seen in its original location. Kitteredge went on to gain fame as an artist, with his works exhibited at the Whitney Museum in New York.

A co-operative canning plant was set up by the government in Snowflake in the mid-1930s, giving local farmers a market for surplus corn, beans, cabbage, cucumbers, pumpkin, squash and meat.

In St. Johns, brick making was revived during the Depression, 50 years after the pioneers had fired their own building materials from local clay.

The Lone Pine Dam was a Depression-era project that did not turn out well. Because federal law required the owners of an existing irrigation system in Snowflake-Taylor to support any new project that might be built in the area, there were bitter disputes. Farmers who already received irrigation water were reluctant to sign up to pay for a new project that might not work. "The old timers knew there was something wrong with the formation of the stream bed of the Show Low Creek," wrote S. Eugene Flake in a letter republished in James Madison Flake's biography. "They had seen floods enter the channel at the headwaters that had scarcely carried through the 13-mile canyon to its confluence with the Silver Creek." Nevertheless, a new irrigation district was formed in 1933 and a loan and grant of $148,000 was obtained to build a new reservoir on Show Low Creek between Show Low and Snowflake.

The Taylor Stake history tells the story of a minor triumph in the construction of the ill-fated reservoir. Two well-fed lively

1,800-pound gray horses were unable to move a large rock. "One of the boys said, 'If you will get those gray horses out of the way I'll hitch old Buggs to the rock and take it out.' Old Buggs, [was] a lanky, raw boned, brown sorrel gelding. ... Several of the fellows guessed their lunches that Buggs could or couldn't move the rock. ... The 12-year-old fellow moved around something like a modern-day teen dancer, tightened his tugs and moved to the left about a 45 degree turn, then turned back till he found the most likely position for moving the rock. He tried it several times and then fastened his sharp shoes into the clay, twitched his ears, groaned like a bull moose and threw his 1,400 pounds into the effort and the rock came loose from its moorings and literally slid up the bank and out of the way."

Thirty-five men worked to build the Lone Pine Dam to a height of 95 feet, according to the Snowflake Stake history. "Soon thereafter the basin filled and water ran out the spillway for several days. Then the lake began to shrink and the engineers began searching for the cause. The basin continued to empty till almost dry. We found in the basin great holes comparable to ice cream cones turned point down that measured more than thirty feet across. The water could be heard gurgling and crashing down, down, down, to where no one knew. Geologists and engineers were sent in by the government to study the phenomenon and they, after days of study, concluded there was a fault running across the basin and that the water was falling some 200 feet to the Coconino" sandstone formation.

"They tried using a mixture of clay and water to caulk the holes found in the reservoir," the Snowflake Stake history says. "However, this did not seem to remedy the situation and the dam continued to lose water." A delegation from Snowflake went to Washington in hopes of getting the debt canceled. While the Reconstruction Finance Corp. was not willing to forgive the debt entirely, it was willing to release the bonded indebtedness of the landowners and take repayment as the irrigation district made money on the sale of electricity.

The dam was left in place for flood control purposes, but never achieved its purpose of collecting water for irrigation.

The Lone Pine Dam was not the only troublesome water impoundment project during the era. Harnessing Porter Creek near Lakeside was a long undertaking. The Mormons built a dam to restore Scott Reservoir in 1924, but it was washed out before it could be used. Reconstructed in 1927, it lasted one season. It wasn't rebuilt until 1942. This time, with federal financing and engineering, the dam was successfully completed in 1943.

The WPA hired Arizona writers to produce a book called *Arizona, A State Guide*. The following are some of their accounts of the White Mountains:

   ◉   Springerville to Clifton Road: "For 135 miles, as it winds and twists over mountains, abounds with game, the road is wide enough for only one car (car going down backs to a turnout if another car approaches from below.)"

   ◉   Springerville-Eagar-McNary Junction-Fort Apache-San Carlos..." "Graveled road bed ... mountain covered; sometimes blocked by snows in winter or washes during heavy rains; inquire locally."

   ◉   Holbrook-Snowflake-Show Low-McNary Junction Road: "Graveled road bed; subject to blocking by snows in winter; washes dangerous during rainy seasons, limited accommodations."

   ◉   Show Low: "Because of cultivated plots between each store and residence, Show Low (population 450) looks more like a farming community than a town. Almost all of its buildings are frame and though few of them were constructed before 1880, they are so weathered and worn that they appear older." The account noted that the largest Indian ruin was on the Whipple Ranch in the center of town.

   ◉   Lakeside: "(425 population) Mormon settlement of sturdy houses and few business buildings. It serves an agricultural area devoted chiefly to stock raising though some vegetables, barley and alfalfa are grown."

   ◉   Pinetop: "(37 population) is another Mormon community surrounded by sheep and cattle raising area."

Relaxed homesteading laws encouraged locals, as well as outsiders, to claim government land during the Depression. Anthon Johnson, the first child born in Lakeside and the treasurer of Navajo County in the 1950s and '60s, spent much of the Depression establishing the rights to 160 acres of Forest Service land near town. He initially filed for the land about the time he married in 1928, building a summer cabin without a fireplace. The family rented in Lakeside during the winters, but raised livestock and crops on the land in the summer. It took 10 years to get full title. The parcel was sold back to the Forest Service in 1954 for $5,000, according to an archaeological survey conducted by Pat Stein.

If Things Can Get Worse

While the Depression was tough all over, it was very bad on the Apache reservation. "Schools were poorly attended and crumbling, not enough lands were under cultivation, federal appropriations were miserly, Apache morals – in the eyes of the superintendent and the Lutheran missionaries — had shown little progress, drinking was rampant, tuberculosis and trachoma afflicted numerous Indians, and adequate housing and decent employment opportunities were in short supply," the *Mixed-Bloods* book says using testimony from a congressional hearing that was held in Whiteriver.

"For most Indians, poverty was not a new experience," says *The New Deal in Arizona*. But the Depression made things much worse. Many Apaches had been relying on off-reservation jobs, but they were often the first to be laid off in a downturn. Also, the unions, fostered by the New Deal, often reinforced discrimination against Indians, particularly in Arizona's mines. As jobs disappeared and cattle prices fell, the average annual wage for an Indian worker dropped to $81.

But the Civilian Conservation Corps helped some Apaches. "In most states, minorities suffered discrimination in CCC enrollment," the *New Deal in Arizona* says. "In Arizona, however, Indians took advantage of a special CCC division setting aside employment on reservation land."

There were no actual camps on the White Mountain Apache Reservation. The enrollees lived at home and went to work every day, notes *The CCC in Arizona's Rim Country*. The Indian workers were different in another way. Most were over 30.

"In 1934, the [Office of Indian Affairs] ranked the Fort Apache agency, led by William Donner, among the top five in the [Indian Emergency Conservation Work] program and second in Arizona," says *The New Deal in Arizona*. "Within a year, though,

... inspectors were criticizing the program as sloppy, expensive, unsatisfactory, incomplete and wrong."

When some New Deal programs attempted to revive Apache culture, including folklore, dances and crafts, the Wisconsin Synod of the Lutheran Church, which had missionaries on the reservation, strongly disapproved of the "paganism."

Despite some negative opinions, much was accomplished. A high school was built in Cibecue, so that 70 students could stay with their families instead of living 40 miles away at boarding school in Whiteriver.

The New Deal brought advances in legal rights to Apaches. The Indian Reorganization Act of 1934 affirmed the rights of Native Americans to local self-government. The White Mountain Apache Tribal Constitution was approved in 1938. The government lifted the ban on the practice of Native American religions in 1935.

A controversial New Deal program on the reservation involved some heavy-handed attempts to match demand for grass with the drought-diminished supply. "In some instances the livestock reduction program was fairly simple, as at Fort Apache where wild horses were considered the chief cause of range depletion," according to *The New Deal in Arizona*. "Estimated to number about 5,000, wild horses were difficult to find and eliminate. By June 1934, about 800 had been captured and, though a few were kept as saddle horses, most ended up at local fish hatcheries or dog food processors in Phoenix and Tucson."

Another Depression-era project that did not last involved Kinishba, an ancient Indian pueblo on the Apache reservation, which had been built by Mogollon inhabitants in about 1160 A.D. and abandoned two centuries later. Bryon Cummings, who founded the University of Arizona Department of Archaeology and rose to become president of the university, had a vision. He wanted to use his academic and political connections, along with Depression-era funding programs, to turn the ruin into a National Monument that would serve as interpretive center and tourist attraction.

Though the site had been known as the Fort Apache Ruin for decades, Cummings christened it Kinishba, an anglicized version of the Apache word for brown house, according to John R.

Welch, who published the story in the Spring 2007 *Journal of the Southwest*. Cummings sought the help and permission of Interior Secretary Ray Lyman Wilbur, and promised artifacts would be stored at the Arizona State Museum, also a New Deal project.

With federal funding lined up, Cummings arrived at the site with his students in 1931 and began to hire Apaches as laborers. With their taboo against unnecessary contact with the dead, Apaches were reluctant to work at the site. They called the archaeologists "bini'dayilsole, meaning 'they blow in their faces' referring to burial excavators clearing loose sediments with focused exhalations," Welch wrote.

But because of the offer of $1.50 a day, between 10 and 27 Apaches showed up each morning to work on the project. Those workers, along with 26 students who received class credit for the field work, excavated the site. They also rebuilt the pueblo and constructed a museum. Cummings was a master at getting help from the New Deal programs. The CCC boys in Pinetop peeled timbers for the project.

The goals, methods and philosophy of archaeologists have changed a great deal since the 1930s. This reconstruction work would not be undertaken by modern archaeologists, who would consider the pursuit of tourist dollars beneath their dignity, as well as harmful to science.

Though he was making excellent progress on the ground in the White Mountains, Cummings was losing the war in other theaters. The archaeologist was getting old. He was hospitalized in Phoenix in 1934 and was forced to retire in 1938 at age 78, when the Depression-racked University could no longer afford many of its senior faculty. Undaunted, Cummings pushed ahead with private funding and opened the Museum in 1940. But the National Park Service, already awash with monuments in the Southwest, resisted taking responsibility for the site despite support from Arizona's legislative lions like Carl Hayden.

Kinishba started a slow slide down the government food chain, falling into the control of the Bureau of Indian Affairs, then the Recreation Department of the Apache tribe. Cummings' improvements gradually turned into ruins themselves. Ironically, the old professor was right: in the unforgiving environment of the White Mountains, everything eventually has to pay its own way. As artifacts of the New Deal themselves move toward the status of antiques, perhaps a generation of archaeologists far enough removed from the embarrassment of the primitive techniques of the pioneers of their discipline will come to value Cummings' enterprise.

Timber: The Lumber Market Crashes

The stock market crash of 1929 did not immediately halt all the nation's business, but the shock waves were soon felt in the lumber market even in remote Arizona.

"In the latter months of 1929 our sales had been running about two hundred thousand dollars a month," wrote James McNary, president of the Cady Lumber Company. "Within six months, they had fallen off to about thirty thousand dollars a month and that income was mostly from the sale of ties to the Santa Fe. ... In 1930, we had to close down our Flagstaff plant and also the Standard plant, which we had acquired in 1928, and greatly curtail our production at McNary."

"In the summer of 1930, I made a trip through our entire sales territory, including Oklahoma City, Ft. Worth, Dallas, Waco, Kansas City and Chicago; spent a week motoring through Michigan with our sales manager for that state, and on to Pittsburgh and several other Eastern industrial centers," McNary wrote. "I was gone a month. Our sales managers at all points had been alerted to the fact that the president of the company would visit them soon and to try to at least, secure an order for a carload of lumber as a compliment to him. In Michigan I visited a number of large industrial operations which had been our customers, and spent three days in Detroit visiting every lumberyard in the city. I returned home at the end of the month without an order for a single carload of lumber."

The company went into receivership, but was able to continue with reduced operations at McNary thanks to help from the Santa Fe Railroad, which bought railroad ties, and the Standard Oil Company of California, which sold fuel for locomotives and Caterpillars in exchange for receiver's certificates.

"Flagstaff was a flourishing little city of about 6,000 people," McNary wrote. "Our employees were drawn from the local population, and, with the closing of the plant, were eligible for public

The University of Arizona used New Deal programs to excavate and reconstruct a Mogollon pueblo near Whiteriver. They named it Kinishba.

relief. At Standard, the workmen were mostly drawn from the little rural communities around the town and they were not completely dependent on the continuous operation of the plant for their livelihood. McNary is a company town, the company owning every building in the community, including mill buildings, store, post office, hospital, schools, churches, and every residence both in Hilltown and Milltown. Our employees consisted of about one-fourth Anglos, one-fourth Spanish-American, one-fourth colored, and one-fourth Indian. Except for the Indians, who drifted away when there was no work, our people were completely dependent upon the operation of the lumber plant for their livelihood. As the depression gradually became more acute, it was necessary to reduce expenses drastically by cutting salaries, reducing wages, and shortening the hours of operation of the plant to the lowest possible point. At no time during the Depression did we accept public relief for the community of McNary. Our employees were given free rent and barely enough wages to keep body and soul together, supplemented by credit at the store when necessary."

After the Depression, the company was reorganized as Southwest Lumber Mills, Inc. Preparations were made to re-open the Standard mill, but a fire consumed the equipment and the town was abandoned. With another name change to Southwest Forest Industries, and a paper mill near Snowflake, the company eventually became one of only a handful of Fortune 500 companies based in Arizona. Employing up to 1,000 men, the McNary mill soon cut out most of the lumber within a radius that permitted easy collection of logs by truck. It began to plan to extend the railroad deeper into the forest to a remote logging town on the eastern edge of the Reservation, which would be called Maverick during the short

419

period of its existence.

Some Businesses Thrived

One business that thrived during the Depression in remote Apache County was bootlegging. "Local consumption was probably about the same, per capita, as it had always been and was only a small part of the booze that was being produced in the hill country of Apache County," says the St. Johns Stake history. "Most of the output found its way to the larger towns. There is no way of knowing the amount of moonshine produced, but a review of its effects on the local economy would indicate that it was substantial."

The stake history goes on to tell the story of the seven Stuart boys, who were perhaps the most successful bootleggers in the county. The brothers used cattle as pack horses to avoid leaving car tracks. They tied their kegs high in windblown trees to give their product smoothness by simulating the rolling motion of ships. At least that was their marketing claim.

Sheriff M. L. Hall bagged two of the brothers one night by creeping up on a dugout in the woods where they were bottling. "Tim and John were down in the hole pinting it out and passing it up to Charles, who was receiving the bottles and placing them in boxes," the stake history says. "Noticing the shadowy form of the sheriff approaching in the darkness, Charles called a warning to his brothers and disappeared into the night. His warning was in vain, for a sudden gust of wind blew his words away." The sheriff took over Charles' role in the bottling operation and arrested the two remaining brothers when they came out of the hole.

"An Apache County man, John Leverton even brought in a man from Oklahoma to make Whiskey for him," according to an account in the Woolford family history. "We delivered our goods to McNary in a Model T Ford," said Leverton. "If the Pro-Eyes (Prohibition Officers) were there, we'd know it. The sheriff in McNary would let us know and if there was any danger we'd take it in at night on pack mules. Two kegs on each mule. Take four or five mules. We'd take in 100-150 gallons, the bootleggers, or wholesalers as we called them, came out to meet us. They would buy the whole load. Paid us $10.00 a gallon. In that day and time that was a lot of money. It would take about an hour in town and our whole load would be sold."

The bootleggers weren't so much hardened criminals as people trying to make a living during the Depression. One man recalled his father, a former sheriff of Lincoln County, New Mexico, selling booze from his house near Vernon.

"Another old-timer, while reminiscing of the old days, declared that the repeal of the Eighteenth Amendment ruined the two most profitable endeavors that Apache County ever had," the stake history says. "It put the bootleggers out of business and worked a hardship on the lawyers who had gathered here to defend them."

Conclusion

Like most humans who came to the White Mountains, the boys from the CCC soon found a need to leave. In their case, the call came from World War II. Already organized and accustomed to camp life, they became good soldiers. Many local Anglos, Hispanics, blacks and Apache men also went to war. The valiant service of Native Americans finally persuaded Arizona to give the original inhabitants the right to vote three years after the war ended.

In the following years, generations would continue to come to the High Country and move away. And like Aldo Leopold, they would deeply regret that the White Mountain area was no longer exactly like it was when they first arrived.

Acknowledgements

The authors gratefully acknowledge the help of many people who assisted during their 20-year adventure to research and produce *Story of the American West,* including Max and Sport Baca, Roman Candelaria, Martha McNary Chilcote, Robert A. Clark, Barb Davis, Bruce Donaldson, Vicki Duraine, Sheryl Eaton, Myna Frestedt, the family of William and James Madison Flake, the Rev. Arthur Guenther, Atella Haws, Tom Henderson, Shirley Jones, Marty LaMar, Marion Elizabeth Menhennet, William Parker, the Penrod Family, the Peterson Family, Edgar Perry, Mary Riley, Bonnie Rogers, Tim Snider, Jacqueline Woolford Solomon, Clair Thomas, Eva Watt, Mary and Melvin Wendrick and Guy Wilhelm.

In addition, the staff members of these museums: Casa Malapais, Fort Apache, American Museum of Natural History, Museum of the American Indian, Smithsonian Institution, Heard Museum, Little House Museum at South Fork, Butterfly Lodge, Sharlot Hall Museum in Prescott, the White Mountain Historical Society Park in Springerville, the Southwest Museum in Los Angeles and the tribal museums at Zuni and Hopi. Also, the community museums in Holbrook, St. Johns, Show Low, Snowflake, Pinetop-Lakeside, Taylor and Winslow.

The authors also acknowledge the assistance of staff members at these libraries, New York Public Library, Library of Congress, National Archives, University of Southern California, University of California at Los Angeles, Long Beach State, University of Arizona, Arizona State University, Arizona Historical Society, Northland Pioneer College, the Arizona State Library and the municipal libraries in Phoenix, Tucson, Pinetop-Lakeside, Show Low, Newark, Bayonne, N.J., Jersey City and Los Angeles. Also, the staff members at county courthouses in Socorro, N.M, Prescott, St. Johns and Holbrook. In addition, the Arizona Game and Fish Department, National Forest Service and Petrified Forest National Park.

A special thanks goes to literary agent Jodie Rhodes, who believed in this book, researchers Joyce L. Jauch and Rita Ackerman, and librarian Vickie Morgan at the Larson Memorial Library in Lakeside, AZ.

Selected Bibliography

The American Heritage Book of Great Adventures of the Old West

American Indians of the Southwest, Bertha P. Dutton

Among the Apaches, Frederick Schwatka

An Apache Odyssey: Indeh, Eve Ball

Anasazi, Ancient People of the Rock, David Duench and Donald G. Pike

Ancestral Hopi Migrations, Patrick D. Lyons

Ancient Ruins of the Southwest, David Grant Noble

Anza and the Northwest Frontier, J.N. Bowman and R.F. Heizer

Apache Agent, the Biography of John P. Clum, Woodworth Clum

The Apache Diaries, A Father and Son Journey, Grenville and Neil Goodwin

Apache Indian Baskets, Clara Lee Tanner

The Apache Indians, In Search of the Missing Tribe, Helge Ingstad

Apache Indians, Raiders of the Southwest, Sonia Bleeker

Apache Indian Scouts, H.B. Wharfield

The Apache Kid, William Sparks

Apache Navaho and Spaniard, Jack D. Forbes

Apache Odyssey, A Journey Between Two Worlds, Morris Opler

Apache Reservation, Richard J. Perry

The Archaeology of Arizona, Paul S. Martin and Fred Plog

Arizona as it Was, Hiram C. Hodge

Arizona Memories, edited by Anne Hodges and Rennard Strickland

Arizona Place Names, Will C. Barnes

The Arizona Rangers, Bill O'Neal.

Arizona Was the West, James R. Jennings

Arizona, A Cavalcade of History, Marshall Trimble

Arizona, a State Guide, Works Progress Administration

Arizona's Dark and Bloody Ground, Earl Forrest.

Arizona's Honeymoon Trail, Norma Baldwin Ricketts

Arizoniana, Stories from Old Arizona, Marshall Trimble

The Basket Weavers of Arizona, Bert Robinson

Before the Dawn, Nicholas Wade

The Biographical Album of Western Gunfighters, Ed Bartholomew

Black Jack Ketchum: Last of the Hold-Up Kings, Ed Bartholomew.

Bleed, Blister, and Purge, Volney Steele

Book of the Hopi, Frank Waters

The Book of the Navajo, Raymond Friday Locke

The Buffalo Soldiers, William H. Leckie

Butch Cassidy: A Biography, Richard Patterson

Canyon Country Prehistoric Indians, F.A. Barnes and Michaelene Pendleton

Cap Mossman, Last of The Great Cowmen, Frazier Hunt

The CCC in Arizona's Rim Country, Robert J. Moore

Changing Woman of the Apache, Sydele Golston.

Concho, The Enchanted Pearl, E.M. DeGlane

Cooley: Army Scout, Arizona Pioneer, Wayside Host, Col. H.B. Wharfield.

Coronado, Knight of Pueblos and Plains, Herbert E. Bolton
The Crooked Trail to Holbrook, Leland J. Hanchett, Jr.
Cycles of Conquest, Edward H. Spicer
The Diaries of John Gregory Bourke, Edited by Charles M. Robinson III
Dictionary of Prehistoric Indian Artifacts, Franklin Barnett
Digging into History, Paul S. Martin
Don't Let the Sun Step Over You, Eva Tulene Watt
Down Through Arizona
Early Western Travels, 1748-1846, Edited by Reuben Gold Thwaites
Edward F. Beale & the American West, Gerald Thompson
Elijah was a Valiant Man, Arvin Palmer
Emma Lee, Juanita Brooks
Encyclopedia History of the Church of Jesus Christ of Latter-day Saints
Firm as the Mountains, a Review of the Early Mormon Settlement
The First Hundred Years of Nino Cochise, As told to A. Kinney Griffith
Francois X. Aubry, Trader, Trailmaker and Voyager, Donald Chaput
The Freight Rolled, James R. Jennings
From Indian Trails to Jet Trails, Snowflake's Centennial, Albert J. Levine
A Gallery of Western Badmen, William Waters
General George Crook, His Autobiography, Edited by Martin F. Schmitt
Geologic Highway Map of Arizona, Arizona Geological Survey
Geology of Arizona, Dale Nations and Edmund Stump
George Scarborough, Life and Death of a Lawman, Robert K. DeArment
Geronimo and the End of the Indian Wars, C. L. Sonnichsen
Geronimo!, E.M. Halliday
Geronimo: His Own Story, S.M. Barrett and Frederick Turner
The Ghost Dance, James Mooney
Gold and Silver in the West, T. H. Watkins
Handbook of American Indians North of Mexico, Frederick Webb Hodge
Handbook of North American Indians, Smithsonian
Handcarts to Zion, LeRoy R. Hafen and Ann W. Hafen
Historic Pueblo Indian Pottery, Francis H. Harlow
Historical Atlas of Arizona, Henry P. Walker and Don Bufkin
Historical Atlas of the Outlaw West, Richard Patterson
Historical Atlas of the United States, National Geographic Society
History of Arizona, Thomas Edwin Farish
A History of the St. Johns Arizona Stake, C. LeRoy & Mabel R. Wilhelm
Homol'ovi: A Cultural Crossroads, William H. Walker
Hoofprints on Forest Range, Paul H. Roberts
The Impact of the Frontier on a Jewish Family, Floyd S. Fierman
In the Great Apache Forest: The Story of a Lone Boy Scout, James Schulz
In the Trail of the Wind, American Indian Poems, edited by John Bierhorst
Indian Land Cessions in the United States, Charles C. Royce
The Indian Races of North and South America, Charles De Wolf Brownell

James Madison Flake, Pioneer, Leader, Missionary, S. Eugene Flake
Journal of Jesse N. Smith
The Journey of Coronado, Pedro Castanada
Kit Carson's Autobiography, edited by Milo Milton Quaife
The Land Looks After Us, Joel W. Martin
Landscapes of Arizona, Terah L. Smiley, J. Dale Nations, et. al.
Life of Tom Horn, Government Scout and Interpreter, Tom Horn
Like A Brother, Grenville Goodwin's Apache Years, Neil Goodwin
Lost Bonanzas, Harry Sinclair Drago
Lost Mines of the Great Southwest, John D. Mitchell
Man and Wildlife in Arizona: The American Exploration, Goode P. Davis
Man Corn, Christy G. Turner II and Jacqueline Turner
Memories of Fred Lindsay Adams, Fred Adams
Memories of McNary, edited by Martha McNary Chilcote
Mickey Free, Apache Captive, Interpreter, and Indian Scout, Allan
    Radbourne with research by Joyce L. Jauch.
Mixed-Bloods, Apaches, and Cattle Barons, Thomas R. McGuire
Mogollon Culture in the Forestdale Valley, Emil W. Haury
Mormon Polygamous Families, Jessie L. Embry
Mormon Polygamy, a History, Richard S. Van Wagoner
The Mountain Men and the Fur Trade of the Far West, LeRoy R. Hafen
My Life as an Indian, James Schulz
Myths and Tales of the White Mountain Apache, Grenville Goodwin
The Navaho, Clyde Kluckhorn and Dorothea Leighton
The New Deal in Arizona, William S. Collins
The New Deal in the Southwest, Peter Bermingham
New Keys to Reading Apache, White Mountain Apache Culture Center
North American Indian, Edward S. Curtis
O.K. Corral Postscript: The Death of Ike Clanton, Rita K. W. Ackerman
On the Border with Crook, John Gregory Bourke
On the Road to Nowhere, Karen Miller Applewhite
Once They Moved Like the Wind, David Roberts
Origin and Development of the Pueblo Katsina Cult, E. Charles Adams
The Outlaw Trail: History of Butch Cassidy, Charles Kelly
Outlawry and Justice in Arizona, Sunnyside High School, Tucson
The Ox-Bow Incident, Walter Van Tilburg Clark
Pages from Hopi History, Harry C. James
The People Called Apache, Thomas Mails
Personal Narrative of Explorations, John Russell Bartlett
Personal Narrative of James O. Pattie, James Ohio Pattie
Plumed Snake Dance, James Schulz
Prehistoric Indians of the Southwest, H. M. Wormington
Prehistoric Textiles of the Southwest, Kate Peck Kent
Prehistory of the Southwest, Linda S. Cordell

Primitive Drinking, Chandler Washburne
Questers of the Desert, James Schulz
Recollections of a Western Ranchman, William French
Saints and Savages, Helen Bay Gibbons
Sand County Almanac, Aldo Leopold
The Scouts, Time-Life Books, Keith Wheeler
The Show Low Arizona Stake, A Compilation
The Slaughter Ranches and Their Makers, Mary Whatley Clarke
Snake-Dance of the Moquis, John Bourke
The Soldiers, Time-Life Books, David Nevin
A Son of the Navahos, James Schulz
Southwestern Archaeology, John C. McGregor
The Spanish Borderland Frontier 1513-1821, John Francis Bannon
Spanish-Americans of New Mexico, Nancie L. Gonzalez
Stalking the Past, Prehistory of the Petrified Forest, Anne Trinkle Jones
Studies in Southwestern Ethnolinguistics, Dell H. Hymes, William E. Bittle
Survival of the Spirit, Chiricahua Apaches, H. Henrietta Stockel
Take Up Your Mission, Charles S. Peterson
Taylor's Centennial Stories 1878-1978
That Hashknife Kid, Clarence W. Durham
The Arizona Sheriff, Major Grover F. Sexton
They Never Surrendered, Bronco Apaches, Douglas V. Meed
This is My Life, James G. McNary
This Land These Voices, Abe Chanin
Through Indian Country to California, John P. Sherburne's Diary, Gordon
Timeless Heritage: A History of the Forest Service in the Southwest
To the Inland Empire: Coronado, Stewart L. Udall
Top O' The Pines, Gene Luptak
Treasures of Pioneer History, Kate B. Carter
A Tribute to the Lakeside Pioneers, Published by Karen LaDuke
Vanished Arizona, Martha Summerhayes
Walter Reed, Doctor in Uniform, L.N. Wood
Warrior Woman, the Story of Lozen, Peter Aleshire
Western Apache Heritage, Richard John Perry
Western Apache Language and Culture, Keith H. Basso
Western Apache Material Culture, Alan Ferg
Western Apache Witchcraft, Keith Basso
The Western Apache, Winfred Buskirk
William J. Flake, Pioneer - Colonizer, Osmer D Flake
Wisdom Sits in Places, Keith H. Basso
With the Invader: Glimpses of the Southwest, Edward Roberts
Women of the Apache Nation, H. Henrietta Stockel
The Works of Hubert Howe Bancroft
Wyatt Earp - The Untold Story, Ed Bartholomew

Zane Grey - A Biography, Frank Gruber
Zane Grey's Arizona, Candace C. Kant
A Zuni Atlas, T.J. Ferguson and F. Richard Hart
Zuni Origins, David A. Gregory and David R. Wilcox
These volumes by Zane Grey: *Arizona Ames, The Dude Ranger, The Hash Knife Outfit, Man of the Forest, Nevada, To the Last Man, Under the Tonto Rim* and the short story "The Wolf Tracker."
These volumes by Edgar Rice Burroughs: *Apache Devil, The War Chief, A Princess of Mars, The Gods of Mars* and *The Warlord of Mars.*
The archives of the Bureau of Land Management, the National Register of Historic Places and the Sharlot Hall and Show Low museums.
These periodicals: *National Geographic, Albuquerque Democrat, Albuquerque Sunday Herald, American Anthropologist, American Antiquity, American West, Apache Chief, Apache Critic, Apache Review, Arizona and the West, Arizona Citizen, Arizona Highways, Arizona Historical Review, Arizona Republic, Arizona Silver Belt, Century Magazine, Chicago Natural History Museum Bulletin, Deseret News, Falcon, Florence Enterprise, Forever Frontier, Holbrook Argus, Journal of Anthropological Research, Journal of Arizona History, Journal of the Royal Anthropological Institute, Journal of the Southwest, Los Angeles Times, New Mexico Historical Review, New York Times, Orion Era, Phoenix Gazette, Pioneer News, Plateau, St. Louis Globe-Democrat, Socorro Bulletin, Southern Vineyard, Southwestern Journal of Anthropology, St. Johns Herald, The Kiva, Smoke Signal, Snowflake Herald, Time, The Way of St. Francis, Weekly Arizona Miner, White Mountain Independent* and *Yuma Sentinel.*
Two papers by Kent Lightfoot: *An Archaeological Survey of Nicks Camp ...,* and *Mormon Sociopolitical Development in Northern Arizona...*
Native American Mitochondrial DNA Haplogroups, Kaestle and Smith
The Central Siberian Origin for Native American Y Chromosomes, American Society of Human Genetics, Fabricio R. Santos and others
Multidisciplinary Research at Grasshopper Pueblo Arizona, Longacre
The Behavioral and Archaeological Contexts of NA14,803
Western Apache Dwellings, Bruce R. Donaldson
Will Croft Barnes and the Apache Uprising of 1881, Paul J. Scheips
Videos produced by Richard Lynch and the Little House Museum.
Manuscripts: *Background History of the Lakeside-Pinetop Area*, Ben S. Hansen; *History of Holbrook and the Little Colorado Country*, Harold C. Wayte Jr.; *History of the Woolford and Hall Families*, Jacqueline Woolford Solomon; *Adair, Arizona -- A Brief History*, Kay L. Read; *John Smith Harris in Arizona*, John V. Wilhelm.
Oral history: Atella Haws, Martha McNary Chilcote, Mary Riley, Edgar Perry, Lewis Peterson, Marion Elizabeth Menhennet, Grace Carlisle.
Numerous pamphlets and family history manuscripts listed on the website, www.StoryOfTheAmericanWest.com

Index

More Complete Index Online at:
www.StoryOfTheAmericanWest.com

About the Authors

Carol Sletten moved to the White Mountains when she was in her early twenties and has studied Apache culture ever since — through scholarship, conducting newspaper interviews, friendships and community projects. She taught Apache students, hiked on the reservation, visited sacred sites and attended ceremonies.

Carol learned about the area's history while working as an illustrator, reporter and oral history specialist – skills she acquired while studying art and writing at the University of Iowa.

She is grateful that her daughters, Heather and Selena, were able to grow up in a house surrounded by natural wonders. Carol and her husband, Eric Kramer, live and work in that same old rustic White Mountain cabin.

Eric Kramer is a successful journalist who rose to supervisory and management positions at the Associated Press, United Press International and Dow Jones & Co. while maintaining ties to rural Arizona and its community journalism.

As Global Desk Editor for Dow Jones & Co., he managed editing operations in New York, London and Singapore. Publication credits include the *New York Times, Washington Post, Arizona Republic* and most major newspapers.

He holds a bachelor of science in journalism from the University of Kansas and a master of business administration from St. Peter's College, Jersey City, N.J.

———————

www.StoryOfTheAmericanWest.com

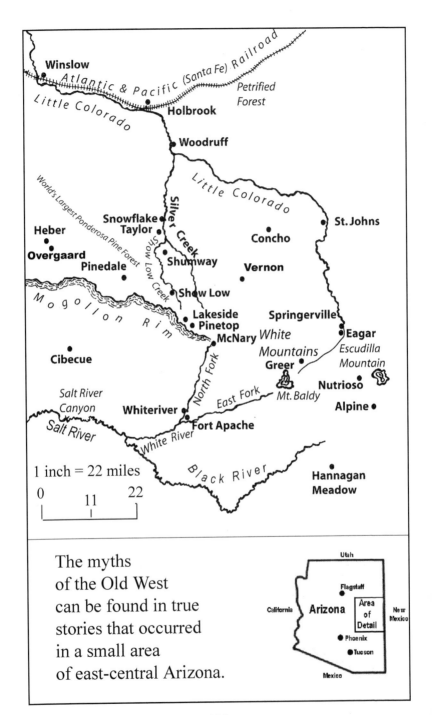

Winslow

Atlantic & Pacific (Santa Fe) Railroad

Little Colorado

Holbrook

Petrified Forest

Woodruff

Little Colorado

World's Largest Ponderosa Pine Forest

Heber

Snowflake
Taylor

Silver Creek

St. Johns

Overgaard

Show Low Creek

Shumway

Concho

Pinedale

Vernon

Show Low

Mogollon Rim

Lakeside
Pinetop
McNary

Springerville

Eagar

Cibecue

White Mountains

Escudilla Mountain

North Fork

Greer

Nutrioso

Salt River Canyon

East Fork

Mt. Baldy

Alpine

Whiteriver

Fort Apache

Salt River

White River

Black River

Hannagan Meadow

1 inch = 22 miles

0   11   22

The myths
of the Old West
can be found in true
stories that occurred
in a small area
of east-central Arizona.

Utah

Flagstaff

California

Arizona

Area of Detail

New Mexico

Phoenix

Tucson

Mexico